Industrial Policy for Agriculture in the Global Economy

Industrial Policy
for Agriculture
in the
Global Economy

S. R. JOHNSON and S. A. MARTIN

Editors

 CARD Publications / Iowa State University

Iowa State University Press / Ames

Industrial Policy for Agriculture in the Global Economy is a copublication of Iowa State University Press and the Center for Agricultural and Rural Development (CARD), Iowa State University. In the interest of providing important information to scholars and policymakers in a timely fashion, the Publications Office of CARD has provided camera-ready copy for this book to Iowa State University Press.

Printed on acid-free paper in the United States of America

First edition, 1993

Library of Congress Cataloging-in-Publication Data

Industrial policy for agriculture in the global economy / S. R. Johnson
    and S. A. Martin, editors. —1st ed.
        p.   cm.
    "CARD publications."
    Includes bibliographical references.
    ISBN 0-8138-2279-3
    1. Agriculture and state—United States—Congresses. 2. Industry
and state—United States—Congresses. I. Johnson, Stanley R.,
1938–   . II. Martin, Sheila (Sheila A.)
HD1755.I53   1993
338.1'873—dc20   93-23803
                                                            CIP

Contents

Foreword

Agriculture provides for the most basic of human needs. Because the products of agriculture are essential to the survival of society, government, as part of its larger function in overseeing society, has a clear stake in the development and advancement of agriculture. As agriculture and the social, economic, and technological factors that surround it have evolved, the proper roles for government and the private sector in shaping the direction of the agricultural industry have changed as well.

Agriculture and its social, economic, and technological environment in the United States have reached a critical stage. Many of the assumptions upon which current agricultural policy has been based are no longer valid. The rural and agricultural structures that government intervention was designed to support no longer define American agriculture. Agricultural technology has surpassed the boundaries that characterized the industry a half-century ago. Clearly the time has come to take a fresh look at what government can and should accomplish as a partner with the private sector in American agriculture and rural communities.

The papers collected in this book were presented at a conference held at Iowa State University in Ames, Iowa, on September 16 and 17, 1992. Conference organizers sought to strengthen understanding of the development of modern agriculture and the policies that influence it. This was accomplished by asking questions about industrial policy in other sectors and nations, and developing implications for American agriculture. Specifically, the conference sought to identify conditions favorable to the growth and development of industries, to evaluate current industrial policy as a strategy for promoting agricultural and rural development, and to identify institutions necessary for formulating and implementing a more successful and effective contemporary industrial policy for agriculture.

To enrich the conference discussion on these topics, leaders from academia, government, and industry were invited to prepare papers and present their views. The discussion included formal responses to the papers and a free and informal exchange among conference attendees. This volume contains the papers used to stimulate the discussions. The synthesis paper by D. Gale Johnson and the conclusion chapter summarize the issues raised by the conference and incorporate the substance of what was a lively and useful debate of industrial policy and the future role for government and the public sector in U.S. agriculture.

Significant policy change and sustained effort by government require the participation of all affected parties. For this reason, leaders from government, private industry, trade and consumer associations, international organizations, and academia were invited. A strong representation from among each of these groups of policy stakeholders provided for effective and comprehensive discussion of the subject. This combination of individual perspectives from the various components of the agricultural industry greatly added to the substance and impact of the conference. The dialogue on the basic issues raised in the conference will almost surely continue as we move toward the development of the 1995 Farm Bill.

Iowa State University, it should be noted, was an apt setting for this discussion. Four major centers of the university are involved in agricultural technology design and evaluation, industrial development strategies, and institutional and industrial development. Researchers from these centers, the Meat Export Research Center, the Center for Crops Utilization and Research, the Leopold Center for Sustainable Agriculture, and the Center for Agricultural and Rural Development contributed to the conference, and assisted in conference development and organization.

For decades, rural communities and U.S. agriculture have been guided by an industrial policy that was conceived in the 1930s. It may be time for a major revision of this policy. This is clear from the economic performance of the rural sector, the prominence of environmental concerns, and the increasing globalization of agriculture. We hope that this conference has enlightened the agricultural policy process and will lead the way to shaping new and more effective industrial policy for American agriculture.

JOHN RUAN
Chair, World Agriculture Development Foundation
Chair and CEO, Ruan Industries

Acknowledgments

THE CONFERENCE "Industrial Policy for Agriculture in the Global Economy" was sponsored jointly by the Cooperative State Research Service (CSRS) of the U.S. Department of Agriculture and the Center for Agricultural and Rural Development (CARD) at Iowa State University, in cooperation with the World Agriculture Development Foundation, Des Moines, Iowa.

The conference was participatory. We wish to express appreciation to the agricultural and rural leaders who participated, for their contributions and for their ongoing interest in shaping policy and institutions to better society. The conference participants, along with their affiliations, are listed at the back of this volume.

This book was copyedited by Kathleen Glenn-Lewin, formatted by Ruth Bourgeois using Ventura® desktop publishing software, and proofread by Christianna I. White. We express special appreciation to Kathy, Ruth, and Chris for their careful and timely assistance.

Introduction

S. R. JOHNSON

S. A. MARTIN

Developments in a number of arenas are creating major opportunities for agriculture and rural communities. Among these are biotechnology, engineering, low-cost telecommunications, distribution and management systems, and changing dimensions of market organization. To seize these opportunities for improving agricultural productivity, profitability, and vitality, nations and regions are trying to find ways to build on the rapidly expanding findings in science and in management research and development (R&D). Success in implementing development initiatives based on these new results will depend upon capacities for assessing potential applications of technology, for enacting a science policy that encourages advancement in areas favorable to agriculture and rural communities, and for developing institutions consistent with adoption of new technologies and market trends. This combination of assessment, policy, and institutional change underpins the ability of modern industry to grow and adapt.

Just as the rapid advance of science and technology is challenging agriculture to create new products and new applications in industry, changes in political systems, economic systems, and communications and transport technologies are challenging the traditional framework of policy for agriculture and rural communities. As world economies integrate, trade increases. Ideas and science flow more easily across national and regional borders. International communication is possible in nearly real time and at relatively low cost. Capital, scientists, and managers also flow freely across borders. In this dynamic environment, how can nations and regions organize and manage their natural resource endowments? How can they foster specialized developments in science in such a way that agriculture, related industries, and rural communities remain an engine for sustained, reliable economic growth? Is this the long-sought key to the development of agriculture and rural economies?

Although these questions refer specifically to the future of agriculture and rural economies, similar questions have been addressed on the future of other industries and the communities that depend upon them. Discussions about the viability of specific economic sectors often lead to a debate of the merits of government intervention designed to alter the fate of these sectors, commonly referred to as *industrial policy*. The papers in this book extend the industrial policy debate to include agriculture and rural communities. While studies of agricultural and rural development policy rarely have been couched in the terms of the traditional industrial policy debate, it is clear that analysis of the role of government in agriculture and rural development is in many ways parallel to analysis of industrial policy for other industries. Industrial policy may be a useful framework for addressing growth and development of agriculture and rural communities as influenced by the many governmental interventions now in place in the United States and other developed nations.

Concepts of Industrial Policy

Industrial policy has been debated among economists, policymakers, and planners for decades (Adams and Bollino 1983; Adams and Klein 1983; Grossman 1990; Krugman 1990; Norton 1986; Solo 1983; Shapiro and Taylor 1990; Wachter and Wachter 1981). While the terminology for what is now called industrial policy may have changed, the question most fundamental to the debate has not: Should government intervene in the operation of the market? Although the discussion surrounding industrial policy often involves more specific issues, it is based upon defining the appropriate role for government in an economy driven primarily by market forces.

No definition of industrial policy is universally accepted. In some sense, all policies that alter economic activity, transferring resources between sectors or collections of agents, be they passive or active, can be considered industrial policy. Using this definition, the entire set of tax, trade, procurement, and regulatory policies applied by the various government agencies, regardless of their targets, can be called an industrial policy. Given this interpretation, most of U.S. industrial policy is macroeconomic, aimed at stimulating domestic economic activity, international trade, and commerce, rather than specific industries.

By contrast, many argue that an industrial policy is a coherent set of measures aimed at a specific industry or sector with a particular set of objectives (Goldstein 1987). Other analysts reserve the term *industry-specific policy* for this more narrow definition. By this definition, very few industrial polices have been applied in the United States at the federal level. This is in contrast to industrial policies of European nations and of Japan, and the initiatives of state and local government, which often include industry- or location-specific initiatives to stimulate growth and economic activity (Bollino 1983; Grossman 1990; Krugman 1983; Lugar 1985).

A number of economic and noneconomic objectives are pursued with the instruments of industrial policy. Broad objectives include promoting economic growth, creating jobs, increasing wages, or improving the trade balance. Other objectives might be sector-, industry-, or population-specific. They include expansion of particular industries, redistribution of income, advancement of particular technologies, or development of specific geographic areas. These more specific policies are often based on the belief that industrial advantage can be created by the right set of conditions and policies (Porter 1990). The organization of an economy and the objectives it pursues, some argue, will affect the direction of industrial development (Tyson 1992).

Specific measures that are designed to influence an industry or sector arise from the choice of policy strategy. Norton (1986) identifies two strategies pursued by proponents of industrial policy. A "modernization" strategy attempts to accelerate the movement of resources into industries with considerable potential for future market growth and competitiveness. A "preservationist" strategy tries to prevent the collapse of a declining industry, and the unemployment (and political strife) that may accompany such decline. A third strategy might be called "stabilizing," or "transitional." This strategy is used to accelerate the flow of resources to their most productive uses. It differs from the modernization strategy in that it seeks to remove obstacles to structural adjustment rather than actively influencing markets and controlling the decisions of the private sector. Some policies reflect a mix of these strategies, on the one hand picking "winner industries," while on the other hand providing transitional aid to declining industries (Adams and Klein 1983). The transitional aid often is needed to provide political support for the modernizing strategy (Competitiveness Policy Council 1992).

Many tools can be used to pursue the strategies of industrial policy. Similar tools can be applied in competing strategies, although they may be directed toward different markets or agents and seek to affect different sets of incentives. While the strategy choice of policymakers and economists often depends upon what they observe and believe about the efficiency of markets and the effectiveness of policy, most economists agree upon a preference ranking for the tools of industrial policy. In descending order they are (1) market-perfecting infrastructure; (2) government promotion of savings, investment, R&D, and education; (3) trade and development policies for whole industries; and (4) firm-specific polices (Tyson 1992). The reasons for this preference ranking concern notions of market failure, externalities, and the difficulties of economic management by government that are addressed in Chapter One.

Industrial Policy for Agriculture and Rural Development

The development of agriculture in the United States has been driven largely by economic policy and by science and technology. Beginning with the mechanization of agriculture in the nineteenth century, technological advances changed farming methods, decreased costs of farm production, and reduced consumer prices for food. Agricultural science was organized through the U.S. Department of Agriculture, the land-grant colleges, and the private agricultural companies. Advances in plant and soil science, veterinary medicine, and agricultural chemicals led a transformation of American agriculture. This transformation set in motion a series of social, economic, and political forces that would contribute to the complex set of institutions and policies that comprise the agriculture industry today (Cochrane 1979). Although it was led by science and technology, this transformation was in large measure due to government policies designed to stabilize prices and income.

Transition in American agriculture can be viewed as a continuous, recurring cycle. Although background details change from one cycle to the next, the same basic process occurs. Advances in agricultural science and technology, arguably stimulated by government policy–related incentives, lead to economic and social consequences. These put political pressure on the established institutions and force them to evolve in response to the demands for change by clients and the political system. This process generated the current system of farm price and income supports and production controls, which resulted when farmers and other interest groups sought policies to address their concerns that the treadmill of technological advance would outpace the average farmer, and that the continuing exodus of labor from farming communities would empty rural communities and smother rural economic activity.

As the transition of American agriculture has continued, developments in biotechnology, genetic engineering, distribution and communications, management systems, and market organization have rendered existing institutions, rural community structures, and policies obsolete. Current U.S. policy toward agriculture and rural communities is in many respects based on the technologies, social structures, and markets of a half century ago. While policies have changed in emphasis and degree, the institutions and interest groups engendered by these policies have failed to evolve as quickly as the industry. The consequently piecemeal approach to agricultural policy has resulted, particularly in the past two decades, in an increasingly preservationist strategy that seeks to maintain obsolete institutions, industry and community structures, and the associated economic and social relationships.

These developments in U.S. agriculture and in rural communities underlie the need to reformulate agricultural policy. An innovative approach is required—one that is not totally conditioned by existing institutional structures, but that builds a new foundation for the role of government in agriculture and rural development. To build this new structure without relying upon outdated preservationist policies, a unifying frame of reference is required. Coordination of all aspects of the industrial policy—objectives, strategies, and tools—is aided by a strong framework within which the relevant issues can be debated.

The foundations of the industrial policy debate can provide this framework for the development of a new set of policies for agriculture and rural communities. These foundations supply a body of economic and institutional theory to apply, a rich literature to consult, and a history of success and failure to examine. The framework can provide a point of reference for decisions on policy for industries other than agriculture, and for regions other than rural America. The industrial policy framework can provide a new perspective from which to view the problems of agriculture and rural development.

Contents of This Volume

Each of the conference papers in this volume fulfills at least one of three functions for defining the framework of industrial policy and applying it to the problems of agriculture and rural community development. Some identify market failures in agriculture and rural economies (or other industries and the communities upon which they depend), describe policies that might correct the market failures, and discuss the success with which these policies have been applied. Other papers review economic outcomes of a policy process that is the result of a political-economic equilibrium based on existing institutions and structures. Still others propose changes in the institutional framework that could alter current agricultural policy and make it more effective for industrial development and rural communities.

The opening paper defines the scope of the discussion and provides background for the conference. In this paper we aimed to review the approaches to industrial policy and to expand these ideas to incorporate the concepts of political-economic equilibrium. The expanded framework for industrial policy also considers nontraditional instruments based on the new developments in institutional economics for influencing the development of agriculture and rural communities.

The three papers in Part II evaluate the results of established agricultural policies and their effects on the growth of agriculture and rural communities.

Advances in agricultural science have provided an engine for growth; however, the process and direction of scientific development has changed. Recent advances in assessing the benefits of these developments on sectoral and regional growth in a general equilibrium framework provide an opportunity for reevaluating the traditional role of government in the development and diffusion of new technologies, as well as in managing incomes and prices.

In Part III, the authors focus on a number of established public institutions. The discussion centers upon how these institutions have affected industrial development and how they have responded to changing demands. Institutional inertia is often to blame for gaps between an institution's function, which is determined by its structure, and the demands placed upon it, which are influenced by social, economic, and technological changes. Each paper contains a discussion of how design innovations might improve institutional performance.

The papers in Part IV examine recent experiments in economic growth and regional development. New strategies for rural development stress recognition of regional advantages and the strengthening competitive advantage. Rather than trying to emulate the development of regions with different social, economic, and natural resource characteristics, rural areas must learn to base their economies and their industrial policies on their traditional strengths: small- and medium-sized enterprises, entrepreneurial spirit, extensive educational networks, and a strong sense of community. In designing these development policies, rural American communities can learn from experiments in less-developed countries that have confirmed the importance of governance structures in enacting successful development policy. The traditional grass-roots activism of rural America may be a key factor to successful industrial development.

If institutions are to meet the changing demands of a dynamic social and economic system, information networks that encourage the communication of these demands must be a part of their design, and they must be flexible enough to respond to change. The papers in Part V focus on policies and programs created by institutions designed using these criteria. Able to respond to market signals as well as to market failure, these institutions exemplify the benefits of counting institutions and their design among the tools of industrial policy. While these experiments provide clues to the direction of change required for a new industrial policy for agricultural and rural development, they are part of a system of policies that has become outdated. To become truly effective, they must be integrated into the new framework for agricultural and rural development policy.

The two papers in Part VI summarize the issues raised in the conference presentations and the discussions that they provoked during the industrial policy conference. The failures of the existing framework of agricultural and rural development policy are highlighted, and recommendations for basing government intervention on a new framework that includes institutions—as well as more traditional instruments in the industrial policy for agriculture and rural development—are put forward.

This conference was organized with the hope of improving understanding of the role of science and industry policy in the development of agriculture, related industries, and the rural sector. By identifying the factors and institutions that control growth in agricultural productivity and the industry, and by better understanding the institutional requirements for the development of industries in general, regions and nations can structure their industrial policies more effectively. Specifically, these policies can be formulated as a system rather than on a piecemeal basis. The result of a more integrated, coordinated industrial policy—based on modern concepts of institutional economics and the political-economic equilibrium that defines sustainable forms of government intervention—will be an improved capacity for stimulating the growth of agriculture and the agricultural industry, as well as that of the rural communities that still depend so heavily on agriculture.

References

Adams, F. Gerald, and C. Andrea Bollino. 1983. "Meaning of Industrial Policy." In Adams, Gerald F., and Lawrence R. Klein, eds., *Industrial Policies for Growth and Competitiveness.* Lexington, Mass.: D. C. Heath.

Adams, F. Gerald, and Lawrence R. Klein. 1983. "Economic Evaluation of Industrial Policies for Growth and Competitiveness: Overview." In Adams, Gerald F., and Lawrence R. Klein, eds., *Industrial Policies for Growth and Competitiveness.* Lexington, Mass.: D. C. Heath.

Bollino, C. Andrea. 1983. "Industrial Policy: A Review of European Approaches." In Adams, Gerald F., and Lawrence R. Klein, eds., *Industrial Policies for Growth and Competitiveness.* Lexington, Mass.: D. C. Heath.

Cochrane, Willard W. 1979. *The Development of American Agriculture: A Historical Analysis.* Minneapolis: University of Minnesota Press.

Goldstein, Harvey A., ed. 1987. "Why State and Local Industrial Policy? An Introduction to the Debate." *The State and Local Industrial Policy Question.* Chicago: Planners Press.

Grossman, Gene M. 1990. "Promoting New Industrial Activities: A Survey of Recent Arguments and Evidence." *OECD Economic Studies* 14.

Krugman, Paul R. 1983. "Targeted Industrial Policies: Theory and Evidence." In *Industrial Change and Public Policy: A Symposium Sponsored by the Federal Reserve Bank of Kansas City.* Kansas City: Federal Reserve Bank of Kansas City.

Lugar, M. I. 1985. "The States and Industrial Development: Program Mix and Policy Effectiveness." Working Paper, Duke University, Institute of Policy Sciences and Public Affairs, Durham, N.C.

Norton, R. D. 1986. "Industrial Policy and American Renewal." *Journal of Economic Literature* 24(March):1–40.

Porter, Michael. 1990. *The Competitive Advantage of Nations.* New York: Free Press.

Shapiro, Helen, and L. Taylor. 1990. "The State and Industrial Strategy." *World Development* 18(6):861–78.

Solo, R. 1983. "Industrial Policy." *Journal of Economic Issues* 18(3).

Tyson, Laura D'Andrea. 1992. *Who's Bashing Whom.* Washington, D.C.: Institute for International Economics.

Wachter, M. L., and S. M. Wachter, eds. 1981. *Toward a New U.S. Industrial Policy.* Philadelphia: University of Pennsylvania Press.

PART I Redefining Industrial Policy

TRADITIONAL VIEWS of the objectives, strategies, and tools of industrial policy are narrowly defined by neoclassical economic theory. A more encompassing view of industrial policy considers the institutions that define the roles played by political and economic agents and that define a political-economic equilibrium. An even broader view of industrial policy examines the dynamics of the constitutional and cultural framework that produces the rules or institutions, and how these dynamics affect the outcome of the political-economic equilibrium. Institutional change then comes to play an important role in industrial policy and industrial growth and development.

1 Industrial Policy for Agriculture and Rural Development

S. R. JOHNSON
S. A. MARTIN

There is little consensus among economists and policymakers on what can and should be accomplished by government intervention in the marketplace. The role for government intervention in special situations is acknowledged by most economists despite a general belief that the market is usually the best mechanism for allocating resources and guiding the development of industry. For example, in the wake of the OPEC oil crisis of the 1970s, economists broadly agreed that although new technologies could provide some relief from the associated structural problems, there was no assurance that market processes could swiftly effect the changes required for industrial adjustment to the new economic environment (Adams and Klein 1983b). In fact, many economists advocated an explicit industrial policy—assisting the response to higher energy prices and playing a key role in associated adjustments (Diebold 1980).

Although acknowledging an important role for government intervention in selected situations, most economists have resisted targeted policy as an alternative to market forces for determining industry growth and development. Even economists who believe that competitive advantage can be created by government action refrain from recommending specific interventions. Because the benefits and costs are so difficult to anticipate, informed opinion about a particular industrial policy or strategy is difficult to formulate (Tyson 1992). In fact, industrial policy

S. R. Johnson is Charles F. Curtiss Distinguished Professor of Agriculture, Iowa State University, and Director of the Center for Agricultural and Rural Development. S. A. Martin is Senior Economist at the Center for Economics Research, Research Triangle Institute.

in the United States seems historically to have been crisis-driven. This may be yet another reason to hesitate before endorsing it as a common recipe for managing economic growth and development.

Arguments against all but the least intrusive industrial policies are difficult to ignore. Formal economic analyses generally show that policies empowering the government, rather than market forces, are inferior. While it can be shown that an optimal policy targeting specific market failures can be beneficial, the optimal policy is often difficult to define and of questionable administrative feasibility. Beyond their conceptual complexity, the information requirements for public guidance of successful policies targeting growth and development of specific industries can be prohibitive. The cost of the necessary information and the political nature of the debate over what industries should be targeted suggest that it is not likely that industrial policies designed by bureaucrats and enacted by lawmakers will approach optimality (Krugman 1983). In short, the support from standard theory for industrial policy as a fix for market failure is cautious at best.

Despite these concerns, the industrial policy debate has expanded. Well-known academic economists and policy advisors such as Robert Reich (1982), Paul Krugman (1990), Lester Thurow (1992), and Laura D'Andrea Tyson (1992) have contributed to the discussion of industrial policy. Their cautious support of industrial policy is conditioned on the need to keep in check political forces that might lead to a policy strategy that does not resemble a careful, informed intervention, but reflects instead the effects of political pressure for a fragmentary, non-coherent set of initiatives that benefit a number of interest groups. Rather than defining an industrial policy assuming insulation of the policy process from political pressure, perhaps the definition of industrial policy should be expanded to include all of the political and economic institutions and agents that influence the final outcome. This expanded view of industrial policy encompasses the political-economic equilibrium and the factors that influence it.

A political-economic equilibrium is the balance of political and economic interests that follows from the interaction within the policy process of all agents and their "personalities." These personalities are derived from the constitutional structure and informal institutions that define an agent's objectives and the scope of the agent's political and economic role. The political-economic equilibrium is characterized by the resulting set of policies, just as price and quantity characterize an economic equilibrium.

Viewing industrial policy in a political-economic equilibrium framework permits its examination on three levels. On the first level, only the economic equilibrium is considered. Industrial policy is guided by a body of economic theory describing market failure and limiting the tools of industrial policy to economic mechanisms that influence economic efficiency. On the second level, the political-economic equilibrium is considered within the existing institutional setting. Given the rules that define the roles of agents and institutions in political and economic markets, changes in political power or economic processes can alter the equilibrium. This analysis has been guided by the literature on rent-seeking behavior (Tullock 1967; Krueger 1974; Buchanan 1989). On a third level, the political-economic equilibrium is considered in a more dynamic context. It is altered by changes in the features of the constitution that empowers groups and defines the scope and the roles of agents in the political and economic markets. This broadest view of industrial policy is considered in the emerging literature on individual and organizational rights (McMillan et al. 1991; Scully 1992).

Industrial Policy for U.S. Agriculture

Agriculture is one of the few U.S. industries for which an at least de facto long-term national industrial policy has been in place. (Others include the utilities and defense.) However, government intervention in agriculture represents an industrial policy in a loose sense compared to European and Japanese approaches. The set of policies for agriculture encompasses diverse goals: economic, environmental, educational, community development, and others far removed from mainstream industrial policy instruments. Many of these interventions and their goals conflict with one another. Still, the extensive government intervention in agricultural markets and in technology development and adoption is unique among industries in the United States, and perhaps it represents an opportunity for applying a new framework for policy formulation and implementation (Urban 1991).

There are a number of ways to describe the industrial policy for U.S. agriculture. Generally, in assessing industrial policy, it is useful to view the essential characteristics of the market activity in the sector compared to the nature and scope of governmental intervention. The selected indicators of sector characteristics and industrial policy shown in Table 1.1 provide perspective for the resources committed by government as compared to the size and activity of the agricultural sector in the United States.

There were approximately 107,000 farms in 1990 that had gross annual sales greater than $250,000. Slightly more than two million farms had gross annual sales of less than $250,000. Gross receipts to agriculture were $169 billion in 1990, split roughly evenly between crops and livestock. Annual farm income in 1990, measured both as cash receipts and as net farm income, was $61.82 billion and

$50.87 billion, respectively. These indicators of economic performance for U.S. agriculture reflect a secular decline in the number of farms, with distribution becoming increasingly skewed toward relatively smaller farms (many of which are part-time). Annual gross farm receipts have moved up relatively slowly in recent years and at rates lower than the general rate of inflation, reflecting in part productivity increases. Net farm income in 1990, although higher in nominal dollars than in most years during the 1980s, was lower in real terms than during the decades of the 1970s and 1980s (FAPRI 1992).

Industrial policy for agriculture is suggested by three sets of summary indicators: Commodity Credit Corporation (CCC) costs, research and extension expenditures, and receipts of checkoff programs. The CCC costs are mostly for direct farm subsidies and in 1990 were $8.11 billion, approximately 15 percent of net farm income. Public research and extension expenditures reflected a rough 2:1 split between the states and the federal government, with federal spending of $1.15 billion and state spending of $2.45 billion. The checkoff programs have been authorized in recent federal legislation and implemented by a number of commodity associations on the basis of general producer referenda. Total checkoff program expenditures were $190 million in 1990. Clearly the level of activity of government and quasi-government organizations in U.S. agriculture is high.

Other aspects of the industrial policy for U.S. agriculture are not easily quantifiable or summarized. These include patent laws that influence the pattern and levels of private research expenditure, a legal environment that has resulted in high levels of concentration in livestock and grain processing and distribution, marketing orders and agreements that restrict production and interregional trade, ethanol subsidies, and border protection for numerous commodities, including sugar, meat products, and peanuts. Government programs not directly related to agriculture are also important for the industry; examples are roads, communication, and other infrastructure investments that could not be supplied at current levels without significant public support.

In a number of respects, the industrial policy for U.S. agriculture has been successful. Productivity has increased, costs of production have declined, the price of food to U.S. consumers is low and stable, and the agricultural sector has been a consistent source of export income. Alternatively, an indirect goal of U.S. agricultural policy that has not been successful is the maintenance of economic activity in rural areas. The increasing recognition that U.S. agricultural policy is not—despite the high federal and state cost—a rural or regional development policy, and that it is benefiting a relatively small number of farms, could imply significant change for the coming agricultural legislation, the 1995 Farm Bill.

Table 1.1.   Indicators of sector characteristics and industrial policy for U.S. agriculture

Sector Characteristics (1990)

Number of Farms
Sales less than $249,999	2,033,399
Sales more than $250,000	107,021
TOTAL	2,140,420

Farm Receipts (Billion Dollars)
Crops	$76.82
Livestock	84.07
Other	8.10
TOTAL	$168.99

Income Measures (Billion Dollars)
Net Cash Income	$61.82
Net Farm Income	50.87

Industrial Policy (1990)

CCC Costs (Billion Dollars)
Deficiency Payments	$4.18
Conservation Reserve	1.63
EEP	.24
Other	2.06
TOTAL	$8.11

Check-Off Programs (Million Dollars)
Beef	$43.15
Dairy	76.67
Pork	31.35
Other	39.10
TOTAL	$190.27

Research and Extension (Million Dollars)
Federal	
Extension	$355
Research	791
State	
Extension	861
Research	1,597
TOTAL	$3,604

SOURCES: FAPRI (1991); U.S. Agricultural Census; Agricultural Marketing System; Huffman and Evenson (1992).

An Expanded Framework for Industrial Policy

Available reviews of the recent experiences with industrial policy developed on the basis of market failure raise questions about the role of government and the constitution of the state that empowers individuals, agents, and institutions (Adams and Klein 1983a; Grossman 1990). In fact, there are serious questions for industrial policy in the United States and in other nations: Where does it start? Where does it stop? Answers to these relatively simple questions involve political-economic equilibrium and serve to broaden the scope for analysis of industrial policy. These constitutional or institutional dimensions provide a framework for investigating industrial policy that extends beyond the traditional concepts of market failure (Buchanan 1989; Laffont and Tirole 1991).

Figure 1.1 sketches the relationship between the constitutional roots of society, private activity, the functioning of markets, and the public sector. The lightly dashed square identifies factors that make up the constitution or social contract forming the foundation for the society or state. These can be viewed as defining individual and institutional rights: civil, political, and economic. The rules by which the state is constituted empower individuals and institutions and provide a structure for political, social, and economic activity (Buchanan 1989; Laffont and Tirole 1991). The institutions, defined both as organizations or agents and as sets of rules or norms for behavior, together with the constitutionally prescribed individual rights, govern and regulate the functioning of the public and private sectors, and the organization of markets (Williamson 1975, 1985). The market and the public and private agents operating in the existent "rights environment" organize economic activity and yield economic performance. Performance is broadly evaluated in terms of economic growth and equity.

The traditional view of industrial policy involves the roles of the public and private sectors, and their interplay through the market. Thus, at one level, outlined in the darkly dashed box of Figure 1.1, industrial policy deals primarily with market failure of one type or another. At another level, encompassing the entire structure of the figure, industrial policy can address institutions, the political economy of policy, as well as the more familiar aspects of market failure within an existing institutional setting.

In summary, Figure 1.1 suggests three alternatives for industrial policy in a market economic framework:

- Policies balancing the public and private sectors, given the institutions and the constitution of the state, to achieve increased economic performance. This is the customary framework for industrial policy to address market failure.

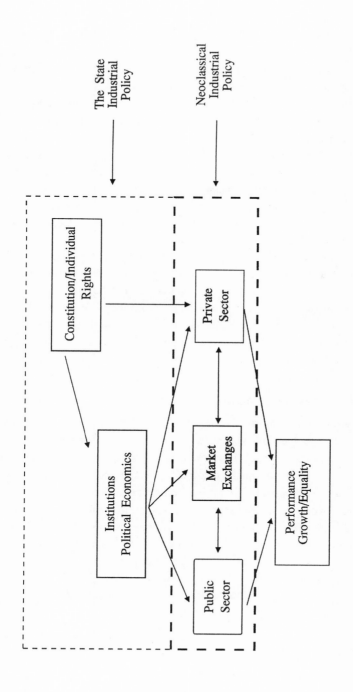

Figure 1.1. Industrial policy, markets, and the state.

- Policies evolving from the political-economic equilibrium. The industrial policy, in this case, is conditioned by the constitutionally implied decision spaces for economic and political agents. Rather than being constrained to the economic sphere, these decision spaces include political markets and the activities that affect their outcomes, such as rent-seeking behavior.
- Policies that consider constitutional and institutional changes, with resulting adjustments in political-economic equilibrium. In national contexts, these constitutional features as determinants of policy and economic growth are receiving increased attention (McMillan et al. 1991). In short, the principles on which the state is constituted affect the role and power of economic and political agents and institutions. These measures are the broadest in scope since they involve manipulation of the factors conditioning the political-economic equilibrium.

Clearly there is more to the explanation of growth and equity in economies and industries than the simple concept of market failure. Still, this concept provides a powerful tool for guiding and evaluating industrial policy. Perhaps it is only when the investigation of economic and industrial policy is expanded to include concepts of political-economic equilibrium and the constitutional and institutional framework defining political, economic, and civil rights that the secrets of sustained economic development and growth will be revealed.

Market Failures and Industrial Policy

The traditional and more narrow view of industrial policy—that which is limited in scope to the darkly dashed box in Figure 1.1—can be guided by neoclassical economic theory. In a traditional market economy model, market efficiency is assured by the characteristics of perfect competition and constant returns to scale. Government interventions to increase efficiency, when legitimate models of real-world economic systems deviate from perfect competitions, are considered. These issues of market failure have been reviewed extensively in the existing literature on industrial policy (Krugman 1983; Urban 1983; Grossman 1990). We discuss several types of market failure that have arisen often in the context of industrial policy for agriculture and rural development. Strategies and tools of industrial policy are discussed as they are traditionally defined by their role in correcting market failure.

Causes of Market Failure

A market unfettered by government intervention might not always result in the most efficient allocation of resources. Conditions under which pure market outcomes might not lead to pareto-optimal results include imperfect competition and externalities in production or consumption. Under these conditions, government intervention is required to achieve an optimal resource allocation.

Imperfect Competition. Large fixed costs of entry and economies of scale are features of many modern industrial activities. Fixed costs may take the form of specialized capital equipment, research and development investment, or the purchase of a license or patent. Perfect competition is unlikely to emerge in such industries, because the market is not large enough to support many producers of the size required for efficient production. In selected cases, the market will not support even a single firm if fixed costs are prohibitively high.

Agriculture traditionally has had many small producers who have little influence over price. However, mechanization and technological advances have led to larger and larger farms as efficient methods of agricultural production become cost effective only when applied to larger and larger scale. Arguments that agriculture will become a concentrated industry have been used to support government intervention to preserve the economic viability of small- and medium-sized farms. And, many of the agribusinesses in the United States are highly concentrated; for example, in meat processing and in grain handling.

Policy toward industries with economies of scale must balance the need to protect consumers from the exercise of market power against the need to promote efficient production. If antitrust policy is so strict as to prevent even one firm from operating at minimal efficiency, then the industry may not develop. In the case of agriculture, the subsidization of small- and medium-sized farms sometimes is justified as a way to rein-in the market power of producers that otherwise would become too powerful. And for agribusiness, exposure to foreign competition is becoming increasingly used to counter monopoly power. The important question, in terms of economic efficiency, is whether the cost of the subsidies and/or the loss of the domestic market to foreign competitors is smaller than the cost of the inflated prices that might dominate a concentrated agricultural market.

External Economies. Externalities arise when the actions of one economic agent affect the well-being of others in ways not mediated by the marketplace. Unless the government intervenes, the agents causing the externalities have no reason to take into account their effects on other agents. Externalities in consumption occur when the utility of one consumer depends on consumption levels of others. Externalities in production occur when the actions of one producer affect another producer's cost of production. Pollution of groundwater is a negative externality resulting from the use of pesticides. Although the productivity of a downstream farm might decline, the farmer using the pesticide has no incentive to consider this effect when deciding whether to apply the pesticide.

One type of positive externality that is widely discussed in the context of rural development policy is called *agglomeration economies.* Agglomeration economies exist in industries in which location near suppliers, customers, or other producers reduces cost or stimulates demand. These externalities are particularly important in industries in which specialized inputs and information networks are necessary for efficient production. Although firms base location decisions on the cost advantages to themselves, their decisions can affect the cost and demand conditions of other firms in the area. Government policies that promote industrial clustering in order to build a critical mass of industrial activity are based on the assumption of agglomeration economies.

External economies also often are cited as a rationale for government intervention in research and development. Knowledge has value that is difficult to appropriate, and intellectual property rights are imperfect as instruments for internalizing the external benefits of knowledge generation. A scientific breakthrough might have implications much broader than the realm within which the funding company operates or within which patent protection can capture the returns. Furthermore, personnel with specialized knowledge of the results of research commonly move between firms, providing the benefit of their training to companies that have not paid for it.

The agricultural extension program and the system of land-grant universities that developed and spread agricultural science over the past century is the most notable example of government support for research and development in agriculture. For example, while private seed companies have contributed to the development of new plant varieties, much of the basic research in the past has been conducted at agricultural experiment stations that were publicly supported. These expenditures can be supported by pointing to their positive and inappropriable externalities.

Government Intervention. One of the pervasive causes of distortions between the idealized model of a competitive economy and economic reality is governmental intervention within the market. Economic incentives are distorted by government policies of all types: taxes and subsidies that are not neutral, procurement, minimum wage laws, price controls, trade barriers, and others. These policies often are developed to accomplish objectives other than economic efficiency. In the presence of these distortions, it can be argued that further intervention is justified (Lipsey and Lancaster 1956). However, the responses to failure due to market distortions must be designed carefully so as not to create additional distortions and associated costs to the economy. Modification of the existing policy to address the major causes of the distortion is often the best economic solution. If this approach is not politically feasible, other approaches can be considered that reduce the distortion and that themselves do not cause additional distortions.

Goals and Strategies of Industrial Policy

Within the darkly dashed box of Figure 1.1, the only industrial policies that are defensible by the standards of economic efficiency are those that correct market failure in a way that causes the fewest distortions of market signals (Corden 1974). However, several factors make it difficult to limit the scope of government intervention to correction of market failure. First, it is difficult to detect market failure, to measure its cost in terms of economic efficiency, and to determine which industrial policies will correct the distortion. Second, instruments that are cost-free, in terms of taxes and subsidies, might not be available to policymakers.

Furthermore, the goals of industrial policy often extend beyond the correction of market distortion. If economic efficiency given the current institutional setting were to be the main criteria for judging the performance of the economy, then correction of market failure would be the only goal of industrial policy. However, economic efficiency is only one of many criteria by which economic performance is judged. And, within different constitutional or institutional settings there can be different regimes for efficient exchange. Also, there are other performance criteria, including economic equity, economic growth, and business cycle stabilization. In view of these criteria and the frailty of the concept of efficiency when institutions are variable or in play, several alternative strategies for industrial policy have emerged.

Industrial policies of the presidential administrations of the 1980s and early 1990s have sought to promote economic efficiency by correcting market distortions. That is, with respect to antitrust and trade negotiations, the official goal has been to seek reductions in impediments to entrepreneurship and to domestic and international trade, with industrial development and change left largely to market forces (Adams and Klein 1983b). However, a number of other government policymaking bodies have enunciated goals that go beyond removing market distortions and achieving national economic efficiency. For example, state governments have been active in attempts to influence the location and growth of technologically sophisticated industries (Martin 1992).

Norton (1986) identifies two strategies pursued by proponents of industrial policy. "Modernizers" seek to accelerate the movement of resources into industries that are up and coming or are likely to be competitive in the future. "Preservationists" are concerned with forestalling the collapse of a declining industry, and the unemployment (and political strife) that may accompany such decline. Some policies reflect a mix of these strategies, on the one hand picking "winner industries" and transferring resources to encourage their development, while on the other hand providing transitional aid to declining industries (Adams and Klein 1983b). A third strategy might be called "stabilizing," or "transitional." These policies aim to accelerate the flow of resources to their most productive uses. This strategy is consistent with the correction of market failure in the sense that it seeks to remove obstacles to structural adjustment.

The modernization and preservation goals of industrial policy have parallels in the literature on agricultural and rural development. Johnson et al. (1989) note that some rural development strategies propose to revitalize rural communities through policies that work against market forces to restore the structure of rural life as it existed three or more decades ago. Alternative development strategies recognize that agriculture cannot create economic activity sufficient to support the growth of rural communities. These strategies actively seek diversification to augment the shrinking level of economic activity related to agriculture (Krikelas 1992).

Redistribution of income is a goal of industrial policy that does not fit well into either preservation, modernization, or transitional strategies. Still, redistribution is a common goal of industrial policy. It involves the idea of working toward greater equity, be it among individuals, firms, regions, or nations. Some policies are redistributive by design; others are redistributive only by accident, often resulting in redistributions away from equity. Redistributive aspects of industrial policy are important, however, because they are designed to change the comparative levels of economic performance over time and across nations and states (Bergman and Goldstein 1987).

Redistribution may conflict with other goals of industrial policy. On the federal level, for example, policies designed to target the most efficient industries may benefit regions that already are doing relatively well economically, at the expense of regions dependent on industries in decline. National goals of regional equity in this case clash directly with national goals for promoting efficient and growing industries (Eads 1981; Bell and Lande 1982).

Industrial Policy Tools under Alternative Goals

A number of measures are available to implement an industrial policy strategy. Even when industrial policy is defined in its most narrow, market equilibrium sense, there are many tools from which to choose. Commonly used tools include taxes and subsidies, preferential tax treatment for certain types of investment, public funding of infrastructure or education, and trade policy. Each of these affects economic incentives and can be employed in an array of industrial policy strategies.

Policy Tools for Industrial Modernization

Modernization, or winner-picking, strategies are used more often in Japan and France, for example, than in the United States. Winner-picking strategies attempt to identify high-growth industries in which the country might be able to gain a comparative advantage (Adams and Bollino 1983; Bollino 1983). Tools often used in this strategy include research and development (R&D) funding, tariff protection, infrastructure development, procurement policy, and antitrust policy.

Public support for research and development is perhaps the type of industrial policy most easily defended in the name of market failure (Arrow 1962; Merrill 1984; Pack and Westphal 1986; Folster 1991). Knowledge has many of the characteristics of a public good, particularly in the case of basic research. In agriculture, government traditionally has funded basic research and has made the results freely available through agricultural extension to maximize its social benefits.

R&D policy for picking winners channels research funding to particular technologies that have been chosen as strategic for the selected industries (Beltz 1991). Another justification for government funding of R&D is the associated risk. Government funding of R&D is designed to spread the risk over taxpayers rather than concentrating it with a single investor (Rothwell and Zegveld 1984). Furthermore, government-funded R&D often is targeted toward technology that will be used in the provision of public goods, such as defense and public infrastructure.

Trade policy has been an important avenue through which U.S. policymakers have intervened in the market with the intent of correcting market failures or distortions. The reduction of trade barriers through the General Agreement on Tariffs and Trade (GATT) since World War II has removed distortions caused by government intervention. Strategic trade policy for stimulating growth in high-technology industries has been promoted within a modernizing industrial policy strategy (Tyson 1992).

Tariffs are imposed sometimes to protect new industries in response to claims of dynamic economies of scale, the so-called infant industry argument for tariff protection. Tariff policy often has been industry-specific (Wescott 1983); however, rather than pursuing the goal of correcting market failure, tariffs and other nontariff barriers have been applied most often to save industries that no longer have a comparative advantage. Thus, tariffs are also a major tool of the preservationist strategy for industrial policy and often result from the political-economic equilibria that include powerful trade associations.

Policy Tools for Industrial Preservation

Measures to provide aid to industries that have lost competitiveness, or to firms threatened with bankruptcy, are associated with the preservationist goal of industrial policy. Most of the direct assistance to firms in the United States falls under this policy category (Adams and Klein 1983a). These policies are sometimes indirect, industrywide policies, such as tariff protection of textiles, and sometimes they are direct, firm-specific policies such as the loan guarantees provided to Lockheed, General Dynamics, and Chrysler.

Preservation policies often are rationalized by the potential loss to society from unemployment, impacts for related industries, or risks to national defense if the industry or firm is allowed to fail. However, the long-term costs of maintaining industries that are no longer competitive may be high. These costs include not only that of the subsidy, but also the opportunity cost of employing resources in activities that ultimately are less productive. For example, resources spent on preservationist policies that amount to simple income transfers might be better spent on aiding the flow of resources—including labor—into more productive uses.

Policies that provide temporary assistance to industries that have the potential for modernization and structural adjustment can be distinguished from policies that are mainly the result of lobbying and rent-seeking activity on the part of the potential losers. Managerial and technical assistance often are provided to modernize industries that are competitive. While this is a preservationist policy in the sense that it attempts to maintain the industry, it does so by attacking the cause of the industrial decline; it emphasizes regaining competitiveness, with that government assistance as temporary. Unfortunately, many temporary programs build political constituencies and are ultimately more permanent than intended.

Policy Tools for Industrial Transition

Transition assistance is designed to speed the flow of resources to uses in which they are more productive. This type of policy relies heavily on market incentives and on the removal of impediments to resource flows. An often cited form of transitional assistance accelerates the flow of labor from declining industries to those in which skilled labor is scarce. These worker training programs have enjoyed varied success. One notable success is the Japanese experience of finding alternative employment for unemployed shipbuilders (Adams and Klein 1983a). Measures commonly employed in the transition strategy may fall outside narrowly defined market-based industrial policy. For example, a change in patent policy allowing government scientists to collect royalties from discoveries while on government contracts will give added incentives to target research toward commercial uses. Similarly, relaxation of antitrust policy that allows firms to pool R&D risk encourages investment in projects that would not be funded otherwise, given imperfections in the capital market. These measures change institutions (property rights and laws against collaboration) and therefore fall within the realm of what has been termed the most broad definition of industrial policy.

Institutions and Industrial Policy

Industrial policies do not emerge or change as economists or policymakers discover and attempt to fix market failures or distortions. Rather, industrial policy is more likely a result of a political-economic equilibrium in the context of the rules by which the state is constituted. The equilibrium may involve the regulatory agency, the legislative body, the participants in the industry, the consumers and interest groups, and the technology, demographics, and other factors that condition the relationships among these players in the political and economic processes guiding the economy.

Each of the interest groups or agents has, in fact, a personality, which is defined by its disposition, talents, self-interest, motivations, and vehicles for action. This personality is derived in part from the rights assigned by the constitution or given over by the individual participants (Olson 1965; Williamson 1975; Johnson 1985; McCubbins 1985; Faux 1987; Spiller 1988). These individuals, firms, interest groups, agencies, and elected bodies participate in both political and economic activity. The resulting balance of personalities, power, and interrelationships conditions the policy process, resulting in a political-economic equilibrium.

If this rationale is accepted as the primary basis for industrial policy—and in particular, for industrial policy for agriculture—analysis can proceed outside the concept of market failure. The features of the constitution that empower these groups or define the scope for their political and economic activity can be studied and formally evaluated. The appropriate framework for this analysis, at least in its basic stages, is cross-country (McMillan et al. 1991; Scully 1992). The equilibrium is also conditioned and influenced by institutional and technological innovations, by which it is continually redefined. These two types of innovations, institutional and technological, are viewed for this discussion in their broadest sense. Examples include newly organized contingency markets, international trade agreements facilitated by developments in communications and transportation technology, technologies related to new-product development, and many others.

The political-economic equilibrium is dynamic, reflecting and adapting to change, some of which may occur in response to internal dynamics and interactions among the players, just as fluctuations in supply or demand (or their interaction) affect an economic equilibrium. Given this understanding, the analysis of industrial policy can proceed to a broader level, investigating the implications of these conditioning factors for changes in the political-economic equilibrium, along with the consequences for economic intervention. Political-economic equilibrium, as a guide to industrial policy and factors responsible for change, can incorporate results of more standard economic theory and measures to address market failure.

The Political-Economic Equilibrium

Modern analyses of government regulation and the conditions that underlie the role of government in market economies concentrate on what is called *agent theory* (Weingast 1984; Laffont and Tirole 1991). This agent theoretic approach identifies the players, collective and individual, the scope for their activity, and their rational behavior given constitutional, organizational, informational, and other conditions. For agriculture, the framework for government intervention and major institutions or players involved can be represented (Fig. 1.2). The elected, or legislative, body is Congress; in particular, the Senate and House agricultural committees. The agency responsible for the administration of industrial policy for agriculture is the U.S. Department of Agriculture (USDA). Other agencies influencing agricultural industry policy include, for example, those that regulate financial institutions, public and private transportation systems, and trade.

The industry participants are the farmers, if agriculture is narrowly defined, or agribusiness in general if a broader industry definition is used. The broader the industry definition, the greater the role for agencies other than the USDA in administering the industry policy. With the broader definition, the firms or industry participants themselves may have monopoly power that they wish to preserve or enhance. More likely, however, the firms or industry participants will organize to form interest groups. These interest groups in turn affect the agency and Congress

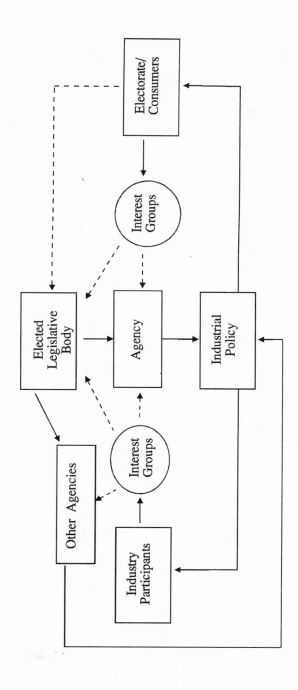

Figure 1.2.   Government regulation, the institutional setting, and industrial policy.

through direct and indirect means, with the objective of developing an industrial policy that is favorable to their constituents.

A parallel structure for influencing policy toward agriculture involves the electorate, or consumers. Members of the electorate can influence the legislative body directly or can organize in interest groups. These groups represent the interests of their constituents to the legislative body and the agency, encouraging objectives of industry policy that are somehow beneficial. Also involved, although not represented in Figure 1.2, are interest groups that represent participants in industries related to agriculture. Consideration of these interest groups would complicate this brief sketch for describing the political-economic determinants of industry policy. Figure 1.2 is thus intentionally stylized to focus on the agents most active in the design and implementation of industrial policy for U.S. agriculture.

Agents and Their Personalities

The agents contributing to industrial policy for agriculture behave in ways important to the policy that has evolved, and that may influence the adaptation of policy in response to external stimuli. Clearly it would be possible to dwell at length on these agents and their constituencies (Laffont and Tirole 1991). This discussion will simply indicate the importance of the organizing principals for the agencies and the ways in which agencies might influence the processes that result in the industrial policy.

Congress. The U.S. Congress represents the electorate and regulates agriculture primarily through its associated committees. The agriculture committees do not have exclusive rights for the governance of the sector, however. Environmental aspects and other impacts of sector activity bring agriculture into direct consideration by other committees. Aspects affecting the personality of Congress and the committees relative to the agricultural policy include the seniority system, the committee structure (e.g., commodity subcommittees), the resources available for staffing and the control of staff, and the interlinkages of key committee members with other important committees (e.g., those directing appropriations).

These observations on Congress are not novel, but they suggest structural features of the forum in which decisions are made within congressional committees. Organization of the committees by commodity makes them particularly vulnerable, for example, to interest-group pressures. And, the laws for campaign financing, seniority, and a host of other factors condition the types of decisions that can be expected from the committees, and the ways in which committees adapt to influences external to the political equilibrium. In short, the role of the Congress in industrial policy and as a decision forum guarantees that policy will not be directed to a single purpose. Instead, the goals of a number of interest groups will be considered and balanced. The result is a policy that is likely to simultaneously pursue preservation, modernization, and transitional goals.

U.S. Department of Agriculture. The USDA is a bureaucracy, with all of the associated behavioral implications of a bureaucracy (Weingast 1984; Williamson 1985). Among the important features relative to its performance in agricultural policymaking are the roles of the organizational leaders; organization-specific goals that reflect both the interests of the members of the bureaucracy and the industry; standard operating procedures, including processes by which decisions are made; time perspectives; incentive systems within the bureaucracy; and other factors. The personalities of an agency and its members characterize the decision-making process and are reflected in decisions to intervene in the industry. The situation for the USDA is perhaps made more complex by its set of responsibilities. Unlike other federal agencies, it has industry-specific charges. These include regulation, education, and technology development, as well as the execution of policies concerned with direct transfers, whether by maintenance of barriers to entry or the management of government subsidies.

Interest Groups. For agriculture, the array of interest groups reflects not only consumers but also the diversity of participants in the industry. These include commodity associations, general farm organizations, farm worker groups, agribusiness promotion groups, and environmental groups. Reasons for their energy, activity, and power have been the subject of a long stream of research (Olson 1965). Olson's theory on the logic of collective action, for example, implies that for a given issue, the smaller the interest group, the higher the per capita stake and therefore the higher the incentive of its members to affect regulatory outcomes. Interest groups also cooperate with each other and attempt to influence their respective agendas and priorities.

The primary focus of interest group activity, however, is the actions of the elected officials and the agency responsible for regulating the industry. Interest groups have many means available for influencing the public decision makers and, in turn, the industry policy. These include

- Bribes or alternative forms of indirect compensation
- Promises of future employment opportunity
- Political support (i.e., delivering constituency votes)
- Cultivation of personal relationships

- Management of information and publicity
- Transfers through political action committees

This list is incomplete, but it serves to highlight the instruments that these organizations have for intervening on behalf of their constituents. The interest groups, too, are bureaucracies, with elected boards, executive staffs, and associated principal agent problems. In some cases, organizational continuity and the design of intervention efforts appear almost entirely given over to the staff or executives. The staffs and executives may use the organization and the form in which the decisions are made for their personal and organizational interests, as well as for the interests of their constituents.

Industry Participants. Alternative definitions of the agriculture industry yield different observations on the homogeneity of its participants. Broad definitions that include the highly concentrated agricultural processing and distribution system suggest that the firms themselves may operate as interest groups to preserve benefits from the regulatory agencies and, arguably, monopoly power of various types. Many large agricultural firms, for example, have a legislative liaison staff and purchase legal assistance designed to influence legislation and the administration of industrial policy. At the other extreme are the farms, which probably most closely approximate the competitive model. The farms and agricultural laborers tend to organize their political activity through interest groups that address particular aspects of their economic activity. These interest groups naturally focus on regions, commodities, and other orientations, as consistent with the ideas and concepts of Olson.

Dynamics and Capacity for Change

One particularly striking aspect of the political-economic equilibrium responsible for industrial policy for agriculture is its potential for rigidity. The different agendas of the elected officials and the bureaucrats in the regulatory agencies, along with the principal agent problem within the interest organizations, all argue for resistance to radical change. In fact, it seems fair to assume that the changes that do occur are more likely to be forced from outside the immediate system. However, even in the case of external stimuli, the response from the system may be defensive rather than adaptive. For example, one of the immediate responses to a possible change could be a coalition within the existing system to preserve the structure of the industry. This type of resistance can be costly if the existing equilibrium is characterized by wasteful policies. The result may be that the agents, in maintaining the existing industrial policy and resulting allocation of resources, find themselves sharing a smaller pie.

Not all of the agents in the political-economic equilibrium are resistant to change. For example, interest groups concerned about the relationship between agriculture and the environment may aggressively pursue an altered industrial policy. Alternatively, agribusinesses and farms that are in a position to take advantage of economies of scale or size may find it advantageous to change the policy. Similar motivations may apply to companies altering the industry through investments in research and development and gaining benefits through market power. Advantages of change to selected participants in the industry include enhanced competitiveness in international markets, increased market share, reduced impacts on key environmental indicators, and increased occupational safety.

Changes in industrial policy also can be initiated by anticipated external events. Examples include changes in demographics that affect political representation, multinational agreements that alter markets and market opportunities, development of new technologies, and the emergence of new constituency groups. Evidence of forward-looking industrial policy is provided by the heavy public and private investment in research and development in areas considered to be winners. Forces for change in industrial policy also can come from within as constituents of interest groups change priorities.

The political origins of industrial policy may help to explain why many agricultural policies appear to work against each other. Industrial policy for U.S. agriculture will change; the question is simply when a major adjustment will occur. Many would argue that we are nearing the threshold of change due to the failure of agricultural policy to further rural development, as well as to the continued internationalization of markets, the reduction of barriers to entry, the recent advances in technology, and the pressures on agriculture from other sectors. The broader constitutional-institutional model, combined with the concept of political-economic equilibrium and with the more traditional ideas of market failure, offers significant opportunity for shaping this policy.

Conclusions

The review of industrial policy for U.S. agriculture suggests several windows at which those interested in effecting changes in the performance of the sector, or in the industrial policy itself, might stand for guidance. Recall that the general goals for industrial policy have been classified as (1) preserving or restoring the existing structure for the industry, thereby maintaining the existing political-economic equilibrium; (2) transition, or accommodating and increasing the efficiency of adaptation to change (primarily external); and (3) modernizing in anticipation of external changes that will affect the structure of the industry and its political-economic equilibrium, and that will position the sector to take advantage of possibilities for increased economic performance. The windows for guidance of activity to support these general goals of industrial policy obviously are not mutually exclusive. It is instructive, however, to consider the set of alternative windows as a basis for understanding the academic, political, and other initiatives under way relative to industrial policy for agriculture.

The first of these windows is for economic analysis. Opportunities for economic analyses of industrial policy are extensive and still underexploited. Issues for the development of industrial policy include market failure–based assessments of the economic impacts of alternative interventions, and analysis of these interventions in multiple contexts (*second best*). To address these issues, both compensatory policies and policies to correct the market failures are options. The value of economic analysis of these policies for the industry is clear; better information about the consequences of interventions can result in policies that alter the political-economic equilibrium, leading to improved efficiency and growth.

The second window is for political-economic equilibrium analysis. The analysis in this case would concentrate on empowerment, the behavior and function of organizations and agents affecting the industrial policy, the institutional structure in which decisions are made, and other aspects of the constitutional and regulatory setting. This framework, commonly called the new institutional economics, has been applied to the behavior of interest groups and the bureaucracy, but its use as an analytical tool is in its infancy. Participants in the policy process can benefit from this analytical framework, which is suggested by the merger of organizational, economic, and constitutional methods. The participation and dynamics of interest groups, the impact of agency (USDA) organization, linkages of USDA with other agencies of government, and interactions among the decision processes of interest groups all can be predicted and better assessed through the use of this approach.

The third window is for constitutional, or more fundamental, change. This may be the most speculative area for inquiry, yet it has the potential for assessing and predicting the most radical changes to industrial policy. Through this type of agricultural policy initiatives, the most sweeping industry changes can be made. For example, concern for the lagging growth and performance of rural areas could lead to a distinction between the industrial policy for agriculture and a regional development policy for rural areas. After fifty years of a basically consistent policy, concerns about the environment and changing political dynamics of agricultural representation, along with changes in technology and agricultural institutions, may provide the stimuli for a major rethinking of agricultural policy. At this window is guidance on how the institutions that forge the new industrial policy for agriculture might be constituted to better accommodate change and better contribute to sustained growth of the sector.

References

Adams, F. Gerald, and Lawrence R. Klein, eds. 1983a. *Industrial Policies for Growth and Competitiveness.* Lexington, Mass.: D. C. Heath.

_____. 1983b. "Economic Evaluation of Industrial Policies for Growth and Competitiveness: Overview." In Gerald F. Adams and Lawrence R. Klein, eds., *Industrial Policies for Growth and Competitiveness.* Lexington, Mass.: D. C. Heath.

Adams, F. Gerald, and C. Andrea Bollino. 1983. "Meaning of Industrial Policy." In Gerald F. Adams and Lawrence R. Klein, eds., *Industrial Policies for Growth and Competitiveness.* Lexington, Mass.: D. C. Heath.

Arrow, K. J. 1962. "Economic Welfare and the Allocation of Resources for Invention." In R. Nelson, ed., *The Rate and Direction of Inventive Activity.* Princeton, N.J.: Princeton University Press.

Bell, M. E., and P. S. Lande. 1982. *Regional Dimensions of Industrial Policy.* Toronto: Lexington Books.

Beltz, C. A. 1991. *High Tech Maneuvers: Industrial Policy Lessons of HDTV.* Washington, D.C.: AEI Press.

Bergman, Edward M., and Harvey A. Goldstein. 1987. "Advocates, Institutional Arrangements, and Industrial Policy." In Harvey A. Goldstein, ed., *The State and Local Industrial Policy Question.* Chicago: Planners Press.

Bollino, C. Andrea. 1983. "Industrial Policy: A Review of European Approaches." In Gerald F. Adams and Lawrence R. Klein, eds., *Industrial Policies for Growth and Competitiveness.* Lexington, Mass.: D. C. Heath.

Buchanan, James M. 1989. *Explorations into Constitutional Economics.* Texas A&M University Economics Series, College Station.

Corden, W. M. 1974. *Trade Policy and Economic Welfare.* Oxford: Clarendon Press.

Diebold, William, Jr. 1980. *Industrial Policy as an International Issue.* New York: McGraw-Hill.

Eads, George C. 1981. "The Political Experience in Allocating Investment: Lessons from the United States and Elsewhere." In M. L. Wachter and S. M. Wachter, eds., *Toward a New U.S. Industrial Policy.* Philadelphia: University of Pennsylvania Press.

FAPRI. 1992. *U.S. Agricultural Outlook.* Center for Agricultural and Rural Development, Iowa State University, Ames.

FAPRI. 1991. *U.S. Agricultural Outlook.* Center for Agricultural and Rural Development, Iowa State University, Ames.

Faux, J. 1987. "Industrial Policy and Democratic Institutions." In Harvey A. Goldstein, ed., *The State and Local Industrial Policy Question*. Chicago: Planners Press.

Folster, Stefan. 1991. "The Art of Encouraging Innovation." Stockholm: Industrial Institute for Economic and Social Research.

Grossman, Gene M. 1990. "Promoting New Industrial Activities: A Survey of Recent Arguments and Evidence." *OECD Economic Studies* 14.

Huffman, Wallace E., and Robert E. Evenson. 1992. "Technology and Agricultural Development: How Public Policy Enhances Scientific and Economic Programs." Paper prepared for "Industrial Policy for Agriculture in the Global Economy" Conference, September 16–17, Iowa State University, Ames.

Johnson, Stanley R. 1985. "A Critique of Existing Models for Policy Analysis." In Zuhair A. Hassan and H. Bruce Huff, eds., *Agricultural Sector Models for Policy Analysis*. Ottawa, Ontario: Agriculture Canada, 195–224.

Johnson, S. R., D. Otto, H. Jensen, and S. A. Martin. 1989. "Rural Economic Development Policies for Midwestern States." In Harrell R. Rodgers, Jr., and Gregory Weiher, eds., *Rural Poverty: Special Causes and Policy Reforms*. New York: Greenwood Press.

Krikelas, Andrew C. 1992. "Why Regions Grow: A Review of Research on the Economic Base Model." *Economic Review* 77(4):16–29.

Krueger, A. O. 1974. "The Political Economy of the Rent-Seeking Society." *American Economic Review* 64(June):291–303.

Krugman, Paul R. 1983. "Targeted Industrial Policies: Theory and Evidence." In *Industrial Change and Public Policy: A Symposium Sponsored by the Federal Reserve Bank of Kansas City*. Kansas City: Federal Reserve Bank of Kansas City.

———. 1990. *The Age of Diminished Expectations: U.S. Economic Policy in the 1990s*. Cambridge, Mass.: MIT Press.

Laffont, Jean-Jacques, and Jean Tirole. 1993. "A Theory of Incentives in Procurement and Regulation." Cambridge, Mass.: MIT Press.

Lipsey, R. G., and K. Lancaster. 1956. "The General Theory of the Second Best." *Review of Economic Studies* 63:11–32.

Martin, S. A. 1992. "The Influence of State Technology Incentives: Evidence from the Machine Tool Industry." Ph.D. dissertation, Department of Economics, Iowa State University, Ames.

McCubbins, M. 1985. "Legislative Design of Regulatory Structure." *American Journal of Political Science* 29:721–48.

McMillan, J., G. C. Rausser, and S. R. Johnson. 1991. "Freedoms and Economic Growth." Institute for Policy Reform Working Paper (November), Washington, D.C.

Merrill, Stephen A. 1984. "The Politics of Micropolicy: Innovation and Industrial Policy in the United States." *Policy Studies Review* 14:445–51.

Norton, R. D. 1986. "Industrial Policy and American Renewal." *Journal of Economic Literature* 24(March):1–40.

Olson, M. 1965. *The Logic of Collective Action*. Cambridge, Mass.: Harvard University Press.

Pack, H., and L. E. Westphal. 1986. "Industrial Strategy and Technological Change: Theory vs. Reality." *Journal of Development Economics* 22:87–128.

Reich, Robert B. 1982. "Industrial Policy: Ten Concrete, Practical Steps to Building a Dynamic, Growing, and Fair American Economy." *The New Republic* 186(March 31):28–31.

Rothwell, Roy, and Walter Zegveld. 1984. "Designing and Implementing Innovation Policy." *Policy Studies Review* 3(3-4):436–43.

Scully, Gerald W. 1992. *Constitutional Environment and Economic Growth.* Princeton, N.J.: Princeton University Press.

Spiller, P. 1990. "Politicians, Interest Groups, and Regulators: A Multiple-Principal Agency Theory of Regulation (or 'Let Them Be Bribed')." *Journal of Law and Economics* 33(1):65–101.

Thurow, Lester. 1992. *Head to Head.* New York: William Morrow and Co.

Tullock, G. 1967. *Toward a Mathematics of Politics.* Ann Arbor: University of Michigan Press.

Tyson, Laura D'Andrea. 1992. *Who's Bashing Whom.* Washington, D.C.: Institute for International Economics.

Urban, Peter. 1983. "Theoretical Justifications for Industrial Policy." In Gerald F. Adams and Lawrence R. Klein, eds., *Industrial Policies for Growth and Competitiveness.* Lexington, Mass.: D. C. Heath.

Urban, Tom. 1991. "Agricultural Industrialization: It's Inevitable." *Choices* (4th qtr.):4–6.

Weingast, B. 1984. "The Congressional-Bureaucratic System: A Principal-Agent Perspective." *Public Choice* 44:147–92.

Westcott, Robert T. 1983. "U.S. Approaches to Industrial Policy." In Gerald F. Adams and Lawrence R. Klein, eds., *Industrial Policies for Growth and Competitiveness.* Lexington, Mass.: D. C. Heath.

Williamson, O. 1975. *Markets and Hierarchies: Analysis and Antitrust Implications.* New York: The Free Press.

_____. 1985. *The Economic Institutions of Capitalism.* New York: The Free Press.

PART II Agricultural Policy and Economic Growth

AGRICULTURAL POLICIES resulting from the current institutional framework have been successful in reaching some goals for the sector, but unsuccessful in reaching other, sometimes competing goals. In the following pages, Duane Acker discusses how a national agricultural strategy has emerged from the divergent interests of the U.S. Congress, agricultural producers, and consumers. Although these interests often work at cross purposes, the U.S. Department of Agriculture must find a way to coordinate them in a systems approach to policy.

Wallace Huffman and Robert Evenson document the profound improvement in agricultural productivity attributable to agricultural extension and other public policies that encourage public and private R&D. Consumers have been the main beneficiaries of public research through lower prices of food and other consumer goods. Maureen Kilkenny and Gerald Schluter compare the welfare effects of investments in agricultural technology to those of simple income transfer payments. They find that spending on agricultural research and extension is more productive than spending on direct transfers. Further analysis shows that while real GDP can be increased by direct subsidies, current real gains do not outweigh their costs, which are passed to future generations via an increased budget deficit.

2 Research and Development in Agriculture: Coordination of Policies with Diverse Aims

DUANE ACKER

I appreciate being at this conference, and I commend John Ruan, Stan Johnson, and Iowa State University for pulling this group together. We come to these kinds of sessions to "fill our buckets," to get some concepts that we might not have been exposed to before. Or maybe we were exposed to them a few years ago and now reinforcement is in order to trigger a memory. We might pick up an idea we can use as an individual or a business or, perhaps more importantly from the standpoint of society, something we can use for a whole industry, or an entire geographic area. That's really what we hope—and would expect—to achieve at these kinds of sessions.

It's my job to talk a little about research and development in agriculture. As assistant secretary of agriculture, I have a long list of aims facing me. Of course, we have the aims of 535 members of Congress, in the Senate and the House; we have the aims of multiple congressional committees; we have the aims of the administration; we have the aims of the environmental groups and people concerned about human nutrition or food safety; we have the aims of the family farmer; we have the aims of the sustainable agriculture segment of U.S. production agriculture; we have the aims of commercial farmers; and certainly we have the aims of the individual commodity groups. At the same time, we are plagued—like all institutions—by being part of an establishment; we sometimes have a hard time

At the time of this presentation, Duane Acker was Assistant Secretary of Science and Technology, U.S. Department of Agriculture. He has headed two USDA agencies and was President of Kansas State University from 1975 to 1986.

31

listening and hearing what is being said by these several constituencies. Personally, I spend a lot of my time reading and listening. I also speak whenever I can, in order to describe our programs to people, and also to stimulate responses.

There are two primary things I want to talk about here: first, why science is important to the agricultural industry; and second, how it relates to some form of accepted national agricultural strategy—an overview, perhaps, which must balance the aims of trade policy, domestic farm policy, environmental policy, dietary and health policy, and the overall economic or business policy of the country.

Let's look first at where we are right now. The facts and figures of the U.S. agricultural system are staggering. In 1950, one American farmer produced food and fiber for 27 people; in 1990, the production was for 128 people. This increased efficiency has been passed on to the consumer in lower food costs. In 1950, the average consumer spent 21 percent of his/her disposable income on food. In 1990, the figure was one of the world's lowest—11.8 percent.

In addition, agricultural efficiency has made the United States a strong competitor in international trade. Of those 128 people for whom one American farmer produces food and fiber, about 30 live outside the United States. Food and fiber production represents one of the few segments of our economy in which there is a favorable balance of payments. The aggregate net contribution of agricultural exports to the U.S. balance of payments for the years 1980 through 1989 was $166 billion. The contribution in 1989 alone was more than $18 billion.

This success was created by more than native ingenuity and natural resources. In the period following World War II, the power of science was harnessed to give U.S. agriculture a dramatic boost in productivity. Through research, a combination of genetic improvement, the application of fertilizers, and the use of chemicals to control insects, diseases, and weeds, helped agriculture achieve striking increases in yields.

But that was in simpler days, when the goal was merely to produce enough food and fiber and to deliver it to the consumer. Today's agriculture and agricultural research are being asked to fill many roles and meet many obligations. These are the "diverse aims" mentioned in my title. To me, the only way we can have any chance of meeting these diverse aims is to have a national agricultural strategy—a plan for the future.

Elements of a National Agricultural Strategy

In the 1990s, those of us in agriculture, and in society as a whole, are facing major responsibilities which challenge our experience and our ingenuity.

American agriculture no longer operates in splendid isolation from the rest of the world, with the only requirement being to produce enough food and fiber for our domestic consumers.

The first step in a modern agricultural strategy has been to discard the idea that the primary goal of agricultural research, for the country or for the individual farmer, is limited to increasing production volume of wheat, corn, soybeans, cotton, cows, and hogs. We recognize now that agriculture's contribution to our nation and our world extends beyond providing the needed volume of food and fiber.

Let me get more specific. What do I see as the essential components of a national agricultural research strategy? First off, these elements are no big secret. They are drawn from the 1990 Farm Bill, from the oft-stated priorities of President Bush and Secretary Madigan, from USDA agency mission statements, and even from my own past writings.

Agricultural research priorities must be interlinked with other U.S. policies. These include trade, domestic farm policy, the environment, diet and health, and the overall national economy.

Trade Policy

These days, we hear a lot of talk about negotiations to gain and keep markets. That's trade policy. But my point is that there must be a strong and consistent *research* policy to back it up—to keep U.S. agriculture competitive in both quality and price.

First, we must identify what markets we are talking about gaining and keeping. Then we must look at what factors would allow us to increase the size of those markets. The markets in which we are most interested in helping agriculture compete include the domestic consumer market for new and improved products; value-added products for global markets; and new nonfood, nonfeed agricultural products, which hold such great promise today.

Domestic. Domestically, consumers are looking for products with improved nutrition—products with lower cholesterol, fewer calories, and the same, if not better, flavor. In addition, they want new and improved products that offer more convenience, lower costs, longer shelf life, and year-round availability. Research can help agriculture respond to these consumer desires.

Our record in the Agricultural Research Service is a good one. Permanent-press cotton has made life easier and has helped the cotton industry compete with synthetics; grape growers sold three million boxes of the "Flame" seedless red grape in 1983, compared to 250 thousand boxes in 1980; and the enzyme lactase in LactAid has helped the three out of ten Americans who can't digest milk products, and has increased sales of milk-based products 2–3 percent. We must remember that our goal is to provide products with the qualities consumers want. Maybe we should change semantics a bit and think less about consumers and more about *customers,* the people who make daily decisions whether or not to buy our frozen orange juice, permanent-press cotton, or Oatrim muffins.

And customers include markets for industrial use as well. For example, 100 percent soybean oil printing inks recently have become commercial. Not only can inks made from this renewable resource be made at a lower cost than petroleum-based inks, but soy-based pigments penetrate the paper more completely, and *stay* there. Total market potential for 100 percent soy-based ink could approach almost 100 million bushels a year.

Global. In the global economy, trade in agricultural products traditionally has been in the bulk commodities. But today, as more and more countries enter that arena, we need to look for new exports, particularly the so-called value-added products, in order to secure and maintain our market share.

Right now, although barely 31 percent of U.S. food exports are considered high-value, consumer-oriented processed products, this is the most rapidly growing segment of agricultural exports. It doesn't take any genius to figure out that if we increase that percentage of processed goods, we are increasing jobs here at home.

And while research is working to develop processed agricultural products that meet foreign tastes or cultural requirements or climatic conditions, the administration is working to remove trade barriers so these products can move freely into an open global marketplace. The North American Free Trade Agreement we have been hearing so much about lately is part of that effort. Not only will it increase U.S. agricultural exports by $2 billion—especially in meat, dairy, grain, and fruits—but it will open up other markets as well.

The population of Mexico is one-third that of the United States, yet its gross national product is only 5 percent of ours. A free-trade agreement will help Mexico export more to the United States, thus adding cash, income, and purchasing power to Mexico's economy. And experience shows that one of the first things people do with elevated income is to spend a higher percentage of it on more food, and higher-quality food.

Research not only creates new trade opportunities, but it can help save or improve old ones. Specifically, research is helpful because it can find ways to overcome concrete obstacles to trade that are based on technical problems rather than political considerations.

For example, following the U.S. ban on fumigation with ethylene dibromide, Japan prohibited the import of U.S. grapefruit because of possible fruit fly contamination. Then, an Agricultural Research Service–led research team developed a replacement treatment using cold temperatures that killed the fly larvae without damaging the quality of the fruit. As a result, Florida growers ship six million cartons of grapefruit a year, worth about $70 million. Similarly, Japan also now accepts more than $15 million worth of U.S.-grown cherries from the Pacific Northwest because agricultural research found a way to control the codling moth.

Other areas in which research can make a difference are quality, grading, and shipability. Choosing to direct research into these areas can have significant impact on the marketability of particular agricultural products. For example, the European market for sweet corn has been increased significantly since research found a way of combining increased sweetness with shrink-wrapping to maintain the corn's sweetness during shipping.

New Uses. Targeting markets both at home and abroad, nonfood, nonfeed uses of agricultural products represent the largest totally new agricultural market. It is also the area in which research can make the most startling contributions.

Domestic Farm Policy

In fact, consider some of the contributions this type of research can make right here at home. Research policy also should be directed so that it acts as an arm of domestic farm policy. The search for alternative uses of commodities that are in surplus has become a research priority.

Let me take a moment to mention the 1992 Yearbook of Agriculture. Its title this year is *New Crops, New Uses, New Markets.* It is a book that will really open your eyes to the possibilities and the realities of this area of research. And the yearbook is just the tip of the iceberg. The 1990 Farm Bill authorizes the creation of an Alternative Agriculture Research and Commercialization Center under USDA. It is designed to foster cooperation between the public and private sectors in taking promising ideas for new uses from the research phase to the new product phase.

For example, a number of new uses have been found for cornstarch in the past few years. Cornstarch has been converted to products like Superslurper, which can absorb more than 1,600 times its own weight in moisture. Superslurper is being used in products from diapers to fuel filters, from batteries to laundry bags. And along the way, it has helped create new jobs, especially in rural areas, as well as having created a new use for corn. With additional uses for a variety of crops, demand comes closer to supply, and less government support may be needed.

Other research aims include improving production efficiency. Most agricultural research is scale neutral. It usually applies to the small-farm operator as much as it does to the large farm. As a result of scientific improvements in technology and management, agricultural efficiency in this country is now at an all-time high. For crops, production per acre is now 27 percent higher than it was ten years ago. For livestock, efficiency is 26 percent higher.

Environmental Policy

One result of this increased efficiency is less purchased input in relation to output. This is good for the farmer's bottom line and good for the environment. Heightened environmental awareness in this country has increased the need for knowledge about environmental influences. For example, research and education emphases are as much on fertilizer or chemical application efficiency as on efficacy. Work on the delivery efficiency of irrigation water must include studies of the impact on soil erosion. Americans today are demanding that agriculture be carried out without damaging the environment, but also without sacrificing the abundance that we have come to expect.

Ensuring the continued competitiveness of U.S. farming while minimizing environmental impact has been recognized as a primary mission of agricultural research in this country. Research is being called on to develop the management techniques and technologies that are environmentally neutral or, in fact, positive. Farmers support these changes as much as anyone. They and their children drink the water from wells and eat the crops grown from farmland, and they share our environmental concerns.

Research contributes not only at the level of farming itself, which science can help make "cleaner," but also in using renewable resources to produce products that are currently made from nonrenewable resources—products like synfuels, plastics made from wheat or corn, and ink from soybeans. Again, new uses come to the fore.

Perhaps one of the most important contributions to which research can be directed is to provide scientific bases for policy decisions and regulations that relate to the environment. For example, Bill Riley, administrator of the Environmental Protection Agency under President Bush, has said that EPA is committed to "follow good science wherever it may lead" in building a firm foundation for environmental regulation. Research can also provide an important balance, making it clear how regulatory and legislative changes will affect agriculture and the economy.

Citizens—read that as "voters" and "taxpayers"—are demanding changes; they want to see active protection of the environment. If we do not provide the science upon which to base sound decisions, then decisions will simply be made without it—not the wisest course by which to steer agriculture, the environment, or the economy.

Diet and Health

As far back as its original charter, part of USDA's research mission has been understanding what it takes in the way of nutrition for people to stay healthy. In 1893, Congress appropriated $10 thousand to "enable the Secretary of Agriculture to investigate and report on the nutritive values of various articles and commodities used for human food." Changes in our domestic dietary and health policy also create different demands for research. Growing interest in foods with greater nutritional value pushes research to find or develop healthier foods; for example, meat with less fat or melon with more vitamins.

Whether we are talking about breeding a new crop variety that is naturally superhigh in a vitamin or developing a new technique that prevents the vitamin from being removed during processing, we turn to research for help. Furthermore, it is in the interest of U.S. agriculture to know every detail possible about the health consequences of the food items we produce. We should never take a defensive posture, but should insist on being the first to know the impacts of our products.

The National Economy

Research and development. Notice how those two words always seem to be served up together, like peanut butter and jelly, or ham and eggs. Research is essential, but without development, it looks pretty lonely on the plate, not a filling or nutritious meal. They need each other.

Research is meant to be put to use. Government also realizes that publicly financed research needs the positive support of private industry to move new technology from the laboratory out into the marketplace. So a total research policy must include a way to transfer technology. Congress recognized the benefits of promoting such interaction with the private sector when it passed the Bayh-Dole Act of 1980. This law not only permits, but encourages, the development of public-private agreements to make commercial use of federally funded research.

One current tool for such transfer is the Cooperative Research and Development Agreement, commonly referred to as CRADA. These public-private partnerships not only provide for the swift transfer of technology from lab to market, they also provide direction and support for research.

Reflecting technology transfer's presence on Agriculture Secretary Ed Madigan's short list of priorities, the USDA leads this country's government agencies in embracing partnership and cooperation between research and industry. Currently, USDA has signed 286 CRADA agreements, 246 through the Agricultural Research Service and a goodly number in the Forest Service as well. And another 40 are in the pipeline. As a result, USDA, agribusiness—and of course the American public—have all benefited.

If we are to achieve the full economic benefits of our research, the United States must develop it into high-quality products and services, and bring them to the market ahead of the competition. This is not rhetoric, it is policy, and better than that, it is funding. In 1992, the budget for commercialization research was $4.5 million; the 1993 appropriation is $7.5 million.

A Systematic Approach to Action

All of this means that those of us in agriculture and agricultural research have a lot spread out in front of us. And like any hungry person with an empty plate at a full buffet table, it's a question of where to start—and how much to take of each dish.

Within USDA

That's why I believe the key word, particularly for USDA with its national responsibilities, is coordination. I can assure you that the secretary and I and the science and education administrators are working closely together. We are keeping our eyes trained on the big picture—all the diversity, all the needs, and of course, all the resources. Our approach is to keep the four science and education agencies working toward the same general goals—though of course, some of them may take slightly different routes in getting there.

As assistant secretary, one of my goals is to spend efficiently. At the same time, I know that I can't dictate to fifty extension directors, or fifty experiment station directors. Even if it were possible, I wouldn't want to. That's not the way I like to operate, and it's not good for the system. The people in Iowa should have input into decisions on the money, time, and effort devoted to swine research or to urban 4-H in their state.

But on the national level, I favor a systems approach. Both federal and state research and extension programs are part of a public system. I want to take a close look at what's going on. See where the successes are, identify bottlenecks, and focus resources. We need a *national* research and development program, but one that is built systematically, commodity by commodity, problem by problem.

And USDA certainly will not ignore the valuable international research community. Recently, the Bush Administration adopted a national policy on international science, education, and development that mandated a larger role for USDA's science and education agencies in these areas. The policy emphasizes the new worldwide importance of agriculture as the means to revitalize and expand the economies of many countries. It also recognizes the crucial importance—and self-interest—of U.S. participation.

University and USDA scientists are involved in a number of aggressive programs:

- Under the Consultative Group on International Agricultural Research (CGIAR), USDA cooperates with the international agricultural research centers, hubs for research around the world. They support a broad research network which extends from CIMMYT, the wheat and maize center in Mexico, to ICRISAT, the Center for Arid Crops Research in India. But just because these centers cover most of the major food crops in the developing nations does not mean that the United States does not have much to learn from the research being conducted. We do. In particular, we work with these centers as focal points for the preservation of genetic diversity.

- Under BARD (the Binational Agricultural Research and Development Fund) the United States and Israel have been benefiting jointly from formal international research collaborations. Established in 1977 with a jointly furnished $110 million endowment, BARD has been a good investment in the future of agriculture for our two countries.

- On a broader scale, my most recent experiences in this area have been with the Office of International Cooperation and Development. OICD's mission statement says that it will help to strengthen food and agriculture systems of other countries, as well as to bring technology to this country.

These international collaborations are win-win efforts: they bring both direct and indirect benefits to U.S. agriculture. These benefits can take the form of new technology and genetic material improving U.S. agriculture; or, because a strong agricultural system is a key to economic growth in developing countries, they can deliver increased economic growth and buying power for potential U.S. customers.

Outside of USDA

That leads me into what those of you who are outside of USDA can do. Talk to us! "The squeaky wheel gets the grease" has become a cliche, but it's hung around this long because it's true. We in government are not mind readers—and we're not in the business of granting wishes—but we can listen to you and work with you to come up with some answers and some compromises.

We all have to learn to look at things in new ways. Think seriously about CRADA and international partnerships. Then, once you know where you want to go, work to develop political support for that goal among experiment station directors, deans, extension directors, and the industry research community. If you can coordinate and set priorities among yourselves, you have a better chance of getting funding or legislation. If you present a united front, consensus is powerful.

The Future

I began my remarks with the assertions that agriculture has been one of the bright stars in the U.S. economic constellation, and that agricultural research and development historically have contributed megavolts to that light. But our current illumination doesn't hold a candle to our potential brilliance if we can reach a consensus on a strategy for our nation's agriculture.

The modern world is complex and now demands more of agriculture and the publicly financed research sector than simple production volume. Yet, diverse aims do not have to be conflicting ones; sometimes working toward one goal can advance another. Contemplating the future of agriculture and research and development, we also have to consider trade and markets (domestic and global), domestic farm policy, the environment, domestic health policy, and the overall national economy. They are real and necessary parts of the world in which we operate. But this mutuality does not weaken or limit agricultural research; it energizes and expands it. It gives it many more arenas in which to show its strength and serve our citizens.

The USDA is committed to working in cooperation with representatives of every other aspect of agriculture: the private sector, farmers, industry, consumers (customers!), universities, and international researchers. We will use tried and true ways, new ways, and ways yet unthought of to foster a sustainable, reliable, and competitive agricultural system and a viable rural America—to ensure that our mutual future remains bright.

3 The Effects of R&D on Farm Size, Specialization, and Productivity

WALLACE E. HUFFMAN
ROBERT E. EVENSON

The United States has a long history of innovation in public policy. These innovations have affected the economics of research and development, farming, and other activities. Public policies have affected the distribution of resources in agriculture (e.g., land and population), the structure of farming (e.g., average size and specialization of farms), and the rates of growth in output and change in productivity. Indeed, a major industrialization of farming has occurred during the twentieth century.

Research and development are productive activities that use highly skilled labor and lead to advances in science and technology. In the United States there is a long history of joint public and private R&D activities for agriculture. In contrast, in most developing countries the public sector has been the primary source of advances in science and technology.

The objectives of this paper are (1) to review the development of public policy and its effects on advances in science and technology that have led to growth of farm output, farm productivity, and structural change; and (2) to present new estimates of the impacts of public policies on farm productivity and structure. Included is background information on major policy innovations and changes in agriculture; a summary of what we know about how public research, extension,

Wallace E. Huffman is Professor of Economics and Agricultural Economics at Iowa State University, Ames. Robert E. Evenson is Professor of Economics at Yale University, New Haven.

education, and farm commodity policies affect farming; new estimates of the effects of public policies on farm productivity, specialization, and size; and, finally, some conclusions.

Some Background

Over the long term, major innovations have occurred in policies dealing with science and technology and the economics and structure of farming.

Science and Industrial Policy

Beginning in the seventeenth century, editors of professional journals established policies for making scientific discoveries available relatively quickly and inexpensively to the scientific community. They also offered support to authors whose priority claims to ideas and findings are unfairly challenged. This institutional innovation means that the first scientist to publish a view, discovery, or finding gets credit for the discovery. This policy establishes incentives for rapid communication and exchange of ideas among scientists, enabling a building block approach to advances in science. Today this policy generally is applied in U.S. patenting. A valid patent application must be novel (new), useful, and nonobvious. It must remove from secrecy the essential features of the invention, or disclose the discovery in exchange for a monopoly on use for seventeen years. Patent documents reference prior patents and scientific publications in much the same way as scientific papers cite earlier work.

Other important institutional innovations leading to R&D for agriculture can be identified (Table 3.1). Between 1787 and 1842 a number of legislative acts were passed that refined and strengthened U.S. intellectual property rights, especially those dealing with patents (Huffman and Evenson 1993). The U.S. Patent Office was established in 1836 to handle patent applications. The property rights bestowed through a patent were important to the early development of the U.S. farm machinery industry. By 1900, the manufacturing of farm machinery was the single largest U.S. manufacturing industry.

Early commissioners of the Patent Office also took an interest in improving the technology of agriculture beyond patentable inventions. For example, the office coordinated the importation of new seeds and plants, and it began collecting and publishing agricultural statistics and performing chemical analyses of agricultural products. These activities were transferred to the U.S. Department of Agriculture when it was established in 1862. The land-grant college system also was established in 1862, followed by the state agricultural experiment stations in 1887

Table 3.1.   Major institutional innovations affecting advances in agricultural sciences and technology

Date	Innovation
17th Century	Royal Society of London and editor, *Philosophical Transactions*, established precedent that the first scientists to publish a view, discovery, or finding get credit for the discovery. This policy established incentives for rapid communication and exchange of ideas among scientists.
1836	U.S. Patent Office established to handle patent applications and issue patents. Valid patent application must show novelty, usefulness, and nonobviousness. It must remove from secrecy the essential features of the invention or disclose the discovery. Early patent office activities included agricultural research.
1862	U.S. Department of Agriculture established to administer federal issues dealing with agriculture and to conduct agricultural research.
1862	Morrill Act passed, giving federal land to each of the states for the establishment of colleges for teaching agricultural and mechanical arts. The act established the land-grant college system.
1887	Hatch Act provided federal aid to help support one or more agricultural experiment stations in each of the states to conduct original research, establishing the state agricultural experiment system.
1914	Smith Lever Act established a federal-state cooperative extension service to disseminate among the people useful information relating to agriculture and home economics.
1930	Plant Patent Act passed so that asexually reproduced plants could be patented, provided they met the regular requirements for a patent. Sexually reproduced plants were not covered.
1970	Plant Variety Protection Act provided patentlike protection to sexually reproduced plants, excluding some vegetables. Later amended to expand coverage. The act contains an important exemption; farmers whose primary farming business is not seed sale can use own harvested seed for planting and sale to others.
1980	*Diamond v. Chakrabarty* decision, in which U.S. Supreme Court ruled that microorganisms were patentable. This was extended to cover most biotechnical innovations.
1985	*ex parte Hibberd* decision extended the Chakrabarty ruling to plants, seeds, tissue culture, hybrid plants, and hybrid seeds. Utility patents are now granted for innovations to crops reproduced both asexually and sexually.

and Cooperative Extension in 1914. These institutions became important parts of the U.S. system of research and development.

Living material initially was excluded from U.S. patent protection, but in 1930 the Plant Patent Act was passed. It provided for patenting of asexually reproduced plants, as long as they met regular patent requirements. Sexually reproduced plants were not covered by patentlike protection until the Plant Variety Protection Act of 1970. Plant Variety Protection Certificates can be issued to an applicant showing that a variety is distinct, uniform, and stable. Farmers, however, are covered by an important exemption in the act. Farmers whose primary occupation is growing crops for nonseed purposes can use their harvested seed for planting and selling to others what is known as bin-run seed.

During the 1980s, patent protection was extended to advances in science or technology contained in living organisms. In the case of *Diamond v. Chakrabarty*, the U.S. Supreme Court ruled that microorganisms were patentable. In 1985, the *ex parte Hibberd* decision extended the Chakrabarty ruling to plants, seeds, tissue cultures, hybrid plants, and hybrid seeds. Utility patents are now granted for innovations to crops reproduced both asexually and sexually. The property rights and the economics of the different property rights in plant materials differ in important ways; for example, the nature of the innovation is not disclosed in protection certificates, hence novelty is not an important characteristic. The first animal patent was granted in 1988 for the "Harvard Mouse" (Office of Technology Assessment 1992, 395), and genetically engineered animals are now serving as important models for research on diseases occurring in people (*Science* 1992). Further animal patents are, however, being delayed temporarily while a number of issues are resolved.

Other policy innovations have been important to the structure of farming. Some major structural features of U.S. farming were put in place more than a century ago. In particular, the federal land distribution policy established by the new nation was one that emphasized sale or transfer of large quantities of public land to smallholders or farmers. The best known of these policies was the Homestead Act of 1862, which gave each citizen the right to homestead 160 acres of unoccupied land. Furthermore, the private property rights that were defined in U.S. land distribution policy were transferable and enforceable. By the 1890s, private property rights in land and many other natural resources were secure. That access to land and other resources, combined with an open immigration policy up to 1921, brought waves of European immigrants to America.

A number of other major public policies affecting the structure and economics of farming can be identified (Table 3.2). A low-cost national transportation system

Table 3.2.   Other major public policies affecting the structure and economics of farming

Date	Legislation/Provision
1776–1862	Federal land distribution policies enacted to sell or transfer large quantities of public land in small parcels to establish small private farms. The best-known provision was the Homestead Act of 1862.
1820–1890	Combinations of state and federal policies to build canals and railroads resulted in reliable and cheap transportation of agricultural commodities from the Midwest to population centers and seaports.
1921	Free-immigration policy of United States ended; quotas were first imposed limiting annual immigrant rate to national origin of U.S. population at an earlier date.
1933	Agricultural Adjustment Act provided the first comprehensive agricultural supply management program. In early programs participation by producers was mandatory. Regular revisions of this policy led to the current U.S. food and agriculture policy.
1961	Agriculture Act initiated a voluntary program for program commodities (except tobacco, sugar, and peanuts), and in 1965 emphasis was placed on bringing U.S. crop prices in line with world prices so that international trade would be possible.
1985	Food Security Act imposed much tougher soil conservation provisions as a condition for federal commodity program participation.
1992	North American Free Trade Act promises to establish a free-trade area covering Canada, United States, and Mexico, wherein a wide range of final commodities could move across national boundaries tariff-free.

was established during the nineteenth century, making possible shipments of farm products from the Midwest to the population centers and seaports. Direct interventions in agricultural production and marketing first occurred following the Great Depression of the 1930s. The Agricultural Adjustment Act of 1933 started a long-term policy of federal management of production (and prices) of major agricultural commodities. The early programs largely required mandatory participation by producers of a commodity. This, however, was changed, starting in 1961. All programs except that for tobacco are now voluntary. Starting in 1965, the management of the farm commodity program shifted to bringing U.S. crop prices in line with world prices so that international trade (i.e., exports) would be possible. The 1985 Food Security Act contained for the first time fairly restrictive soil conservation provisions that program participants must meet.

The North American Free Trade Act (NAFTA) of 1992 provides new possibilities for specialization and trade. It establishes a free-trade area covering Canada, the United States, and Mexico, wherein a wide range of final commodities can move across national boundaries duty-free. International mobility of labor, however, is not part of NAFTA provisions.

Structure, Organization, Technology, and Performance

No matter how the past century is divided, major changes have occurred in agriculture. A century ago there were about 4.9 million U.S. farms; 39.3 percent of the 70 million people lived on farms, and a total of 64.9 percent of the U.S. population lived in rural areas (Dahmann and Dacquel 1992). In 1940 there were more farms, 6.1 million, yet only 23 percent of the population (now 132.2 million) lived on farms and 43.5 percent lived in rural areas. By 1990 the number of farms had fallen to about two million; only 2.2 percent of the U.S. population (246.1 million) lived on farms, and about 30 percent of the total population was living in rural areas. The share of the U.S. labor force employed in farming is similar to the share of the U.S. population living on farms, and it shows a similar dramatic decline during the past century.

Farm output (measured using weighted real prices) in 1990 was 5.6 times larger than a century ago and 2.6 times larger than fifty years ago. Thus, the average rate of growth of real farm output was 1.72 percent per annum (compounded) during the past century and 2.06 percent for the past fifty years (Fig. 3.1). Although the index of inputs under the control of farmers has increased significantly during some subperiods, it was only slightly larger in 1990 than in 1890 (0.14 percent), and it was essentially the same in 1990 as in 1940.

The composition and quality of inputs have changed, of course. A century ago 87 percent of the farm inputs were supplied by farmers; only 12 percent were purchases of intermediate inputs from nonfarmers (Kendrick 1961, 347). In contrast, in 1990 more than 45 percent of the farm inputs were purchased from nonfarmers (USDA 1991, Table 3.1). Furthermore, the technologies embodied in inputs have changed dramatically over the past century or half century. The science and technologies embodied in new seed varieties, breeding stock, farm chemicals, farm machinery, and information systems are much different than in the distant past (Office of Technology Assessment 1992).

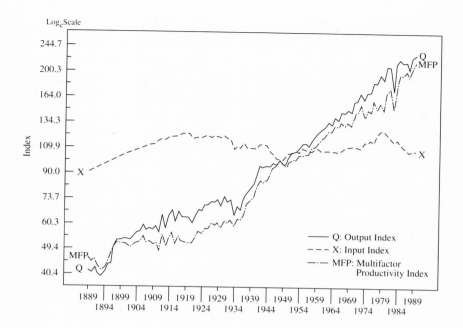

Figure 3.1. U.S. (real) farm output, farm input, and multifactor productivity,
1989–1990 (1948 = 100).

But how can large growth in farm output occur without significant growth in
farm inputs? The primary answer is that farm productivity has been increasing.
For the past century, multifactor farm productivity (MFP), the average product of
inputs under the control of farmers, has increased by an average rate of 1.6 percent
per annum (compounded). For the past one-half century the rate of increase in
multifactor productivity has been 2.1 percent per annum. Given that multifactor
productivity need not have changed at all over time, these average rates for the past
fifty and one hundred years are very high. In fact, Jorgenson and Gollop (1992)
show that the rate of MFP increase and the share of output growth that is due to
MFP during the post–World War II period is large for the farm sector relative to
other sectors of the U.S. economy.

One of the main consequences of an increase in multifactor productivity is to
shift the aggregate supply curve for farm output to the right. In Figure 3.2, S
represents the original supply curve for Q, and S′ represents the supply curve after
a one-time change in productivity. The new market equilibrium will be at a lower

market price and a larger quantity consumed. With the change in productivity, the change in consumer surplus is represented by the area B + E. Thus, consumers receive a large share of the net benefit from the new technology or productivity change. This is a common outcome for competitive sectors.

Average farm size and extent of specialization have changed markedly. The average size of farm, based on an index of real output, was 1.6 times larger in 1940 than in 1890, but 8.5 times larger in 1990 than in 1940. The average rate of increase in farm size (using the output measure) was only 0.9 percent per annum (compounded) from 1890 to 1940, but it was 4.3 percent per annum during the past fifty years; hence, the average rate of increase over the past century was 2.6 percent per annum. In 1940 most farms raised both crops and livestock, and livestock production was organized around many small herds and flocks. During the past fifty years, livestock production and to a lesser extent crop production have become increasingly specialized on a few much larger farms.

Geographically and within producing units, livestock production has experienced dramatic increases in concentration during the past fifty years. The commercial broiler industry did not exist in 1930 and was quite small in 1950. U.S. broiler production increased by a factor of 4.2 between 1950 and 1965, and by a factor of three between 1965 and 1989. Total U.S. broiler production is now roughly equal to beef and veal production. In 1989, U.S. broiler production was centered in Arkansas, Georgia, and Alabama, and producers in those three states accounted for 44 percent of total production. The two largest firms accounted for about 23 percent of total production.

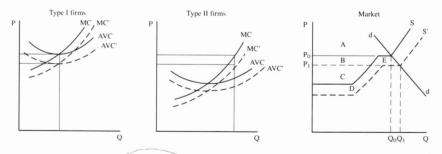

Figure 3.2. Effects of scale-neutral technical change on welfare.

For beef cattle finishing, the primary center of activity in 1950 was in Illinois and Iowa, where many small feedlots with fewer than 100 head on feed per year accounted for 17 percent of total beef cattle slaughter. The second largest center was in the Great Plains states of Nebraska, Kansas, and Colorado, where feedlots were much larger and weather conditions were better for year-round cattle finishing. These three states accounted for 14.1 percent of the total. California producers accounted for 10.6 percent and Texas producers, for 5 percent.

During the late 1960s and 1970s, the center of U.S. cattle finishing began to move to the high plains. In 1989, the states of Nebraska, Kansas, Colorado, Oklahoma, and Texas accounted for 60.9 percent of total finished beef. Production has become concentrated in very large feedlot operations. In 1988, the top four cattle feeding businesses had average marketings of almost 700 thousand head and accounted for about 12 percent of total U.S. slaughter cattle.

Shifts in the locations of dairy and pork production have been less dramatic, but the average size of these production enterprises has increased. Some of the companies that have been successful in large-scale broiler production have been experimenting with large-scale swine units; for example, in North Carolina. This approach to organizing production is being tried in other states.

The growth in the average size of farms, the increased reliance on purchased nonfarm inputs, specialization of production in large units that are sometimes vertically integrated, and use of more sophisticated technologies, management, and credit systems are major changes in farming that have occurred largely during the past fifty years. These changes are the reasons why farming in the United States can be described as becoming increasingly industrialized.

Changes in farming during the past decade look small relative to those over the past fifty or one hundred years. They are, however, important and significant. During the 1980s, the number of U.S. farms decreased by about 20 percent. Real farm inputs decreased 15 percent, but real output grew 19 percent and multifactor productivity grew 34 percent. Although the decade was one of hard financial times for the farm sector, growth of output and multifactor productivity continued much as they had during prior decades.

The State of Knowledge

Schultz (1953), Kendrick (1961), and Denison (1962) performed pioneering studies into the sources of growth in agriculture. Much additional research has followed.

General Findings

Science and technology policy is important, and it should promote research and development in such a way that linkages occur between advances in general science and practical problems and possibilities. Furthermore, public and private research activities should be largely complementary, rather than competitive, activities. The R&D enterprise can be viewed as a multilayered set of activities that progress via a building block approach, in which needed blocks are drawn from various layers. General sciences (chemistry and biochemistry, general and molecular biology, physics, mathematics, economics) are located at the core. Pretechnology sciences (plant and animal physiology, zoology and genetics, environmental sciences, entomology, agricultural economics) are located in the next layer, followed by applied sciences (plant and animal breeding, plant and animal pathology, agronomy, horticulture, animal science, farm management) and technology development and commercialization (Huffman and Evenson 1993).

This multilayered organization of R&D produces core advances in basic science that are primarily of a public-good nature and that must be undertaken largely by the public sector (the research agencies of the federal government, the public state agricultural experiment stations, and universities). On the outer boundary, the new technology is of a type that can be developed and sold largely by private firms motivated by profit. In the intermediate layers, a mixture of public and private activities occurs.

In a successful R&D system, activities proceed at all levels simultaneously. Advances within one layer are held up frequently because of a missing building block being "constructed" in another layer, and the stock of knowledge and technology is most likely growing because of the public-good nature of the discoveries and advances. In the short run some independent activity may occur in a layer or field of science or technology, but over the long term advances in science and technology can occur only when linkages among at least some of the layers exist and function well. If practical problems are going to be solved, basic information or knowledge must be transferred and, most likely, adapted.

The pretechnology sciences serve as a catalyst and critical linkage both to the general sciences and to applied sciences and technology development (Huffman and Evenson 1993; Huffman and Just 1992). Because new technology development by the private sector depends critically on advances in science undertaken in the public sector, public and private R&D activities should be complementary.

Much of agricultural technology has geoclimatic specificity. A considerable amount of experimental and on-farm evidence shows that the performance of plants and, to a lesser extent, animals is affected by local geoclimatic conditions (Evenson

1989; Huffman and Evenson 1993; Griliches 1960). Geoclimatic conditions affect growth processes, nutrient and water availability, and type and extent of pathogenic and general environmental problems. This has several implications: (1) new technology that is successful in one state or region will not necessarily outperform other technologies or spill over into other regions or states; (2) a national index of public agricultural research activity obtained by simply adding together contributions from the individual states is an imperfect measure of useful public research affecting the productivity of agriculture in any one state or region; (3) each state must conduct some of its own agricultural research (which might be only adaptive in nature) in order for its farmers to obtain new technologies that advance their competitiveness relative to farmers growing similar commodities in other states and regions; (4) the potential size of the market for a new technology differs depending on its adaptability to particular geoclimatic conditions; and (5) generally it is most profitable for private-sector firms to develop and sell technologies that can be used intensively in large areas and where new purchases are made regularly (say, annually).

Because of the geoclimatic heterogeneity of farmland and the dispersal of production among a large number of independent units, the process of adopting new agricultural technologies is relatively complex and time-consuming. Griliches (1960) showed that when farmers considered replacing open-pollinated seed corn with hybrid corn, they first experimented by planting a relatively small share of their corn acreage to hybrids. Even after the switch proved profitable, it took several years before they planted 100 percent of their corn acreage to hybrids. The process seems to repeat itself as new and superior hybrid corn varieties replace older ones. Studies have shown, however, that schooling of farmers and agricultural extension play important roles in the adoption process, and that additional schooling and information increase the rate of adoption of superior technologies (Huffman 1974; Rahm and Huffman 1984; Wozniak 1984; and Huffman and Mercier 1991). Wozniak (1991) also has examined substitution possibilities between public and private extension or information in the adoption of agricultural technologies.

Inventions for U.S. Agriculture

There is evidence to show that technology policy has affected the rate of innovation for agriculture. First, industrial inventions can be linked to potential use in agriculture. Although it is not a simple matter to attribute inventions in one sector of our economy or from abroad to use in agriculture, a system developed at Yale University using Canadian data can be used to aid in this process (Evenson et al. 1990). In this project a concordance was developed by which inventions made and manufactured (IOM) can be mapped into an industry of use (IOU). Table 3.3 presents estimates of the proportion of inventions in sixteen industries that are used by five different industrial classes of farms. Note that a relatively large share (over 50 percent) of the inventions in the agricultural chemical and agricultural machinery industries have been used on field crop farms. The feed industry has a large share (about 65 percent) of its inventions used by livestock farms.

Because the information in Table 3.3 is expressed as a percentage of the IOM (origin sector), it does not give a good sense of the absolute importance of the flow of inventions into farming. Table 3.4 provides a historical summary of the number of inventions intended for use on farms of different industrial classes. This classification system contains six three-digit SIC farm types, each including several four-digit SIC farm types. It should be noted that many inventions assigned to a three-digit class are not further assigned to a four-digit class. Thus, there are two levels of specificity in this classification scheme, one at the more detailed four-digit level and one at the broader three-digit level.

The first seven columns of Table 3.4 report on the total number of patents intended for use by farms, including foreign ones, by decade starting with the 1920s, along with the number intended for use by farm industrial type. Note that the number of patents intended for use dropped during the 1930s (largely because of the Great Depression) and 1940s (because industrial efforts were being devoted to World War II). During other decades, the number of patents intended for use in agriculture ranged between 800 and 924. Patents intended for use in agriculture tailed off again during the 1980s. Those intended for use by field crop farms numbered 332 during the 1980s, the lowest number since the 1940s. The number of patents intended for use by horticultural farms and by combination farms generally has been increasing for each successive decade.

Table 3.4 also presents information on the extent of use of foreign-origin patents (imports) in U.S. agriculture for the 1970s and 1980s. This information is summarized in the share of patents granted to foreign-origin inventors. It is clear that the import ratios differ among the farm types, being lowest for livestock, fruit and vegetable, and horticulture farms and highest for field crop farms. The import ratios increased dramatically from the 1970s to the 1980s.

The import ratios reflect three factors primarily. First, the total number of inventions worldwide applicable to crop farms is much larger than the number applicable to livestock farms. The reason is that significant commercial livestock production occurs only in high-income countries, but crop production occurs everywhere. Second, there are fundamental differences in technologies and their

Table 3.3. Sources of private-sector inventions intended for use in U.S. agriculture, 1978–1988

Sending Sector	Proportion of Sending Sector's Inventions Used				
	Livestock Farms (.011)	Other Animal Farms (.012)	Field Crop Farms (.013)	Fruit and Vegetables (.015)	Horticulture Farms (.016)
Food Industries	.049	.006			
Feed Industries	.641	.003			
Rubber and Plastics	.020		.009	.003	.011
Leather	.008	.048		.014	
Clothing and Textiles	.002	.004	.021	.008	.002
Wood Industry	.005	.229	.039		
Paper Production	.033		.002		
Fabricated Metals	.017	.004	.010	.008	.006
Agricultural Machinery	.088	.002	.510	.005	.004
Other Machinery	.011	.004	.072	.032	.015
Electrical Products	.002	.001	.007	.008	.001
Stone, Clay, Glass	.010		.003		.003
Agricultural Chemicals	.049		.566	.020	.034
Other Chemicals	.015	.001	.029	.004	.001
Other Manufacturing	.005	.005	.039	.004	.004
Construction	.115	.019	.019	.040	.239

SOURCE: Huffman and Evenson (1993).

Note: The numbers in parentheses are codes from the Standard Industrial Classification, or SIC codes.

Table 3.4.   Inventions used by the U.S. agricultural production sector, selected years 1920–1989

Farm Type (and SIC code)	Average Annual Inventions Patented							Import Ratio	
	1920s	1930s	1940s	1950s	1960s	1970s	1980s	1970s	1980s
011 Livestock Farms (Total)	204.4	166.3	96.6	178.3	211.3	230.9	202.3	.21	.40
0111 Dairy Farms	25.0	22.5	14.3	21.7	23.8	28.5	23.8	.28	.55
0112 Cattle Farms	13.0	10.4	7.6	17.2	23.3	27.8	25.9	.20	.41
0113 Hog Farms	6.1	8.5	2.6	8.2	10.9	9.7	10.0	.09	.48
0114 Poultry Farms	76.9	54.8	25.4	50.0	44.6	38.9	34.3	.17	.31
0115 Sheep-Goat Farms	0.1	0.1	0.2	0.3	0.5	0.7	1.0	.90	.13
012 Other Animal Farms (Total)	39.7	23.3	14.2	20.5	19.7	22.6	26.7	.18	.19
0121 Bee-Keeping Farms	13.4	8.9	5.5	7.2	5.4	6.4	10.5	.09	.22
0122 Horse Farms	18.2	7.6	3.7	5.6	6.8	8.2	8.4	.26	.14
0123 Fur Skin Farms	0.7	0.2	0.1	0.4	0.3	0.3	0.2	.00	.00
013 Field Crop Farms (Total)	443.6	320.4	227.3	423.3	383.8	406.7	332.0	.26	.47
0131 Wheat Farms	32.5	23.8	13.9	23.4	29.0	33.3	29.2	.27	.46
0132 Small Grains Farms	4.4	5.9	7.0	11.1	15.9	15.3	10.6	.47	.47
0134 Corn Farms	8.9	7.3	7.5	11.5	9.9	10.6	9.1	.16	.52
0135 Forage-Hay Farms	8.8	6.2	6.1	18.1	17.4	15.4	16.7	.26	.58
0137 Tobacco Farms	1.0	1.4	1.1	2.0	3.5	3.5	4.6	.13	.78
0138 Potato Farms	6.8	4.4	3.3	6.0	3.4	3.6	2.6	.20	.21
015 Fruit and Vegetable Farms	43.8	37.9	23.1	57.5	68.2	64.9	35.7	.15	.31
016 Horticultural Farms (Total)	23.0	31.9	16.4	32.6	37.7	56.3	57.1	.21	.33
0161 Mushrooms	1.7	2.8	1.5	4.2	4.6	4.8	4.7	.17	.40
0162 Greenhouse Products	6.2	9.2	4.3	6.7	8.1	10.7	11.0	.26	.30
0163 Nursery Products	2.2	2.7	1.4	3.4	4.4	7.4	6.2	.21	.27
017 Combination Farms	68.1	67.3	57.5	106.5	138.4	142.4	150.2	.35	.60
All Farms	824.6	647.1	435.1	819.1	859.1	923.8	804.0	.25	.45

SOURCE: Huffman and Evenson (1993).

transferability. Some inventions are highly location-specific and of little value in other countries. Third, the competitiveness of foreign inventors seems to have risen markedly in the 1980s relative to the 1970s. Not only has the foreign-origin share risen, but domestic inventions intended for use by most types of farms declined sharply for the 1980s, especially for field crop farms.

Before the 1970 Plant Variety Protection Act, the development of new crop varieties was primarily the result of public research, except in the case of hybrid corn (Huffman and Evenson 1993). With protection to new varieties granted by the act, private seed companies have expanded their R&D efforts toward developing new varieties. Table 3.5 indicates the absolute size of the plant breeding and related plant development research effort going into crops for the private and public sectors in 1989.

The private sector is investing heavily in corn research. About one-half of all the private-sector, Ph.D.-level plant breeders/geneticists, and about 40 percent of the plant-related biotechnology researchers, are focused on corn varietal improvement. In field crops, soybean breeding research is second in importance. For corn and soybeans—where the seed purchased commercially each year amounts to 100 percent and 60 percent, respectively—the number of Ph.D.-level, private-sector plant breeders is now much larger than the number in the public sector. However, for wheat and forages, where the use of commercially purchased seed is lower, there is a larger number of public-sector plant breeders than private ones.

Table 3.6 shows the rate at which plant variety protection certificates (PVPCs) have been granted for major field crops and forages and for selected vegetables from 1971 to 1991. The rate of issue generally has been increasing for each crop since the period 1971–1974. The largest number of PVPCs has been issued for soybean varieties, a total of 499. Very few PVPCs were granted to hybrid corn varieties until the latest subperiod, 1987–1991, when 115 were granted. In vegetables, relatively large numbers of PVPCs have been granted to peas and garden bean varieties. The far right column of Table 3.6 shows that PVPCs have been granted primarily to varieties developed by private-sector companies, with the exceptions being oats and wheat.

Effects of Public Policies on Farm Productivity

Considerable empirical evidence now exists about the effects of public research, extension, education, and farm commodity policies on agricultural productivity. Much weaker evidence exists about the effects of these policies on the structure of agriculture, including farm size and specialization.

Table 3.5.   Ph.D.-level scientific personnel involved in plant breeding, 1989 (full-time equivalent)

| | No. in Plant Breeding Research | | |
| | Breeders/Geneticists | | Private |
Crops	Public[a]	Private	Biotech
Field crops			
Corn	36.6	256.9	90.1
Sorghum	12.2	22.8	—
Wheat	38.4	25.2	1.1
Other Small Grains/Cereals	39.4	14.8	0.7
Soybeans	32.7	59.7	17.3
Other Oil Crops	14.9	13.0	10.5
Alfalfa	27.1 }	28.3	2.1
Other Forage Legumes	9.3 }		—
Forage Grasses	27.1	1.6	—
Cotton	15.2	11.1	7.2
SUBTOTAL	252.9	433.4	129.0
Fruits, Vegetables, Nursery, Greenhouse			
Fruits and Nuts	47.4	0.3	—
Vegetables	81.1	108.3	31.4
Flowers and Nursery	13.2	16.4	—
SUBTOTAL	141.7	125.0	31.4
Other Crops	22.2	22.0	91.5
TOTAL	416.8	580.4	251.9

SOURCES: Column one is from James (1990). Columns two and three are from Kalton, Richardson, and Frey (1989).

[a]Combined scientists in USDA-ARS and SAES.

In our forthcoming book (Huffman and Evenson 1993) we summarize evidence from past studies and present new evidence from our most recent work.[1] In particular, econometric evidence covering more than a decade of farm production shows that investments in public and private agricultural R&D have made positive and significant contributions to U.S. multifactor productivity and growth of output. Hence, growth in output and changes in productivity have occurred more rapidly as a result of investment in agricultural research than they would have in its absence, other things equal.

Table 3.6. Plant Variety Protection Certificates issued in the United States by crop, 1971–1991

	1971–1974	1975–1978	1979–1982	1983–1986	1987–1991	Total Issues	Percentage Public
Field Crops and Forages							
Corn (Field)	0	1	6	40	115	162	0.6
Sorghum	—	—	—	—	—	3	0.0
Wheat	13	42	60	30	97	242	30.2
Barley	0	12	2	23	5	42	7.1
Oats	0	11	5	1	8	25	56.0
Soybeans	34	69	135	155	106	499	15.8
Alfalfa	0	3	21	16	31	71	18.3
Cotton	22	31	38	31	53	175	13.1
Vegetables							
Lettuce	14	17	14	15	33	93	0.0
Garden Beans	32	39	21	29	—	121	0.0
Peas	20	48	46	61	—	175	0.0

SOURCE: USDA, *Plant Variety Protection Official Journal.*

Our most recent work uses states as units and covers the years 1950–1982. Included are data from forty-two states (excluding the New England states, Alaska, and Hawaii). By pooling observations for these forty-two states across thirty-two years, we obtain a relatively large body of evidence and sample size. States were the selected unit of study because many of the important decisions on funds and organization of public agricultural research are made at the state level. Also, the use of state units permits us to examine channels of influence that are untraceable using national aggregate data; for example, spillover effects of research conducted in one state on the productivity of agriculture in other states, and subtle interaction effects between different types of research.

As we puzzled over why aggregate multifactor productivity for states in the Corn Belt performed relatively poorly compared to those in other regions during the postwar period, we became convinced that it was useful to divide the U.S. farm sector into separate crop and livestock sectors. The biology of plants and animals is vastly different, the degree of sensitivity of plant and animal technologies to local geoclimatic conditions is different, and the potential for advances in the science and technology of crop and livestock production through R&D seemed likely to be different. A summary of some of our findings follows.

First, in a successful R&D system, research in the pretechnology sciences and the applied sciences should be complementary—additional investments in one type of science raise the productivity of the other type of science. Our evidence, however, is mixed on this issue. In estimated equations explaining crop- and livestock-sector multifactor productivity, we looked for positive coefficients on interaction variables containing pretechnology and applied agricultural research. In the equation for crop-sector MFP, the coefficient on the key variable was positive as expected. In the equation for livestock-sector MFP, however, the coefficient on the key variable was negative. The negative sign is evidence that public livestock research projects in the pretechnology and applied sciences act as substitutes for each other in affecting productivity.

Our findings also showed larger marginal products and rates of return to investments in public pretechnology science research than to applied research. The magnitude of the difference was larger in the livestock sector than in the crop sector. These differences suggest a type of misallocation of public resources allocated to scientific research in the different areas.

Second, some individuals have suggested that private R&D substitutes for or crowds out public agricultural research. With growing real investments in private R&D, this substitution would imply a lowering of the productivity of public agricultural research. In some of our early work we examined this issue by including interaction variables between public and private research (see Evenson 1991).

The evidence is mixed and it, too, differs between the crop and livestock sectors. In the estimated equation for crop-sector MFP, the coefficient of the key variable is negative, implying substitutes between public and private research. However, the magnitude of the effect changes with the share of public agricultural research that is focused on enhancing biological efficiency. As the share invested in biological efficiency increases, the strength of the substitution effect is reduced and the relationship shows potential for becoming complementary. In the equation for livestock-sector MFP, the coefficient of the key variable is positive, implying complementarity. The tendency is strengthened as livestock research focuses increasingly on enhancing biological efficiency. Thus, the evidence is mixed about whether public and private research are complements or substitutes in affecting agricultural productivity, and in our most recent work we have chosen to exclude interaction variables containing public-private research. This imposes a type of "neutrality of effect" between public and private research. The issue, however, merits more examination in light of the interactions between research in the pretechnology sciences and applied sciences, and the more rapid growth in private, rather than public, agricultural research.

Third, farmers' schooling and agricultural extension have been positively related to adoption rates for superior new technologies, as well as to enhanced quality of allocative decisions by farmers. Our findings show a strong positive impact of farmers' schooling on productivity in the crop and livestock sectors, and on aggregate multifactor productivity. Furthermore, farmers' schooling and public commodity-oriented extension are substitutes in affecting productivity. These results are supportive of findings in earlier studies. When the impacts of public extension on productivity were evaluated at the beginning of the study period, they were found to be positive and significant. However, because the level of schooling increased approximately 50 percent during the study period, and because extension and education were substitutes, the positive impact of public agricultural extension eroded to approximately zero by the end of the study period. Public investment in schooling individuals who become farmers has made traditional public agricultural extension largely an unproductive activity in the United States, at least as it relates to increased productivity.

Fourth, much speculation, but not much empirical evidence, exists about the effects of government commodity programs on agricultural productivity. Our results show that higher support prices for crops and milk generally increase productivity. These results are in line with some other speculation (e.g., Quance and Tweeten 1972).

The relative importance of these effects of public policy on growth in multi-factor productivity can be summarized (Table 3.7). Public agricultural research is the single most important source for the crop sector, and private research and extension are second. In the livestock sector, private R&D is the dominant source over all others.

Fifth, although Griliches (1963) attributed a significant proportion of the increases in U.S. agricultural productivity during the period 1940–1960 to economies of scale, few later studies of productivity have reexamined the issue. One exception is Evenson and Kramer (1988). Using the Huffman-Evenson data set, they examined productivity, farm size, specialization, and share of older farmers. Their arguments about the economics of structural change were built largely on an earlier paper by Kislev and Peterson (1982).

The Evenson-Kramer study found that the real nonfarm wage rate, an opportunity cost of labor used on farms, and government farm programs were the primary factors driving U.S. farm size and specialization during the period 1950–1982. Public and private agricultural research appeared to be retarding farm size and specialization. Griliches (1992) recently raised again the issue of the likely

Table 3.7.   Sources of growth in multifactor productivity for U.S. agriculture, 1950–1982

Growth/Source	Crop Sector	Livestock Sector
Total Growth	.626	.513
Explained	.323	.409
Public Research	.225	.072
Public Extension	.156	.087
Private R&D	.151	.457
Farmers' Schooling	-.106	.064
Government Programs	.014	.047
Other Variables[a]	-.117	-.318
Unexplained	.303	.104

SOURCE: Huffman and Evenson (1993).

[a]The contribution of the 15 regional dummy variables to growth is .4078 - .4054 = .0024 for the livestock sector and -.3442 + .3724 = .0285 for the crop sector.

importance of economies of scale in explaining increases in U.S. agricultural productivity. Thus, more study seems warranted of this issue, and of how structure and productivity affect each other.

Public Policy and Farm Productivity, Size, and Specialization

This section presents new evidence about the effects of public policy—research, extension, education, and commodity programs—on farm productivity, size, and specialization. In particular, changes in farm size and specialization may be an important part of a more detailed story about productivity changes in U.S. agriculture during the post–World War II period.

Average farm size seems most likely to be determined by technology, human capital, the labor market, and farm commodity program policies. Specialization may be determined largely by the human capital of farmers and by transaction costs. Kislev and Peterson (1982) present a theory of farm size wherein available technology and the nonfarm wage rate (or opportunity cost of the labor of farmers) are key determinants. In particular, when the nonfarm wage rate increases, the average size of farm must increase to provide a comparable return to "unpaid" farm labor (also see Huffman 1980 and Barkley 1990).

Much earlier, Coase (1937) and Stigler (1951) presented a theory of firm size and specialization in which interfirm and intrafirm transaction costs are important determinants. When transaction costs fall, small farming units are put at a disadvantage against larger producing units. When costs associated with interfirm transactions fall, firms generally become smaller and more specialized, other things equal. In particular, food processing and feed manufacturing shift to nonfarm firms, and the farms become more specialized on basic farm production. When the cost of intrafirm transactions falls or that of interfirm transactions increases, firms generally conduct a more diverse set of activities. Sometimes vertically integrated firms become very large. The entrepreneurial and organizational skills of farmers undoubtedly also affect the size of transaction costs.

The literature on human capital has shown that additional schooling by farmers enhances their allocative ability (e.g., Huffman 1974, 1985) and can be expected to reduce the intrafirm transaction costs associated with less specialization or more diversity. When the nonfarm wage is held constant, additional schooling of farmers tends to increase diversity, and possibly to increase farm size. Applied research can be expected to affect farm size and specialization through the type of new technologies developed. Applied livestock research is expected to be more favorable to larger farm size and greater specialization than is applied crop research. The primary reason is the differing sensitivities of plants and animals to geoclimatic conditions. New animal technologies can be scaled up relatively easily to quite large operations (e.g., with confined growing, laying, feeding, milking, and finishing) without significantly harming productivity in the process. In crop production, attempts to scale up lead to larger negative consequences for productivity. The primary reasons are that the timing of field work is critically determined by local climate and weather, and thus additional land area can be obtained only by accepting a greater range and diversity of geoclimatic conditions.

The Econometric Model

In trying to tell a more complete story about farm productivity and structural change, we constructed an econometric model in which several variables could be taken as jointly determined. In this paper we treat six variables as dependent, and we use a six-equation model of productivity and structural change. Our units of observation are state aggregates for forty-two U.S. states, 1950–1982.

The dependent variables, or variables to be explained, are crop-sector MFP and specialization, livestock-sector MFP and specialization, average farm size, and aggregate MFP. Two separate indexes of specialization are defined because we believe that the policy-induced tendencies to specialize are different for crops than for livestock. The specialization index addresses individual farm-level specialization, not regional specialization of a commodity to a particular state. For example, a farm defined in the Census of Agriculture as a poultry farm may produce an increasing share of a state's total poultry output as a result of changes in research, extension, education, labor market, or farm commodity policy. Thus, our specialization index uses the share of a state's total farm output due to a major commodity, *plus* the share of total output of that commodity produced by its farm commodity type. Farm types and major commodity groups are poultry, dairy, general livestock, cotton, fruit and vegetable, and general crop. A larger value of our crop specialization index indicates that a larger share of crop output is being produced by crop-farm types than is being produced by livestock and combination crop-livestock farm types.

The farm-size variable is an index of the average (real) services obtained from relatively fixed capital used in farming. It is the annual service flow from cropland-equivalent farmland and from farm machinery and breeding stock. This measure of farm size differs from a size measure based strictly upon land area. Our measure is not strictly natural resource–based because it also includes services from reproducible capital, and it seems to better approximate a critical dimension of farms that is more closely associated with capital needed for annual production than with land area (or value).

Our model is multi-equation and interrelated. Some equations contain regressors that are determined or explained by the whole system, and economic disturbances, or shocks, are likely to have common same-year effects across equations. In the reduced-form specification of the model, each equation has one dependent variable that is "explained" by the complete set of independent variables. These latter equations contain more policy-relevant parameters than do the structural equations.

The six-equation structural model used in this analysis contains some significant simplifications, although it is more complex than other reported models of productivity. The equations for crop and livestock specialization and farm size contain only one dependent/endogenous variable. (See Table 3.8 for a complete list of the variables and a brief description of each.) The practical implication of this structure is that productivity does not feed back to specialization and size. Furthermore, we use a somewhat abbreviated set of public policy variables to explain specialization and size. The productivity equations contain three or more dependent/endogenous variables, and a full set of independent variables for public policy and weather. Crop (livestock) MFP is assumed to be affected by crop (livestock) specialization and farm size, and state aggregate multifactor productivity is assumed to be affected by crop and livestock specialization and farm size. The model is estimated by three-stage least squares to take account of random regressors in the productivity equations and the cross-equation correlation of economic disturbances. The reduced-form coefficients are derived mathematically from the structural coefficients.

The Results

The fitted structural model provides new insights about how farm size and specialization affect productivity, and it offers some information about the determinants of size and specialization. Because a number of the same independent variables affect farm size and specialization as well as productivity, the coefficients of the dependent variables in the structural equation provide an estimate of the short-term impact of these variables, holding size and specialization constant. In a longer-term context, size and specialization may change as a result of a change in policies or other exogenous variables. The reduced-form coefficients of the model provide estimates of these long-term impacts and are easier to interpret for policy purposes. Reduced-form coefficients are reported in Table 3.9.

Table 3.8.   Definitions of six-equation model variables

Endogenous	
MFP	Multifactor productivity: Divisia output index divided by Divisia input index, 1.00 for national mean 1949–1952 (crop, livestock, and aggregate).
SPECIAL	Specialization Index: Index representing the extent to which farms specialize in the production of a single major agricultural commodity (derived from the farm-type data in Census of Agriculture and interpolated between census years) (crop, livestock), indexed to be 1.0 in each state averaged over 1949–1952.
SIZE	Index of average farm size: Index representing the real service flow from cropland-equivalent farmland and from other farm capital stocks (e.g., machinery, breeding stocks). This index is 1.0 in each state averaged over 1949–1952.
Exogenous	
APP	Stock of public applied research in 1984 dollars, total lag of 33 years, trapezoidal shape weights 7 rising + 6 constant + 20 declining. Research spill-ins from similar subregions and regions are included (crop, livestock).
SC	Stock of public pretechnology science research in 1984 dollars. Lag pattern and spill-in as in APP (crop, livestock).
EXTG	Public extension stock having a commodity focus in days per year, total time lag of 3 years (.5, .25, .25), adjusted for number of geoclimatic subregions (crop, livestock).
SCH	Schooling of farmers: average years of schooling completed by rural males 15–65 years of age (interpolated between census years).
PRIVG	Private agricultural research stock in 1984 dollars, total lag of 33 years, trapezoidal shape 7 + 6 + 20, adjusted for the number of geoclimatic subregions (crop, livestock).
ST	Ratio of the number of private agricultural research and extension staff to the number of public staff in 1970.
NPSUPPORT	Government crop price support: weighted ratio of support price to market price for crops.
NPSUPMLK	Government milk price support: weighted ratio of milk support price to milk market price.
NDVERSION	Government crop diversion payments: equivalent price ratio of direct government crop acreage payments.
DROUGHT	Drought dummy variable: equals 1 if rainfall is less than 1 standard deviation below normal, and 0 otherwise.
FLOOD	Flood dummy variable: equals 1 if rainfall is more than 1 standard duration above normal, and 0 otherwise.
PREPLANT	Cumulative rainfall, February through July.
WAGENF	Real wage rate for production workers in manufacturing.
OVER65	The share of the farm operators that are 65 years of age or older.
TIME	Trend.
REGION$_i$	Share of a state's agricultural land classified in each of 16 geoclimatic regions.

Table 3.9. Reduced-form coefficients for the underlying exogenous variables: six-equation model of productivity, specialization, and size

	Crop Sector		Livestock Sector		Aggregate	
	ln MFP	ln SPECIAL	ln MFP	ln SPECIAL	ln SIZE	ln MFP
Public Research						
ln APPC	0.021	0.981			-0.081	-0.027
ln APPL			-0.325	-0.227	0.134	-0.109
ln SCC	0.176	-1.602			0.141	0.148
ln SCL			0.249	-0.063	-0.116	0.082
Private Research						
ln PRIVGC	0.090	3.035			-0.122	-0.020
ln PRIVGL			0.285	0.214	-0.035	0.140
Public Extension						
ln EXTGC	0.008	-1.335	-0.027	0.129	0.055	0.032
ln EXTGL	0.056	-1.114	0.086	-0.205	0.037	0.006
Farmers' Schooling	0.665	1.058	0.386	0.671	0.045	0.093
Gov. Farm Programs						
NPSUPPORT	0.665	7.544	0.864	0.671	-0.037	0.430
NPSUPMLK	-1.091	-0.617	-0.325	-2.751	-0.331	0.136
NDVERSION	-0.202	0.529	-0.439	1.377	0.382	0.209
Nonfarm wage (ln)				-0.522	0.107	-0.268
Percent Farmer $\geq$ Age 65	-1.3×10^{-7}	-3.4×10^{-5}	-6.4×10^{-7}	-6.4×10^{-7}	-9.1×10^{-7}	-9.1×10^{-7}

Note: Derived from model reported in the text. Model evaluated at the sample mean for some variables.

Of central interest in the structural model are the estimated coefficients for specialization and size in the productivity equations. Holding specialization and the independent variables constant, larger farm size increases productivity in the livestock sector and in aggregate. This result is generally consistent with Griliches' (1963) earlier finding that economies of scale were an important source of increases in farm productivity. In the crop sector, larger size reduces productivity gains. This result is consistent with the adverse effects of greater geoclimatic heterogeneity and the difficulty in getting field operations completed in a timely manner when size increases.

Increases in crop and livestock specialization, holding farm size and the independent variables constant, have differing impacts on productivities. An increase in livestock specialization increases livestock and aggregate agricultural productivity. In contrast, an increase in crop specialization reduces crop and aggregate productivity. The major consolidation of livestock production over the study period into larger, more specialized farm units supports the model finding that greater livestock specialization increases productivity. The negative effects of greater crop specialization on productivity are, perhaps, unexpected. Research over the past decade or more, however, has shown that crop pest problems are magnified by monoculture, and continuous row-cropping is known to increase rates of soil erosion significantly over that from crop rotations that include small grains and meadow (Tegene et al. 1988). Crop-sector productivity might also be affected adversely by greater crop specialization because of the reduced use of animal waste as a soil enhancer. Of course, the possibility exists that differences in effects of size and specialization on productivity are partially a result of our methods of creating separate crop and livestock sectors.

Given the specification of our structural model, the structural and reduced-form equations explaining size and specialization are the same. In the model, productivity does not feed back to farm structure, so the results in Table 3.9 are directly relevant here. Several policies have similar impacts on crop and livestock specialization. Additional schooling of farmers reduces specialization in crops and livestock; however, inasmuch as the coefficients of schooling and the nonfarm wage have opposite signs, the effects of schooling appear to be associated with the greater skill of more educated farmers in running a diversified farming business successfully. Also, a larger investment in private R&D increases both crop and livestock specialization. Private R&D focused on the livestock sector has aided farmers greatly in preventing livestock disease. This appears to be the single most important factor enabling farmers to specialize in large-scale finishing operations for broilers, swine, and cattle.

In the crop sector, private R&D leading to larger and more technically sophisticated farm machinery has undoubtedly encouraged crop specialization. R&D in the agrichemical and seed industries also has yielded technologies that encourage specialization in row crops, especially corn, soybeans, and cotton. Additional applied agricultural research by the public sector has tended to increase specialization, too, but this effect is much stronger for crop specialization than for livestock specialization.

Investment in public pretechnology science research and commodity-oriented public extension have different effects on specialization in the two sectors. Their coefficients are negative in the equation for crop specialization but positive for livestock specialization. Exactly why these effects occur is unclear.

The government commodity programs have affected farm specialization, according to the results of the model. Higher support prices for crops increase specialization. A higher price support for milk has had a positive effect on crop specialization but a negative effect on livestock specialization. A larger cropland diversion payment has increased livestock specialization but has not had any significant effect on crop specialization.

The effects of variables on average farm size is the last set of relationships to be examined. Both the nonfarm wage rate and farmers' schooling have positive and statistically significant effects on size. These results are in line with the predictions from Kislev and Peterson's (1982) model, as well as from the human capital–allocative ability model. Farmers' average schooling level and the real nonfarm wage increased by about 50 percent over the study period, and they appear to have been major sources of the increase in average farm size over the study period (also see Barkley 1990). Increases in public agricultural extension also have had positive and significant effects on farm size.

The effects of research on farm size are mixed. Larger private crop- and livestock-oriented R&D has reduced farm size. This may come as a surprise to some. This finding is certainly contrary to beliefs that farms have been forced to become larger because private industry produces and sells only technologies that can be used on large farms.

In the equation explaining size, the coefficient of public applied crop research is negative, but the one for crop pretechnology science research is positive. For public, livestock-oriented applied and pretechnology science research, the coefficients are also opposite in sign, but they run just the reverse of the public crop research variables. Hence, as a group these coefficients of public research do not show strong positive or negative effects on farm size.

Two of the three coefficients of the government farm program variables have statistically significant effects on farm size. A larger diversion variable causes a larger farm size, but a larger milk price support variable reduces size. The crop price support variable has no significant effect on farm size in our model; this latter result differs with some popular beliefs.

Conclusions

The United States has had a long history of growth and development through a mixture of public- and private-sector activities. The U.S. Constitution established basic citizen rights and the right to ownership and transfer of private property. The property to which ownership rights are attached has been expanded gradually over time, especially in the area of intellectual materials. Real transaction costs associated with enforcement of property rights have stayed modest, primarily through technological advances. In the United States, considerable integrity exists in most private property rights.

U.S. policies have aided the development of a joint public and private system of research and development. The not-for-profit sector has enabled research in the general and pretechnology sciences. The private sector has been given largely the role of applied research and technology development and commercialization. Both the public and private sectors engage in technology transfer to producers, consumers, and governments, as well as in forwarding problems from clientele groups to applied researchers. The boundaries of these activities have shifted over time as policies and technological innovations occur and the natures of the clientele groups change.

Evidence from data spanning more than a century shows that public policies that encourage public and private R&D have had positive impacts on U.S. multi-factor farm productivity. In this paper, we have provided new empirical evidence that changes in farm size and specialization are part of the story for agricultural productivity. Larger farm size and greater specialization have, however, been more favorable to livestock productivity than to crop productivity. The primary reasons are differences in biology, effects of geoclimatic conditions, and the need for land surface area by producing units. Labor (through linkages and mobility between the farm and nonfarm jobs) and education (through schooling for rural people) policies have been more important determinants of farm size than has R&D policy or government commodity programs. Public policies for education of rural people and private R&D were shown to be important determinants of farm specialization.

Although we have made some advances here, our knowledge continues to be incomplete. We would like to know more about how agricultural research, extension, education, and government commodity policies affect the growth and development of rural communities. As the average size of U.S. farms has grown over time, the average amount of labor per farm has remained relatively constant. This has meant a dramatic reduction in the density of the farm population but an improvement in incomes over what they would have been without the large reduction in farm labor and population. This reduction will continue.

The prospects for the rural nonfarm areas are better. The major problems of U.S. inner cities most likely will continue into the foreseeable future. This makes rural nonfarm life relatively attractive. In order to reduce and prevent areas of rural poverty in the future, a high-quality education for rural children and ties of rural people to modern communication systems seem critical. They are handles to future opportunities for socioeconomic mobility.

Note

1. See Antle and Capalbo (1988) for more of the technical details on measurement of agricultural productivity.

References

Antle, J. M., and S. M. Capalbo. 1988. "An Introduction to Recent Developments in Production Theory and Productivity Measurement." In S. M. Capalbo and J. M. Antle, eds., *Agricultural Productivity*. Washington, D.C.: Resources for The Future.

Barkley, Andrew. 1990. "The Determinants of the Migration of Labor out of Agriculture in the United States: 1940–85." *American Journal of Agricultural Economics* 72:567–73.

Coase, R. 1937. "The Nature of the Firm." *Economica* 4:386–405.

Dahmann, D. C., and L. T. Dacquel. 1992. *Residents of Farms and Rural Areas: 1990.* Current Population Reports: Population Statistics, Series P-20, No. 457. Washington, D.C.: U.S. Government Printing Office.

Denison, E. F. 1962. *The Sources of Economic Growth in the United States and the Alternatives before Us.* New York: Committee for Economic Development.

Evenson, R. E. 1983. "Intellectual Property Rights and Agribusiness Research and Development." *American Journal of Agricultural Economics* 65:967–75.

_____. 1989. "Spillover Benefits of Agricultural Research: Evidence from U.S. Experience." *American Journal of Agricultural Economics* 71:447–52.

_____. 1991. "Two Blades of Grass: Research for U.S. Agriculture." In J. Antle and D. Summer, eds., *Essays on Agricultural Policy in Honor of D. Gale Johnson.* Presented at conference honoring Johnson, May 3–4, 1991, Chicago.

70

Wallace E. Huffman and Robert E. Evenson

_____. 1992. *Research and Extension in Agricultural Development.* San Francisco: ICS Press for the International Center for Economic Growth.

Evenson, R. E., and R. A. Kramer. 1988. "Public Policy, Technology, and the Structure of U.S. Agriculture: Some Econometric Evidence." Paper, Yale University, New Haven, Conn.

Griliches, Zvi. 1960. "Hybrid Corn and the Economics of Innovation." *Science* 13:275–80.

_____. 1963. "The Sources of Measured Productivity Growth: United States Agriculture, 1940–1960." *Journal of Political Economics* 71:331–46.

_____. 1992. "Source of Agricultural Economic Growth and Productivity: Discussion." *American Journal of Agricultural Economics* 74:762–63.

Huffman, Wallace E. 1974. "Decision Making: The Role of Education." *American Journal of Agricultural Economics* 56:85–97.

_____. 1980. "Farm and Off-Farm Work Decisions: The Role of Human Capital." *Review of Economic Statistics* 52:14–23.

_____. 1985. "Human Capital, Adaptation Ability, and the Distributional Implications of Agricultural Policy." *American Journal of Agricultural Economics* 67:429–34.

Huffman, Wallace E., and Robert E. Evenson. 1993. *Science for Agriculture.* Ames: Iowa State University Press. *Forthcoming.*

Huffman, Wallace E., and Richard E. Just. 1992. "Structure, Management, and Funding of Agricultural Research in the United States: Directions and Likely Impact." Paper, Department of Economics, Iowa State University, Ames.

Huffman, W. E., and Stephanie Mercier. 1991. "Joint Adoption of Microcomputer Technologies: An Analysis of Farmers' Decisions." *Review of Economic Statistics* 73:541–46.

Jorgenson, Dale W., and F. M. Gollop. 1992. "Productivity Growth in U.S. Agriculture: A Postwar Perspective." *American Journal of Agricultural Economics* 74:745–50.

Kendrick, J. W. 1961. *Productivity Trends in the United States.* National Bureau of Economic Research. New York: Princeton University Press.

Kislev, Y., and W. Peterson. 1982. "Prices, Technology, and Farm Size." *Journal of Political Economics* 90:578–95.

Office of Technology Assessment. 1992. *A New Technological Era for American Agriculture.* Washington, D.C.: U.S. Government Printing Office.

Quance, Leroy, and L. G. Tweeten. 1972. "Policies, 1930–1970." In A. G. Ball and E. O. Heady, eds., *Size, Structure, and Future of Farms.* Ames: Iowa State University Press.

Rahm, M., and W. E. Huffman. 1984. "Adoption of Reduced Tillage." *American Journal of Agricultural Economics* 66:405–13.

Schultz, T. W. 1953. *The Economic Organization of Agriculture.* New York: McGraw-Hill.

Science. 1992. "Animal Models Point the Way to Human Clinical Trials." Vol. 256:772.

Stigler, George J. 1951. "The Division of Labor Is Limited by the Intent of the Market." *Journal of Political Economics* 59.

Tegene, A., W. E. Huffman, and J. A. Miranowski. 1988. "Dynamic Corn Supply Functions: A Model with Explicit Optimization." *American Journal of Agricultural Economics* 70:103–11.

U.S. Department of Agriculture. 1991. *Economic Indicators of the Farm Sector: State Financial Summary, 1990.* Rockville, Md.: ERS-NASS.

Wozniak, Gregory D. 1984. "The Adoption of Interrelated Innovations: A Human Capital Approach." *Revised Economic Statistics* 66:70–79.

_____. 1991. "Joint Information Acquisition and New Technology Adoption: Late Versus Early Adoption." Paper, Department of Economics, University of Tulsa, Tulsa, Okla.

4

The Effects of Farm Productivity and Income Support on the Rural Economy

MAUREEN KILKENNY
GERALD SCHLUTER

Public support for agriculture ranges across a variety of approaches, from spending on agricultural research and extension to direct income transfers. This support varies over time. In 1982, support for agricultural research and education amounted to $1.0 billion, while income support totaled $1.2 billion. By 1986, support for agricultural research and education remained at $1.0 billion, yet income support had risen to $13.4 billion (Webb et al. 1990). This paper compares how these two types of support affect rural economic activity and income. The costs and benefits of productivity improvements and of farm income transfers are traced through input-output and income-expenditure links using a computable general equilibrium (CGE) model that highlights rural/urban and farm/nonfarm interdependencies. Using the model, we find that a dollar spent on agricultural research and extension over the years 1982–1986 results in 2.26 percent annual total factor productivity growth, and it appears to stimulate a ninety-cent net additional real economic activity economywide. The equivalent amount of money spent on direct transfers stimulates only ten cents of rural net additional real economic activity; it actually costs the whole economy an additional twelve cents real output foregone for every dollar transferred over the same five-year period.

Maureen Kilkenny is Assistant Professor and member of the Economics Institute, University of Colorado Department of Economics, Boulder. Gerald Schluter is Leader of the National Aggregate Analysis Section, Economics Research Service, U.S. Department of Agriculture, Washington, D.C.

Another question we consider is whether or not there exists a pattern of subsidies to rural industries that dominate a *laisser-faire* economic policy. We define an "optimal industrial policy" as the mix and level of production-signaling subsidies that would move resources into particular sectors, at the expense of others, increasing real gross domestic product (GDP) and nominal income (and thus tax revenues) enough to cover direct costs and deadweight losses. Our investigation indicates that real GDP could be increased by government intervention in favor of rural industries that supply agricultural inputs, process agricultural products, and provide household services. However, the current real gains would come at a cost to future generations. An increased government budget deficit would shift costs to the future.

The Model

To simulate the effects of different policies we have developed a rural/urban computable general equilibrium model (R/U CGE) (Kilkenny, forthcoming). The U.S. economy is described by a system of equations representing the behavior of producers, consumers, government, and other economic decision-makers.

The entire economy is aggregated into urban (metropolitan) and rural (non-metropolitan) market areas and six aggregate sectors: agriculture, primary/extractives, agriculture-linked, manufacturing, household services, and business services (Table 4.1). We employ the standard theoretical assumptions that producers face market prices, input costs, and factor prices; they choose the level of supply and mix of inputs to maximize profit. The production technology is given, and product-augmenting productivity growth is modeled as an exogenous phenomenon.

The model also explicitly tracks payments by producers to suppliers of labor, land, and capital as income to households. Members of households residing in rural areas work on rural farms and in rural industry as well as commute to work in urban industries. Urban households work in urban industries. Both types of households receive dividends, interest, and rent from both regions, and purchase most of their household services from within the region in which they reside. Household consumers demand the mix and level of goods and services to maximize utility.

In the present study, we assume that markets for goods, services, and factors of production are regionally circumscribed; that is, there is limited mobility between rural and urban regions. We do not allow for complete economywide market clearing at a single economywide price, so results must be interpreted as pertaining to the short run (less than five years). For example, labor is not modeled

Table 4.1.   Industry composition of sectors

Sector Rural/Urban Model	BEA Commodity Number (85 Table)	Activities Included
Agriculture	1–2	Field and orchard crops, livestock, dairy
Primary & Extractives	3–10, 31, 37–38	Forestry, fisheries, mining, refining, primary metal and steel
Ag Inputs & Processing	14–15, 27, 33, 44	Fertilizer, pesticides, farm and garden machinery, food and feed processing
Manufacturing	13, 16–64 NEC; 80–81	Durable and nondurable goods
Household Services	68, 74–77, 79	Utilities, eating and drinking places, health, education, amusements, local government
Business Services	11–12, 65–67, 69–73, 78	Construction, trade, finance, insurance, transport, federal government

as relocating frictionlessly from rural activities to urban activities in response to a change in the wages offered in either region.

Wages are assumed to be bounded from below at the reservation wage in each regional labor market. In effect, we assume L-shaped labor supply curves: perfectly elastic supplies of labor up to 108 percent of the benchmark levels of employment (when unemployment rates were over 7 percent), after which it is perfectly inelastic and only wage increases can occur (the economy "overheats"). Labor is demanded as long as the value of its marginal product meets or exceeds the market wage. Thus, increases in productivity raise labor demand and employment, while decreases in subsidies lower labor demand and employment.

According to these assumptions, a change in policies can change local employment rates or cause interregional wage differentials that are not dampened by migration. Furthermore, a change in regional household income will be reflected in local markets for household services in particular, because we also stipulate that most household service sector demands are met by local supplies.

The government collects indirect business taxes, profit taxes, social insurance taxes, real estate taxes, tariffs, and income taxes. It purchases commodities and services, provides transfers to households and businesses, spends on farm programs, and loans money to foreign countries. The shortfall of endogenous revenues over mostly exogenous expenditures is the government deficit. The deficit is financed by borrowing in capital markets; so, all else equal, an increase in the deficit will reduce the amount of loanable funds available for private investment.

The model is computable in the sense that it is constructed using real data and solved on the computer. It is general in the sense that the model represents the behavior of not just one type of economic agent, but all types of agents in the economy. The equilibrium solution of the model is the set of prices and quantities that no agent has an incentive to change. All prices are determined by the interaction of suppliers and demanders in each market. Also, the government alters market outcomes by levying taxes, providing some services, competing in the market for loanable funds, and transferring income. Finally, foreign trade can affect the level and value of economic activity.

The benchmark version of the model is calibrated so that the solution replicates the data for rural and urban USA in 1982. To show the effect of a change in policy, the model is solved again using the new specification, and the solution is compared to the benchmark solution. For programs that span a number of years, the model is solved sequentially, one year at a time. Each year's solution is the initial condition for the next year. The cumulative effects of the policy are shown as the difference between solutions in the terminal year and the benchmark year.

Simulation Results

This section presents the results of three basic simulation analyses using the R/U CGE model. In the first simulation we incorporate an annual increase in productivity and an annual expenditure on research and development, each year for five years. The rates of research and extension spending and productivity growth are the ones observed between 1982 and 1986. No other exogenous variables are assumed to change. The idea is not an attempt to project or track the U.S. economy over the same period, only to focus on the implications of public spending that result in productivity growth. The first simulation experiment is called the invest-in-productivity scenario.

In the second simulation we model increases in direct income transfers to rural households of the same amount as that spent on research and extension in the first experiment. This simulation experiment is called the income transfer scenario. In essence, we are looking at the implications of a shift in policy reallocating research and extension expenditures to direct income transfers.

In the third simulation experiment, we solve endogenously for the mix and levels of production subsidies that would maximize real gross domestic product (real GDP). We call this the optimal industrial policy scenario.

Invest-in-Productivity Scenario

From 1970 to 1982, total factor productivity in agriculture grew an average of 2.26 percent per year (Capalbo and Vo 1988). From 1982 through 1986, combined federal, state, and local expenditures on infrastructure, which includes research and extension, averaged $2.658 billion per year (Webb et al. 1990, 296). The first simulation experiment assumes that for the observed rate of expenditure 1982–1986, agricultural productivity grew at the historical rate of 2.26 percent per year for five years. The model is used to focus on how this expenditure and productivity growth affects rural and urban sectoral activity, prices, employment, and other indicators.

Table 4.2 presents some simulation results for the invest-in-productivity scenario. The obvious outcome is an extra 11.27 percent real agricultural output beyond what there would have been without productivity growth. Note, however, that this increase is less than 2.26 percent compounded for five years, since suppliers also respond to falling market prices. The lower market price following the supply shift is a benefit to *consumers*. The benefits of productivity growth in traded sectors such as agriculture are usually passed on to other sectors in the form of lower market prices. Indeed, agricultural product prices are over 5 percent lower.

Higher productivity means that fewer resources are needed to produce the same or even more agricultural output. On balance, farm-sector income falls. This is one of the reasons why agricultural research and extension are considered public goods. The benefits of increased supply (and lower product prices) are captured by the public, not by private farmers, so it is appropriate that the costs are assumed by the public (through taxes and government spending).

There are also significant effects for industries linked to agriculture, either directly upstream (selling to) or downstream (buying from) agriculture. Increased farm production stimulates demand for farm inputs. Sale prices of farm inputs rise, while costs to ag-input industries remain relatively unaffected. Measures of value added per unit rise in the farm input–producing industries of the ag-linked sector. In farm output processing industries, lower agricultural product input prices also

Table 4.2.   Results of invest-in-productivity program for five years, rural USA

Sector	Output	Percentage Change		
		Value Added	Ag. Prod. Prices	Capital Rental Rate
Agriculture	11.27	-12.28	-5.74	-2.4
Primary & Extractives	*	*	*	*
Ag Inputs & Processing	3.49	2.29	-0.59	5.9
Manufacturing	*	*	*	*
Household Services	1.89	1.64	1.25	3.6
Business Services	1.31	0.60	0.78	1.9
Rural CPI	100.68			

Change in rural real GDP: $5.95 billion (1982 dollars)
Total additional rural employment: 403,700

Note: Asterisk indicates not significantly different from zero (less than ±0.5%).

cause value added to rise. This is borne out by the model's estimate that ag-linked value added rises by more than 2 percent. This increase in value-added signals a 3.49 percent expansion of output from ag-linked industries. Rural employment in ag-linked activities rises by 92,100 full-time equivalents (see Fig. 4.1), and the rental rate on capital in the sector rises 5.9 percent.

Another reason why U.S. farmers may not benefit from technological improvements and supply growth is that there is little unmet domestic demand for the traditional agricultural output. This is the consequence of Engel's Law: As income increases, the proportion spent on food declines. Therefore, the main outlets for increased U.S. agricultural output are overseas. The simulation shows nearly half of the additional product going to exports, and that means expanding agricultural exports by 37 percent over the benchmark level. This underscores the importance of free trade to American agriculture. Under current conditions there is no vent for this much surplus; the gains associated with the invest-in-productivity policy would accrue almost entirely to importing countries, inasmuch as U.S. prices would have to fall dramatically to clear markets. The modeling assumption, however, is that world prices are exogenous; thus, the impact of increased trade for decreased commodity prices does not occur in the simulation. In effect, we have simulated a post–successful GATT scenario in which U.S. agricultural exports can increase. That is, the United States becomes even more competitive because of improvements to productivity.

The effects of the invest-in-productivity policy on rural employment are compared to those of the other two policy scenarios in Figure 4.1. As history has long shown, productivity growth in agriculture releases labor from farms. This has been an engine for domestic industrial growth in the past. A modern concern is that this may also imply the demise of rural communities.

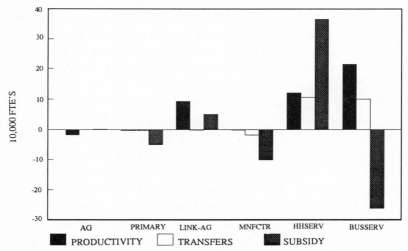

Figure 4.1. Change in rural unemployment, three scenarios.

Our simulations indicate that agricultural productivity growth and the resulting labor release are not necessarily bad for the rural economy. More agricultural inputs are used; more agricultural processing and trade occurs. These ag-linked industries expand employment, and rural incomes rise. This also increases demands for nonagricultural commodities. Ultimately, there are more, rather than fewer, job opportunities in rural areas. The model simulations of the invest-in-productivity scenario show that rural employment rises by over 400 thousand jobs (Table 4.2), which reduces rural unemployment to 6 percent from the benchmark rate of over 8 percent. Most of this additional employment is in the business-services sector: construction, finance, trade, among others.

Rural value-added (nominal) increases by $9.69 billion. All that additional rural employment and income stimulates rural household- and business-services sector activity. Employment rises 119,800 and 214,300 in the household and business sectors, respectively, resulting in 1.89 percent and 1.31 percent increased real output. The rural cost of living rises slightly (0.68 percent), reflecting a Dutch Disease type of phenomenon.[1] Real rural product increases $5.95 billion (1982 dollars), which is less than nominal value added due to the price increases.

Urban activity is also stimulated. Economywide, real gross domestic product is increased by $12.02 billion (1982 dollars). This can be interpreted as the net real gains, or benefit, of the invest-in-productivity policy over the five-year period. The five-year cost in terms of budgetary outlay totals $13.29 billion, to give an economywide benefit:cost ratio of 0.90. However, the government outlay stimulates additional economic activity. This raises tax revenues sufficiently so that the net affect on the government deficit is to reduce it by $1.51 billion. This reduces the drain on loanable funds, and more is available for private investment.

Income Transfer Scenario

The second policy experiment simulates what would happen to the rural economy if the expenditure on research and extension instead were provided as a pure income transfer to rural households to spend as they chose. This is similar to a decoupled farm subsidy policy in that the transfers do not affect the allocation of resources directly. That is, direct income transfers do not distort prices or otherwise signal agricultural production. Some analysts believe that rural areas need injections of income to survive. Our simulation results (Table 4.3) indicate that such income transfers do stimulate the rural economy, but not as much as an invest-in-productivity policy, and they occur at significantly higher costs economywide.

The transfer policy experiment gives the same $2.658 billion dollars that was spent on agricultural research and extension to rural households instead, each year for five years. First, the good news. The income transfers increase rural household income by more than 2 percent, which stimulates the demand for rural services. Rural household service sector activity increases by 1.67 percent. Rural employment expands 0.95 percent, by 106,000 in the household services sector and 100,600 in the rural business services sector (Fig. 4.1). These are the only expanding sectors, however, and rural real product increases only by $1.35 billion (0.3 percent). For the same outlay under the invest-in-productivity policy, rural real product increased $5.95 billion, more than four times as much.

Now the bad news. This policy adds $10.79 billion to the budget deficit, and it causes a $2.48-billion reduction in investment and a $1.61-billion decrease in real GDP economywide. The benefit:cost ratio for the transfer policy is thus negative: ⁻0.12. These results contrast starkly with the invest-in-productivity

Table 4.3.   Results of transfer program for five years, rural USA

| Sector | Output | Percentage Change | | |
		Value Added	Ag. Prod. Prices	Capital Rental Rate
Agriculture	*	*	0.33	*
Primary & Extractives	*	*	0.23	-0.61
Ag Inputs & Processing	*	*	0.52	*
Manufacturing	-0.88	*	0.26	-1.10
Household Services	1.67	1.45	1.17	3.15
Business Services	0.61	*	0.53	0.90
Rural CPI	100.70			

Change in rural real GDP: $1.35 billion (1982 dollars)
Total additional rural employment: 182,700

Note: Asterisk indicates significance of less than ± 0.5%.

policy, which provides static economic gains and could well underlie larger dynamic gains. The potential for dynamic gains arises with the invest-in-productivity policy because more investment is possible. Investment is the basis for future productivity growth.

An Optimal Industrial Policy?

The third experiment lets the model determine the mix and level of production-signaling subsidies that would maximize economywide real GDP given the benchmark level of employment, land in farms, and capital in use. In other words, it attempts to identify the optimal industrial policy.

We define industrial policy as the means by which government encourages resources to move into particular sectors or to promote some parts of the economy at the expense of others. By maintaining the initial level of employment, we focus exclusively on the effects of reallocating existing employees across industries. This is an optimal industrial policy if the reallocation gives net real GDP gains that outweigh the direct costs; that is, one that has a benefit:cost ratio of at least unity.

Arguments for an industrial policy were reviewed by Johnson and Martin in their leadoff paper for the industrial policy symposium. A basic question when considering an industrial policy is this: if expanding such industries were to be profitable, why does private business not do it? Why must the government intervene at all? We wondered if spatial constraints might result in less-than-optimal rural activity and designed the model to investigate this. The R/U CGE model incorporates two of three main types of factor market distortions that may justify government intervention: factor immobility (between regions) and factor price differentials (Magee 1971).

Selected results of this scenario are presented (Table 4.4). The implication is that if rural agricultural input and processing, along with household service industries, were subsidized by the sum of $15.08 billion, economywide real GDP could be increased. The increase is insignificant, however, amounting to only $520 million additional real GDP. Rural wages rise by 2.7 percent, while the cost of consumer goods falls and real rural purchasing power increases.

Rather than subsidizing production agriculture, the simulation points to the value of targeting the ag-linked sector. This finding is consistent with the popular argument that the government should promote the expansion of industries that (1) have high value added or pay high wages (e.g., manufacturing); or (2) are basic or linkage industries that supply inputs to many other domestic sectors (e.g., agriculture). The ag-linked sector includes the food processing industries. These

Table 4.4.   Results of industrial subsidy program, rural USA

Sector	Subsidy	Percentage Change		
		Output	Value Added	Ag. Prod. Prices
Agriculture	*	-1.06	3.85	2.13
Primary & Extractives	*	-10.83	4.28	*
Ag Inputs & Processing	$4.30 bil.	1.97	3.79	-0.60
Manufacturing	*	-6.54	3.23	*
Household Services	$10.78 bil.	9.46	3.98	-3.21
Business Services	*	-3.17	3.56	1.68
Rural CPI		99.53		

Total additional subsidies: $15.08 billion
Change in rural real GDP: -$2.80 billion
Change in economywide real GDP: $ 0.52 billion

Note: Asterisk indicates significance of less than ±0.5%. No change in employment by assumption.

industries have been shown to have some of the largest input-output multipliers (Schluter and Edmondson 1989). Previous efforts to capitalize on this fact by emphasizing processed agricultural products have, in fact, given mixed results (Brown 1992; Barkema et al. 1990). Some of the trade-offs implied by these previous analyses are borne out in our simulation: while the subsidy stimulates a 3.2 percent increase in exports of processed agricultural products, it crowds out raw product exports (-8.6 percent). Furthermore, the 2.6 percent increase in nominal rural value added is an illusory gain. The subsidized price increases erode the nominal gain. After adjusting for price changes, real rural product, land, labor, and capital income is barely (and negatively) affected.

This set of subsidies does not constitute an optimal industrial policy. There are negative side effects. One, the real GDP gains arise not in the rural industries but in urban ones. The expansion in rural ag-linked activity undermines the urban ag-linked sector. The urban ag-linked sector contracts, releasing labor and capital to urban manufacturing, where labor is more productive in real terms and earns higher wages. Two, the policy does not help the rural economy substitute away from imports, nor does it help to expand exports. Three, the subsidies add more than $15 billion to the government budget deficit and show a benefit:cost ratio of only 0.03.

The real GDP increase is limited by assumption: we are solving the model only for a policy that would *reallocate existing resources* across sectors. To allow additional employment would complicate interpretation of the results. However, these results show that the factor market distortions in rural areas lead to a less efficient economy. More output could be produced with the same resources if government subsidies were used to attract labor and capital into rural ag-linked and household services activity. The current real gains, however, can be achieved only by borrowing against our future, as is indicated by the budget deficit.

Conclusions

We have attempted to answer the question, Which is the better rural development policy: public spending for agricultural research and extension, or equal spending for direct income transfers to rural households? Our criterion for *better* is that the policy must induce more real economic activity. Greater economic activity implies expanded consumption and higher national income, expanded consumption and investment, and less unemployment. Our simulations with a computable general equilibrium model suggest that research and extension that results in productivity gains of more than 2 percent per annum is a much more effective way to stimulate the rural economy.

The computable general equilibrium model we use to simulate how the economy responds to different policies is characterized by market segmentation. In particular, labor is confined to the labor markets in the rural or urban regions in which laborers reside, and households make most of their purchases in local markets. This implies that our results refer to the shorter run, the time within which people may become unemployed but not move to another region to find work. In the longer run, migration will take place, and even more gains might result from policies that promote growth.

Furthermore, although we model the policies year-to-year in a recursive way, we do not explicitly model dynamic effects. Also, we assume the historically observed pattern rather than make an explicit model of how spending on research and extension relates to productivity growth. We also attribute all of the observed productivity growth to government activity. In fact, much of what accounts for productivity is embodied in the inputs supplied by the private sector. Thus, even though we are using the most broadly defined measure of outlay, we may be underestimating the costs of achieving those productivity gains by ignoring the private costs of research and development. Also, we do not take into account how changes in policies that change relative profitability across industries will change expectations, and thus the pattern of investment across industries. We can only identify which policies allow total investment to grow rather than shrink.

Our model is further characterized by the assumption that demand for U.S. exports is perfectly elastic, allowing exports to expand without lowering U.S. export prices. In this context, the world market is simply a vent for the surplus agricultural product made possible by increased productivity. The results suggest gains from agricultural research and extension are very sensitive to this assumption. Unfortunately, it is plausible that demand for U.S. exports is inelastic, and it may remain so if the GATT is not passed. In that case, even the gains from research and extension could be significantly smaller, because expanded exports would require lower market prices, thereby canceling the estimated income gains.

The lessons we have learned from simulating different agricultural and rural industrial policies can be summarized in four main points. First of all, dollar for dollar, investing in productivity-enhancing activity is a better way to obtain more real output than simply shifting purchasing power from urban households to rural households using income taxes and farm income transfers. Second, free trade and open markets for U.S. agricultural exports are critically important to the success of this strategy. Productivity growth in agriculture pushes farm labor and other resources out of the sector unless there is a market for the products where demand is elastic. Third, the immobility of labor between regions provides some justification for rural industrial policy. The recommended intervention and the benefits of such intervention, however, are so small that it is probably not worth opening Pandora's Box, in terms of the rent-seeking activity and other counterproductive behaviors that the policy might stimulate. Fourth, there is no free lunch. The monies spent on any policy must come from somewhere, or be borrowed today and paid back tomorrow. We must be mindful of the budgetary implications of increased government spending. Public borrowing may crowd out private investment, and future generations must pay the government debts incurred today. Spending today that induces increased private investment, however, such as our invest-in-productivity scenario, will help lighten that burden on the future and thus may be most worthwhile.

Note

1. The term *Dutch Disease* refers to the situation in which a boom in a traded goods sector (due to an exogenous shock such as a resource discovery or a technological breakthrough) induces a reallocation of resources away from nontraded service sector activity and into the booming trade industry. Usually the shift in the supply of nontradables (such as household services) leads to increases in their price. Since such services are the majority of the consumer bundle, the cost-of-living index rises (Corden 1984). The phenomenon was named after it was observed in the Netherlands following the discovery of North Sea oil.

References

Barkema, Alan D., Mark Drabenstott, and Julie Stanley. 1990. "Processing Food in Farm States: An Economic Development Strategy for the 1990s." *Economic Review* (July-August).

Brown, Dennis M. 1993. "Changes in the Red Meat and Poultry Industries: Their Effect on Nonmetro Employment." AER 665. Agriculture and Rural Economy Division, Economic Research Service, U.S. Department of Agriculture, Washington, D.C.

Capalbo, Susan, and Trang Vo. 1988. "A Review of the Evidence on Agricultural Productivity and Aggregate Technology." In *Agricultural Productivity: Measurement and Explanation*, S. Capalbo and J. Antle, eds. Washington, D.C.: Resources for the Future.

Corden, W. 1984. "Booming Sector and Dutch-Disease Economics: Survey and Consolidation." *Oxford Economic Papers* 36(3):359–80.

Kilkenny, Maureen. 1993. "Rural/Urban Effects of Terminating Farm Subsidies." *American Journal of Agricultural Economics* 75(4). *Forthcoming*.

Magee, Stephen P. 1971. "Factor Market Distortions, Production, Distribution, and the Pure Theory of International Trade." *Quarterly Journal of Economics* (November):623–43.

Schluter, Gerald, and William Edmondson. 1989. "Exporting Processed Instead of Raw Agricultural Products." Staff Report No. AGES 89–58. Agriculture and Rural Economy Division, Economic Research Service, U.S. Department of Agriculture, Washington, D.C.

Webb, Alan, Michael Lopez, and Renata Penn. 1990. *Estimates of Producer and Consumer Subsidy Equivalents: Government Intervention in Agriculture, 1982–87.* Statistical Bulletin #803. Agriculture and Trade Analysis Division, Economic Research Service, U.S. Department of Agriculture, Washington, D.C.

III

Public Roles in Industrial and Rural Development

GOVERNMENT HAS a long history of intervention in agriculture. The four papers that follow discuss the roles of different branches of the public sector and critically evaluate past public-sector policies. The continuing federal commitment to agricultural science is contrasted in Peter Eisinger's paper with a bleak picture of the federal commitment to rural development. Today, changes in the technology of agriculture have forced many rural communities to search for alternative sources of economic activity. Despite the need for increasing and diversifying the economic base, federal outlays for rural development have declined, and no coherent, consistent federal policy has emerged.

The federal retreat from rural development has forced state governments to experiment with a wide array of economic and rural development initiatives. The most popular among these focus on the promotion of science-based activity; many have asked universities to act as catalysts for the development of science-based industrial development. Irwin Feller discusses the motivation, strategy, and design of these science and technology programs, and he makes observations about the prospects and limitations of state governments to effect changes in a state's industrial structure. Michael Crow examines the ability of universities to fill the new role that states are imposing upon them, and he sets forth a number of criteria by which universities more capable of filling this role might be designed.

Industrial policy has been more common in Europe and Japan than in the United States. The view that government can and should have a greater role than economic management alone has produced a number of industry- and region-specific policies in these nations. Henry Ergas evaluates these policies in the European Community and considers how the lessons learned from the experiences of other countries might be applied to a new framework for industrial policy for U.S. agriculture.

5 The Federal Role in Rural Development Policy

PETER EISINGER

By most measures of economic well-being, rural Americans are substantially less well off than their metropolitan neighbors. Unemployment and poverty rates are both about one-third higher than in metropolitan areas; rural income is 25 percent lower; and rural housing represents a disproportionate share of substandard housing (Center for Community Change 1990, 3; Lazere et al. 1989, 25). So limited are opportunities for the good life in the countryside of certain parts of the nation that several hundred thousand rural dwellers each year have begun again to leave their homes for urban destinations.[1]

Rural economic distress has long been a concern of the federal government. Particularly since the Depression, federal government has spent considerable sums in the effort to stimulate economic growth in the countryside. Yet without denying that there has been significant progress in combatting rural poverty, building the infrastructure of modern economic life, and extending health care, there still remain intransigent disparities between metropolitan and nonmetropolitan populations. To some at least, the problem lies in shortcomings of the federal programs.

In congressional hearings on rural economic development in 1989, U.S. Rep. Fred Upton of Michigan wondered why it is that "with so many programs already on the books, rural America is as bad off as it is." The answer, he suggested, is that many federal programs discriminate against rural areas: per capita federal spend-

Peter Eisinger is Director, LaFollette Institute of Public Affairs, and Professor of Political Science and Public Policy, University of Wisconsin at Madison.

ing for all functions in 1985 amounted to $3,192 in urban counties, but only $2,478 in rural counties. To make matters worse, he argued, "even funds earmarked for rural recipients *just do not reach rural areas*" (U.S. Congress 1989, 97–98).

Programs specifically targeted for rural development purposes also dried up in the Reagan years. A report by the Center for Community Change (1990, 3) attributes the rural crisis in part to the 67 percent real decline in federal spending for rural development during the 1980s. For example, funding for programs administered through the Farmers Home Administration fell from four billion dollars in 1981 to less than one billion dollars in 1988.

Grave as these figures are, it would be difficult to argue seriously that the failure of federal programs to spend enough in the countryside or to target rural areas more precisely are root causes of enduring rural problems. Structural weaknesses in the rural economy—stagnant farm income through the 1980s, the high concentration of low-skill manufacturing jobs vulnerable to low-wage foreign competition, lack of modern communications and transportation infrastructure, and a comparatively poorly educated and trained work force—are more likely the prime factors. Yet charges of waning and indifferent federal interest suggest at least that the federal role in rural development is worth examining. How adequate has it been? To what degree has federal assistance been targeted to the most needy rural places? Can any responsibility for rural underdevelopment be attributed to a lack of federal effort or focus?

The Adequacy of Federal Rural Development Programs

Adequacy, of course, is a subjective standard. Yet the notion provides a way to start to think about the scope, consistency, coherence, and variety of Washington's rural development programs. At first glance, federal efforts to assist rural areas and people seem substantial. In his testimony Representative Upton identified 125 such programs, ranging from the highway construction funds administered through the Appalachian Regional Commission, to rural electrification, to the price supports of the Commodity Credit Corporation (U.S. Congress 1989, 101–5). A report by the General Accounting Office counted at least eighty-eight programs, administered by thirteen different federal agencies, that have some rural development implications (U.S. General Accounting Office 1989). A Department of Agriculture task force identified seventy-eight different nonfarm programs in the USDA alone that bear directly or indirectly on rural development (U.S. Department of Agriculture 1989).

Not only is there clearly a large number of contemporary programs, but the historical record suggests a varied and long tradition of federal interest in stimulating rural development and well-being that extends back to the preconstitutional period. The story can be traced from the Northwest Ordinance and the canal-era land grants, through the Morrill Act of 1862 and the 1916 Highway Act, to the New Deal programs designed to conserve soil and provide farm credit (Eisinger, forthcoming). The most important of the rural development programs, both in the contemporary period and historically, have provided support for infrastructure: roads, electricity and telephone networks, water and sewer facilities.

If the sheer number and variety of federal programs were sufficient to satisfy the adequacy test, then it would be reasonable to judge national rural development efforts favorably. But several other characteristics of rural development policy suggest that the federal effort has been distinctly mixed. Specifically, the adequacy of federal initiatives to foster rural economic well-being can be challenged on the following grounds:

1. Federal spending in rural areas has focused on individual income redistribution and farm programs rather than on community development.
2. Federal outlays for rural development were generally lower at the beginning of the 1990s than they were just before Ronald Reagan was elected president.
3. In its focus on infrastructure, Washington has failed to address, in a consistent way, a particularly fertile area for economic development, namely, rural small-business capital needs.
4. The federal effort is limited in the sense that existing programs are small relative to the problems, and the effort as a whole lacks coherence.

Let us examine each of these.

Rural Spending Priorities

A recent analysis of federal spending for all purposes in metropolitan and nonmetropolitan counties indicates that the latter are far less likely to be the recipients of federal monies that stimulate development (Dubin and Reid 1988). Two-thirds of federal spending in rural counties in 1985 came in the form of income transfers, including retirement benefits, welfare payments, medical benefits, unemployment compensation, and farm support. These expenditures have little long-term development value, serving instead to boost short-term income circulation. In contrast, only 48 percent of federal spending in metropolitan counties came in the form of income transfers.

Aggregate federal spending for direct development purposes, including investment in public infrastructure and human resource development, commanded roughly equal proportions in metro and nonmetro counties (4 and 6 percent, respectively),[2] but there was more than a 2:1 metropolitan advantage in spending for procurement (mainly defense goods) and research and development. As Dubin and Reid (1988, 6) point out, such expenditures may "help build an area's research facilities or industrial capacity. When they do, they produce genuine and lasting economic development, though this effect is incidental to their principal objectives."

Among federal rural programs, the emphasis has always been on farm programs rather than development. Yet farming has declined as a source of rural employment. Only 9 percent of rural workers are employed in farming, and only about 20 percent of nonmetropolitan counties depend for their economic life mainly on farming. Yet as the USDA task force pointed out, "Agricultural initiatives often dominate the attention of USDA management while concerted action on equally worthy rural development objectives is given less attention" (U.S. Department of Agriculture 1989, 16–17).

Declining Federal Outlays

A number of the federal grant and loan programs used to support rural development, including most of those administered by the Appalachian Regional Commission, the Tennessee Valley Authority, the Economic Development Administration, and the Farmers Home Administration, were targeted for elimination in the Reagan years. The proposed cuts were part of a larger New Federalism agenda that sought to reduce the size and scope of the national government by devolving much domestic policy responsibility to subnational governments.

The White House was unable to persuade Congress to cut these programs entirely, but in most cases their funding levels decreased sharply in the early 1980s. Table 5.1 shows the funding history in the Reagan years for the major programs targeted specifically to rural development. Note, for example, that appropriations for six of the eight programs were lower at the beginning of the 1990s than in 1980. Losses ranged from the 91 percent cut in loan guarantee authority for the Business and Industrial Loan Program to the 9 percent decrease in the Water and Waste Treatment Loans. All but the Secondary (rural) Highway Program have risen from mid-decade low points, however.

Small Business Capital. It is widely agreed that the most fertile job generators in the economy are small businesses. Yet much of their development potential goes

Table 5.1. Appropriations for selected targeted rural development programs

	1980	1982	1984	1986	1988	1990	1991
				(in millions of dollars)			
Farmers Home Administration							
Water and Waste Treatment Grants	290.0	125.0	90.0	109.4	109.4	212.0	300.0
Water and Waste Treatment Loans	700.0	375.0	270.0	325.4	330.3	535.0	635.0
Community Facility Loans	240.0	126.2	130.0	95.7	95.7	125.0	125.0
Business and Industrial Loans	1073.8	300.0	300.0	95.7	95.7	100.0	100.0
Appalachian Regional Commission							
Nonhighway Programs	126.6	62.1	49.1	32.7	37.6	46.0	44.0
Tennessee Valley Authority							
Economic and Community Resources	12.4	16.8	20.8	14.0	14.0	21.0	21.0
Department of Transportation							
Appalachian Highways	228.7	107.6	110.8	61.7	67.0	—	—
Secondary Roads	772.9	387.0	500.0	650.0	475.0	400.0	—

SOURCE: National Governors' Association (1988); and Office of Management and Budget, *Budget of the United States*, annual.

unrealized, for it is among this group of firms that the gap between capital needs and resources is most acute. Lack of access to capital and undercapitalization are key factors in the high rate of small-business failure. Thus, for many economic development practitioners it follows that government loans and loan guarantees are most productively employed when they are targeted to the small-business sector.

There is evidence that the rural credit shortfall is especially acute: although roughly a quarter of the U.S. population resides in rural America, rural banks and credit institutions control only 15 percent of the savings (Stanfield 1983, 1936). As recently as a decade ago 40 percent of all rural counties had no savings and loan institutions, and 65 percent had no mortgage bankers (Rauch 1985, 473). Rural advocates in Congress are convinced that the lack of credit for small-town businesses is a key barrier to economic growth (U.S. Congress 1989, 5–6). Federal attempts to close the small-business capital gap in rural areas, however, have been inconsistent at best.[3]

One rural business credit program, the Rural Loan Program (Title IIIA) of the Economic Opportunity Act of 1964, provided sixty-six thousand loans to low-income farmers, nonfarm rural dwellers, and rural cooperatives for new and expanded businesses and farm improvements, but it was abolished after only seven years (Levitan 1969, 228). The major remaining program devoted exclusively to the provision of credit guarantees for rural business is the Business and Industrial Loan Program, now administered by the recently established Rural Development Administration in the Department of Agriculture. This is an extremely small program (it guaranteed only about sixty loans per year during the late 1980s), and it has tended to focus mainly on large firms. More than 40 percent of the loans guaranteed from 1986 to 1988 were over one million dollars, and more than half the dollars involved went for loans of more than two million dollars. Funding for the program is less than one-tenth of what it was during its peak in the Carter years (Center for Community Change 1990, 51–52).

The Small Business Administration runs a variety of programs designed to channel credit to small firms regardless of their location, but none of these programs is targeted specifically to rural enterprises. Rural and small-town banks are notoriously reluctant to participate in SBA loan guarantee programs because the administrative costs do not justify the small scale of the loans and the small number of transactions. According to the Center for Community Change (ibid., 63–64), the SBA itself tends to focus on the large end of the urban small-business sector. It guarantees few loans of less than $25 thousand, almost none of which are to businesses in rural areas. The U.S. General Accounting Office (1989, 35) calculated that rural areas get less than their proportional share (based on the percentage of the U.S. population that lives in rural counties) of SBA funding in five of the seven small-business programs for which rural data were available.

In short, the focus of federal rural development assistance has been on the subsidy of the infrastructure of modern industrial society rather than on a more targeted, microinterventionist strategy in the small-business sector. If the former is undeniably important, it is also a relatively blunt tool for stimulating business investment and encouraging permanent job creation. In the words of one member of Congress, when it comes to the small-business credit gap, the federal government "is selling rural communities short" (U.S. Congress 1989, 6).

Limited Effort

If the federal effort to stimulate rural development is calculated as an aggregate over time, then the record appears impressive. Take, for example, support for the construction of modern water and waste disposal systems, probably the single most important federal rural economic development program. Between 1961 and 1988 the Farmers Home Administration channeled approximately $9.8 billion in loan guarantees and $3.1 billion in grants to over twenty-nine thousand water treatment and waste disposal projects in rural communities (U.S. Congress 1989, 144). Yet these impressive numbers notwithstanding, the task of providing clean water to rural dwellers is far from complete.

A majority of rural water systems are presently out of compliance with the federal Clean Water Act and the federal Safe Drinking Water Act. The executive director of the National Rural Water Association estimates that approximately 80 percent of the rural water systems must add treatment facilities to meet current standards. The estimated cost for these improvements to existing water and waste systems ranges between $3.5 billion and $6.1 billion (ibid., 1989, 147–48). These figures do not include cost estimates to construct new systems for areas still served by wells.

Federal grant activity for development purposes in any given year is relatively sparse. Table 5.2 shows the number of rural and nonrural counties that received selected development grants in selected years. Rural counties, which account for 78 percent of all counties, include all those located outside of designated metropolitan statistical areas (MSAs). (This is a rough measure that probably understates the actual extent of rural America, since large numbers of very small towns and farmsteads are located in the outlying parts of counties included in MSAs). Quite small numbers of both metropolitan and nonmetropolitan counties receive grants in any given year through the four Economic Development Administration (EDA) programs shown in Table 5.2, but nonmetropolitan counties did especially poorly in comparison to their urban counterparts.

Water and waste disposal grants were more numerous than grants awarded under the Economic Development Administration. Only in the former program did nonmetropolitan counties receive a slightly higher proportion of grants than metropolitan places, but the annual activity in both types of counties is still relatively small. The conclusion of a recent GAO report that "relatively few federal programs pursue rural development as a primary objective" (U.S. GAO 1989, 60) is particularly true with respect to the EDA initiatives.

Not only is federal grant activity spotty in any given year, but the whole approach to rural development has lacked coherence. Concern over fragmented efforts led Congress to pass the Rural Development Policy Act of 1980, which called on the executive branch to enunciate a coordinated and comprehensive rural strategy. In the first (and only) report pursuant to this mandate, however, the secretary of agriculture under President Reagan challenged the notion that responsibility for a development strategy lay primarily with Washington. New Federalism doctrines called for devolution of authority to state and local governments. "The Federal role," wrote Secretary John Block in transmitting the report to the Congress, "becomes one of support rather than direction. . . ." (U.S. Department of Agriculture 1983). By the end of the decade, however, lack of federal leadership caused the rural revitalization task force to conclude, "Rural policy at all levels of government consists of a collection of programs that, however useful individually, do not add up to a coherent and consistent strategy to achieve any well-understood goals" (U.S. Department of Agriculture 1989, 3).

Interestingly, there has been a recent federal attempt to redress this lack of coherence, but so far it has borne little fruit. In 1990 the federal government established pilot rural development councils in eight states to bring officials from the state, local, and federal governments together with private-sector representatives to coordinate rural development efforts and think strategically about policy. Yet as Radin (1992, 126) concludes in her examination of these bodies after their first year in operation, "Despite much rhetoric, few [councils] were able to develop a comprehensive view of their state's entire rural development landscape as is suggested by the concept of strategic planning. Rather, they moved modestly, 'testing the waters' before proceeding further."

Table 5.2.   Distribution of selected development grants among metropolitan and nonmetropolitan counties

	1983		1990	
	Metro County Recipients	Nonmetro Country Recipients	Metro County Recipients	Nonmetro County Recipients
Water and Waste Disposal	71 (10.3%)	298 (12.2%)	67 (9.8%)	320 (13.1%)
EDA Public Works	65 (9.5%)	74 (3.0%)	43 (6.3%)	94 (3.8%)
EDA Technical Assistance	91 (13.3%)	13 (0.5%)	50 (7.3%)	35 (1.4%)
EDA Economic Development Assistance	27 (3.9%)	10 (0.4%)	34 (5.0%)	2 (0.1%)
Special Adjustment	4 (0.6%)	3 (0.1%)	31 (4.5%)	57 (2.3%)
	(N = 686)	(N = 2446)	(N = 686)	(N = 2446)

SOURCE: Bickers and Stein (1991), FAADS data archive.

Targeting Rural Development

By setting federal rural development programs against some standard of adequacy, a picture emerges of a long and varied history that is nevertheless marked by gaps or overlooked opportunities, lack of coherence, and inconsistent—even declining—fiscal commitment. To what degree, however, is development spending targeted to the most rural places, and among those, to the most distressed? Even if federal development assistance is less than adequate, is it at least focused where the need is greatest?

Targeting program funds, or fiscal redistribution, has long been an objective of federal intergovernmental assistance. Formulas based on various need or distress factors are the basis for distribution in such programs as education aid to disadvantaged children and community development. Nevertheless, political pressures to spread program benefits more widely are intense, leading often to a diffusion effect in which the original targeting objectives are compromised significantly. For example, in his study of the Community Development Block Grant Program, Rich (forthcoming) concludes that targeting to needy places, needy neighborhoods, and needy people all declined over the course of its history. Similarly, distribution criteria for the programs for rural development established by the Public Works and Economic Development Act (PWEDA) of 1965 had become so broad by the mid-1970s that 85 percent of the U.S. population lived in counties eligible to receive such funding (Eisinger 1988, 101). Four of these PWEDA programs are included in the analysis that follows. In general, Dye (1987, 443) has observed that "the research literature on targeting has produced a stable and durable set of findings over the last decade: Federal aid allocations to local governments are only weakly related to measures of social need and fiscal capacity." Significantly, nearly all these studies have focused on the distribution of urban, not rural, programs.

Altogether, five development programs were chosen to study rural targeting patterns (Table 5.2). These programs do not constitute a random sample of all rural development programs; rather, they offer a range of major and minor initiatives that meet three criteria:

1. Distribution of funds is not driven by formula; instead, federal granting agencies have some discretion in making awards in these programs, although the degree of discretion varies by program according to targeting criteria.
2. The programs may be used to generate direct development impacts; that is, to support or plan for job creation and to encourage business investment.

3. Each involves actual grants rather than loans or loan guarantees; data for the latter two sorts of intergovernmental aid are rarely available by subnational jurisdictions.

Annual federal outlays, by county, for each of these five programs for the period 1983–1990 were derived from archives compiled by Bickers and Stein (1991). Although county governments themselves were rarely the actual recipient jurisdictions, the county unit provides the only way in this data archive to control for ruralness. Besides, to look at counties as the units within which development grants are made makes good theoretical sense: development grants are likely to have spillover economic effects beyond the boundaries of municipal grant recipients, and counties represent a reasonable way to measure a labor market area, especially in rural parts of the country. Thus, it is interesting and important to know how different counties fare in the competition for federal development resources.

Data on program outlays provide an unusually fine-grained opportunity to study distribution: as Rich (n.d.) observes, most efforts heretofore to study federal spending distribution have had to do so with highly aggregated data, such as outlays by broad function rather than specific program. The Bickers-Stein data are drawn from Census Bureau tapes called the Federal Assistance Awards Data System, which begins in a form useful for comparative purposes only in 1983. The archive includes only grants, not loans or loan guarantees, which limits the analysis of rural development programs to some extent.[4]

Two of the programs, Water and Waste Disposal System (WWD) Grants and the EDA Public Works initiative, provide funds for infrastructure, sorely lacking in many rural areas. This is especially true of good water and sewer systems, which are crucial to an area's development potential. As Robin Tallon, a member of Congress from rural South Carolina, points out,

> A quality water and sewer system is the first thing a company looks for in relocation and it's a community's first demonstration that you are ready, willing, and able to meet that company's future needs. It's the first test and for far too many communities in my State and District it becomes the last one. . . . Water and sewer lines are what it takes to move a community from rural to rural developed. (U.S. Congress 1989, 6)

Of the five grant programs, only WWD grants, administered by the Farmers Home Administration, are currently aimed specifically at rural communities. In 1961 Congress gave FmHA authority to make such grants, hitherto limited to individual farms or farmers, to small communities of fewer than twenty-five hundred people. In 1972 the program was expanded to include communities of fewer than ten thousand. Water and Waste Disposal is the single largest develop-ment grant program targeted to rural areas.

The other four programs are administered by the Economic Development Administration. These programs originated as part of the federal effort to combat underdevelopment in Appalachia and other rural regions, but they have long since lost their exclusive rural focus. Although they now serve a broader constituency, they are nevertheless targeted to areas experiencing "severe economic distress."

Public Works grants, the major EDA program, provide funding for a variety of infrastructure projects, including water and sewer systems, but also industrial park development, tourism amenities, and port facilities. Technical Assistance and Economic Development Assistance are two minor programs that provide funds to support economic development demonstration projects, feasibility studies, re-search, and planning efforts. The fifth program, Special Adjustment, is perhaps the most flexible of all federal economic development initiatives. It is designed to provide resources to communities experiencing some sort of severe economic dislocation, such as a plant or military base closing, or long-term economic deterioration. Monies may be used, among other purposes, to construct public facilities, provide public services, pay for technical assistance, train or retrain workers, or establish a revolving business loan fund. In the 1990 Defense Authorization Bill, Congress added $50 million to this otherwise relatively small program to help communities deal with dislocations caused by cutbacks in federal defense spending.

In general, all five of these programs—but particularly those administered by the EDA—concentrate their resources on places in metropolitan counties and on more populous counties. Table 5.3 shows the size of the average grant, by program, in metropolitan and nonmetropolitan counties in 1990. In only one case, Economic Development Assistance, was the average grant to recipients in nonmetropolitan counties higher than in metropolitan counties. Simple correlation coefficients indicate that at least for three of the programs, recipients in larger counties get larger grants.

Other data support the finding that federal development efforts focus on larger, not smaller, places. Not only were the data for 1983 virtually identical (the correlation coefficients were somewhat more robust), but the same results were obtained by correlating county population size not with the size of the grant but simply with the likelihood of receiving a grant. The counties were also divided according to the size of their county seat to explore grant activity in very rural places. Counties in which the seat consists of fewer than five thousand people tended to get smaller grants than those that had seats of 5,000–20,000. Counties

Table 5.3.   Rural targeting of federal development programs, 1990

	Average Metro County Grant (Dollars)	Average Nonmetro County Grant (Dollars)	Correlation (*r*) between Grant and County Population (1980)
WWD	650,164	534,298	.00
Public Works	1,146,952	750,554	.19[a]
Technical Assistance	72,095	62,465	.14[a]
Economic Development	137,058	150,000	.18[a]
Special Adjustment	874,280	467,656	.03

[a] $p < .001$.

with seats of more than twenty thousand in population tended to get the largest grants. Smaller places stood less chance of receiving any grants at all.

If small places do less well in the federal grant competition than large places, does the same hold true for less-well-off rural places vis-a-vis their more prosperous rural counterparts? To assess the degree to which federal grants are targeted to need, both the dollar amounts of the grants and the likelihood of receiving a grant were regressed on various indicators of need, controlling for county population. Need indicators included the percentage of the county population below the poverty line, county income rank nationally, and population change. Table 5.4 shows the results of the calculations in the case in which the dependent variable is dollars granted.

There are two plausible hypotheses regarding the relationship of grant activity to population change. One is that population decline signals diminished economic activity and elicits development intervention. The other is that rapid growth generates needs, particularly for infrastructure and planning. In the former case we would expect negative coefficients; in the latter, positive. In effect, however, the coefficients in the first column of Table 5.4 show that the relationship between grant activity and population change is nonexistent. To the degree that population growth or decline indicates need, federal development programs are not responsive.

Grants are, however, related to poverty and income rank, even when size is controlled, although the direction of the relationship varies depending on the program.[5] A positive relationship between either (1) the percentage of persons living in poverty or (2) county income rank and grant activity indicates that funds

Table 5.4.   Targeting development grants to needy counties, controlling for
              county populations, 1990

	Population Change, 1980–86		Percentage of Persons below Poverty, 1979		Per Capita County Income Rank, 1985	
	(standardized beta coefficients and level of significance)					
WWD	.019	(.28)	.014	(.02)	.065	(.000)
Public Works	-.014	(.43)	.051	(.004)	.048	(.009)
Technical Assistance	.018	(.31)	.026	(.14)	-.065	(.02)
Economic Development	.010	(.55)	-.005	(.79)	-.056	(.002)
Special Adjustment	.006	(.76)	-.008	(.63)	-.045	(.02)

are disproportionately allocated to jurisdictions in high-need counties. A negative relationship indicates that funds are allocated to healthier (i.e., low poverty and high income rank) jurisdictions even when size is held constant.

Although the simple coefficients are small, many are statistically significant. Water and Waste Disposal grants and EDA Public Works grants tend slightly to be distributed to jurisdictions in less-well-off counties. The greater the percentage of people below the poverty line and the worse the rank on the income scale, the more likely it is that a jurisdiction in the county will receive such funds. The allocation of grant funds in this program is, to some degree, attentive to need.

Three of the EDA grants, in contrast, are allocated disproportionately to communities in better-off counties, a finding that indicates that severe economic distress provides little assurance of attention in the allocation process. Although the regressions show that there is no statistically significant relationship between grant activity and county poverty level, there is a small, but significant, relationship between grants and a better income ranking.

At least where the three EDA grants are concerned, the pattern in which jurisdictions in slightly larger (Table 5.3) and better-off counties (Table 5.4) get grants may be characterized as one in which the rich get very slightly richer. There are several plausible explanations for this pattern of advantage building on advantage. One is that jurisdictions do well in the grant competition when they have various bureaucratic resources that enhance their ability to write applications, perform the necessary planning exercises, and lobby the granting agency. There is some evidence in the political science literature to support this hypothesis.

Saltzstein (1977) and Rich (1989) have shown, for example, that local entrepreneurial skills and resources are important independent of need in successfully winning federal grants.

A second possible explanation is that the allocation of federal grants in programs not constrained by entitlement formulas or rigorous targeting criteria is responsive to political pressures. Let us suppose that the grant allocation process is open to influence by members of Congress. Within any given congressional district, it is reasonable to expect that all things being equal, a member of Congress will seek to channel federal aid to those jurisdictions that can provide some political benefits in return. Thus, one could explain the finding that larger jurisdictions tend to do better than smaller places in getting the EDA grants by the fact that within the congressional district they have more votes.

Neither of these hypotheses is easy to test using county-level aggregate data; thus, these initial efforts are essentially speculative. A series of simple correlations between grant activity (measured in two ways: whether a jurisdiction within a county received a grant or not, and the amount of the grant) and various measures of bureaucratic and governmental capacity showed no support for the first hypothesis. Capacity was measured by local tax revenues per capita, local government employment per ten thousand people, and local government expenditures per capita. The coefficients that measure the relationship between capacity and grants were extremely small (generally in the .02 or .03 range), mostly negative, and rarely statistically significant. When the variables are combined in a multiple regression equation controlling for population size and need variables, there is no support for the capacity hypothesis, at least insofar as the concept is measured here.

No single regression model explains much variance. A county's metropolitan status is the major, or only, significant variable in explaining the receipt and distribution of EDA program grants. Table 5.5 shows a typical model, this one regressing EDA Economic Development Assistance grants on the need, capacity, and population variables in 1990.[6] It is possible, of course, that larger places tend to receive larger grants simply because they have more people to serve and therefore need to build larger facilities. Population here serves as an indicator of demand. This explanation would be more appealing if population were an important factor empirically in explaining the distribution of Water and Waste Disposal Grants, which go to fund infrastructure projects. But population is not a significant variable in that regression equation. Furthermore, the grants for which population is important mostly involve assistance for planning and for research and demonstration projects. These are unlikely to vary with population in the way that size and, therefore, cost of an infrastructure facility might vary.

Table 5.5.   Multiple regression of need, capacity, and population on economic
              development assistance grants, 1990

	Standard Beta	Beta	Standard Error	Significance
Local Government Expenditures				
Per Capita, 1981–1982	.048	1.830	.944	.05
Local Taxes				
Per Capita, 1981–1982	-.011	-.362	.684	.59
Local Government Employment				
Per 10,000, 1982	-.008	-.917	3.085	.76
Percent Persons under				
Poverty, 1979	.078	186.132	64.463	.004
County Per Capita Income				
Rank, 1985	-.065	-1.255	.582	.03
County Metropolitan				
Status	.102	4,336.176	897.119	.000
County Population, 1980	.129	.009	.001	.000

SOURCE: Independent variables are from *County and City Data Book, 1988.*

Population functions not only as an indicator of demand but also of where the votes are. This is a slim, but plausible, reed upon which to consider a political explanation. The association of population and grants suggests that members of Congress may push agencies to allocate grants in a way particularly sensitive to the needs of the most populous communities in the representatives' districts, because that is where federal aid from the congressional pork barrel might be expected to generate the greatest electoral payoff.

Although it is the bureaucracy that does the actual allocation of federal grants (in this case, the Economic Development Administration), we do know that bureaucrats are not immune to congressional influence in deciding whether or not to approve a grant.[7] Indeed, as Hird notes (1991, 429), "Evidence suggests that legislators channel federal projects to their constituents in forms ranging from high-tech science . . . to water resource projects. . . ." If bureaucrats are responsive in these ways, then it is plausible to argue that they may be responsive to influence as to *which applicants* in a district actually receive grants. This political feature helps to explain what it is about large places that makes them more successful in attracting grants than smaller places when other explanations, such as those that focus on the capacity advantage that large places might have, wash out.

Conclusions

Federal involvement in rural economic development has been extensive, measured both across history and by the scope of the contemporary programmatic commitment. Yet the portrait that emerges under more careful examination suggests that Washington's efforts have an amorphous and inconsistent quality. They have lacked coordination and, particularly in the era of the New Federalism, programs for rural development have had to operate in an uncertain and often hostile funding climate.

Rural economic development has remained a poor cousin in its claims on federal programs for rural areas, most of which focus not on development but on farm support and individual income transfers. Those programs that do support economic development have taken a relatively unidimensional approach by concentrating overwhelmingly on the construction of basic infrastructure facilities and networks as a way of encouraging private investment and job creation. Rural economic development has not been a field in which imaginative policy approaches have been common. Finally, development funds rarely have been carefully targeted to rural areas, or to the most needy rural places.

As in many other areas of national concern, the federal government has neither a *theory* to support a coherent national rural development policy nor an inclination to develop one. That is to say that national leadership has failed both in justifying adequately national intervention or a national role in the rural development process and in developing a multidimensional, coordinated approach to rural development. Just as Washington has no theory to support a national industrial policy, the notion that rural development concerns might require novel approaches, a coherent and coordinated effort by the central government, and careful long-term planning is anathema in a government long used to piecemeal, incremental, and ad hoc initiatives.

In the 1980s, the states experimented with a bewildering array of entrepreneurial approaches to economic development. Many of them grounded their efforts in strategic planning exercises that laid out what were essentially state-level industrial policy initiatives. Toward the end of the decade the states turned particularly to the issue of rural development, understanding perhaps that stimulating economic growth and prosperity in the countryside called for different approaches than those used in urban areas (John 1987; Smith 1988). But the national government has never exhibited such energy or imagination where economic development, either urban or rural, is concerned. As the century comes to a close, it is likely that the states will carry the major burden in the rural development arena, while Washington, despite its massive resources, remains an uncertain player.

Notes

I wish to thank Ken Bickers for his generosity in providing the federal outlay data used in this study, and Kristin Stout and Kurt Sippel for their assistance in managing this large dataset.

1. Between 1982 and 1987, over half of all nonmetropolitan counties in the United States lost population. Net annual out-migration from nommetropolitan counties ranged from about 350,000 to over 630,000 between 1983 and 1986. This contrasts with net growth of about 350,000 per year in nonmetropolitan counties in the 1970s. Data are reported in U.S. Department of Agriculture (1987, 3); and Reid and Frederick (1990, 10).

2. As we shall see in the next section, an analysis of several of the major programs reveals that funds for rural development tend to go disproportionately to local governments in metropolitan, rather than rural, counties.

3. The USDA disputes the notion that a rural credit gap is a function of the absence of capital or of discrimination by lenders against rural businesses. The department argues, rather, that "lack of borrower information about where and how to find financing, and the unfamiliarity of lenders with rural areas, may better explain complaints about credit shortages by rural entrepreneurs" (U.S. Department of Agriculture 1989, 10).

4. Three of FmHA's major programs involve loans or loan guarantees: WWD Loans and Loan Guarantees, Community Facility Loans, and Business and Industrial Loans. This is also the case with respect to the four major programs of the Rural Electrification Administration under the U.S. Department of Agriculture.

5. The percentage of persons ranking below the poverty line and the county's national income rank are related to one another at the .72 level of significance.

6. No regression of the various independent variables against any particular grant program produces a model that explains more than 5 percent of the variance. With very minor variations, they all resemble one another in relative magnitude of their standardized coefficients. Copies of regression analyses are available on request from the author.

7. Arnold (1979, 207) shows that bureaucrats administering grant programs are disproportionately responsive to applicants from districts whose congressional representatives control the budget of the administering agency.

References

Arnold, R. Douglas. 1979. *Congress and the Bureaucracy.* New Haven, Conn.: Yale University Press.

Bickers, Kenneth, and Robert Stein. 1991. *Federal Domestic Outlays, 1983–1990.* Armonk, N.Y.: M. E. Sharpe.

Center for Community Change. 1990. *Searching for the "Way that Works": An Analysis of FmHA Rural Development Policy and Implementation.* Washington, D.C.: Aspen Institute.

Dubin, Elliot, and J. Norman Reid. 1988. "Do Federal Funds Help Spur Rural Development?" *Rural Development Perspectives* 5:2–7.

Dye, Thomas. 1987. "Targeting Intergovernmental Aid." *Social Science Quarterly* 68:443–46.

Eisinger, Peter. 1988. *The Rise of the Entrepreneurial State.* Madison: University of Wisconsin Press.

Eisinger, Peter. 1993. "Creating a Better Rural Countryside." *Forum* 8. Forthcoming.

Hird, John. 1991. "The Political Economy of Pork: Project Selection at the U.S. Army Corps of Engineers." *American Political Science Review* 85.

John, Dewitt. 1987. *Shifting Responsibilities: Federalism in Economic Development.* Washington, D.C.: National Governors' Association.

Lazere, Edward, Paul Leonard, and Linda Kravitz. 1989. *The Other Housing Crisis: Sheltering the Poor in Rural America.* Washington, D.C.: Center on Budget and Policy Priorities.

Levitan, Sar. 1969. *The Great Society's Poor Law.* Baltimore: Johns Hopkins Press.

Radin, Beryl. 1992. "Rural Development Councils: An Intergovernmental Coordination Experiment." *Publius* 22:111–27.

Rauch, Jonathan. 1985. "Rural America's Reach into the Federal Pocketbook May Be Sharply Curtailed." *National Journal* 17:470–73.

Reid, J. Norman, and Martha Frederick. 1990. *Rural America: Economic Performance, 1989.* Agriculture Information Bulletin No. 609. Washington, D.C.: U.S. Department of Agriculture.

Rich, Michael. 1989. "Distributive Politics and the Allocation of Federal Grants." *American Political Science Review* 83:193–213.

———. n.d. *National Goals and Local Choices: Distributing Federal Aid to the Poor.* Unpublished manuscript.

Saltzstein, Alan. 1977. "Federal Categorical Aid to Cities: Who Needs It Versus Who Wants It?" *Western Political Quarterly* 30:377–83.

Smith, Stewart. 1988. "Six Ways States Can Spur Their Rural Economies." *Rural Development Perspectives* 4:8–14.

Stanfield, Rochelle. 1983. "Rapid Economic Growth of Rural Areas Brings Drawbacks along with Blessings." *National Journal* 17:1932–37.

U.S. Congress, House Committee on Agriculture. 1989. Hearings before the Subcommittee on Conservation, Credit, and Rural Development. Printed in *Rural Economic Development.* 101st Congress, First Session. June 6, 8, 13, 20, 22, 27, and 29.

U.S. Department of Agriculture, Rural Revitalization Task Force. 1989. *A Hard Look at USDA's Rural Development Programs.* Washington, D.C.: Government Printing Office.

U.S. Department of Agriculture. 1983. *Better Country: A Strategy for Rural Development in the 1980s.* Washington, D.C.: Government Printing Office.

_____. 1987. *Rural Economic Development in the 1980s: A Summary.* Washington, D.C.: Government Printing Office.

U.S. General Accounting Office. 1989. *Rural Development: Federal Programs that Focus on Rural America and Its Economic Development.* Washington, D.C.: Government Printing Office.

6

The University as a Catalyst for Scientific and Industrial Development

MICHAEL M. CROW

The questions of what a university is and what its responsibilities are to society have been debated long and heatedly, both within institutions themselves and in society at large. This debate often has focused on the need to distance the university from the general society, most particularly from those aspects of society linked most closely to commerce. This distancing takes on many forms, but generally it is manifested in the on-going debate about how or if universities should help to secure and maintain national scientific preeminence and, hence, national economic competitiveness.

Because universities are organizations that evolve very slowly, and are organizationally conservative, we cannot consider the question of how a university can best serve as a catalyst for scientific and industrial advancement without considering the historical development of the modern university and its culture. To do this I will first consider the factors behind the founding of the modern European university, the organizational creature from which the American university is directly descended; then I will discuss the factors leading to the evolutionary offshoot that developed in the United States between 1865 and 1990: the American research university. It is my hope that some understanding of the evolutionary patterns in the university enterprise will help illustrate that universities have long catalyzed scientific and industrial advancement, in addition to advancing the basic

Michael M. Crow is Vice Provost for Research at Columbia University, New York City. Previously he was Director of the Institute for Physical Research and Technology, Iowa State University.

social design of our society. Understanding how these institutions have treated change in the past is important to understanding how they might catalyze scientific and industrial change in the future. This is particularly true given the role and identity struggle that many universities appear to find themselves in today.

From this historical perspective, this paper will outline how a university can best serve to stimulate scientific and industrial advancement in the twenty-first century. But first, a little history.

The Development of the University Model

In the Middle Ages in Europe, a handful of cities served as homes to small, loosely coupled groupings of teachers and students struggling to develop organized higher learning.[1] Built around the philosophies of animism, scholasticism, and other less than enlightened views of the world, universities in Leipzig, Pisa, Prague, Heidelberg, Bologna, and other cities focused their academic energies on theology, law, and medicine. These were thought to be the disciplines worthy of teaching, but poorly taught they were. The institutions were badly designed, poorly funded, and focused on unfounded ideas. The result was nearly uniform failure, along with dawning recognition that universities must be based on principles, practice, and philosophies grounded in something other than the temporal. At the same time, it was believed that they must be relevant to society.

Beginning in the early fourteenth century, with the rediscovery of the Latin classics and the revival of Greek learning after 1450, the concept of knowledge itself began to be seriously redefined. With that redefinition most of the medieval "universities" were discredited, and they crumbled. New universities, built around the long-dormant ideals of humanism, were established, and in those fledgling institutions the notion of scholarship began to emerge as a revered and honored profession.

Universities then began the process of pulling society away from a millennium in which the institutional advancement of knowledge and ideas had been lost. The process was not an easy one, but it was the "modern universities" in Glasgow, Aberdeen, and Dublin, together with the new colleges at Oxford and Cambridge (established between 1496 and 1516) and the new universities at Genoa (1471), Munich (1472), Uppsala (1477), Copenhagen (1479), Wittenberg (1502), and Frankfurt (1506) that led the way.

Led by humanist professors teaching from the classics, these universities literally reshaped the world and laid the intellectual foundation for the shaping of modern society. Rejecting the pedagogy of the past and focusing on the careful intellectual development of philosophy and new social designs, they served as the catalyst for change and advancement on a very large social scale—a scale previously unknown outside of religion. In this way, universities firmly established themselves as agents of change and social advancement. In these modern universities professors declared the humanities to be superior to medicine, law, theology, and other practical arts (the old subjects of the now-defunct medieval schools). Their declaration was followed by the wider-scale design of European universities as centers for scholarship, protected from influence by outsiders but imbued with the goal of helping society through an emphasis on the humanities.

In this area of science, these new universities became the organizational homes for a small group (numbering in the hundreds) of fundamental scientists operating in Europe between 1500 and 1850. During this period a handful of scientists, funded by the Crown and by private benefactors, made great progress in understanding our natural world and shaping our designed world. This model for science, in which lone investigators charted a course though the physical and natural unknown, also became a basic model of the European university. Today this somewhat antiquated model remains the foundation of the American university. It is this model that fuels the debate over how or whether universities should attempt to catalyze scientific and industrial advancement.

Transfer of the European Model to the United States

When colleges began to be established in America in the seventeenth and eighteenth centuries, the model of the modern (post-1500) European university was nearly uniformly adopted.[2] Liberal education in the classics, scholarship without external influence, and general support for religion and society were the stated objectives of nearly every young college in the country. These nascent colleges hoped to contribute to continued social advancement and evolution through the production of great minds and great scholars. Science was a part of this training but was not, for the most part, a separate area of emphasis. Hopes were realized locally through classically trained intellectuals such as Thomas Jefferson (William and Mary), Alexander Hamilton (Columbia), James Madison (Princeton), and John Jay (Columbia), who among others designed the American society in which we live today. Such social engineering served as the catalyst for the design of the nation and its capitalistic economy, and thus laid the foundation for many of the unique characteristics of America. Furthermore, this university design produced an elite cadre of loyal alumni satisfied by the wisdom and insight gained in the college days, and dedicated to the furtherance of the *European model* of higher education.

More than two hundred years later, as the design process was beginning to move into a second phase (of transforming colleges to universities and building new universities from the ground up after 1860), we were presented with alternative models, such as the Morrill Act of 1862 that sought to marry practical education in engineering and agriculture with the modern liberal university. Why? The answers are long and complicated. Suffice it to say that universities are institutions that, in spite of their conservative nature, reflect the environment in which they exist. Like all organizations, they are a function of their environment. And as America changed in response to massive working-class immigrations, continental expansion, and rapid industrialization, the American university was tugged toward change in response to the environment.

The design and social setting of America itself, a socially mobile and highly innovative society spread out across a continent several times the size of Europe, was one indicator that the traditional European model of a university would not meet all the social and intellectual demands of the American setting. Furthermore, the standard American version of a European humanist-focused university, successfully transplanted to many American colleges before the revolution, had evolved to some extent on its own. This was particularly true in the area of increasingly specialized studies in the sciences, along with correspondingly expanded curricula. Such programs at Yale and Harvard were developed early (before 1860) and were driven by wealthy alumni wanting to see more science, and greater fame and industrial development as a result.

It should not be surprising, then, that by the end of the Civil War, with an eye toward the esteemed European model, the leaders of fifteen American universities began to design a new type of university, the research university. Certainly history tells us that the emergence of research universities in the United States was at least in part a replication of a German model for focused scientific and scholarly efforts. While it is true that there was a strong link between the German model and the design both of Johns Hopkins University in the 1870s and of elements at other schools, the process of developing the American model was in fact influenced by many sources and was thus a unique design configuration.[3]

The Evolution of the American Research University

The fifteen evolving research universities came from a varied evolutionary pool. They included well-established private colleges built on the European model

(Harvard, Princeton, Pennsylvania, Yale, and Columbia); five large-scale state university experiments (Illinois, Michigan, Wisconsin, Minnesota, and California); and five new American research universities, each designed as such from the outset (MIT, Cornell, Hopkins, Stanford, and Chicago). These institutions differed from all other schools in the United States in that, between 1870 and 1900, they moved forward as research universities.

According to university historian Roger Geiger, these fifteen were different because of four significant factors.[4] First, they were highly competitive, and they built a series of complex interrelationships among themselves for purposes of both competition and cooperation. Second, rapid growth of knowledge in disciplines and changes in the nation's intellectual and economic environment placed new demands on select colleges, particularly those with some science-related research capability. Third, the fifteen schools were uniformly larger (in the numbers of students and faculty), richer, and physically more well endowed than other U.S. schools during this period. Finally, each of these schools, for various and complicated reasons, determined to make research a priority of their overall mission, affecting all faculties, not just those of science. This priority was realized before 1900 through massive private and public investment in university expansion and university science and technology.

Not unlike the handful of European universities that developed in the late fifteenth and early sixteenth centuries into centers of humanism and scholarship, these select American universities evolved and changed in the late nineteenth century to create a system of national research universities. By 1935, these national research universities had become the world's leading centers in agriculture, basic physical sciences, medicine, and engineering. In addition, they became large-scale producers of graduate degree holders, particularly of the Ph.D.[5]

Since 1900, these fifteen universities have represented a new type of university that other schools have emulated, many successfully, and they represent a distinctive model of American organizational innovation and academic scholarship. Without exception, these universities have developed and maintained some of the finest centers for liberal education in America. At the same time they have built and developed close research ties with industry. Those industries have ranged from big manufacturers of all types, to agricultural and natural resource interests, to literally hundreds of small spin-off companies, particularly from MIT and Stanford. Suffice it to say that each of these schools has been involved heavily in the business of supporting business through applied and basic research. Over the years these schools have contributed a new wave of innovation to industry, and new scientific advancements critical to society as a whole or to industrial activity. Contributions have included the following:[6]

- The standard malaria preventative pill (University of Chicago, 1950).
- The first atom smasher (University of California, Berkeley, 1931).
- The recombinant DNA technique that revolutionized the field of biology and spawned the modern biotechnology industry (Stanford University; University of California, San Francisco, 1974).
- The documentation of the acid rain problem in North America (Cornell, 1972).
- The first scientific research into the design of airplane and ship propellers (Stanford University, 1890s).
- A computer technique for calculating airflow that simplifies the process of aircraft design by reducing the need for costly and time-consuming wind-tunnel testing (Princeton University, 1986).
- The sound motion picture (University of Illinois, 1922); the FM radio (Columbia University, 1939).
- Modern laser eye surgery (Stanford University, 1963).
- The technology (fluidized-bed reactor) that made possible modern, high-volume production of gasoline (Massachusetts Institute of Technology, 1930s).
- The first successful blood tests for cancer (Columbia University, 1936).
- Modern design codes for concrete buildings and bridges through research into concrete strength and durability, and refinement of design techniques (University of Illinois, 1900 to 1970s).
- The Minnesota Multiphasic Personality Inventory, the most widely used psychological test in the world, which is critical in the evaluation of psychiatric patients (University of Minnesota, 1930s to present).
- The first antitoxin for botulism poisoning (University of Illinois, 1919), and the research that led to the adoption of safety standards for the modern canning industry.
- Carbon-14 dating, which has revolutionized the ability to date ancient artifacts (University of Chicago, 1949).
- A material that induces new bone to grow, facilitating the healing of bone injuries (Harvard University, 1981).
- The first external heart pacemaker (Harvard University, 1952).
- The chemical synthesis of penicillin (Massachusetts Institute of Technology, 1957).

- The chlorinated water purification system that has been adopted by every major municipal and industrial water supply system in the United States and many other parts of the world (Johns Hopkins University, 1926).
- The growth of the multi-million-dollar California wine industry by developing dozens of new grape varieties and improved methods of growing and handling vines and making wines (University of California, Davis, 1960s to present).
- The discovery of Vitamin E (University of California, San Francisco, 1923).
- The identification of the cause of rheumatic fever (Columbia University, 1920s).

In addition, all of these schools responded to national needs in World Wars I and II with major applied research and directed basic research programs. Programs such as Lincoln Laboratory (MIT), The Applied Physics Laboratory (Hopkins), The Applied Research Lab (Harvard), Brookhaven Laboratory (Columbia), Los Alamos Lab (University of California), and many others were developed by these fifteen universities. These programs represented major use of the American academic science base in pursuing large-scale national interests. Such uses of the science base have become characteristically American.

This new type of university proved to be not only a center for liberal education, scholarship, and social design, just as the European university model prescribed, but also a center for intense science, engineering design, and new systems design on a grand scale, drawing on heavy interaction with government and industry. This new model for the American university provided for both the practical and the aesthetic. The design was a unique American adaptation to a unique environment. Through this design the American research university model became the model to emulate; in many ways it became the dominant paradigm in higher education.

The Research University Model in America

The American research university model had become firmly established by 1935, and with fifteen new large-scale research universities fully integrated into the U.S. National System of Innovation and another twenty-five universities transforming themselves into research universities, the country was technologically well positioned for success at the outbreak of World War II.[7]

As a part of the national response to the war, universities were called upon to produce large numbers of trained personnel, develop large-scale basic research programs, and deploy large-scale applied research organizations. Partly as a result of the overwhelming scientific successes of the university community in the war effort and partly out of a realization that large-scale public science and technology investment could have on-going social and economic benefits, a plan was proposed for the development of a permanent, federally funded, academic science and technology research community. Based on the experiences of wartime, and to some extent on those of the agricultural experiment stations, it was felt by many, most notably Vannevar Bush, the wartime director of the Office of Scientific Research and Development, that a "social contract" between the government and the research university should be established.[8] The contract, presented to President Truman in July 1945 and debated until 1950, called for full funding of the academic research enterprise for the benefit of the people of the nation.[9] Peter Likins, president of Lehigh University, recently characterized the basic contract in the plain terms understood by President Truman, by suggesting that the president's briefing on the scheme went something like this:[10]

"Look, Harry, here's the deal. The United States government promises to finance all legitimate research required to satisfy the curiosity of America's scientists, and they in turn promise to deliver military security, public health, and economic prosperity to the American people."

While somewhat hyperbolic in tone, Likins believes, and I agree, that this was the basic social contract. Universities would receive substantial and relatively unencumbered financing from the government in return for delivering life, liberty, and a strong American economy. While extremely naive in its design, this social contract was developed and implemented in response to the perceived social profit that might be gained by enhancing a great American asset, the research university.

With the federalization of U. S. academic science after 1950, largely as a result of the establishment and funding of the National Science Foundation (1950), the Office of Naval Research (1946), the Atomic Energy Commission (1947), and several other federal research programs that were heavily dependent on the research university community, and with the investment of the Department of Agriculture and of the National Institutes of Health, the pieces were in place for rapid expansion of the research university community. This rapid expansion also was fueled by tremendous investments from the defense establishment and NASA, particularly in graduate education and research.

All in all, the university research community was fully funded to catalyze scientific and industrial advancement, and catalyze it did, or at least so it appeared. By the period 1965–1975 America had developed the largest technology-based economy in the world, the most productive agricultural system in the world, a defense technology base which has proven to be more than adequate, an unparalleled health-care technology base, and a consistently high standard of living. By all accounts, this is a record of which the social contract writers of the 1940s and the research university architects of the late nineteenth century would be proud.

Turbulence in the American Research and Technology Development Environment

Since 1975, the U.S. National System of Innovation, including the universities, has witnessed significant stresses. These are the result of environmental change on two levels, within the world economy and within the university community itself.

On the first level the United States, with its National System of Innovation fully designed and implemented, has met some formidable competition in Asia and Europe. These places, ravaged by the war we survived intact, redesigned and rebuilt for economic competition, as opposed to military competition, built heavily around government and industry attempts to catalyze industrial advancement. Their efforts presented the first real challenge to American economic dominance in this century.

On the second level, in the university community itself, things had grown nearly out of control. By 1975 there were one hundred universities competing with each other for the resources necessary to be a research university, and more than fifty agricultural experiment stations were working on many of the same problems and competing for the same resources. Within this network of institutions, "Science for the sake of science" had become an important motto, in true European university tradition, and the conflict between the humanist core and the large science and technology programs that had developed over the previous decades was growing in intensity. In a word, the American research university system was adrift. It had grown large and cumbersome, and it was involved in serious internal fighting over the mission and role of the institutions themselves in science and technology. Furthermore, the science community lacked direction and purpose in terms of setting priorities and focusing on the common good, or even in defining the common good. Add to this literally thousands of individual scientists trained and produced by the system itself, each expecting their individual research funding, almost as an entitlement from the government, and the conditions for a less than fully productive system began to be realized.

In the period between the mid-1970s and the early 1980s, efforts were initiated that essentially began the process of revising the social contract between universities and the government. Although these efforts continue and their focus increasingly has become directed toward the establishment of a national technology policy, the question of the role of the universities in catalyzing science and industry has not been resolved.

True to their heritage and design, universities as a community have resisted attempts by the government to revise the social contract and move research universities toward a larger role in commercial technology development and technology transfer. The howling from individual research investigators in response to the notion that more funding from the National Science Foundation should be devoted to organized centers (which by design would cooperate with industry) has been loud and has continued for more than ten years. On individual campuses, the debate as to the proper role and function of the university in stimulating economic development has been characterized by asperity and divisiveness.

The debate comes at a time when national and state leaders say it is time for change and time for us to reexamine our institutions and their roles, particularly in light of the continued vulnerability of the American economy to external, technology-based threats. The university research community has been asked by the nation to do much more in the past, and it has met those challenges. Now it is being asked to do more in very different ways, and the system, involving both the university response and the national science and technology policy process, is filled with uncertainty.

A key to understanding some of the pathways to continued scientific and economic success is to look at the historical development of these institutions in the context of the present dilemma. The dilemma is that there are one hundred major universities, all measuring themselves against the same resource model, and all trying to be the same great center for humanism and for science and technology. The stresses that our needs impose on this one model are enormous. Also, the inflexibility of the model may result in the model devolving. What is needed is a more flexible model, or a series of models that allow for variations.

Replicating the Model

The research university paradigm is one that, like all paradigms, can exist only for a short while in an unchanged or unadapted state. In the case of the fifteen universities that led the development of the American model, it is fair to say that in many ways each of these schools grew from a national center of scientific and technological knowledge to become an international center, each with immense research funding (hundreds of millions of dollars per year), extensive international connections, and enviable centers and programs in research and development. As they have evolved, other American universities have elected to focus their own design efforts on replicating the same model, all in hopes of growing to "greatness."

Consider, for example, the ten or fifteen former teachers' colleges that have set their sights on becoming a research university. Most of these schools grew from small colleges in the 1940s to comprehensive colleges of 20,000–30,000 students in the 1970s, and later to add a medical or law school, becoming endowed universities by 1980. To succeed, these schools must compete with such institutions as Cornell University, which was designed and funded from day one to be a broadly focused research institution, or with Johns Hopkins, which has had an active, funded, science-based research program for one hundred years. Why does the faculty at erstwhile teachers' colleges and universities believe that its role and function in life should be identical to that of faculty at state schools such as the University of Illinois, or the University of Michigan? Because faculty members at these institutions were trained in the same traditions of scholarship and research, often at the very research universities they are emulating. Tradition says that as a faculty member, one's job is to produce new knowledge, store and synthesize knowledge, and pass on that knowledge, with insight, to able-minded students. This tradition is based on more than five hundred years of practice, and as such it represents the core of university culture.

Most faculty members at American research universities believe it is their duty to mold and shape their institutions according to the original American research university model, while protecting the European tradition of humanism (something often in conflict with technology and economic development), uninfluenced scholarship, and societal design. The conflict herein lies at the heart of the basic question of this paper: How can universities catalyze science and industrial advancement that will benefit the nation and be true to their ultimate societal goals, while at the same time being measured by a standard that recognizes differences between them?

To some extent the approximately one hundred American research universities operate today like their distant European ancestors, as if they were located in isolated towns, each with the responsibility of building new knowledge and bringing about the renaissance in its own area. This operating mode forces universities to judge themselves against those who have implemented the research university model before them, leaving American society and industry with a particular dilemma. Does it really take hundreds of centers of research in the materials sciences, or in agricultural biotechnology, to produce the requisite new knowledge and new people in these fields; or does it take just a handful of well-funded centers of excellence in targeted areas to provide the knowledge and technology that society and the economy need. The answer to both extremes is certainly no, but the solutions are much less clear.

It seems that many universities are stuck in an evolutionary rut, maybe even in what biologists would call an evolutionary dead end. Can one hundred or so research universities, all trying to be the same thing and living off the same resources, become or maintain themselves as national centers for new scientific and technical knowledge *and* centers for liberal education and humanism? Can everyone do both and do them well?

America today is a nation with its social design in place, its economy in transition, its standard of living in steady state, and its way of life challenged. We have hundreds of universities, thousands of colleges, and millions of students in college. These institutions of higher education have played a critical role in our national success and could play a role in our national economic decline. The university contribution to our national economic problems comes from our recent inability as a community to continue to evolve new institutional designs, and with these designs, new approaches to serving society. We continue to operate under the assumption that to be a great university we must be both a center for humanist scholarship and a world-class science, engineering, and medical research center. Each university simply cannot do it all. More importantly, America today needs to catalyze its scientific and industrial sectors if we hope to maintain our society into the long-term future. There is a need for new university organizational designs and new approaches to supporting both science and industrial development.

Designing Universities for Scientific and Industrial Advancement

For a university to be a successful catalyst for scientific and industrial advancement, it must adapt to be of the greatest value to its constituents and "owners," as opposed to being of the greatest value to a given discipline or faculty group; thus, each institution must first determine and define its ownership, and from this its purpose. Given that I can't do this alone for even one university, I can only speculate, with confidence, that those defined purposes, when looked at carefully, will in fact differ from one another. Some universities will want to serve the world, others will want to serve industry, and still others will choose particular subregions of the country. Given these overall differences, it would seem reasonable that designing a university in terms of science and industrial advancement would also result in meaningful and significant differences.

It is from these differences and their meaning, in terms of organizational design for science and industrial advancement, that a number of new types of research universities can be imagined. Each of these types of institutions could have a different role and responsibility in terms of science and industrial advancement. The differences would not represent evolutionary steps in a class of organizations but would reflect distinctly different classes or types of institutions. As such, institutions within a given class could be compared, but between classes there would be little value in comparison.

While the development of any organizational design guidelines is problematic, let me suggest that the U.S. National System of Innovation could benefit from a set of research universities that considered the following design criteria.

Design for and Build on Differences. There isn't need for or money to finance one hundred, two hundred, or more research universities all cut from the same cloth. It is time to recognize that each institution can work to stimulate scientific and industrial advancement from their individual strengths and individual environment. Within the National System of Innovation, there is a need for research universities of several distinct orientations. Such orientations require different approaches to research, including disciplinary, interdisciplinary, topically focused (all agriculture or all manufacturing or all space technology), and focused by area or region (international, national, regional, urban area). Such foci could permit the development of classes or types of research universities ranked not only by funding profiles, as the Carnegie Foundation presently does, but according to accomplishments within a given focal area.

For instance, where are the national agricultural universities in the United States? Defined as institutions concerned about the whole of agriculture as science, industrial development, and trade, there are none. We have a number of agricultural schools, each trying to be the same thing. Maybe what we need are four or five nationally or internationally focused agricultural universities and a few regionally focused schools. What we don't need is a set of agricultural schools all with the same agenda.

Enhance Linkages between Humanism, Science, and Technology. Science and technology advancement without purpose and assessment can have as many negative effects as positive effects. There must be an improved linkage between the heart and soul of our universities and their role in advancing science and technology. The need for this linkage would be true at each type of research university. At the national research universities, the questions of designing alternative technological futures must be a part of the science program. At national

agricultural universities, broad questions of social design, sustainable development, global change, and population control would be a facet of all research and
would be a fundamental characteristic of the university as a whole. As such, a
university can maintain its humanist core while linking it to its specific science and
technology objectives.

Accept Social Responsibility for Scientific and Industrial Advancement.
Universities have always been as involved in the design sciences as in the physical
and natural sciences. The design sciences focus on building our artificial world,
socially and physically. A part of our artificial world is the political economy that
sustains our society, and its design has been heavily embraced by universities. Just
as university ideas about designing new political and economic institutions should
be brought forth, so should all the ideas and technologies that embody new
knowledge in the design sciences. A university has as much social responsibility
for transferring to society a new vaccine or a new design of the social security
system as it does for transferring a new bioengineered corn variety to industry. All
of this knowledge, insight, and technology equally merits transfer. If that transfer
is to society, it should be responsible; if it is to industry, it should also be
responsible. Responsibility in this case means that the idea, know-how, or technology is transferred in such a way that consequences have been considered and
an attempt has been made to understand and, if necessary, mitigate the consequences of transfer. Design steps should be taken to accept such responsibility.
Universities that accept full responsibility for designing new social institutions and
studying them cannot accept only partial responsibility for science and technology;
for example, engaging only in inventing and taking no part in transfer and
assessment.

**Recognize that Technology Drives Science as Much as Science Drives Tech-
nology.** The notion that the R&D process is linear—proceeding from basic science
to development—is dead. Get over it. Universities have contributed and should
continue to contribute to both fundamental science and technology, realizing that
there is a knowledge exchange relationship between both. Regarding technology,
this in-volves remembering that a technique or a process isn't a technology until it
is in practice and has diffused through industry. Accordingly, universities should
not pursue science as superior to technology or the reverse, but rather should
consider each of them to be equal pursuits with alternative transfer routes.
Likewise, some universities could focus on technology, others on science, and
others on science and technology in selected areas.

Recognize that Industry Is What Universities Make It. Universities are the principal producers of new personnel for industry. For decades, universities have served as a key source of new scientific and technological ideas. If as a nation we are unhappy because our industry is not as competitive as we would like, we should look at our universities and say, why? Why don't we emphasize design more; why have we not yet developed nonpolluting, completely recyclable livestock production? The answer, at least in part, is because we haven't developed managers, engineers, and scientists with experience in doing what needs to be done. In part it is because we have inadequate mechanisms for knowledge and technology transfer. If universities want to catalyze change in society, demonstrate it, and then get the word out, they will need focused energy, resources, commitment, and vision.

For instance, if a state or a region is concerned because it lacks agricultural diversity or innovativeness in making new industrial products from agricultural feedstocks, then look at what the idea factory (the university) is producing. Is the university demonstrating new pathways, evaluating the economic and environmental issues, and working to transfer the new idea? Or is the university built around fragmented and isolated single investigators who on their own cannot accomplish the full set of tasks at hand?

Universities can't sit back and say, "If industry could only do it right." Universities have to define what is possible and what is needed and then just do it, making certain that in doing it, they work to attain successful transfer.

Specialize and Cooperate. Why are Iowa State, Cornell, U.C. Davis, Purdue, Illinois, and other agricultural research schools all attempting to build large-scale agricultural biotechnology programs? Because they think that the only way to be great is to be broad and deep. What is wrong with being *narrow* and deep? These schools should focus on that which they can do better than anyone else, and then cooperate with the rest. Within these areas of specialization, the complete spectrum of activity should be pursued. Beyond these areas of specialization, faculty members should work with others at other universities and in industry.

Integrate R&D for Economic Growth and Sustainability. The majority of our National System of Innovation is built around economic assumptions regarding neoclassical economic growth: growth is good, and it is driven by technology. For instance, in agriculture the vast majority of U.S. university research enterprise is focused on enhancing productivity. Such a focus could prove disastrous in the long run. Universities must develop not only a focus on sustainability, as Iowa State and others are doing, but the means of building economic growth and environmental sustainability as *equal criteria* in R&D. Such development requires a rethinking of disciplinary research boundaries and a significant shift toward establishing broader research agendas.

Build a Unified Research Culture. If a university is going to be a national research institute, then its entire faculty should be involved toward that end. Such an effort would focus on the nation as a whole and on a broad set of basic science areas. If a university is going to build itself into a national agricultural teaching and research center, then all of its elements should have a strong thrust toward that goal. Universities should determine their desired niche and work to develop a unified, interdisciplinary approach to that niche.

Developing a unified research culture within a university does not mean limited thinking and lack of diversity among scholars and their ideas. It does mean unification of purpose. If the purpose is to be a great agricultural research university, then the research culture should develop around that topic. This means chemists and botanists working to understand the fundamentals of photosynthesis, ecologists working on sustainability and environmental issues, and other similar foci. It doesn't mean nothing else would be taught or researched, but it does mean that there is a dominant theme.

Develop Means for Knowledge and Technology Transfer. When transferring a new design concept about how the U.S. government should support the price of agricultural commodities in the world market, the ideas are written and published for wide distribution. When transferring a new soybean variety, a designed product, the university must decide how best to assure that this new "technology" will be adopted into the marketplace.

Each of these cases requires certain procedures and rules that protect the interests of the university, its owners, and the funding source. Such procedures should be established at each university, thus enabling it to best serve the constituents it has chosen, including those constituents trying to survive in the complex proprietary environment of industry.

Appropriate means for those universities attempting to stimulate industrial advancement must include mechanisms for (1) transfer to proprietary entities, (2) spin-off of new enterprises from the university itself, (3) nurturing new businesses, and (4) the conduct of proprietary research. Innovative means must be carefully considered and should not be rejected out of hand.

Design for Flexibility and Change. American research universities are built on a five-hundred-year-old philosophy and are, for the most part, organized to emulate a model that was designed before 1900. There are very few, if any, secular organizations that have such an ancient design. Designing for flexibility and change does not mean that the past models must be rejected. The argument is that a key design criteria should be to establish flexible and change-tolerant structures of university organization. This might mean organizing fields of emphasis differently, establishing interdisciplinary faculties, or developing rigorous external (academic and non-academic) reviews of university programs.

The University as a Catalyst

The design criteria presented in the previous section are critical to designing the catalytic university of the future. Universities have risen to address societal needs numerous times in the past. History is clear about that. What is not clear is whether or not universities, as organizations, can adapt and change fast enough to meet the challenge of the global economy in the twenty-first century. The heritage of humanism in the European design code, ingrained in every American university, coupled with the drive for sameness among American research institutions, seems to be placing the United States in a difficult situation. Universities in many ways have become like shopping centers, providing a home for individual faculty and disciplines to pursue their own versions of the academic science model. This environment has discouraged the development of uniqueness and variation in the university community and has weakened our national scientific and technical base.

Looking specifically at agricultural science and technology at universities, the realities are perhaps even harsher. The focus of scientific and industrial advancement seems to have been almost totally on enhancing agricultural productivity. The result is about fifty or sixty universities chasing after the same objective. At some universities this has meant focusing the research program on those commodities most productive in the surrounding region, and it has most certainly meant the narrowing of the research agenda at most of these schools.

I know from my own experience that in 1985 the research infrastructure for developing new industrial products from agricultural feedstocks at Iowa State University was very limited. How, in a leading agricultural state with such immense potential, could the State of Iowa have so limited its agricultural R&D enterprise? There are many possible answers, but one is that Iowa State University was underdesigned and lacked unique flexibility. This was through no fault of the university's leaders, but rather was the result of attempting to do what everyone else was doing. A simple replication model. This same pattern was repeated throughout the nation at more than forty other agricultural land-grant universities.

This organizational pattern presents the national agricultural enterprise with a dilemma, as the world's agricultural and industrial economies continue their rapid evolution to a truly global marketplace. How can so many agricultural universities, each attempting to do the same thing, provide the kind of diversity in knowledge and technology that will maintain the American economy?

It is time to consider serious organizational analysis within the university agricultural research community. This organizational analysis should consider the past, take what is needed, and move on to a *new* organizational design. The need is here, and the time is right. Universities *can* change and should do so now. Our environmental, economic, and scientific and technological future hangs in the balance.

Notes

1. The history reviewed in this section has been drawn from the recent volume by William Manchester, 1992, *A World Lit Only by Fire: The Medieval Mind in the Renaissance*, Boston: Tamma Brown & Co. Also Hastings Rashdall, 1936, *Universities of Europe in the Middle Ages*, three volumes, Oxford.

2. This section draws heavily from the following works: R. Veysey, 1965, *The Emergence of the American University*, Chicago: University of Chicago Press; Richard Storr, 1953, *The Beginnings of Graduate Education in America*, Chicago: University of Chicago Press; Earl D. Ross, 1942, *Democracy's College: The Land Grant Movement in the Formative Stage*, Ames: Iowa State College Press; Edwin E. Slosson, 1910, *Great American Universities*, New York: McMillan. In addition, I found particularly useful text by Roger L. Geiger, 1986, *To Advance Knowledge: The Growth of American Research Universities, 1900–1940*, New York: Oxford University Press. Excellent historical background on the transfer of the European university model to the United States and its subsequent development can be found in John S. Brubacher, 1958, *Higher Education in Transition: An American History, 1636–1956*, New York; and Richard Hofstadter and Wilson Smith, 1961, editors, *Documentary History of American Higher Education*, Chicago.

3. Interesting reading in this general historical area includes Jock Barzum, 1959, *The House of Intellect*, New York; and Eric Ashby, 1958, *Technology and the Academics: Essay on the Universities and Scientific Revolution*, New York.

4. Just to put these fifteen universities into perspective in 1992, they represent about 50 percent of all of the university research going on in the United States, and 85 percent of all U.S. patents issued to universities. These fifteen schools have been home to more than 90 percent of all American Nobel laureates, and they represent the vast majority of Ph.D.s granted in the United States in the twentieth century.

5. Based on statistics drawn from a list provided by the Association of American Universities.

6. Transformation into the classification of research university based on research funding and performance profiles provided annually by the National Science Foundation, Science

Resource Studies Division. This division provides and makes available data on individual universities and their research activities, as well as aggregate numbers that permit an analysis of market share. My own analysis of these numbers indicates that by 1990 about forty universities dominated the research arena. For the most part, these forty universities had emerged as research institutions by 1935.

7. Two outstanding summaries of this transition for the United States and the important role of the universities include Bruce L. R. Smith, 1990, *American Science Policy since World War Two*, Bookings Institution; and the long-known classic by A. Hunter Dupree, 1986, *Science and the Federal Government: A History of Policies and Activities*, The John Hopkins University Press. Both texts provide a wealth of information on the design of the R&D system before, during, and immediately following the war. They are essential reading to anyone interested in the history of U.S. science and technology policy.

8. For an excellent summary of the notion of the social contract between the scientific community and the government, see Don K. Price, 1983, *America's Unwritten Constitution*, Louisiana State University Press. Also relevant is Price, 1965, *The Scientific Estate*, Harvard University Press. Of course, it is important to look directly at the original argument for the establishment of the science research funding base in the United States. To do this, consider directly Vannevar Bush, 1945, *Science: The Endless Frontier*, Washington, D.C. There is a later version of this report that was published by the National Research Council in 1990. I have a copy of the regional report that was printed in 1978 by the House Science and Technology Committee, U. S. Congress, Washington, D.C.

9. For a detailed analysis of this debate and its implications, see James L. Pennick et al., editors, 1972, *The Politics of American Science, 1939 to the Present*, revised edition, MIT Press.

10. Peter Likins, 1992, *A Breach of the Social Contract*, paper presented to the Computing Research Association Conference, Snowbird, Utah.

7 The Effectiveness of State Investments in Science and Innovation

IRWIN FELLER

I am tempted to begin an analysis of the relevance of the development, implementation, and impacts of state investments in science, technology, and innovation to industrial policy for agriculture in a global economy by stating that there is none, and then to end. The most prominent feature of these state initiatives has been the support of technology development through establishment of university-based centers of advanced technology and research grant programs. Thirty-eight states provided support for technology/research centers in 1992, and an overlapping set of twenty-eight states supported research grant programs (Phelps and Brockman 1992).

Although identifiable program thrusts toward agriculture and food processing are found in seventeen states (buried within these programs' predominant emphases on microelectronics, communications, information technology, manufacturing technology and industrial processes, and biotechnology), the economic development impacts of the more notable state investments in agricultural technology remain problematic. Cornell University's Center for Agricultural Biotechnology in the New York Center for Advanced Technology Program, for example, started out promisingly, attracting major U.S. Army and National Science Foundation grants for a plant science research center. The center also patented a "gene gun" and sold the rights to Du Pont. More recently, however, the center has lost

Irwin Feller is Director, Graduate School of Public Policy and Administration, and Professor of Economics, The Pennsylvania State University, State College.

its main corporate sponsors as their interests in agricultural biotechnology have waned. The state's agricultural and food processing industries have proved to be too fragmented to provide a stable source of research funding. As a consequence of these developments, the center has had to restructure its sponsor programs and modify its research activities (SRI 1992, I-13).

Ohio University's Edison Agricultural Biotechnology Center (EABC) similarly began with a successful commercial relationship with Embryogen, a private, for-profit partner. Embryogen provided a private-sector match through research contracts and in-kind contributions to the state's contribution to EABC. In return, Embryogen received exclusive rights to EABC patents on microinjection techniques. However, soon after developing a successful line of commercial products, Embryogen, apparently because of difficulties in securing funds for expansion from Ohio-based venture capitalists, merged with another firm, DNX, and moved its headquarters and research facilities from Ohio to New Jersey. Ohio University still receives a revenue stream from DNX for its original license agreements, and it may earn future income from the sale of its founders' stock in the firm, which went public in late 1991. DNX also has retained Embryogen's animal breeding facility in Ohio. With all this, the larger share of the income and employment benefits associated with the firm's expansion will occur outside the state (Weinberg and Mazey 1988).[1]

Shifting the focus from agriculture as a production sector to rural areas as a unit of analysis yields a similar assessment of limited economic impacts. Other than the fact that a number of leading research universities, especially land-grant universities, are located in rural areas, giving them the potential to help expand the local economy, state technology centers were not designed primarily as substate regional growth poles. Indeed, Glasmeier and Kays-Teran (1989) have argued that "as presently constituted, most state high-tech programs not only inadequately address rural development problems, but are actually biased against rural areas."

A similar assessment may be made of the limited and indirect benefits to agriculture or rural areas of growing state interest in manufacturing modernization programs directed at improving the technological competitiveness of small- and medium-sized firms. Their location in rural areas creates spatially distributed benefits of state technology programs, but these benefits are ancillary to an industrial strategy that is not focused specifically on agriculture.[2]

In addition, although attention is being paid increasingly to technological innovations, particularly telecommunications, as a basis for rural area economic development (Center for Rural Pennsylvania 1992), there is little evidence to suggest either that high-technology economic activity has been a distinctive source of economic growth for rural regions, or that rural regions have a distinctive locational advantage for the production of high-technology goods. Development of high-tech industries has been a modest source of economic expansion in selected rural counties, but such development also has been absent in the expansion of many of them. Moreover, the characteristics of high-tech employment in rural areas have not differed appreciably from those of traditional rural manufacturing, nor has much correspondence been found between the industrial sectors targeted by state high-technology programs and the source of high-tech employment growth in rural counties (Glasmeier 1991).[3]

Focusing on state technology development efforts, moreover, has intimations of "back to the future." The bloom is gone from state technology development centers as the cynosure of state economic development strategies. Five to ten years ago one would have opened a discussion of state technology initiatives with an expansive emphasis on the new economic role of the states (Fosler 1988; Schmandt and Wilson 1987), of states as policy innovators experimenting with variants of industrial policy while the national government was stalemated by ideological fetters (Osborne 1988), of the synergies flowing from increased university-industry-cooperation, and of the undisputed regional growth potential of high-tech, sunrise industries. Today most state technology programs are in a defensive posture (Blumenstyr 1992; Lambright et al. 1992). The combined vicissitudes of state fiscal austerity, the unrealized expectations of state officials and unfulfilled promises of university officials, and changes in gubernatorial ideologies that have spawned minimalist public sectors have led states to rethink their support of university-industry research centers and competitive research grants programs. States have reduced the scale of these programs—total appropriations for technology programs declined from $320 million in FY 1990 to $202 million in FY 1993 (Carnegie Commission 1992)—while eliminating some (Michigan) and privatizing others (Massachusetts). This scaling down of expectations and commitments has occurred even as some of the initially projected barriers to effective university-industry-state government collaborative R&D ventures, such as arrangements for intellectual property rights, have proven to be readily surmountable or passable (Feller 1990).

State economic development strategies are directed increasingly at improving the manufacturing efficiencies of small- and medium-sized firms by bringing these firms up to best-practice technology or, more modestly, by closing the gaps between existing practice and average practice (Shapira 1990). The strategy thus is to move small- and medium-sized firms toward the efficient (technological) frontier rather than to move the frontier.

More generally, in considering the impact of public-sector technology programs, the work of Nelson and others suggests that the effectiveness of federal support for technological innovation is conditioned heavily by industry-specific configurations of demand, supply, and market structure variables (Nelson 1982). In a related manner, the writings of geographers such as Buswell (1983) and Malecki (1991) on technology and economic development, buttressed by the Embryogen example, suggest that the location of R&D activities and the production of R&D-intensive products are influenced by a complex, interrelated set of variables. These include economic, spatial, and technological variables that extend well beyond those typically encompassed in state technology development programs. When combined with the conclusion reached by Sears and Reid (1992) following their assessment of research on rural development strategies—that there is little evidence that any single strategy will work everywhere, under all conditions, and that *"patient and careful analysis of each local situation is a necessary prerequisite to effective development programs"*—any review of state technology development strategies intended to elucidate industrial policy for agricultural development must be seen as an analytical scrim, not as a prompter to action (Sears and Reid 1992, 300; italics original).

Finally, a search through state experiences with technology development and innovation for lessons related to agricultural policy is hindered by the absence of an agreed-upon body of codified findings. State investments in technology development have drawn from two different analytical and research traditions: one that relates to processes of economic development, particularly the role of technological change; and another that relates to the objectives, criteria, means, levers, and processes through which state governments can intervene to affect processes, rates, and (presumably) directions of economic growth. The striking resurgence of state policy innovativeness in the 1980s, and the shift in state economic development strategies from smokestack-chasing to demand generation, caused most analysts to focus on processes of state policy formulation (Eisinger 1988; Atkinson 1991). Relatively less attention has been paid to the validity of explicit or implicit theories of economic development, research and development, technological innovation or diffusion of innovation embedded in the design of state programs or their administrative provisions.

The result has been a recurrent, if muted, debate among state officials, planners, and economic development practitioners, and university officials on the one hand, and economists and economic geographers on the other. While there is considerable agreement within the two broad research traditions on what was attempted, far less agreement exists on what these programs have accomplished or on the implications of these experiences for the what and how of state investments in technological innovation as a tool for regional economic development (Osborne 1990; Portz and Eisinger 1990; Feller 1992).

By setting forth these propositions, I have obviously resisted temptation. I have used this introduction instead to suggest the need to shun great expectations, and to prepare to sift through complex choices and contending positions. I would suggest that accounts of state experiences be viewed at best as navigational charts, useful in policy and program design for their identification of shoals and alternative courses along traveled routes, and as limited guides to voyages to new destinations.

State Investment Strategies in Technology Development

Within the industrial policy conference's larger themes, my specific assignment is to address institutional links between and among state government, universities, and the local private sector. Because universities have featured so prominently in state technology development programs, treatment of institutional links inevitably segues into questions of the role of universities in regional economic development and of the character of university-industry R&D partnerships.

Offered here in the form of a value-added contribution to the considerable amount written on each of these topics is an analysis based on a review of recent assessments of selected state experiences, with all the caveats cited above duly kept in mind, and on my participation in evaluations of the National Institute of Standards and Technology's Manufacturing Technology Centers Program and the New York Center for Advanced Technology Program. The analysis is designed to present an operational description of working relationships among the different organizations involved in state technology and innovation programs under different state strategies.

Elsewhere I have argued that state programs have been deficient in their provisions for adequate evaluation designs, that most of the performance indicators have been process measures and/or imperfectly related to economic measures of effectiveness or efficiency, and that claims have been often anecdotal and/or unaudited (Feller 1988). Many evaluations, including several cited in this paper, remain subject to many of the same methodological criticisms. Recent evaluations and internal agency studies, however, are methodological advances over the reportage and case studies that characterized initial accounts of state technology programs; for that reason the recent studies are relied upon here.

In earlier work I organized state strategies into four broad categories: research infrastructure/human capital; generic/precompetitive research; spin-off/product development; and technical assistance/manufacturing modernization. Many of the larger state programs contain elements of each of the first three strategies. As noted earlier, states also are increasingly establishing manufacturing modernization programs (Clarke and Dobson 1991).

As a summary proposition, recent evaluations provide findings that support and reject the effectiveness of each of the three generic strategies; in so doing, they imply considerable variation (and flexibility) in effective working relationships among state governments, universities, and private firms. The evaluations also suggest boundaries to these relationships that are based on the economics of technological innovation, including the technical and economic uncertainties of commercialization of academic research; the pluralistic system of public-sector funding of academic research, which results in state governments having but modest levers on the research agendas of many faculty; and the inherent difficulties encountered by states in attempting to appropriate the benefits of technological innovations within their borders. The evaluations also highlight issues of program implementation with state policies that so shape the behavior of the collaborating organizations that outcomes are logical within the context of program incentives but contrary to state economic development objectives.

State technology programs have tended to express their objective as the stimulation of technological innovation that will lead to the generation of new, commercially viable products and processes. These, then, would be used as a catalyst for the formulation of new firms, the expansion of product lines of existing firms, and the improvement in production efficiency of existing or new firms, all resulting in firm and job creation and retention. Research universities, as Eisinger (1988, 275) has noted, became "pivotal institutions" in state economic development programs; states have allocated the larger share of their technology development program funds to university researchers.

Balancing the state's interest in directing academic research agendas towards commercially relevant technologies has been a perennial task. Most states have relied upon cost-sharing by industrial firms, as well as industrial participation on the boards of state programs or technology centers, to ensure that state funds go to research that has a "commercial," rather than an "academic," orientation. States and participating universities typically have eschewed basic research, venturing at most to speak of the importance of "precompetitive, generic research."

State skepticism about the convergence of faculty research and economic development research agendas was present at the origins of these programs. It continues to this day. Osborne (1990, 57), for example, described the industry-university research center model as seriously flawed because "academia is clearly in the driver's seat; . . . business is not intimately involved in defining the research agenda; . . . little technology transfer takes place." The cutbacks in state support noted above derive in part from this concern.

Among state programs, Pennsylvania's Ben Franklin Partnership Program has been characterized by its short-term orientation toward product development and an aversion to generic R&D projects involving the type of collaboration between research centers and Fortune 500 firms found in the New York and New Jersey programs. Even with this avowed intention to avoid being captured by an academic perspective, Pennsylvania officials have become increasingly concerned about the research orientation of many centers of excellence funded through the four Ben Franklin centers. Many individual research centers are viewed as being engaged in basic and very-early-stage applied research, attracting very large U.S. and foreign multinationals as partners but producing few concrete results for the commercialization or application of technology in Pennsylvania. Accordingly, the state's Ben Franklin Board has initiated major changes in the funding criteria used to allocate state support to the Ben Franklin Centers. The board has reduced support for research centers and required instead that the centers focus their activities on near-term commercialization and application of technology, concentrate their activities upon small- and medium-sized firms, and strengthen their participation in the regional or state infrastructure that supports established or emerging industries in Pennsylvania.

The Ben Franklin Program also offers insights into how administrative practices shape the performance of centers in ways not consistent with overall, if admittedly changing, state economic development objectives. The state has funded its four centers through a combination of core funding and competitively awarded annual allocations. A complex formula that included activities and outcomes related to start-up companies, new products and processes, size of firm, job creation, and matching funds was used to make these competitive allocations. The formula provided strong incentives for centers to select projects directed at product development with new, small firms; it provided fewer incentives for centers to select R&D projects related to process innovations involving the participation of mature, mid-size companies (greater than fifty employees) that led to job retention rather than creation. These mid-sized firms often were found in the state's traditional industries, such as machinery and plastics; their technological need to remain competitive focused on incremental improvements to existing products and processes. Recognizing the unintended consequence of its earlier policies and reflecting a shift in program strategy away from high-tech, small-firm start-ups toward improvements in competitiveness of existing firms, Pennsylvania changed its funding formula in July 1992.

Experiences in Pennsylvania and New York, widely shared with other states, show the difficulties of obtaining specific assessments of program activities directed at technological innovation. For example, in assessing its activities, the Ben Franklin Program has begun to emphasize commercialization (new products being sold in the marketplace or new processes being implemented internally by the sponsoring firm) as outcome measures. The short-term, applied orientation of the Pennsylvania strategy is reflected in the concentration of R&D projects on the development of new products or production processes, with over 92 percent of the projects in each of the Ben Franklin Centers being described this way. Reviews of the centers' operations provide indicators of the percentage of projects that are commercialized. However, as recognized by state officials, these indicators lack economic meaning since they may include product innovations for which only one unit is sold, or adoption of an innovation in a process that leads to few, if any, economic benefits.

Of all the state programs, Texas's Advanced Research Program and Advanced Technology Programs most closely approximate an "academic" model to technological development and innovation. In the Texas strategy, universities are believed to best serve the "economic development needs of their state by achieving excellence in their primary missions of teaching, research, and public service"; they transfer technology from the laboratory "by educating young scientists and engineers" (Ebert et al. 1991).

Reviewed by an external advisory panel in late 1990, the state's two programs received strong endorsement:

> The principal objective of the Advanced Research Program is to stimulate and promote innovative discovery research; for the Advanced Technology Program it is to catalyze technology transfer, especially the transfer of key discoveries and inventions to Texas industry. . . . The reviewers find both programs to be superb, both in principle and in practice, with the objectives clearly being met. Indeed we find the program to be so innovative and distinctive in character that we commend the State of Texas for their introduction. They can well serve as models for many other states in the union (ibid., 1).

Ohio's Thomas Edison Program, which is composed of nine autonomous university-affiliated centers, also has been commended by the National Research

Council. The Council described the program as "generally healthy, vigorous, and well managed," as giving "good value for the state's investment," and as warranting continued state funding (National Research Council 1990).

Although each Ohio Edison center is characterized by a distinctive technology, clientele, mission, and set of activities, the composite activities of the Edison centers, as well as the activities of selected centers, span the prototypical R&D spectrum. Center activities range from the generation of state-of-the-art knowledge and cutting-edge technologies, through short-term problem-solving and applied R&D projects, to company-directed research and human resource training for specific companies. Without seeking to strain analogies between agriculture and manufacturing, in the aggregate, the Ohio centers perform the functions of research, technology development, and technology transfer found in the prototypical agricultural technology delivery system.

As supportive as they are of the respective state programs, the Texas and Ohio evaluations may be challenged on the qualitative character of the reviews, as well as on their implicit search for legitimacy in the standing of the individuals and organizations that authored the reports, rather than on the empirically documented outcomes. To date, the most comprehensive analytical and empirical estimates of the economic benefits from a state technology program are contained in the 1992 evaluation of the New York Center for Advanced Technology (CAT) Program (SRI 1992).

New York's program is organized around nine university-based centers, each specializing in a particular technology. Like the Ohio program, the New York centers, in the aggregate, conduct "commercially relevant" basic research, funded jointly through state, industrial, and other funds; foster technological innovation through the direct transfer of research findings to corporate sponsors via the establishment of new firms and assistance to emerging companies; and provide technical education and training programs.[4]

The authors of the SRI report identify, and then venture to estimate, the economic benefits from the CAT's several activities. Included as economic benefits are external income, technological innovation and increased productivity, increased or retained employment in the state, and improvements in the quality of the technical work force. Specific problems associated with attribution of program impacts in the absence of experimental controls, difficulties in estimating economic benefits from basic research, and potential estimation problems with double-counting outcome measures are treated explicitly. With these qualifications, benefits for each of the named categories were estimated separately.[5] Total economic benefits were estimated at between $190 million and $360 million for 1982–1991. Even with allowances for time adjustments for benefit and cost streams, "these benefits are substantially greater than the State's direct investment of $61 million. . . ." (SRI 1992, S-3). The authors conclude that the "CAT Program has provided a substantial return of the State's investment in terms of both specific, quantifiable short-term benefits and longer-term qualitative benefits, with the consequent implication that continuation of the Program is merited and worthwhile" (ibid., S-9).

A striking aspect of the New York program is that approximately one-third of these estimated benefits occur in the form of externally generated income, primarily federal and other nonindustry research awards; research funding from out-of-state companies; and, to a limited extent, patent and license income from nonsponsors (ibid., II-16). The report thus treats knowledge generation, either in the form of the performance of R&D or through its complementarity with the production of graduate education, as a state economic sector.

Reconsidering State Experiences
with Technology Development Programs

The experiences of Texas, Ohio, and New York do more than offset the prevailing perception of the limited impact of state technology development programs; they raise anew questions of the relative effectiveness of "targeted" technological development programs and general enhancement of the research and instructional capabilities of universities.

Here the limits of basing this review of the effectiveness of state strategies on program evaluations become evident, and a shift in focus to broader analytical frameworks is necessary. Program evaluations monitor outcomes against objectives; they seldom inquire into whether the objectives were the right ones, or whether the strategies employed in attaining these objectives were efficient relative to other approaches.

At this point, attention shifts from comparative program performance to the analytical and empirical underpinnings of state strategies. Allowing for the penchant of faculty to cast their research agendas in the rubrics and objectives of sponsors, and for the necessary administrative criteria and safeguards built into state programs to avoid this situation, the disenchantment of state governments with the limited, slow rate at which state investments have translated into identifiable products and processes follows from something more fundamental: the weak theoretical and empirical understanding of the processes of technological change, and the role of universities as engines of economic growth, upon which programs were designed and expectations formed. States simply have expected too much and in the form of the wrong outcomes. Their analytical and accounting systems emphasize discrete technological products and processes, and thus they do not encompass many of the economic benefits generated by existing programs, much less allowances for "social savings" that are appropriate economic criteria for gauging the economic efficiency of state investments. States have been rightfully, but perhaps overly, concerned about the spatial leakage of economic benefits, failing to recognize that spillovers flow in multiple directions and that state rates of return may still meet investment criteria even after allowance for leakages.

The process of commercializing academic research is risky, expensive, and lengthy. Industrial R&D officials have stated recently their view that commercially successful technological innovations—with a few notable exceptions, such as those found recently in the advent of biotechnology—occur on an incremental basis within corporate environs, not within university research laboratories, and that from industry's perspective, "the primary role for universities is in training and education" (Government-University-Industry Research Roundtable 1991, iv). In their evaluation of NSF-funded university-research centers, Gray et al. (1986, 26) found that "both faculty and industry respondents rated general expansion of knowledge as the most important goal and the more short-term goals of patent and product development as the least important." After reviewing a number of similar studies, Mowery and Rosenberg (1989, 264) have noted that, "although the wide variety of university-industry collaborative programs makes generalization hazardous, the weight of anecdotal evidence . . . suggests that collaborative ventures that focus on applied development work or on technological 'deliverables' in many cases are less successful. The benefits of collaboration . . . are longer-term benefits that rely on the establishment of a relationship lasting a number of years."

Similar findings regarding industry's participation in state-funded programs are found in Rees's (1989, iv) study of state-funded research centers for microelectronics and computer-aided manufacturing technology. Of the 216 firms in the Rees sample, only thirty-five had direct experience with state-funded centers. Twelve of these firms reported that involvement with state technology centers led to the development of prototype products, and twelve also reported that their involvement had led to improvements in production processes. The most common activities of firms participating in the state programs were enrollment by employees in courses, followed by the use of faculty as consultants and the use of students as research assistants or interns. Rees termed these the human resources, or human capital, dimensions to university-industry relationships.

Interpretation of study findings reflects a subtle mixture of economic efficiency criteria and state expectations. According to Rees, the number of reported

positive outcomes is small, but they "represent the type of marginal benefits that
state policymakers should not ignore, particularly when they represent a relatively
small investment by participating companies who made an average annual investment of $27,000 in the centers in 1987" (ibid., 92–93). In a related way, Lugar and
Goldstein's findings (1991, 179) on university-based science parks point to
economic benefits that at best are "slow to be realized" and at worst may be
nonexistent as the park "fails to achieve its promise and objective." This suggests
that this strategy should be approached cautiously. Their observation that university-based localization economies "are especially important in smaller regions
which are not likely to have other sources for generating external economies" (ibid.,
159) does suggest, however, that such a strategy may be the most promising of a
set of limited options.[6]

The issue in assessing the effectiveness of state investments in a university-
based technology development strategy may not be ex post economic rates of return
but the divergence between these returns and ex ante expectations, as well as
divergence between the gestation period of economic benefits and the time
horizons of elected officials.

Institutional Design

What do these experiences suggest about the transferability to agricultural
development of state strategies to promote technology development? State technology development programs have been presented as institution-building undertakings, with the state acting in a brokerage, or catalytic, role to surmount barriers
to cooperation that have stifled links between universities, as suppliers of new
technologically relevant knowledge, and business firms, as transformers of new
knowledge into commercially viable products and processes. States have become
the visible manifestation of what Lambright and Teich (1976, 50) have described
as the "invisible hand of mutual organizational adjustment" that is needed in most
instances to effect the transfer of technology.

Clearly evident in the establishment of state technology development and
manufacturing modernization programs were choices about institutions. In most
cases, the choice was to support technology development through support of
university-based programs, administering these programs through state science and
technology offices or state departments of commerce or economic development
(Lambright and Teich 1989). The choice was almost reflexive; the main administrative issues were the number of centers and the criteria and selection process
used.

As reflected in the experiences and evaluations of state governments, universities, and firms, the choice has resulted in a glass that is half full, half empty. Short-term and long-term regional economic benefits have been documented. State programs have contributed to the expanding (and bending) of university research priorities to closer fits with those of firms. These programs have expanded by a substantial—if imprecisely documented—quantity the number of formal and informal interactions that universities, particularly research universities, have had with small- and medium-sized firms within their states.

But these experiences have also shown the limits of a catalytical, coalition-building strategy. Universities may be flexible institutions in adjusting research priorities, but they break at a certain point. Absent sizable levels of sustained, targeted funding and the establishment of faculties with dedicated missions (the financial and organizational model of the state agricultural experiment stations), there is little evidence to suggest that universities can serve as other than episodic sources of regionally capturable, commercially significant technological innovations.

There also appear to be limits to the span of activities that even those universities that are proven productive partners in state programs are willing to undertake. The SRI study of New York's program describes an evolution in state technology-based economic development strategies. Strategies have moved from an initial emphasis in the early and mid-1980s on university research in relevant technologies (funding for centers of excellence), to technology transfer from university to industry (incentives for university-industry collaboration), to industry-driven research in universities (industry sponsorship of research and programs), to the present policy emphasis on cluster-driven economic development strategies (involving integrated research, education, and business assistance programs). This analysis captures an evolving consensus among state economic development officials that state technology development programs need to be more closely linked with state comparative advantages and with what is termed the regional economic infrastructure.

SRI recommended that centers which have successfully established an effective technology-transfer program take on an expanded set of economic development activities, including support for education and training programs, cooperation in regional development efforts with technology development organizations and regional economic development organizations, participation in industrial attraction and retention efforts, and sponsorship of technology-awareness conferences and seminars (SRI 1992, V-18–19). CAT center directors have opposed this added mandate, contending that these activities would divert them from research and technology transfer and that their organizational capabilities are insufficient for the new activities they are being asked to add.

Given these experiences, state governments are searching for new partners. Reinventing government involves giving new authority to existing institutions or creating new ones; this is precisely what states seem ready to do. Reinforcing a pattern seen in the federal government, where the National Institute of Standards and Technology's Advanced Development Program funds individual companies and joint ventures for precompetitive generic R&D, states are opening opportunities for firms to be the direct recipients of grants. Universities may be included as partners in joint ventures, but no longer are they the prime movers in the state's technology development cosmology.

Similar patterns may be observed in the case of manufacturing modernization programs, where a larger number of diverse possibilities have been considered. Included as institutional performers in federal and state programs are land-grant universities, public and private universities, community colleges, industrial extension services, departments of economic development, and not-for-profit organizations. Although experiences are too recent to permit summative statements, the trend has been to move beyond universities. Pennsylvania's Industrial Resource Centers Program, for example, which focuses on the modernization activities of small- and medium-sized firms, is organized as a series of nine geographically distributed, independent, nonprofit corporations.

Choices of institution and coordination among institutions are likely to become more pronounced issues as states simultaneously shift their technological development strategies and attempt to integrate their technology development and manufacturing modernization programs. States in effect are attempting to recreate the prototypical agricultural technology delivery system, with its components of mission-oriented basic research; product- or process-specific applied research; and developmental research, dissemination, education, and organization building, as found in the state agricultural experiment stations and among extension specialists and county extension agents.

Teething problems and competition among institutions are being encountered in these endeavors. Pennsylvania has found that some research centers have disengaged from the state's program following new requirements to emphasize technology transfer and to work with small- and medium-sized firms. More generally, the emerging situation has been described by Shapira et al. (1992, 19) as follows:

> When funding potentials become large, or when budget cutbacks loom, ugly intrastate political battles are likely to ensue. Some point specifically to

educational institutions as being particularly inclined to fight for funding, although university presidents may be skeptical at hearing about the relevance of industrial extension to their missions. Coordination between technical schools, community colleges, and universities is crucial to a balanced technology services program, but there may be divisions analogous to class distinction that retard collaboration. Similarly, funding battles between agricultural extension and industrial extension have been reported, as have tensions between federal and state programs.

Conclusions

Experience with state technology development programs and emerging experience with federal and state manufacturing modernization programs attest to the mixed records of specific state programs and specific technology development strategies. This mixed record also relates to the characteristics of the interorganizational links that states have sought to develop with and between universities and firms. State experiences point to the potential and feasibility, but also to the limits and risks, of either imposing upon institutions tasks that they cannot perform (without harming the performance of other missions), or of having these institutions seek out these expanded roles.

Several reasons exist for the difficulty in formulating definitive assessments. Many of these relate to methodological and data issues encountered in program evaluation. In particular, the absence of quantifiable data on economic impacts related to technological innovations is a major source of state disenchantment. But, as noted, the absence of data is a two-edged sword, raising the possibility that states have underestimated systematically the benefits from the university-industry research model that they are currently abandoning in the belief that the strategy has failed to contribute to state economic development.

Indeed, what I believe to be the salient finding from recent evaluations is not the disappointments and general sense of limited success that states have had with the university-based centers or the competitive research grant model, but the positive endorsements and documented economic benefits that the approaches have received. Moreover, the findings from the New York State evaluation noted earlier suggest that these programs may have contributed to state economic development. They may have done so both in ways that have not been adequately measured, given the limitations of existing evaluation undertakings, and in ways that have been summarily and incorrectly disregarded, such as strengthening the overall educational and research capabilities of universities.

An element of political irony surfaces here. In their early years, state technology programs probably benefited politically from the difficulties associated with rigorous program evaluation; few means existed to scrutinize public claims of short-term economic impacts, particularly related to job creation or retention. Now they likely suffer politically from the crude state of evaluation, which I believe understates the range and magnitude of their benefits.

But the difficulty of assessing the past performance of these programs and of their place in present and future state economic development strategies is more than a matter of evaluation design. In part, too, the difficulty includes the absence of a stable reference point in assessing or prescribing state development strategies. The underlying theories of how state governments should proceed in fostering economic development continue to undergo rapid change. The initial major change from supply-side to demand-side approaches to economic development has been overtaken by a new "third wave" paradigm. According to this perspective, states have had to shift from being a direct supplier of resources (e.g., direct sources of loans, or of information) to developing organizational arrangements.

The substantive merits of the third-wave framework aside, what is striking to an outside observer is the speed of new theoretical paradigms relative to the flow of evaluative knowledge of what does or does not work. The rate of change—three waves in a decade—creates a sense of intellectual unease about whether what is being observed is cumulative learning, theoretical fads, or the political pursuit of novelty.

More is gained politically by novelty and action—certainly at the outset of a new administration—than by waiting for the effects of prior administrations to affect relationships that require lengthy gestation. Programs are initiated or terminated at rates far slower than new theories are articulated and disseminated. This situation is compounded by the lag between much of what has been written about these programs and the significant strategic and administrative changes now under way in many programs as a result of major budgetary cutbacks and the increased skepticism of state officials about the benefits from these programs.

Ideas, like waves, form, crest, crash, and ebb with rapidity and totality; programs form slowly, crest, but most often linger even while new programs emerge, producing an eclectic array of approaches often funded and operated in competition with one another. States considering new programs run the risk of adopting yesterday's models.

If the fluid programmatic and political status of the larger state programs is kept in mind, then the decade of experience with investments in technology development and innovation may be used constructively to establish a realistic set of expectations of the economic benefits that can be generated from state government-industry-university collaboration in technological innovation and manufacturing modernization. They also can be used as warning markers, pointing to the manner in which the specification of program benefits (jobs, growth, development) can not only torque specific program decisions but return to haunt programs as tighter budget accountability or sunset provisions require that they demonstrate what they have said they could and would accomplish. State experiences also serve to establish meaningful time frames for the production of projected benefits by programs.

If, at the end of this analysis, the economic gains seem small relative to the magnitude of improvements sought for a production sector, region, or state, the problem lies not with analysis but with the inherent limitations of state government and universities to effect short-term change in the systemic economic, political, and institutional processes that determine the wealth of nations.

Notes

1. The EABC experience with Embryogen also outlines the complex paths between initiatives and subsequent outcomes. As DNX opted not to exercise its first-option rights under its initial agreement with Ohio University, the university began to license other firms. Learning from its experiences with Embryogen, the university's strategy is now to attempt to tie the technology to the local area by requiring firms to build facilities in Athens as part of a patent licensing agreement. It also has entered into consortia arrangements with other Ohio universities in developing a statewide capability in biotechnology, which it sees as providing a regionally accessible research infrastructure to support a diverse array of fledgling biotechnology firms.

2. Indeed, seeking guidance from industrial policy in manufacturing for industrial policy in agriculture is a reversal of accustomed roles, given the distinctive U.S. success in blending public and private R&D activities, and federal and state funding of agricultural research and technology transfer, to produce a highly productive agricultural sector (Evenson 1982). As this paper turns to state experiences with science and innovation for guidance in industrial policy for agriculture, national discussions of the need for expanded federal support of manufacturing modernization programs frequently invoke agriculture and agricultural extension as a model for emulation.

3. "The dynamic CEC (computer, electronics, communication) high-tech sectors and those most influenced by national policies (DDS) (defense-dependent sectors) contribute little to development of a technological base of employment in rural counties. While there have been modest increases in the presence of these industries within the nation's rural communities, shares of CEC and DDS sectors in rural areas are still substantially below comparable figures for the nation. All regions show small amounts of this type of rural employment, but it is doubtful that these dynamic sectors will play a significant role in changing the long-standing compositions of high-tech jobs in rural areas. . . . " (Glasmeier 1991, 186–87).

4. The New York and Ohio centers differ somewhat: the CATs tend to be codeterminous with a research university, and therefore to be oriented toward the performance of basic research, while the Ohio centers are consortia of research universities, comprehensive universities, and community colleges, and thereby conduct a broader range of activities.

5. New York's CAT program review encountered difficulty in estimating the benefits of technological innovations. The SRI review of the New York program identified more than one hundred specific instances of transfer from specific CATs to specific companies that were commercialized or incorporated into commercial activities. "However," according to the report, "the centers have not been able to obtain information on the value to companies, in terms of additional revenue or reduced costs, that has resulted from these transfers" (SRI 1992, II-21). It is noted that "such data may be very difficult to obtain since companies are often unwilling to divulge information on the value of specific new technologies, estimation methods are not well-developed in industry, and the long-term benefits from the technology over the lifetime of a product or process are not easily observed."

6. They phrase the strategic implications of their findings as follows: "Park developers must consider not only the existence of a research university, but also the strength of various departments and research institutes, and the organizational arrangements between the research park and the university. It may be that investments in universities will have to precede investments in research parks before the latter can be successful" (Goldstein and Lugar 1992, 260).

References

Atkinson, Robert. 1991. "States Take the Lead: Explaining Reformation of State Technology Policies." *Economic Development Quarterly* 5:33–44.

Ben Franklin Partnership Program, Strategic Investment Committee. n.d. *An Analysis of the Research and Development Component of the Ben Franklin Partnership Program.* Project report. Harrisburg, Pa.: Author.

Blumenstyr, Goldie. 1992. "States Re-Evaluate Industrial Collaborations Built around Research Grants to Universities." *The Chronicle of Higher Education* 38(25).

Buswell, R. J. 1983. "Research and Development and Regional Development: A Review." In *Technological Change and Economic Development*, ed. A. Gillespie. London: Pion Limited.

Carnegie Commission on Science, Technology, and the Government. 1992. *Science,Technology, and the States in America's Third Century*. New York: Carnegie Commission.

Center for Rural Pennsylvania. 1992. *Telelinked Business: A New Horizon for Rural Pennsylvania*. Project report. Harrisburg, Pa.: Author.

Clarke, Marianne, and Eric Dobson. 1991. *Increasing the Competitiveness of America's Manufacturers: A Review of State Industrial Extension Programs*. Washington, D.C.: National Governors' Association.

Ebert, James, Craig Fields, and James Wyngaarden. 1991. *Evaluation of the Advanced Research Program and Advanced Technology Programs*. A Report to the Texas Higher Education Coordinating Board.

Eisinger, Peter. 1988. *The Rise of the Entrepreneurial State*. Madison: University of Wisconsin Press.

Evenson, Robert. 1982. "Agriculture." In *Government and Technical Progress*, ed. Richard Nelson. New York: Pergamon Press.

Feller, Irwin. 1988. "Evaluating State Advanced Technology Programs." *Evaluation Review* 12:232–52.

_____. 1990. "University Patent and Technology Licensing Strategies." *Educational Policy* 4:327–40.

_____. 1992. "American State Governments as Models for National Science Policy." *Journal of Policy Analysis and Management* 11:288–309.

Fosler, Scott. 1988. *The New Economic Role of American States*. New York: Oxford University Press.

Glasmeier, Amy. 1991. *The High-Tech Potential: Economic Development in Rural America*. New Brunswick, N.J.: Rutgers, the State University of New Jersey.

Glasmeier, Amy, and Amy Kays-Teran. 1989. "Rural Area Development: Competing for the Chips." *Forum of Applied Research and Public Policy* (Fall):53–57.

Goldstein, Harvey, and Michael Lugar. 1992. "University-Based Research Parks as a Rural Development Strategy." *Policy Studies Journal* 30:249–63.

Government-University-Industry Research Roundtable. 1991. *Industry Perspectives on Innovation and Interactions with Universities*. Washington, D.C.: Research Roundtable.

Gray, Denis, Elmina Johnson, and Teresa Gridley. 1986. "University-Industry Projects and Centers." *Evaluation Review* 10(6):776–93.

Lambright, W. H., and Albert Teich. 1976. "Technology Transfer as a Problem in Interorganizational Relationships." *Administration and Society*: 29–54.

_____. 1989. "Science, Technology and State Economic Development." *Policy Studies Journal* 18:134–47.

Lambright, W. H., Albert Teich, and Mark O'Gorman. 1992. "The Turbulent Condition of State S&T Programs in the 1990s." In *Technology and U.S. Competitiveness*, eds. W. H. Lambright and Dianne Rahm. Westport, Conn.: Greenwood Press.

Lugar, Michael, and Harvey Goldstein. 1991. *Technology in the Garden*. Chapel Hill: University of North Carolina Press.

Malecki, Edward. 1991. Technology and Economic Development. Great Britain: Longman Group UK, Ltd.

Mowery, David, and Nathan Rosenberg. 1989. *Technology and the Pursuit of Economic Growth*. Cambridge: Cambridge University Press.

National Research Council, Commission to Review the Ohio Thomas Edison Technology Centers. 1990. *Ohio's Thomas Edison Centers: A 1990 Review*. Washington, D.C.: National Academy Press.

Nelson, Richard, ed. 1982. *Government and Technical Progress*. New York: Pergamon Press.

Osborne, David. 1988. *Laboratories of Democracy*. Boston, Mass.: Harvard Business School Press.

_____. 1990. "Refining State Technology Programs." *Issues in Science and Technology*, 55–61.

Phelps, Paul, and Paul Brockman. 1992. *Science and Technology Programs in the States*. Alexandria, Va.: Advanced Development Distribution, Inc.

Portz, John, and Peter Eisinger. 1990. "Biotechnology and Economic Development: The Role of the States." Working Paper No. 1. Madison: University of Wisconsin.

Rees, John. 1989. *Industrial Experience with Technology Research Centers.* Final report prepared for the U.S. Department of Commerce, Economic Development Administration.

Sears, David, and Norman Reid. 1992. "Rural Strategies and Rural Development Research: An Assessment." *Policy Studies Journal* 3:301–9.

Schmandt, Jurgen, and Robert Wilson, eds. 1987. *Promoting High-Technology Industry.* Boulder, Colo.: Westview Press.

Shapira, Philip. 1990. "Modern Times: Learning from State Initiatives in Industrial Extension and Technology Transfer." *Economic Development Quarterly* 4:186–202.

Shapira, Philip, J. David Roessner, and Richard Barke. 1992. *Federal-State Collaboration in Industrial Modernization.* Atlanta: Georgia Institute of Technology.

SRI International. 1992. *New York State Centers for Advanced Technology Program: Evaluating Past Performance and Preparing for the Future.* Report prepared for the New York State Science and Technology Foundation. Menlo Park, Calif.: SRI International.

Weinberg, Mark, and Mary Ellen Mazey. 1988. "Government-University-Industry Partnerships in Technology Development: A Case Study." *Technovation* 7:131–42.

8 Industrial Policy in Europe

HENRY ERGAS

"It is well known," wrote Alexander Hamilton, first U.S. secretary of the treasury, in 1791, "that certain nations . . . enable their own workmen to undersell and supplant all competitors in the countries to which those commodities are sent. Hence the undertakers of a new manufacture have to contend, not only with the natural disadvantages of a new undertaking, but with the gratuities and remunerations which other governments bestow. To be able to contend with success, it is evident that the interference and aid of their own government are indispensable."[1]

Whatever their substantive merits, Hamilton's words have not fallen on deaf ears. Exactly two centuries later, the governments of the twenty-four member countries of the Organization for Economic Cooperation and Development (OECD) spent $100 billion[2] promoting the development of new technologies,[3] and (an admittedly very rough estimate) perhaps that much again on a variety of other subsidies, provided through a range of instruments from public procurement to export guarantees, on firms in "high-technology" industries.[4] Nor are there signs of the enthusiasm for these policies abating in Europe and other developed nations. Far from it:

- In Europe, the Treaty of Maastricht, through a series of amendments to Article 130 of the Treaty of Rome, has strengthened the statutory basis for a European Community–wide industrial strategy, a strategy in which the

Henry Ergas is *Conseiller pour la politique structurelle,* Economic Affairs Division, Organization for Economic Cooperation and Development in Paris.

European Free Trade Area (EFTA) countries will become involved first through association and eventually through membership.

- In Japan, the 1990 vision of the Ministry of International Trade and Industry, while outlining a subtle and broadly market-supportive role for policy, emphasizes the contribution public action should make to "arranging market conditions [so as] to shift smoothly industrial activities and labor forces to sophisticated areas."[5]

- In the United States, "no matter how sharp the disagreements among the candidates or who ultimately wins the [1992 presidential] election," writes an observer of the U.S. political scene, "one outcome at least is certain: in the next administration, the United States will have some kind of national industrial policy."[6]

Yet the substance of these national industrial policies is changing, and changing in important ways. Earlier failures, evolving circumstances, and new thinking about how governments can act (and, to a lesser extent, about how they should act) have each contributed to the themes of change.

These changes in modern industrial policies are at the center of this paper. The focus is on policies to promote new industries and activities, with concentration on the three larger European countries: the United Kingdom, France, and Germany. Together they account for nearly 90 percent of EC expenditure on research and development, and for about a quarter of the research and development outlays of the OECD. These countries differ in many respects, but there are also some important common elements in their experience with, and current outlook on, policies to promote new industries and economic activity. They have, in particular, all engaged in conscious programs aimed at supporting domestic firms in the field commonly referred to as *high technology*.[7] These programs have yielded results which are, at best, modest. The attempt to maintain the goal of these programs while modifying their format is at the core of the current European debate.

Commonalities in Postwar Experiences

The commonality in approaching modern industrial policy at least partly reflects a common experience with these programs in the immediate postwar period. The tradition of government intervention in industry is hardly of recent origin. The direct and systematic attempt by governments to foster technological development and to strengthen the position of domestic firms in high-technology markets received new impetus in the 1950s. Three factors weighed especially heavily: (1) the contributions that scientific and technological capabilities had made to military power in the Second World War, and seemed destined to make to defense in a nuclear age; (2) the close link that seemed to exist between these capabilities and the very high levels of productivity and real income achieved in the United States, links highlighted in the many reports of the European Productivity Agency, set up in the late 1940s to promote awareness of the economic contributions that new methods could make; and (3) the inference that the political and economic future of the European countries was intimately bound up with their ability to master the technologies that the Second World War had brought to the fore.

Developments in the 1960s only heightened these perceptions and incentives. To begin, notably after the orbiting of Sputnik in 1957, the U.S. government dramatically increased its support for technology development. A further spectacular boost came in 1961 with President Kennedy's announcement (in reaction to the Gagarin flight) that the United States would "consider . . . any program now, regardless of its cost, which offers us the hope of being pioneers."[8] By the early 1960s, U.S. defense funding alone accounted for about one-third of all public and private research and development in the OECD area. At least partly due to this support, U.S. firms seemed to be steadily increasing their technological lead, a lead documented in the mid-1960s by the OECD's *Gaps in Technology* series and widely publicized by Servan Schrieber's best seller, *The American Challenge*.[9]

At the same time, seen from Europe, the United States increasingly appeared to be flexing its muscles in refusing or restricting European access to new technologies. In some cases, the U.S. action was based on alleged security concerns, as with the sale of computer technology to be used in the French nuclear program. In others, commercial considerations seemed primary, as in the decision to initially vest the management of INTELSAT (the International Satellite Consortium created, at U.S. initiative, in 1964) in the U.S. agency COMSAT, rather than creating a specialized international organization as the Europeans had proposed. Commercial considerations also seemed evident in the restrictive conditions imposed in 1968 on the launching of the planned European communications satellite.[10] Either way, the U.S. conduct cemented perceptions that independent action in trade, defense, and commercial development rested on technological mastery.

Finally, developments in economic theory seemed to confirm that technical advance was crucial to sustained economic growth. New techniques of growth accounting and of econometric production function analysis proved that economic growth was primarily due to a residual factor, a term immediately attached by many economists and policymakers to technological progress rather than, say, to the effects of liberalizing markets. These results were widely publicized by the OECD, most notably at the first meeting of OECD ministers of science in 1963. Implicit in the conclusions of this meeting was the assumption that a greater policy effort in science and technology would accelerate the growth process. Further support for this presumption came from the equally recent work on innovation and market failure, which concluded that firms, left to their own devices, would underinvest in research and development. This argument gained great respectability from its prominent role in the first report of the Kennedy Council of Economic Advisers, and it was quickly picked up, and widely diffused, by the OECD.

All of this created a climate extremely favorable to large-scale government programs for support of industry development in advanced technology areas. The strongest policy responses came in the United Kingdom and France. These countries, both undergoing the painful process of losing overseas empires and anxious about their status as world powers, were concerned most directly with the links between technological prowess and national sovereignty. Fears about access to U.S. technology clashed with what Raymond Vernon has described as the "powerful psychic and social need on the part of the elite groups . . . to avoid a sense of dependence on outsiders."[11] The result was an escalating series of measures in support of national technological development.

The British Experience

Despite all that has been written about indifference on the part of successive British governments to the needs of manufacturing, and the supposed dominance of the political system and the Civil Service by the interests, or at least outlook, of "the City" (the London-based financial institutions), the United Kingdom led the way in direct intervention as a form of industrial policy. The first postwar governments sought to maintain defense technology capabilities across the board, with projects to develop nuclear weapons, supersonic bombers, interceptor aircraft, and a range of ballistic and tactical missiles. It soon became apparent that these initial plans far exceeded the financial capability of the British economy. Some retrenchment occurred after Duncan Sandys' 1957 Defense Review, which found, among other things, that "an undue proportion of scientists and engineers are engaged in military work."[12] Still, the U.K. defense program remained second only to that of the United States in the period following the Second World War, and it was paralleled by ambitious initiatives on the civilian front, notably in nuclear energy, in telecommunications, and in civil aircraft. Together with the buying power of the nationalized industries, these industry development programs gave the government considerable clout. This clout was used, often bluntly, to restructure the industrial base, especially in the direction of greater concentration.[13] By the 1960s, these programs had evolved into an enormous undertaking, stretching from Concorde to efforts to develop a specifically British nuclear reactor technology (the Advanced Gas Reactor, or AGR) and to foster and maintain a U.K. presence in the electronics and computer industries.

To understand the fate and consequences of these policies, it is useful to reflect on what happens when governments themselves take on these large-scale, mission-oriented programs, which I have defined elsewhere as "[programs] focused on radical innovations needed to achieve clearly set out goals of national importance."[14] (Being older and somewhat wiser today, I rather doubt I would now say "clearly set out.") What most distinguishes these missions, of which the prototype was the Los Alamos program, is the degree of centralization they entail. Their goals are centrally determined; their high cost encourages a narrowing in the range of options explored; and their technical complexity restricts participation in execution to a few technologically sophisticated agents.

This feature of the mission-oriented programs has, in turn, two consequences. First, mission-oriented programs place a heavy burden on administrative capabilities. Their design and implementation typically involve a high degree of administrative discretion; the monitoring of performance relies primarily on administrative processes rather than on the discipline normally exerted by competition in product and factor markets. Also, the very scale of the expenditures involved and the complexity of the goals pursued impose great demands on the standard processes of public administration. These programs are, at the same time, high-risk ventures. In effect, a few large bets are being placed on a small number of races. This inevitably creates the danger both that the wrong bets will be chosen and that the large outlays devoted to these programs will crowd out more valuable alternative uses of the resources.

Seen against this background, two features have characterized the U.K. experience. The first is the sheer scale of the program effort, both in absolute terms and relative to British national income. By even the most conservative estimate, these initiatives, during their 1960–1980 heyday, must have consumed some two-thirds of the U.K.'s research and development outlays—outlays which (until 1969) were greater both in absolute amount and as a share of GDP than those of any U.K. competitor other than the United States. Second is the reliance on policy designs that, by minimizing the use of markets, place the heaviest demand on administrative capabilities. In the product markets, preferential procurement distorted market signals or suppressed them outright. Meanwhile, capital market monitoring and discipline of the firms involved in the programs was weakened in many instances by the willingness of government to salvage weaker firms, or it was removed in others through partial or complete nationalization. In the former case, cost overruns on government contracts and new competitive awards gave government a strong hand in developing the industry.

Even in the best of circumstances, these features of the mission-oriented programs would have taxed the administrative abilities of the state. But in the United Kingdom they fell on an administrative process singularly unsuited to the task. Pervasive secrecy enforced by draconian legislation ("the reasons for secrecy [being] themselves a closely guarded secret"[15]), the anonymity of decision makers cloaked in a practice of management by committee, and the lack of any reward for good performance or any penalty for poor ("the unimportance of being right"[16]) combined to remove both the incentives for success and the mechanisms for detecting and correcting failure. Examining the way policies were made, "we glimpse in operation a system which is extremely centralized without, however, being decisive; and procedures which are extraordinarily time-consuming, yet leave one with no confidence that the evidence has been systematically and objectively explored. . . . [It] is a process of decision-making which is ponderous, ritualized, secretive, and highly unreliable in its results."[17]

And so it proved to be. The most spectacular failures were undoubtedly Concorde and the AGR: together, the net economic loss to the United Kingdom from these programs, measured in today's currency, exceeds $20 billion[18]—an amount equal to nearly two years of all British research and development expenditure in the late 1980s. Programs such as System X, an electronic telephone exchange system; the British high-speed train; ICL, the British computer company; and INMOS, a government-owned semiconductor producer, also compiled large losses, despite the high prices and guaranteed markets they obtained from preferential procurement.

After 1979, successive Conservative governments reversed this mission-oriented industrial policy approach only very partially. Some of the lame ducks inherited from the Labor government have been sold to the private sector, and the direct subsidies provided to firms such as ICL have been reduced substantially. But even in the civilian field, intervention has remained widespread. The now privatized utilities have been required to maintain a preference for U.K. producers, with OFTEL (the British telecommunications regulatory body) intervening to ensure that British Telephone continues to rely primarily on System X. Also, the nuclear system has remained largely protected, funded through a levy on the non-nuclear generators. Finally, preferential procurement and local research and development requirements remain central to the allocation of licenses for North

Sea oil, and the subsidies still flow to the (also privatized) producers of civil aircraft, notably British Aerospace (BAe).

At the same time, Mrs. Thatcher's Conservative government presided over a large increase in defense outlays. Between 1974 and 1983, the share of defense purchases in manufacturing GDP rose from 6 to 12 percent, and in engineering GDP it rose from 17 to 33 percent. Like its predecessors, the government used the leverage provided by the rising outlays to restructure the defense suppliers, intervening in the sale of the helicopter producer Westland to Sikorsky, further strengthening the dominance of the aerospace segment by BAe, and supporting GEC's position in electronics. What evidence there is suggests that the leading British high-technology firms became even more focused on defense markets over the course of the 1980s,[19] and hence, even more dependent on the system of mission-oriented industrial support. This clashed both with budgetary constraints and with the changing international situation; with further major retrenchments in defense outlays considered virtually inevitable, the prospects for the British suppliers of high-technology products, were they to remain so largely reliant on support from the British government alone, could hardly justify optimism.

The French Experience

Industrial policy in France shares a number of similarities with that of the United Kingdom. Here, too, considerations of national sovereignty and prestige weighed heavily in the growth of public support for technological advance. For example, they were certainly at the heart of de Gaulle's interest in promoting research. The industries and activities covered by the industrial or technology policy were also broadly similar to the British experience, most notably in aerospace, nuclear power, and computers and information technology. And, again as in the United Kingdom, large-scale government procurement in these targeted areas, together with direct subsidies to and controls over the firms operating in them, were used to alter the structure of the supplying industries, expanding the scope of the firms currently in favor, often in return for commitments on their part to absorb those making losses. All of this culminated during the first phase of the Mitterand presidency (1981–1983) in what one observer termed the *Lego* approach to industrial policy: chopping newly nationalized firms up and then reconstituting them on the basis of grandiose plans conceived—in splendid isolation from market forces—by the government's "industrial strategists."[20]

Yet there have also been important differences in industrial policy relative to the United Kingdom. To begin, the French programs generally had less ambitious goals than those of the U.K. Already, de Gaulle had cautioned against trying to go it alone.[21] His government was given the task of achieving a degree of national control over technology "without weighing on the balance of payments, and [while] enriching the general economy by applying useful scientific and technological progress to purposes other than defense."[22] Moreover, the major client agencies for the mission-oriented programs, notably the electric, rail, and telecommunications utilities, were mindful of the fact that their continued legitimacy could not rest on technological prowess alone, but had to reflect the maintenance of reasonable standards of cost efficiency, an approach mirrored in their early adoption of marginal cost pricing. These firms were therefore unwilling or at least reluctant to embark on programs that seemed extremely ambitious, or (in most, though by no means all, cases) to perpetuate mission-oriented programs that appeared to have little prospect of success. As a result, the French programs, rather than following the "not invented here" approach taken in the United Kingdom, have frequently involved adopting and adapting advanced technology from overseas, and most notably from the United States, as in the use of the Westinghouse PWR nuclear reactor and the GE CF6-50 jet engine.

At the same time, the character and functioning of the French administrative elite have tended to facilitate the implementation of mission-oriented programs. The highly selective engineering schools (*grandes ecoles*) have acted as a key filter for recruitment into the senior ranks of the administrative system. These same schools have provided the top management of the technologically oriented enterprises. Moreover, each of the major schools has had its own area of exclusive competence (for example, aerospace, power engineering, or telecommunications), and their graduates have tended to dominate both those parts of government involved with that specific competence and the associated firms. Last, but not least, the best graduates from each school—regardless of whether they work in the public or private sectors—have generally been members of the same technical corps or guild, which, with official recognition, monitors and helps to arrange their careers.[23] As a result, the senior decision makers in a government ministry or agency are likely to have shared a socialization with their counterparts in the private sector. The top private-sector manager often will have worked in government and will therefore be sensitive to the constraints this involves, and managerial performance will be monitored not only by the administrative apparatus but by their corps, which will be concerned to avoid failures that could lead it to lose prestige or, even worse, to give up turf. All of this can be seen as reducing the transactions costs involved in the design and execution of mission-oriented programs, notably by better aligning the incentives of each party, facilitating communications between them, and providing peer group sanction against opportunism.

The degree to which these factors have been sufficient to offset the many sources of inefficiency in administrative coordination is difficult to judge. As Jacques Delors, then minister of economics, noted in 1983, few cost-benefit studies have been done, and even fewer published.[24] Even without secrecy laws as stringent as those in the United Kingdom, the compact nature of the French elite has led all too often to concerted attempts to suppress critical analyses[25] while rejecting their findings as jeopardizing "France's industrial imperative; that is, the will to survive of industries exposed to fundamental threats and the will to act of a state confronted by the deceleration of its national growth."[26] Assessments, therefore, must be based on fragmentary evidence, yet a pattern does emerge from the published sources.

First, to the extent to which there have been successes, they have been in areas in which the programs were geared to public procurement, were monitored by their prospective users, and were involved primarily in "stretching" technologies that were already available. Thus, in the nuclear program, the French graphite-gas approach had to be abandoned, but the industry was capable of taking the Westinghouse PWR and reducing its costs by the adaptation, incremental improvement, and repeated implementation of what it made into a highly standardized design. Equally, in telecommunications, the Alcatel E10 electronic switching system was based on a design far simpler than that of any of its competitors, yet it became and (until recently) remained competitive by being the first of these systems to secure economies of large-scale production. Finally, the same holds for the TGV, or high-speed train. It entailed a far simpler approach than the magnetic levitation mechanisms pursued in Germany and Japan and was less versatile than the design sponsored by British Rail, but it was capable of being implemented sooner and on a larger scale. In each of these cases, effective user-supplier cooperation allowed steady improvement in complex technical systems, with the integrated nature of the French elite making this cooperation much easier to achieve.

Second, even in these areas, "each success," notes one of the foremost analysts of French technology policy, "seems to have been inexorably shadowed by a failure."[27] In part, this reflects a commonality of approach: the attempt to achieve scale economies through a crash program of domestic market expansion; the consequent rapid scaling-up of industry capacity, with the industry then experiencing acute financial difficulties when growth slowed in the domestic market. Yet more fundamental factors were also at work: the fact that the products for which world markets were being sought were not clearly technically superior; an insufficient emphasis on marketing and customer service; the difficulty of introducing product and systems engineering technology into contexts where the French "old school tie" does not hold sway; and the tendency to react to difficulties by seeking government assistance rather than by devising and implementing a commercial response. Durable success has, therefore, been a rare phenomenon, notably in the export markets. Thus, these programs have come to entail a financial burden that (despite expedients such as transferring large funding responsibilities onto France Telecom) increasingly conflicts with fiscal constraints.

Finally, none of the mission-oriented programs implemented in industries serving mass—or at least decentralized—markets has come anywhere close to success. In these industries, the public sector cannot act as the leading-edge buyer; that is, as a test for commercial markets. Rather, its interventions have tended to distract the firms involved from the reality of market development. In the computer industry, for example, successive governments have sought to support Bull, a partly state-owned computer manufacturer, through preferential procurement. But the resulting heavy reliance on public markets has tied Bull to a far broader product line than it could sustain, freed it of the need to develop commercial marketing skills, and cut it off from knowledge of market trends. Equally, in VCRs, the attempt to shelter Thomson from Japanese competition may have allowed the French firm to raise its prices, but it did nothing to bridge the cost and quality gap that made it virtually impossible for Thomson's VCRs to be sold outside France. Finally, a large-scale attempt in the mid-1980s to salvage the French numerical machine-tool industry proved no more successful than its British equivalent some fifteen years earlier, although the industry's de facto nationalization did reduce the losses that exit otherwise would have imposed on the firms' former owners.

The 1980s and early 1990s have not seen a fundamental reconsideration of these industrial policies. In theory, governments have become less interventionist since 1983; in practice, however, the French system works much as it always has. Indeed, the consensus seems to be that these policies are all the more essential in the face of stronger competition from Japan. The only real question is about France's ability to bear this "burden" on its own. The key issue then becomes that of the scope for action on industrial policy at a European level. This, however, is conceived as a change in scale rather than in kind of industrial policy.

The German Experience

This approach might at first seem to clash with the traditionally more market-oriented approach to industrial policy adopted in Germany. But the reality of the situation is more complex. It is indeed true that German technology policy has been far more decentralized than policies in the United Kingdom and France. It has also placed greater emphasis on the mechanisms that accelerate the diffusion of technological capabilities throughout the industrial base, and notably to small- and medium-sized enterprises. Then, too, the administration of the programs has relied more heavily on the subnational units of government and on the delegation of functions to independent bodies. These diffusion-oriented policies have centered on the system of industrial standardization, on an extensive network of cooperative research institutions, and on the apprenticeship system. They are important elements in the German story and must take some credit for the high technical level of German industry.[28] Yet there has also been, and remains, an extensive system of direct involvement in large-scale, mission-oriented research and development.

Germany got off to a slow start in mission-oriented industrial policy. The German background paper to the 1963 OECD ministerial was highly critical of direct government involvement in industrial research and development, suggesting that policymakers might want to concentrate on improving the patent system. An OECD review team in 1965 questioned the hands-off approach to industrial research and asked "whether German industry will be able to maintain its current financial independence, or whether international developments will not require government funding and coordination of costly and long-term programs in areas such as computers and automation."[29] The report suggested that, should such pressures become apparent, the U.K. model (then centered on a Ministry of Technology) provided a useful point of reference. By that time, the pressures in favor of a domestic policy of technology promotion were very strong. By the late 1960s significant targeted support programs were under way in nuclear power, computers, and aerospace, with semiconductors and telecommunications joining the list in the 1970s.

The implementation of these programs in Germany has differed somewhat from that of France and the United Kingdom, notably in terms of the nature of the relationships between the funding agencies and the performers of research. By and large, mission-oriented research in Germany is done in industrial firms, with public laboratories playing a minor role. It is the firms that tend to set the research agenda, rather than the sponsors. In telecommunications, Siemens may receive considerable direct and indirect funding from the telecommunications utility, but it would not accept the degree of involvement by that utility in its decision making that accompanies such funding in France and the United Kingdom. Power in the system therefore tends to lie more squarely with the performers. These firms also bear a higher share of the financial risk than do their French or British counterparts.[30]

The mission-oriented programs in Germany, however, do not appear to have been outstanding successes. In particular, the successive measures in support of information technology are widely (and rightly) judged to have been failures, and the continuing difficulties of firms in the industries being targeted have led to growing concentration, with Siemens becoming increasingly dominant in electronics and Daimler Benz becoming completely dominant in the defense market. This lack of success has not seriously jeopardized the legitimacy or stability of these programs. Rather, much as in France, the political debate has centered on whether such actions were not doomed to fail if taken by each European country acting independently. The scale of the effort, and not its conception, has been viewed as the problem, further strengthening the push to a Europe-wide approach to industrial policy.

Multinational Approaches

The developments in Britain, France, and Germany point in a common direction for industrial policy in Europe, that of internationalizing the mission-oriented effort. Repeated attempts to move in this direction have been made in the past; the record of these provides the backdrop to more recent trends. The first such steps were taken even before the ratification (in 1956) of the Rome Treaty with the decision to set up Euroatom as a coordinating framework for the development of European nuclear research. In practice, the French viewed Euroatom primarily as a way of controlling the German research effort and, "[having] consistently expressed more interest in a community for atomic energy than in a common market,"[31] insisted upon it as a quid pro quo for proceeding with the Treaty of Rome. Under the Paris Agreements, Germany could not carry out nuclear research for military purposes. By requiring the Germans to secure all fissile material from Euroatom, the Euroatom Treaty was designed to ensure that any civilian research they did obtain would be subject to a de facto French veto. France was not, however, willing to forego its sovereignty in the nuclear field, and so retained the vast bulk of its own nuclear program outside Euroatom. The Euroatom framework rapidly became an empty box, administered at considerable cost by the European Commission but with little to show for itself.

With the failure of Euroatom, the Commission's direct role in promoting technological development became negligible. But this has not prevented cooperative efforts from proceeding, both through project-specific consortia (as in the Concorde and subsequently the Tornado) and by the establishment of specialized program management agencies (as in the European Launcher Development Organization, ELDO, and the European Space Research Organization, ESRO). In each case, the stated goals have been similar: to achieve greater program effectiveness by pooling resources and complementary skills, to reduce costs by achieving economies of scale, to promote longer-term and cross-border rationalization and specialization, to strengthen the competitive position of European firms in these activities, and to be able to avoid having to rely on "technology from other lands [which] results in a degenerative effect on creative ability, a dependence on external resources, and increases emigration of trained men."[32]

Underpinning these goals has been the presumption that duplication—having similar programs under way in different countries—is harmful, and that joint efforts can reduce costs to all. In practice, the joint programs have rarely, if ever, had this effect. A key factor has been that the major countries have not viewed the cooperative efforts as alternatives to their national programs. Rather, they have seen them as a way of perpetuating and further strengthening domestic capabilities. In other words, they have not been interested in foregoing what they perceive as their own independence; instead, they have looked to the programs to help them maintain a presence in the broader markets across the board. As a French minister of defense put it, "It may seem paradoxical, but our primary goal in cooperation is to retain control and autonomy. . . . Without cooperation, we would have to abandon the presence we now have in all key sectors; we would have to specialize, which would inevitably lead to a loss of independence."

Given this attitude, the participating countries have insisted on what has become known as the principle of *juste retour*. That is, that each country should receive from each program an amount about equal to its contribution to that program. This has had both short-run and long-run effects. The most immediate consequence has been to impose on these programs complex production-sharing arrangements that substantially increase unit costs. In Airbus, for example, the assembly of an airplane starts with the two fuselage sections and the vertical tail stabilizer, produced in any one of six German factories. Then the cockpit, the front, and the central fuselage section come from four factories in France. British Aerospace wings (which themselves rely on inputs from seven other consortium factories) are then added, together with inputs from Spain. Finally, all the pieces are flown to France for final assembly. Economies of scale are almost entirely unexploited, the pace of work is slowed to that of the weakest link, and the desire to avoid outages in the complex supply chain leads to the carrying of excessive inventories.

These costs and delays have been escalated by the administrative procedures put in place by the countries to monitor the implementation of the *juste retour* and to protect their interests. In Concorde, for example, governmental approval was needed even for modifications to the toilet equipment,[34] and cumbersome decision-making machinery, requiring seemingly constant travel by government officials, has been a persistent feature of subsequent major programs. Despite incessant meetings, the ability to actually decide is hampered by the fact that "the government of every country is paralyzed overall for perhaps 10 to 20 percent of the time because of impending elections, a ministerial reshuffle, or a currency crisis . . . [and given] ten governments with uncorrelated periods of paralysis, the days when all are in a position to take decisions are rather few."[35] All of this hardly makes for the flexible response widely considered essential to success in technological innovation.

Seen over the longer run, the *juste retour* has perpetuated the problem the joint programs were intended to correct, namely the duplication of research and production facilities. This has happened first and foremost because the participating countries have insisted on it. For the Concorde, there were two final assembly lines, in the United Kingdom and in France; for the Tornado, separate assembly lines were established in each country; and for the Airbus, Germany successfully demanded that a second assembly line for the A320 be opened either in Hamburg or in Munich. The problem with duplication has been aggravated by the incentives which the *juste retour* principle creates for each country to "defect" from the pooling approach. In effect, countries have tended to get larger shares of the retour when they can bring critical skills to the table. Thus, the greater a country's technological strength relative to that of the other parties, the larger the return it can hope for. The larger countries, in particular, have built up parallel programs to those under way cooperatively, hoping to recoup some of the costs this imposes through a higher return share in subsequent agreements. In the cases for which data are available, the collaborative programs actually appear to have increased total research and development outlays, with unchanged national outlays being joined by rising costs in the cooperative venture.

Given high budgetary costs and the existence of some economies of scale and scope to design and production, the maintenance of duplicative facilities among countries has been paralleled by a trend towards concentration within countries. Thus the "national champion" model has become even more firmly entrenched, with firms such as GEC and BAe totally dominating their fields in the United Kingdom, Thomson and Aerospatiale in France, and Siemens and Daimler Benz in Germany. Because each country has had to be represented in each major contract and there is generally only one firm from each country with the skills required to take part, competition among the firms has been effectively ruled out. There may be competing consortia, but because "the companies which are their nation's sole representative will be members of every consortium . . . [they] cannot lose."[36] The incentives for efficiency have, thereby, been further blunted.

The goals of these collaborative efforts are far from having been met. In case after case, unit costs have risen, the time required for development has lengthened, and genuine rationalization has become even less likely.[37] All of this gives little cause for optimism, yet recent years have seen a determined attempt by the EC Commission to further extend intra-European technological cooperation. The Commission's efforts have relied on three sets of instruments. A first is collaborative research and development programs, aimed at funding "precompetitive" research, initiated by the European Strategic Program for R&D (ESPRIT) in 1984. These programs (modeled after the Alvey Program launched by Mrs. Thatcher's government) assume that collaborative research is necessarily a good thing. Although the funding they provide is small, they do seem to have contributed to a growing number of joint ventures by European companies.

Second, the Commission has been able to buttress direct support for favored technologies with trade protection. Particular emphasis has been placed on controlling competition from Japan, with a series of antidumping and export monitoring measures being used to force Japanese producers to raise European electronics prices by some 20 to 30 percent.[38]

Third, the Commission has to some extent modified its competition policy to accommodate collaborative efforts in high-technology industries. Research and development agreements have been granted a partial exemption from Article 85 of the Treaty of Rome (prohibiting agreements between competitors), and the actual enforcement of EC competition policy—a matter over which the Commission has considerable, and indeed, growing discretion[39]—appears to have erred on the side of leaving the European-owned, technology-advanced firms (as against, for example, IBM) largely unhindered.

Taken together, these instruments provide the Commission with considerable resources, but they have been further strengthened by the Single European Act (1987) and the Treaty of Maastricht. The Maastricht treaty is especially important because it provides, through Article 130, a statutory basis for Community intervention to better exploit the EC's industrial potential. At the same time, a new paragraph added to Article 130f explicitly provides for the unification of Community research and technological development policy, while Article 130h imposes a new obligation on member countries to coordinate their research and technological development policies so as to ensure that national policies and Community policies are mutually consistent. Together with strengthened control (under Articles 92–94 of the Treaty of Rome) over domestic subsidies, and over the Community countries' trade policies (under the Single European Act), these measures could give the EC Commission the leverage over technology policy which until now it has lacked. This is worrying for two reasons.

First, it is clear that the EC Commission intends to make full use of the powers being granted to it. Thus, the Commission's most recent official statement on technology policies argues that, under the principle of subsidiarity, the Commission should have the primary role in all technology development efforts whenever the scale of a program exceeds the resources of individual countries and its effects are felt across countries, meaning that the bulk of the mission-oriented effort would fall under the Commission's responsibilities.[40] There is, however, no reason to believe that the Commission, were its resources substantially reinforced, would act very differently from the national champion model dominant in its member states. Rather, somewhat surprisingly in view of the history, the same statement identified a dispersion of themes, the scattering of resources, and weak selectiveness as "the dangers generally inherent in research activities supported from the public purse," from which it sees a need to further avoid duplication through more rigorous selection. "Actions dealing with technologies of limited importance," declares the Commission, must not be allowed to jeopardize "the resources available for really important projects . . . [such as] microelectronics." Yet the criteria that would be used as the basis for selection and evaluation of these really important projects give no role to factors such as the likelihood of market failure were governments not to act. Instead, it is the increase in competitiveness that is used to justify the involvement of public money in research activities. Even this rationale, however, would not be assessed on cost-benefit grounds. Program evaluation instead would be based on the effect on patents and the technological balance of payments. Such an approach could certainly lend itself to a re-run of some of the most disastrous industrial experiences of recent years.

Second, the procedures envisaged under Maastricht provide the member countries with the degree of control they need to implement a de facto *juste retour*. In effect, the treaty makes acceptance of the EC Commission's framework proposals on research policy conditional on the unanimous approval of the member states under the new, and extremely cumbersome, procedure of co-decision (Article 189b). The Commission, therefore, will face overwhelming pressures to provide something for everyone, with the likelihood that this will lead to a few big projects dispersed throughout the EC. It is difficult to see how this will avoid many of the same consequences that have characterized collaborative programs on research and development and industrial policy in the past.

Conclusions

Three broad conclusions can be drawn from this review of the industrial policy experience in Europe. First, at least in the major European countries, government efforts to selectively promote technologically advanced industries have yielded few positive results. Second, despite this, governments do not appear to have substantially altered their approach to industrial policy, especially in the area of high technology. Third, the desire to continue to pursue these policies makes it increasingly likely that the experiences in the United Kingdom, France, and Germany will be replicated at a European level.

In examining this record for industrial policy, it is fair to wonder whether a different approach to implementation, notably one that placed less burden on the administrative machinery of government, could have led to better outcomes. There may be something in this alternative approach, though the diversity of policies on implementation across the European countries does not seem to have led to a great variety of positive results. It is, however, also fair to ask whether the lack of success does not cast doubt on the fundamental rationale for industrial policy. That rationale may require a rethinking if past errors are not to be repeated.

Three premises for such rethinking appear particularly important. These are (1) that there are technologies that a country somehow needs to have, and which, in the absence of concerted government action, it would not acquire; (2) that these technologies can be discovered by administrative process; and (3) that they will be more effectively secured by a centralized effort than through the duplication and waste that characterizes competitive markets. Yet even taking these premises on board, it may be that industrial policies have grossly overstated the importance of technology to international competition. In a world where human capital is fairly widely dispersed, the ability of any country to persistently derive rents from the command of technological know-how is likely to be very limited. Rather, the ability of firms to compete will depend largely on their organizational capacities—on the ability to mobilize the complex set of resources required, as Alfred Chandler has reminded us, for "constant learning about products, processes, customers, and suppliers."[41] Precisely because this learning occurs within very specific organizational contexts, it is difficult to transfer from one company to another, and hence can provide the durable competitive advantages that firms seek.

Technology policies are not neutral with respect to these organizational and cultural capabilities and conditions. Rather, they tend to distort them, as firms are led to put greater weight on the political process of seeking support and on achieving the technical goals on which the policies focus than on the search for better ways of meeting customers' needs. It may be that this kind of industrial policy generates some advanced technology, but it is unlikely to generate organizations that genuinely know how to compete.

Notes

1. A. Hamilton, 1791, "Report on Manufactures," quoted in F. G. Adams and L. R. Klein, 1983, *Industrial Policies for Growth and Competitiveness,* Lexington, Mass.: Lexington Books.

2. All amounts, unless otherwise indicated, are in U.S. dollars at current exchange rates.

3. This is the share of gross expenditure on research and development (GERD) funds allocated by participating governments.

4. Total subsidies to industry in the OECD area were estimated at around $60 billion in 1989, the latest year for which data are available. However, this estimate reflects substantial under-reporting by some countries and excludes subsidies provided (1) through public procurement (defense procurement alone being some 1.5 percent of OECD GNP) and (2) by subnational units of government. Moreover, it is calculated on a net-cost-to-government basis, and to be comparable to the R&D data (which are on an annual expenditure basis), should be grossed up by a factor of four. National studies suggest that about one-third of this expenditure goes to high-technology industries.

5. See S. Fukukawa, 1990, "Recent Development of Industrial Policy and Business Strategy: Japan," Ministry of International Trade and Industry, Background Information Paper B1-72, Tokyo.

6. K. P. Phillips, 1992, "U.S. Industrial Policy: Inevitable and Ineffective," *Harvard Business Review,* July-August.

7. This term is widely used to refer to the industries with an above-average ratio of research and development expenditures to sales. The U.S. National Science Board defines this group as composed of industrial chemicals, drugs and medicine, engines and turbines, office and computing equipment, aerospace, and scientific instruments. See National Science Board, 1991, *Science and Engineering Indicators—1991,* Washington, D.C.: Government Printing Office.

8. J. F. Kennedy press conference, April 21, 1961, quoted in H. E. McCurdy, 1990, *The Space Station Decision,* Baltimore: Johns Hopkins University Press.

9. Published in French in 1967 and in English by Pelican Books (Harmondsworth) in 1967.

10. The U.S. government was willing only to assure the launch of experimental satellites; operational (that is, commercial) satellites would only be launched if they were judged "compatible" with the INTELSAT system; but the meaning of INTELSAT compatibility had not yet been worked out, and the U.S. government would provide no assurances in this regard. See J. W.

Muller, 1990, *European Collaboration in Advanced Technology,* Amsterdam: Elsevier Science Publishers.

11. R. Vernon, 1971, "The Multinational Enterprise: Power Versus Sovereignty," *Foreign Affairs* 99:736–51.

12. *Defense: Outline of Future Policy Cmnd. 124,* 1957, London: HMSO.

13. For example, those firms that refused to go along with the government's view of how the structure of the aircraft industry should evolve were refused access to government contracts. See especially P. D. Henderson, 1962, "Government and Industry" in *The British Economy in the Nineteen-Fifties,* Oxford University Press.

14. H. Ergas, 1987, "Does Technology Policy Matter?" in B. R. Guile and H. Brooks, eds., *Technology and Global Industry,* National Academy Press.

15. Henderson, 1962, p. 369.

16. See P. D. Henderson, 1977, "Two British Errors: Their Probable Size and Some Possible Lessons," *Oxford Economic Papers* 29:(2)190.

17. P. D. Henderson, speaking on BBC Radio 3, 14 November 1977, quoted in P. Henne Whitehall, 1989, *The Free Press,* New York.

18. See Henderson, 1977 (*Two British Errors . . .*), p. 184.

19. See W. Walker and P. Gummett, 1989, "Britain and the European Armaments Market," in *International Affairs.* Two exceptions are, however, worth noting: Racal, which though originally a defense electronics firm, has diversified successfully into mobile telecommunications (the fact that it was granted one of the two U.K. licenses for cellular mobile telephony helping); and the software firm Logica.

20. The "Lego" analogy was used by A. Grjebine, 1983, in *L'Etat d'urgence,* Paris: Flammarion. Some of the best anecdotal descriptions of the system at work are in E. Cohen and M. Bauer, 1985, *Les grandes manoeuvres industrielles,* Paris: Pierre Belfond, and J. M. Quatrepoint, 1986, *Histoire secrete des dossiers noirs de la gauche,* Paris: Alain Moreau.

21. A point stressed in the memoirs of one of his senior economic advisors, A. Pra, 1978, *Les batailles economiques du General de Gaulle,* Paris: Plon.

22. Michel Debre, cited in E. A. Kolodziej, 1987, *Making and Marketing Arms: The French Experience,* Princeton: Princeton University Press.

23. See especially E. Suleiman, 1978, *Elites in French Society,* Princeton: Princeton University Press, and J. C. Thoenig, 1973, *L'ere des technocrates,* Les Editions d'Organization, Paris.

24. See J. Delors, 1984, "Preface," in J. P. Niche and R. Poinsard, *L'evaluation des politiques publiques,* Paris: Economica.

25. As happened to the Mayer report on the French weapons establishments in the mid-1970s, the Hannoun report on assistance to industry in 1978, and most recently to a 1991 audit study of the Minitel.

26. L. Stoleru, 1973, *L'imperatif industriel,* Paris: Le Seuil. By far the best analysis of how the industrial policy elite responds to criticism remains J. G. Padioleau, 1981, *Quand La France s'enferre,* Paris: Presses Universitaires de France.

27. D. Finon, 1989, *L'echec des surgenerateurs: L'autopsie d'un grand programme,* Presses Universitaires de Grenoble.

28. I have discussed these mechanisms and their operation in Ergas, 1987.

29. OCDE, 1967, *Politiques nationale de la science: Allemagne,* Paris.

30. See R. Sally, 1992, *States and Firms: The Political Economy of French and German Multinational Enterprises in International Competition,* Ph.D. thesis, London School of Economics and Political Science; A. Cawson et al., 1990, *Hostile Brothers: Competition and Closure in the European Electronics Industry,* Oxford: Clarendon Press; and Finon, 1989.

31. M. Jansen, 1975, *History of European Integration 1945–1975.* The University of Amsterdam (Europa Institute Publications).

32. SCL/TPS/217E, 1967, *The Economic Potential for Europe of Applications Satellites,* (ESRO), cited in Muller, 1990.

33. Charles Hernu, September 1984, quoted in Kolodziej, 1987, p. 166.

34. C. Layton, 1969, *European Advanced Technology,* London: George Allen and Unwin.

35. H. Bondi, 1973, "International Collaboration in Advanced Technology," *The World Today* 39:20.

36. Sir Arnold Hall, 1988, "European Co-operation in Armaments Research and Production," *RUSI Journal* 133 (Summer):53–58.

37. See, for example, W. Walker and P. Gummett, 1989, "Britain and the European Armament Market," in *International Affairs;* and K. Hartley, 1988, "The European Defense Market and Industry," in P. Creasey and S. May, *The European Armaments Market,* London: Macmillan.

38. See, for a case study, K. Flamm, 1990, "Semiconductors," in *Europe 1992,* The Brookings Institution, Washington, D.C.

39. See especially V. Korah, 1990, *EEC Competition: Law and Practice,* Oxford: ESC Publishing.

40. Commission of the European Communities, 1992, *Research after Maastricht: An Assessment, A Strategy,* Communication from the Commission to the Council and the European Parliment (SEC (92) 682 Final), Brussels.

41. A. D. Chandler, 1992, "Organizational Capabilities and the Economic History of the Dominant Enterprise," *Journal of Economic Perspectives* 6:79–100.

IV New Approaches to Growth and Development

FOR INDUSTRIAL DEVELOPMENT to be rooted in modern science, linked to the rapidly changing world market, and built upon the existing comparative advantage of agriculture in a region or nation, there must be careful coordination of government expenditures and public policy. The three papers that follow discuss changing concepts of comparative advantage and new views of economies of scale, economies of scope, and the advantages of location that traditionally benefited large firms in urban areas. Gary Anderson, John Melville, and Steve Waldhorn provide guidelines for defining and exploiting a region's comparative advantage. Stuart Rosenfeld focuses on the potential of small- and medium-sized enterprises as sources of competitiveness for rural areas, and Gordon Rausser presents the case for a completely revised view of the path toward industrial development and sustained economic growth.

9 Creating Economically Competitive Regions: The New Comparative Advantage

GARY G. ANDERSON
JOHN MELVILLE
STEVEN WALDHORN

Advances in technology, globalization of competition, and corporate restructuring have changed the global economy. Knowledge is now the dominant source of added value in products and services. Global competition challenges corporations to be world-class in the value of their products and services. To meet this challenge, corporations are restructuring to emphasize core specialties, establishing relationships and alliances with other corporations to produce world-class products and services. With these changes, the comparative advantages of economic regions are now determined by their ability to contribute to the competitiveness of corporations.[1]

These new knowledge-based sources of comparative advantages come not only from the geographic attributes of the region. They also arise from the region's industry clusters, within which enterprises cooperate for mutual competitiveness, and from the economic foundations that provide knowledge-based resources, including human capital, technology, venture and investment capital, advanced physical infrastructure, and an attractive quality of life. Sources of advantage derive, too, from relationships between government, industry, and other regional institutions that provide a supportive environment for competitive business.

At the Center for Economic Competitiveness, SRI International, Gary G. Anderson is a Principal Consultant, John Melville is a Senior Policy Analyist, and Steven Waldhorn is Center Director. SRI is the former Stanford Research Institute, Menlo Park, California.

These new knowledge-based comparative advantages are not static but dynamic; they can be molded with the leadership and collaboration of regional organizations and institutions. A region can enhance its comparative advantages in a three-step process that includes inventorying the present and potential comparative advantages, defining strategies to sustain and develop these comparative advantages, then implementing these strategies through collaborative initiatives among businesses and between business and other regional institutions.

Global Trends and the New Economics

All over the world, in regions as diverse as Arizona, Slovenia, and Hong Kong, a new phenomenon is emerging. Working together, private corporations, public-sector institutions, and governments are creating coalitions and implementing initiatives with the express goal of improving the employment opportunities, economic welfare, and quality of life of their citizens. This approach is being used with success in a variety of economic regions in the United States (Kelley et al. 1992). The basic theme of these initiatives is that a region can offer the opportunities of a healthy economy to its citizens if it possesses comparative advantages that help private enterprises in the region to compete effectively in global markets. These regions have discovered that the types of comparative advantages that are important to corporate competitiveness are not static, but are rather dynamic and can be created and sustained through collaborative regional efforts.

In this paper we attempt to bring together the elements of these efforts, based on the experience of SRI International with many of them, into a framework that demonstrates why these new comparative advantages are important and how regions can create and sustain them. Where possible, we have cited the observations of other authors who are interested in the same phenomenon. However, we must note that those looking for proof that the theories work will have to be patient; the efforts in most cases are too recent to have produced results that can be compared against other regions. Nevertheless, the efforts are widespread enough to be worth examining and understanding.

Over the past twenty-five years, the global economy has changed fundamentally. New technologies, expanding competition, and restructuring corporations have altered the sources of comparative advantage.

- With new technologies, knowledge is now the primary source of added value in products and services rather than raw materials and labor hours.
- Business competition now is carried out on a global basis as corporations strive for success against competitors from all parts of the world.

- Corporations are restructuring themselves to emphasize core competencies, establishing alliances to link their competencies with those of other enterprises.

Knowledge is the Primary Source of Added Value

With rapid advances in technology over the past forty years, the characteristics of products and services have changed. The introduction of microelectronics, information processing software, and advanced materials has altered every aspect of the chain of value-adding operations, from the production of raw materials, through the manufacturing of components, to the assembly of the final product. The parallel chain of innovation, market identification, product development, distribution, and marketing has been altered fundamentally by changes in the technology of collecting, transmitting, and analyzing information; that chain has taken on greater importance in determining the success of the product. The result of these technology-driven changes is that raw materials and labor hours no longer are the sole—or even the primary—determinant of the ultimate value of a product. Knowledge is now the major value-adding ingredient and the major source of competitiveness in products and services.

As a result, the traditional resources that regions offered to industry—and that gave regions their comparative advantages as places for industry to locate and from which to do business—are no longer as important as they once were. The comparative advantages once offered by traditional factors of production, such as raw materials, land, labor, and capital, have given way to new sources of comparative advantage. Today a region's comparative advantage is determined by knowledge-based factors of production, such as trained and adaptable human resources, access to advanced technology, and available risk and investment capital. The proof of this trend is found in the success of regions such as Japan, Singapore, and Hong Kong, which have become economic successes with no raw materials or land to offer, but with the advantages of well-educated workers and access to global markets. By contrast, regions that were able to offer only raw materials and space have been less able to offer a competitive base for global corporations (Reich 1991a).

Global Competition Is Fundamental to Corporate Operations

The advent of new technologies of information management and communication also has changed the geography of competition. Now global markets and global business competition are fundamental factors in corporate strategies and operations. Competitive product development and production is no longer the

province only of traditional industrialized regions but is being carried out successfully within newly developing economies as well. Likewise, information on
market opportunities is available to corporations everywhere in the world. The
result is that business competition is now carried out on a global basis (Ohmae
1990).

Aggressive competition on a global scale means that producers throughout the
world are alert to opportunities for new products and services in any regional
market, and that products and services can find global markets. Likewise, companies in any part of the world can produce a specific product, or a variation that
meets the same need as easily and as quickly as the company that developed the
original innovation. A company that has recognized a specific product opportunity
soon finds itself facing competition for that opportunity from other companies; in
order to maximize the return from its innovation, it must be prepared to compete
in all markets that offer the same opportunity. For companies to succeed, and to
continue to be successful, it is not enough that they produce a product or provide
a service better than other companies in their home region. Now a company must
be among the best in the world in order to maintain its place within its own region
and in the global marketplace (Drucker 1989).

As a result, for a region to attract and retain globally competitive industry, it
must be prepared to offer the industrial operations within its boundaries the ability
to be competitive on a global scale. To attract world-class corporations, a region
must itself be world-class in its ability to support its corporations (Reich 1991b).

Corporate Restructuring Is Altering Economic Relationships
As competition has become more challenging and global markets shared by
global competitors have become the primary factor in business competition,
individual companies have found that traditional organizations and structures no
longer provide the productivity and responsiveness required to maintain their
competitive edge. Not only have they been down-sizing by taking advantage of
new technologies to provide increased productivity and reduce staffs. Corporations also have been shedding their traditional emphasis on self-sufficient operations and vertical integration as a source of efficiency. They have been adapting
to global competition by specializing in the core competencies in which they can
be world-class, and then moving other operations to companies that can supply
particular inputs or provide particular services more efficiently than they can
themselves.

This concept has been extended beyond traditional buyer-supplier relationships to partnering with other companies in corporate alliances. A company that

is strong in, for example, product development will establish relationships with companies having complementary capabilities in manufacturing and marketing in order to produce and distribute the final product. It is now common for a company to identify a product opportunity, then contract with other companies to design particular components, share the manufacturing and assembly operations with still other companies, and establish alliances with yet other companies to market the product (Magnet 1992).

The direct result of this trend is that the boundaries between corporations, and the traditional structures within corporations, have given way to fluid relationships within and among corporations. Regions are finding that these changes in corporate structure make it possible for companies to relocate operations or to establish alliances with companies in other regions if that is necessary to sustain competitiveness. On the other hand, regions that offer a competitive base for a diversified range of industry operations related to some particular product or specialty are in a stronger position to attract and retain enterprises that focus on that particular product or specialty.

Economic Regions Are Taking on New Importance
These changes in the source of added value in products and services, in the competition and market opportunities faced by corporations, and in the structure of corporations and corporate relationships have created a new phenomenon, the *economic region*. Economic regions are defined by economic rather than political relationships. These economic relationships include both those of buyers and suppliers among companies and those between the companies and the economic infrastructure—physical and intellectual—that supports them. This definition of a region in terms of economic relationships was first identified in the 1950s in a study of the economic structure of the New York metropolitan region. That study coined the term *economic agglomerations* to define the gathering of corporations and resources in a region (Hoover and Vernon 1959).

Economic regions are significant in corporate competitiveness and, therefore, in the understanding of new sources of competitive advantage. Within these regions companies maintain close geographic relationships with other companies, and from within these regions companies draw the resources they need to remain competitive. It is for this reason that economic regions have become the fundamental unit of analysis of comparative advantage. Political boundaries do not do an effective job of describing economic regions. In some instances, several economic regions will exist within a political region. In other instances, an economic region may cross political boundaries (Ohmae 1993).

The United States is an example of a political region that is composed of several economic regions. An analysis of the economic regions of the United States shows that in the first sixty years of the twentieth century, the economic conditions of all regions tended to converge. In the past thirty years, however, the economic circumstances of individual regions have moved independently of one another. This change has taken place because individual regions now offer differing sources of comparative advantage to companies located within the region. Within these regions, governments and businesses are realizing that they can rely no longer on national business cycles and national economic policies to assure their economic vitality. Instead, they must establish policies specific to individual economic regions.

Examples of new economic regions that cross political borders within and among countries include the region of Hong Kong and the Pearl River Delta of South China; the industrial regions that now extend across the U.S.-Mexican border; the region from Ann Arbor, Michigan, through Detroit to Windsor, Ontario; the thirty-county area that defines the tri-state New York metropolitan region; and the Silicon Valley/Bay Area region around San Francisco that encompasses three counties and over thirty municipalities. To assure that their individual political jurisdictions can thrive, these economic regions are finding that they must invent new approaches to governance that provide for collaboration and avoid competition among the political jurisdictions within the region.

The dynamics of regional comparative advantage also have changed. Where once comparative advantage was rooted in the natural resources of a nation and was relatively unchanging, comparative advantage is rooted now in the resources of information, knowledge, and experience, which can be changed (Marshall and Tucker 1992). The characteristics of these new sources of comparative advantage mean that the ability of a region to offer a competitive base for corporate operations can be molded by regional action (World Development Report 1991).

SRI has worked successfully with institutions in many regions to enhance the comparative advantage of their regions. These projects have been carried out because the regions have realized that they must be competitive in order to attract and sustain the corporations that provide high-value employment and economic advantages to their citizens. To understand how comparative advantage can be enhanced, it is necessary first to understand the new sources of comparative advantage that have resulted from global trends in technology, competition, and corporate structure.

New Sources of Comparative Advantage

Within the new economics of technological advance, global competition, and corporate specialization, comparative advantage arises from the ability of regions to provide companies with resources that allow them to add value to their products through the application of knowledge. The sources of comparative advantage that provide knowledge inputs to companies can be divided into four categories:

- Geographic attributes that create old and new comparative advantages
- Industry clusters that define the economy of the region
- Economic foundations that support those industry clusters
- Regional leadership and collaboration that influence clusters and foundations

Each of these four categories contributes in its own right to the competitiveness of industry in a region and thus influences the comparative economic advantage of the region. Defining the nature and relative quality of the components of each category is a means for determining the relative comparative advantage of a region at a given point in time. More important in understanding the new economics of comparative advantage is the fact that each of these four categories influences and is influenced by the others, so the comparative advantage of a region is, in fact, the result of a dynamic and constantly changing system of characteristics.

Geographic Attributes

Geographic attributes are important sources of comparative advantage, but they are no longer limited to physical attributes such as land, location, and raw materials; characteristics that determine a region's base of knowledge, experience, and perspective are equally important.

In traditional economics, the physical, demographic, and cultural characteristics of a region—its geographic attributes—were dominant in determining its comparative advantages. The region's raw materials, climate, and location were critical in determining whether it had a comparative advantage in, for example, mining, agriculture, or trade; its demographics determined the size of its markets and the cost of its labor. Even with the new importance of global markets, rapid international exchange of information, and accelerating change in technology and business conditions, these characteristics of the region's geography still play an important part. However, their role now is different. Instead of inexorably determining the economics of a region, they define the region's comparative opportunities for developing global competitiveness.

In the new global economy, new aspects of the region's basic endowments contribute significantly to regional comparative advantage. Among these attributes are the region's location relative to potentially complementary regions (not just relative to potential markets and suppliers), its ethnic base and the implicit cultural relationships, and the market knowledge that has been built up through the region's history.

Complementary Regional Relationships. A new type of economic region is emerging in south China and Hong Kong, in U.S. states bordering on Mexico, and in Eastern Europe. Within this economic region, the connections between complementary capabilities offer opportunities to create new comparative advantages that the respective political regions could not offer. In each of these three examples, one part of the region is characterized by a high level of business knowledge and access to global markets but is constrained by the size of its labor market and/or its geographic limitations.

The case of Hong Kong is well documented. Its earlier rapid growth, rooted in easily available and inexpensive labor, had slowed, while the sophistication of its marketers, managers, and product designers had increased. This knowledge and skill could reach its full potential only when coupled with the large population in the Pearl River Delta of Guandong Province. Likewise, the opportunities for growth in that region of China could be achieved only with the knowledge offered in Hong Kong (CEC 1989a).

Culture and Cultural Relationships. The culture of a region, particularly as it relates to ethnic structure, may offer sources of knowledge-based comparative advantage. Where business success depends on establishing and maintaining credibility and confidence over long distances, such as is the case in corporate alliances and buyer-supplier relationships, a common cultural relationship may be important to competitive success.

Los Angeles offers a good example of how cultural diversity creates regional comparative advantage in the new global economy. Because of its location on the border with Mexico and on the rim of the Pacific Basin, Los Angeles has benefited from emigration from both Latin America and Asia. Now its large Hispanic-American and Asian-American populations give it a source of comparative advantage in linking manufacturing development in northern Mexico with the growing markets of the Pacific.

Market Knowledge. Cultural and locational advantages are working together to offer a new edge for economies that possess knowledge of other markets and sources of supply that enable them to serve as knowledge-based entrepots. A number of economic regions in Eastern Europe possess this attribute that offers to become an important new source of comparative advantage. For example, Maribor is located in Slovenia near the Austrian and Hungarian borders and on natural shipping routes between Western Europe and both Eastern Europe and the Middle East. Its cultural ties and five hundred years of experience in serving eastern markets give it the potential to become a trading center and entrepot linking eastern suppliers with western markets.

Taken together, the physical characteristics of a region's geography have been so dominant in the past that many economists have defined comparative advantage strictly in their terms. These characteristics cannot be ignored because they still play a role in defining or limiting a region's opportunities. However, other attributes that have a basis in knowledge of customers, suppliers, and regional markets are offering new comparative advantages. Nevertheless, these attributes—even when redefined in knowledge-based terms—are not the only or primary source of comparative advantage. New sources are growing in importance based on the industry structure, economic foundations, and governance of a region.

Industrial Clusters

Industrial clusters are an important source of dynamics within economic regions and, in themselves, are an important source of regional comparative advantage.

Industrial clusters are composed of concentrations of competing, complementary, and interdependent firms across several industries. They include component suppliers, service providers, and final product manufacturers. Enterprises in these clusters benefit from and help generate specialized labor pools, readily available suppliers and support services, economies of scale, ease of communication, and efficiency of transportation. This structure, now given the term *industrial clusters,* was identified by SRI in a study of the economic structure of the southern California economy and has been elaborated in other studies (CEC 1988b; Porter 1990).

Traditional economic analysis does not provide accurate information on the characteristics and participants in clusters. Subdividing industries in terms of the type of good or service that each produces, as is done in the Standard Industrial Classification System, simply does not reveal enough about the complex dynamics of regional economic interaction to be useful (CEC 1992a).

Characteristics of Clusters. Complexities of production, specialization in design and development, and the increasing numbers of skills required to produce a final product or service have led successful firms to depend on their ability to establish linkages. They link with suppliers, customers, and alliance partners who together can perform the variety of specialized functions needed for competitiveness more effectively than can any individual firm. Because of the ability of these combinations to respond to change over time and from product to product, clusters are better able to respond through "flexible specialization" to shifting technology and customer needs than could an individual firm (Piore and Sabel 1984).

As important, though more difficult to observe, are the intangible relationships that are developed within clusters. Firms may compete with one another yet still share information, skills, and experience through informal social networks as well as through interfirm movement of employees. Firms that are concerned with the same technologies and markets, though they may not be direct competitors, also have the means to share information about developments in technology or changes in market preferences.

Regions and Clusters. Enterprises that compose clusters generally are located close to one another. Concentrations of enterprises within clusters in a sense define the boundaries of an economic region because of relationships to each other. Ease of access to the other enterprises essential to a firm's success has become more critical. In economic terms, transaction prices increase as the distance between two related firms increases. As a result, the synergy necessary to develop and sustain comparative advantage requires close geographic relationships. Examples of this synergy include "just-in-time" inventory systems and buyer-supplier collaboration in product design and quality management. Firms and industries that are distant from their buyers, suppliers, and competitors seldom generate this synergy.

Some of the most highly publicized clusters are electronics and computer-related clusters found in Silicon Valley and along Route 128 in suburban Boston, Massachusetts. But examples of industrial clusters abound, including

- Los Angeles—aerospace, entertainment, and apparel clusters
- Minneapolis—large-scale computer cluster
- Rochester—optics and optoelectronics cluster
- Tokyo/Osaka—automobiles, microelectronics, camera, and robotics clusters
- Denmark—agricultural and health care products clusters
- Italy—machine tool, ceramic, and ski boot clusters

Forms of Clusters. Clusters take on a variety of different forms, depending on the good or service produced. Many are vertically integrated, with a high concentration of firms involved in raw materials, intermediate components, and final products. This kind of continuum from suppliers to final producers is exemplified by the automobile cluster in the midwestern United States (e.g., iron ore, steel, machinery, chemicals, electronics, parts, automobile manufacturers).

Some clusters are more horizontal in nature, with a high concentration of similar economic activity. This kind of cluster may seem to have unrelated industry components (e.g., R&D operations in biotechnology and computer software in the San Francisco Bay Area), yet it benefits from sharing pools of resources, such as a specialized pool of technicians and administrators ideal for R&D operations. Similar horizontal clusters can form around other functional specialties, such as headquarters operations in New York and Tokyo, production operations in Seoul and Bangkok, or marketing operations in Hong Kong and Singapore.

Clusters sometimes may extend over long distances, including in their sphere of influence "satellite firms" that have succeeded in developing and maintaining close ties to the rest of the cluster. The extended cluster is extremely difficult to sustain unless telecommunications, frequent travel, or similar concerted efforts are made by satellite firms to tap into the synergy of the cluster. Examples of satellite clusters include computer hardware operations in Idaho and Utah linked to primary clusters in Silicon Valley, or software developers and telemarketers in rural Nebraska linked to the telecommunications-based financial services cluster in Omaha. Development of satellite clusters is often a major source of economic vitality in rural or small metropolitan areas (Rosenfeld et al. 1992).

Cluster Life Cycles. Clusters have a life cycle that generates regional economic growth from within. Clusters are composed of individual industrial sectors at various life-cycle states, which produce a composite life cycle for the cluster. Thus, some clusters have existed for some time and are transforming to meet new competitive challenges, such as the computers and software cluster in Silicon Valley. Other clusters are expanding, attracting new firms from other areas as well as generating small firms of their own, such as the telecommunications cluster in Alberta. Clusters may be emerging, generated from the innovation of new technology and supported by the strengths of existing clusters (CEC 1990a). The biotechnology clusters in San Francisco and Boston are examples of recently emerging clusters, generated by scientific discovery within local universities and supported by skills in clean-room processes, micromanufacturing, and equipment development in the existing microelectronics clusters in those regions.

Because of the characteristics of clusters and their dynamics, any successful strategy to enhance comparative advantage must take into account the existing industry clusters in a region. The competitiveness of a region depends not only on the competitiveness of individual firms and the direct exchanges of goods and services necessary for effective business operations, but also on the comparative advantages that arise out of the interchange among firms and the knowledge and experience shared among closely related firms.

Economic Foundations

In order to compete in global markets, regional enterprises require access to knowledge-based economic foundations that provide skilled labor, access to advanced technology, venture and investment capital, appropriate physical infrastructure, and a desirable quality of life.

These foundations, sometimes referred to as economic infrastructure, are the third major source of comparative advantage. In order to compete, individual industry clusters require access to competitive factors of production. In a fast-moving environment of global competition based on the application of knowledge, a number of specific factors are needed for success. Included in these economic foundations are a skilled and adaptable work force, access to technology, availability of risk and investment capital, advanced physical infrastructure, and an attractive quality of life. Each of these factors must be adapted to meeting the needs of the industrial clusters they support.

The importance of these foundations to regional competitiveness was shown in a ground-breaking 1984 SRI study of the Midwest, then becoming known as the Rust Belt. The conventional wisdom was that the midwestern states were losing industry to foreign countries that could offer cheap labor. Instead, SRI found that industry was migrating to other parts of the United States, not overseas. A detailed analysis of measures of the important economic foundations showed that on nearly every measure, the Midwest was losing ground to other regions. Other states were benefiting from industry relocation and expansion because they were more effective in their ability to provide up-to-date training for workers, access to technology through support for university-industry research, availability of capital to support emerging firms, infrastructure to link companies to outside markets through advanced information and transportation channels, and a quality of life that would attract and retain workers (CEC 1984). In more recent projects, the importance of each of these foundations has been shown in more detail.

Skilled and Adaptable Work Force. In order for industry to thrive in changing markets, enterprises must have access to a work force that has the necessary skills to perform new tasks and manage new processes. Institutions must help workers maintain the ability to continue developing skills as technologies and markets change. Finally, workers must have the incentives and structure to perform high-quality work.

As Hong Kong was faced with competition from lower-wage regions for low-skilled manufacturing jobs, its best opportunity was to develop a work force that could undertake value-added jobs in product design and manufacturing management. SRI found that the college and university system in Hong Kong was weak in its ability to train engineers, making it difficult to take advantage of this opportunity. As a result of project recommendations, Hong Kong has established a new polytechnic university with the support of government and business. This new institution is beginning to provide trained engineers to Hong Kong companies, increasing their ability to manage workers producing high-technology goods in the Pearl River Delta area near Hong Kong (CEC 1989a).

In the United States, the role of infrastructure in providing appropriate skills in education was identified in an SRI study done in Baltimore, Maryland. The Baltimore area had a bifurcated economy, with major federal R&D labs on the one hand and a traditional manufacturing sector on the other. Johns Hopkins University viewed itself as a world university not connected to the local economy, and so in general there was very little connection between the world of research and that of business. The study showed that industry was not developing in the region because of this lack of access to appropriately educated workers. When a working coalition of executives from both public and private institutions came to see this as a real issue for the future economic development of the region, it energized a group called the Greater Baltimore Committee. The committee laid out an agenda for a new business school in Baltimore, provided a design for new apprenticeship training programs for the community, and encouraged Johns Hopkins to link its research and education more closely to the needs of Maryland (CEC 1988a).

Access to Technology. In order for industry to compete in the technology-based markets of today and tomorrow, research competence, technology training, and diffusion of new product and process knowledge must be available within the region. A region that can provide this access to technology has a comparative advantage in attracting, retaining, and supporting industry. A major trend in state economic development programs over the past ten years has been the establishment of university-industry research programs to provide technology access.

In New York State, SRI had the opportunity to study ten centers for advanced technology that had been founded eight years previously to stimulate exchange of technology information between universities and industry. SRI found that a number of these centers had been quite successful, not only in supporting industry-focused research in their regions, but also in transferring skills and knowledge to industry and in providing a base for new technology-based companies. These centers had been successful in supporting industry clusters in computer software, financial services, telecommunications, and advanced manufacturing, all significant to the economy of the state. A benefit-cost analysis of this program by SRI and Pennsylvania State University has shown that the direct and measurable economic benefits of these centers, in terms of improving productivity and creating new employment opportunities, were more than four times greater than the state's investment in the programs (CEC 1992b).

A similar program in Alberta illustrates the impact that an effectively structured and managed technology access program can have in helping an emerging industry cluster to become established. The Alberta Center for Telecommunications Research, with research support from the province's two leading universities, and funding and participation by industry, has been helped in the emergence of a telecommunications technology cluster in the province from the region's capabilities in telecommunications equipment manufacturing. Technology access by itself, however, is not sufficient to develop an industry cluster. The Alberta Microelectronics Research Center, though performing excellent research, has not been sufficient to foster growth of a semiconductor industry in the province, even with significant assistance from the provincial government, because it lacks industry partners in the province and thus has no cluster to which to transfer its knowledge and trained graduates (CEC 1990b).

Availability of Capital. For industry to develop and maintain its competitiveness, sufficient capital must be available at an affordable price for all types of business. Necessary forms include venture capital, to support establishment of new firms in emerging markets and technologies, and investment capital, to support the modernization and transformation of mature industry clusters. Availability of such capital is an important comparative advantage for an economic region.

The importance of a pool of venture capital readily available to start-up firms was illustrated in an SRI study of why the Illinois economy is encountering difficulties relative to other regions. In Chicago, a sophisticated financial services industry has been successful in generating venture capital and establishing venture capital investment funds. Nevertheless, Illinois ranks low compared to other states in its generation of new enterprises. Availability of capital includes not only the generation of that capital, but also the ability to transfer it to local industry. Interviews with entrepreneurs and investors indicated that the venture capital community was unaware of local venture opportunities in technology-based start-up companies, and that a conservative banking system was not prepared to extend financing to small companies. Identifying these bottlenecks in availability of capital has led to definition of initiatives to increase awareness of local venture opportunities. These may help to alleviate the problem and help Illinois start small businesses and retain the small businesses that its excellent university system is generating (CEC 1992c).

In the new country of Slovenia, established in 1990 from the ex-Yugoslavian province, the economy is encountering difficulties similar to those of others throughout Eastern Europe who are making the transition to a free-market economy. One major difficulty is that of generating new investment capital to support the establishment and transformation of enterprises in industry clusters that offer promise for the future. SRI identified two problems contributing to this difficulty. First, western investors have been reluctant to invest where potential was not obvious. Second, social pressures to maintain employment by supporting the old socially owned companies have prevented capital from flowing to the most promising new investment opportunities. In *Maribor Jutri (Maribor Tomorrow)*, the community leadership of Maribor, with the assistance of SRI, has defined a set of initiatives to address these problems, among others. The community is developing a strategic plan with which to seek investment from western banks and international institutions to support development of new businesses, and it is working with the national government to restructure and privatize industry so that businesses with the greatest promise will have access to investment support (CEC 1992d).

Advanced Physical Infrastructure. Physical infrastructure is a base for industrial development and so generally has been included in lists of traditional sources of comparative advantage. However, in a global economy composed of technology-based companies, the old definitions have to be expanded. In addition to basic transportation, water, low-cost energy, and waste disposal, economic regions can develop comparative advantages through their ability to provide advanced infrastructure that supports specific industry needs; for example, high-quality, uninterruptible sources of electricity, effective mass transit and high-speed personal and industrial transportation systems, and waste disposal procedures that can handle toxic industrial wastes. Perhaps more important, advanced communications linkages, often called the "highways of tomorrow," must be available to link industry clusters to markets and sources of information within the region and around the world.

A recent SRI study for the State of Oregon is focusing on the telecommunications systems of the state. Two concerns primarily motivated this study. First, in order to provide economic opportunities to rural areas, the state needs an advanced in-state telecommunications system. This system would link rural areas to urban sources of continuing education, and rural companies to established industry clusters on the western coast. Second, for industry in the state to compete in global markets, it must have access to the most advanced international telecommunications capabilities available. A set of public-private initiatives is being designed to provide this source of comparative advantage to industry and to rural regions within the state (CEC 1992e).

Los Angeles is a complex economic region defined by a variety of industry clusters, from aerospace and entertainment to textiles. Developed on the basis of a broad system of modern freeways, the region expanded to absorb a rapidly growing population while sustaining industrial growth. This freeway system was the most advanced in the country when built in the 1950s, but it has reached capacity, and its use is contributing to the pollution problems of the Los Angeles basin. An SRI study of the region's problems and future challenges has illustrated how critically important an advanced transportation system is to maintaining the region's economy and environment (CEC 1991a).

Attractive Quality of Life. For a region to remain competitive, it needs to sustain a high quality of life. That quality is reflected in distinctive regional amenities that are attractive to residents and outside visitors and investors, as well as in strong basic community health, reflected in limited social problems, good availability of housing, and fulfillment of other basic needs that make the region an effective place to live and work.

The value of this comparative advantage is illustrated in the history of development of Silicon Valley and in the emerging problems that now are slowing growth in the region. In the early 1980s SRI studied the development of the region to try to explain how this vibrant economy of advanced industry clusters had evolved. In addition to the other comparative advantages of a strong university system and easy access to venture capital, the climate, housing, and social stability of the region were identified as important in retaining the entrepreneurial and innovation talent and the technical labor force needed to support rapid technological growth (CEC 1985). A current SRI study now indicates that the declining ability of the region to maintain this quality of life is making it difficult for industry to continue to expand in the valley. Increasing pollution, lack of affordable housing, and growing disparities between upper and lower income classes are challenging the future of the valley. The project arising out of this current study is seeking to establish public-private initiatives to identify and address the sources of these problems as a means to revitalize economic growth (CEC 1992f).

Leadership and Collaboration

Comparative advantages in the new economics are not static; they can be positively influenced through strong public-private leadership and collaborative action.

The fourth category of new sources of comparative advantage deals with the environment for business created in an economic region, and the ability of the region to define and undertake specific initiatives to enhance comparative advantages in its industry clusters and economic foundations.

Leaders from government and industry in regions that are seeking to enhance knowledge-based comparative advantages are taking on leadership roles and forming institutions to achieve economic advantage. The emerging trend is one of government and industry working together in a variety of institutional structures and relationships to explicitly define and execute strategies for enhancing the comparative advantages of a region.

A variety of temporary and permanent types of new relationships are emerging. Twenty-five years ago, responsibility for specific economic issues was demarcated strictly between those that were to be handled by government (such as education and regulation) and those that were to be handled by individual companies (such as research and capital formation). Today, those demarcations are becoming more fluid and roles are changing, in a "third wave" of governance (Ross and Friedman 1990). Government is responsible not for "rowing the boat, but steering the boat." Public-private partnerships and coalitions of private companies—sometimes loosely coordinated and assisted by government—are as important in dealing with regional economic issues as were government agencies and individual companies acting separately within their own domains in the past (Osborne and Gaebler 1991).

While it rarely shows up in any typical ranking of regions by comparative advantage, such as those promoted for use in site location decisions, the environment for business in a region is frequently mentioned by business executives as an important comparative advantage. That environment often is reflected in its government leadership and its ability to foster collaboration between government and business. Executives choosing to locate in a region frequently mention as positive factors a supportive attitude toward business and close government-business collaboration. Executives explaining why they are relocating operations or not choosing to expand in a region often mention a negative attitude toward business and an adversarial relationship between government and business. The regional business environment is composed both of specific regulations that make it convenient or difficult to do business economically and efficiently in the region, and of more intangible attitudes of cooperation between government and business.

Equally important, the ability of leadership—both public and private—to define a vision for the region and then work to achieve it, and the ability of the region to form collaborations between government and business and among businesses, will influence the region's ability to enhance its comparative advantages. T. J. Rogers, founder of Cypress Semiconductors, expressed this succinctly in a recent speech to the Joint Venture: Silicon Valley collaborative project:

> When I started in business, success was characterized by adversarial relationships; government was an adversary, suppliers and customers were adversaries, and our competitors were our adversaries in a highly competitive game. Now it is becoming clear that to succeed, we must all find ways to work together as allies.

These new comparative advantages of leadership and collaboration take two forms. First, continuing negotiated dialogue between government and business is necessary to establish regulations that will satisfy both common social needs (sometimes at the expense of business) and the needs of individual businesses to operate within regulations that promote their individual ability to compete, at minimal expense to society. Second, leadership and collaborative action is needed to develop common visions for a region, to establish the structure that will allow the region collectively to adapt to change, and to initiate actions that will improve the quality of economic foundations. Such leadership and collaborative action may come through business and government working together on general regional problems, or through enterprises within industry clusters working together on problems specific to their clusters. Two recent SRI projects illustrate the power of leadership and collaboration as a regional comparative advantage.

Enterprise Florida illustrates how public-private coalitions can be more effective in accomplishing economic objectives than can adversarial relationships among public institutions and private industry. Beginning under the leadership of the Florida State Chamber of Commerce, SRI undertook a study of the Florida economy to define the state's economic base and to project its future. This study indicated that while Florida had been successful in attracting some industry to the state through traditional advantages such as a good climate, low labor and land costs, and lack of an income tax, its economy was still based strongly on the wealth brought to the state by tourists and wealthy retirees (CEC 1989b). In the subsequent project, the state's industry and government came together in recognition of what must be done to put the state's economy on a viable basis. This project has led to the establishment of a new public-private organization called Enterprise Florida, which has taken over many of the functions of the state Department of Commerce. This coalition is managed by a board of directors that includes industry and government leaders and has as its mission the promotion and support of industry in the state (CEC 1989c).

Even before the recent formalization of Enterprise Florida, the coalition already had undertaken an analysis of the state's taxation system. The coalition identified problems of raising revenue without an income tax and recommended a value-added tax that would provide needed revenue without constraining business development (CEC 1990c). Projects are being undertaken within individual regions such as Tampa, Palm Beach County, and Jacksonville under the umbrella of Enterprise Florida for specific initiatives in education and training, technology development, local regulation, and telecommunications networking within and among industry clusters to support efficient exchange of information on product needs, employment opportunities, and industry capabilities (CEC 1992g).

The Arizona Strategic Plan for Economic Development illustrates how leadership and collaboration within industry clusters, with the support of government, can establish the basis for revitalizing the economy of a region. In the first study of this project, SRI identified nine industry clusters, ranging from agriculture and mining to aerospace and electronics, that encompassed the economy of the state and the relationships among its individual firms (CEC 1991b). In the second phase of the project, each of these clusters was organized into a task force. Task forces focused on opportunities for development within the cluster and defined requirements for development of economic foundations that would help industry take advantage of these opportunities. The project now has been formalized into an ongoing structure of cluster working groups under the governor's recently announced Arizona Strategic Plan for Economic Development. Each of these cluster working groups is defining and undertaking initiatives, some within the clusters and some with public participation, to create and improve the foundations needed to compete successfully (CEC 1992h). The value of this collaborative public-private approach already is showing as companies in the region choose to expand locally rather than to relocate operations to other regions, citing the new attitude of cooperation within the state as the justification for their decision.

Strategies for Comparative Advantage

The key proposition of this paper is that comparative advantage is a dynamic phenomenon, not a static set of predetermined conditions. Comparative advantage can be defined, developed, and maintained. This proposition has been proven in regions throughout the world, with the economic success of countries of East Asia, including Japan and the "Four Tigers" of Singapore, Hong Kong, Taiwan, and Korea. Closer to home, it has been proven in economic regions such as Florida, Arizona, Kansas, Nebraska, and Oregon. It is in the process of being validated in regions now undertaking new strategies to improve their comparative advantages. The process by which this can be done can be divided into three steps:

- Identifying actual and potential regional advantages
- Defining strategies to gain and maintain comparative advantage
- Implementing regional strategies for comparative advantage

This process can be illustrated through a case study of a project undertaken by SRI in Omaha, Nebraska, for a committee of business executives organized through the Omaha Chamber of Commerce. While this particular project was not as complex or far-reaching as those in Florida and Arizona, in its elements it offers examples of each of the stages in the process (CEC 1991c).

Identifying Actual and Potential Regional Advantages

To translate comparative advantage from a static set of conditions to a dynamic system of continuous improvement, it is necessary first to define, accurately and honestly, the current comparative advantages of a region, then to determine how current comparative advantages can be enhanced to address future opportunities for the region. The process starts with a quantitative and qualitative inventory of the region, using the four categories of comparative advantage already discussed.

Regional Attributes. The region's geographic attributes, historical circumstances, and cultural relationships must be reviewed to identify the current strengths of the region relative to other regions, and the potential—and limitations—of those attributes to define future opportunities. A region with easy access to other regions, and with a background in trade and marketing services, has the potential to become an international business services center. New York, Los Angeles, and Tokyo are developing in this direction. A region with a central location relative to growing markets has the potential to develop an advanced goods-manufacturing base. Centers in the U.S. Midwest and in some regions of central Europe have this potential. By contrast, a geographically isolated region, or one that is not centrally located, is not likely to be successful as a goods-manufacturing center, but it may have opportunities in such areas as telecommunications, or research and development services.

Omaha lies in a region geographically distant from sources of raw materials and international suppliers, and from most potential markets, though centrally located in the United States. The distance to markets and suppliers indicated that a strategy to develop an advanced manufacturing center would be difficult. On the other hand, a strategy based on transportable services could benefit from the central location without being constrained by lack of access to suppliers and markets for manufactured goods.

Industry Clusters. Because most industrial development arises from within the capabilities and experience of existing industry clusters, a profile or map of industry clusters is the second aspect of the inventory of current and potential comparative advantage. County business patterns data, as coded by the Standard Industrial Classification, can be used to calculate industrial concentration quotients, comparing employment concentration in a region with the national percentage concentration of employment in that industry. These indexes identify concentrations of employers producing final goods and services. This data is supplemented by interviews to determine the relationships among final goods and services producers, intermediate producers, and supporting services. The result is the identification of one or more industry clusters that produce tradable products and services, thus forming the core of the region's economy.

Comparison of the recent growth or decline of these regional clusters with global trends in the industry will identify how clusters are performing relative to current international trends, and which clusters have the opportunity to sustain or regain growth based on projected trends. It can also reveal symptoms of problems in the relationships among companies in the cluster (e.g., is the cluster weak in a particular supplied good or service?) or relationships between clusters and economic foundations (e.g., is a cluster declining because of an insufficient supply of trained workers or technology?).

In-depth interviews of corporate managers within clusters is a means for beginning to build industry coalitions that will be essential at later stages in the process. The interviews will identify individuals who understand and are concerned enough about the health of their industry and their region to take leadership roles in defining and implementing strategies.

In Omaha, a quantitative inventory of employment indicated that the region had a cluster of agriculturally related enterprises in food production and processing, although this cluster essentially had been stagnant for a number of years. The region also had a large and growing concentration of employment in financial services (especially insurance), in financial data processing, and in telemarketing. Interviews with industry executives indicated that these enterprises were linked closely to one another in their shared need for information systems, especially large-scale, real-time databases. In addition, there were a growing number of small businesses in specific niche markets, such as telephone billing, that drew on the same abilities to design and maintain computer-based data systems. Out of this analysis, supplemented by interviews, SRI identified the existence of a cluster of what were called information-intensive businesses.

In these interviews, a number of leaders from both large insurance companies and financial data systems, as well as from small supplier companies and the local headquarters of the regional telephone company, were identified as strongly interested and committed to the prosperity of the region and their own companies, and as seeing the two as intimately connected. These leaders were to become the nucleus of a core of leadership in later stages of the project.

Economic Foundations. An inventory of economic foundations is the third phase in profiling the region's comparative advantages and potential. Here a *quantitative* analysis of the strength of foundations is a basis for *qualitative* analysis. A review of indicator data will reveal the region's strengths in its economic foundations relative to other regions. Such data might include, for example, numbers of graduates and individuals with advanced degrees, numbers of patents issued and grants received by research institutes, creation of venture capital and new business formations, miles of roads constructed and numbers of advanced telephone switches, and levels of income and unemployment.

As with data on employment by cluster, these data are only an indication of potential problems; the analysis must be supplemented by qualitative interviews with the leaders of the institutions that provide and support the economic foundations. In particular, the level of understanding and responsiveness of these institutions to the needs of industry clusters in their region will indicate the quality of the economic foundations relative to industry cluster needs. An important element of this inventory is the identification of potential leaders and participants in the second stage of regional development of comparative advantage.

In Omaha, foundations in advanced education are well-developed for a community of that size. Two universities, one private and one public, are located in Omaha, and the state's central university campus is only an hour's drive away. In addition, two local four-year colleges and two community colleges generate graduates and provide opportunities for continuing education at general and technical levels. However, concerns were expressed in interviews that local graduates in data processing were having some difficulty finding employment in the city. At the college level, the institutions were unable to supply all of the training in data processing that the business community needed. Corresponding interviews with personnel and development managers in local companies indicated that the training being provided was not meeting their needs for software engineers and technicians, and that they were going outside the region to find the entry-level engineers they needed and continuing education opportunities for their employees. The problem seemed to be a combination of lack of communication on curriculum needs and lack of institutional resources to meet the level of needs of the business community. As a result, the inventory of comparative advantage in economic foundations indicated a strong institutional system and a well-educated work force, but some specific weaknesses relative to the needs of the region's fastest growing cluster.

Leadership and Coalitions. Within the fourth area of comparative advantage, the quality of the current economic environment, any problems between potential coalition participants and the strength of current and potential leadership must be assessed. This process is highly qualitative, depending on interviews, discussion and focus groups, and community and town hall meetings, to identify both present problems and future capabilities. The earlier inventories of regional attributes, industry cluster structure and potential opportunities, and strengths and weaknesses in economic foundations are useful tools for structuring discussions and uncovering both differences of opinion and areas of consensus on which leadership and collaboration can be built.

In Omaha, SRI found a long-standing tradition of involvement by the community's business leaders in the affairs of the community, and a positive attitude towards business on the part of government. This involvement made it easier to structure and initiate the project, and it offered the potential for forming coalitions to plan and undertake specific programs once these were identified. In addition, the willingness of the business community to support initiatives and seek the support of government would help initiatives to survive changes in government administrations at the city and state levels. This existence of willing leadership and experience in forming coalitions was definitely a strong source of comparative advantage for the community.

Defining Strategies to Gain and Maintain Comparative Advantage

The second phase in gaining and maintaining comparative advantage is the definition of strategies. This phase can be divided into three steps: development of an encompassing vision, identification of requirements to achieve that vision, and development of specific strategies to meet those requirements. In SRI's experience, these steps are most effective when carried out simultaneously at two levels: the general regional level and the level of the individual industry clusters and economic foundations.

Development of Vision. The principle of developing a compelling, specific vision that also reveals requirements for achieving the vision and defining strategies for its achievement is as new as corporate planning principles and as old as the Old Testament, which notes, "Where there is no vision, the people perish." A vision is both a pragmatic tool to reduce options and alternatives to a manageable and easily understood set of objectives, and a strong motivator for attracting participants to the process of definition and implementation of strategies.

This vision should state what the region will seek to become, how those objectives will meet the values and goals of communities in the region, and what the eventual benefits will be. To be effective, the vision should be shared by the stakeholders in the region: industry and government, the leaders of the institutions providing economic foundations, and the general community. The ability of the community to jointly form a vision for itself is a first measure of the probable success of any resulting initiatives. Initiatives that are undertaken without a vision to provide context frequently fail or are superseded by other initiatives because of lack of overarching objectives. Nevertheless, in SRI's experience, formation of a vision is nearly always possible if a community is truly committed to revitalization.

To develop this vision in Omaha, several steps were taken. First, the analyses of the current comparative advantages and limitations of the region were reviewed with a group of leaders from all segments of the community. Then, in individual interviews with these leaders, a concept gradually emerged of what the region wanted to achieve, what it valued, and how it interpreted the analyses in terms of potential opportunities. Finally, a draft statement of the vision was presented to small focus groups, with each group including representatives from each of the stakeholder categories.

The resulting vision was that Omaha would seek to become a leader in the central United States in information-intensive industries—including insurance and financial data-processing services—and related enterprises, through technical development, training, and application of applied information management systems. In this vision, Omaha defined the industry cluster that it wished to develop, its objective in terms of geographic reach and leadership, and the means by which it would achieve the vision.

Identification of Requirements. Having come to a general agreement on the vision for its economic future, a region then must determine what requirements must be met to achieve the vision, in terms of cluster emphasis and development of economic foundations. Here the close relationship between clusters and foundations is a key factor. For some regions the requirements may be very broad, addressing the needs of several clusters that offer opportunities for regional growth and encompassing all economic foundations. In other regions the needs may be more narrow. In either case, the industry clusters need to work within their groups to identify needs. If several clusters are involved, as was the case in Arizona, each cluster must identify the needs specific to its industry; a collaborative effort is used to identify both common needs across clusters and specific needs within clusters.

In Omaha, the challenge was narrower. After the decision was made to focus on the information-intensive industry sector, it was possible to work with small groups and in individual interviews to define a fairly limited set of requirements. Curricula for entry-level engineers needed to be focused more directly on regional needs; means had to be found to provide continuing education opportunities for current employees at both the professional and technical levels; a larger stream of programmers and technicians was needed; and support had to be available for creating small companies in software services support, as well as new financial systems opportunities.

Development of Strategies. Having identified the specific needs that must be addressed if the industry clusters with greatest opportunities for growth are to thrive, strategies to address them must be developed. Two sources of ideas are available in this strategy development. First, there are the examples of other regions from which to draw. An extensive literature has emerged over the past ten years discussing regional economic initiatives. At SRI, there is also a significant amount of research and applications experience on which to draw in identifying initiatives in other regions applicable to the needs of the local clusters. Second, the community itself, and the various stakeholders who have been involved in the process to this point, also may identify specific ideas that have not been tried in other regions. Here the consultant can work to define a set of alternatives and options for consideration by the community.

In Omaha, a number of locally generated ideas and outside examples of best practices were drawn together, and an outline plan was developed for an umbrella organization called an applied information management institute. This organizational plan combined a number of different concepts. A joint committee of business managers and educators would identify education needs and define new curricula in information technology. A coordinating group among all the educational institutions would address problems of course coordination, transfer of credits, sharing of instructors, and so forth. A funding mechanism would be established to provide support from businesses for new courses that the universities and colleges could not develop with existing funds. A continuing education program with a coordinator would locate courses and instructors and provide training opportunities ranging from short executive courses to longer courses in, for example, specific software packages. Finally, a research program would be designed to identify specific research needs of industry and to fund research in the universities. This would serve not so much as a means to develop major technological breakthroughs as it would to attract professors and enhance the region's reputation as a place where leading-edge information technology was maintained (Nebraska Applied Information Management Institute 1992).

Implementing Regional Strategies

The best regional strategies are those that are implemented through the collaborative efforts of all the stakeholders in the community. With growing funding constraints on government and pressures on business to improve the "bottom line," no individual institutional category can be expected to pull the combined weight of an effective set of initiatives. Some initiatives can be undertaken by umbrella collaborations, such as Enterprise Florida, to provide statewide regulation change and to foster a positive relationship between government and business; some initiatives can be undertaken by focused public-private initiatives, such as an industry-funded university research and education center or an apprenticeship program; and some initiatives can be developed by groups of companies working together, such as in a worker retraining program in which companies in an industry cluster share the costs and benefits, rather than expecting one or two leading companies to undertake training that will benefit other companies.

In Omaha, the Nebraska Applied Information (AIM) Institute was incorporated as a nonprofit organization, with a board of directors including government leaders, presidents of the participating universities and colleges, and executives of the major beneficiary companies. Initial funding has been secured from a core group of companies that will participate in the various programs of the institute, and ongoing funding will be secured from payment for services such as education and training programs. Grants also will be sought from state and federal government education and technology programs, though the program is not dependent on securing those grants. In this sense, the AIM Institute broke some new ground: government is being asked to match the contributions from private industry rather than the other way around, as is usually done in government-sponsored industry programs.

The AIM Institute is now established and is in its first year of operation. Already some benefits are being realized through a closer working relationship between industry and education in the community, as well as through a working group of educators from the various institutions sharing ideas and resources in course development. Both situations arose naturally out of the process that led to formation of the institute. Other programs now are being formulated in continuing education and in research that will be implemented over the next two years. The program also is working closely with the Chamber of Commerce to support both the Chamber's small-business development center and the Omaha 2000 education program to improve elementary and secondary education.

Perhaps the greatest value that has arisen from this midwestern effort is that the community came together to identify a major opportunity for economic development, to organize and start working together in a collaborative manner, and to define and implement a long-range strategy with a specific organization composed of all community stakeholders to lead in the efforts. In this way it was able to translate static comparative advantages to a dynamic set of comparative advantages. These advantages support the competitiveness of local industry and should enable Omaha to respond effectively to current opportunities and new developments as they occur in the future.

Conclusions

Over the past twenty years, the economic rules that governed the prosperity of nations have been turned upside down by the growing importance of knowledge in products, the opening up of markets to global competition, and the restructuring of corporations. Many economic regions, whether circumscribed by or transcending political boundaries, have been finding ways to take advantage of the new rules of global competition by creating new comparative advantages that increase the abilities of enterprises in their regions to compete. What once was experimental now is being confirmed in more and more regions. Through new public-private efforts to encourage development of industry clusters and to develop economic foundations to support industry competitiveness, these regions are building prosperity. It is a prosperity that, like the knowledge-based resources that underpin it, is not diminished by its application, but can be applied in a positive-sum process throughout the world.

A region cannot count simply on its traditional advantages of location and endowments, nor on the serendipitous development of industry clusters and general improvements in economic foundations to gain and maintain comparative advantage. In a world where competition is carried out on a global scale, those regions that create and sustain knowledge-based comparative advantages to support the competitiveness of their industry are most likely to win the fruits of continuing economic vitality.

Note

1. The framework and perspective presented in this paper is based on ten years of work by the Center for Economic Competitiveness (SRI International, Menlo Park, California). As such, it represents the combined views and insights of all staff members. In particular, the contributions of the authors' colleagues—Jim Gollub, Eric Hansen, Doug Henton, Ted Lyman, Jennifer Riggers, Eric Rosenfeld, and Kim Walesh—are acknowledged and appreciated.

References

The purpose of this paper has been to place into a comprehensive framework the experience of SRI's Center for Economic Competitiveness in helping regions to identify and enhance their comparative advantages. Listed here are general references from economic development litera-ture that validate the concepts presented in this paper, as well as SRI reports describing the examples used.

Drucker, Peter F. 1989. *The New Realities.* New York: Harper & Row.

Hoover, Edgar, and Ray Vernon. 1959. *The Anatomy of a Metropolis.* Cambridge, Mass.: Harvard University Press.

Kelley, Kevin, Joseph Weber, Janin Friend, Sandra Atchison, Gail DeGeorge, and William H. Holstein. 1992. "Hot Spots: America's New Growth Regions." *Business Week* (October 19): 80–88.

Magnet, Myron. 1992. "Who's Winning the Information Revolution." *Fortune* 126(12):110–17.

Marshall, Ray, and Marc Tucker. 1992. *Thinking for a Living: Education and the Wealth of Nations.* New York: Basic Books.

Nebraska Applied Information Management Institute. 1992. Institute brochure. Omaha.

Ohmae, Kenichi. 1990. *The Borderless World: Power and Strategy in the Interlinked Economy.* New York: Harper Collins.

———. 1993. "Trade Watchers Should Focus on Regions, Not Nations." *Wall Street Journal,* January 27.

Osborne, David, and Ted Gaebler. 1991. *Reinventing Government: How the Entrepreneurial Spirit Is Transforming the Public Sector.* Reading, Mass.: Addison-Wesley.

Piore, Michael J., and Charles F. Sabel. 1984. *The Second Industrial Divide: Possibilities for Prosperity.* New York: Basic Books.

Porter, Michael. 1990. *The Competitive Advantage of Nations.* New York: The Free Press.

Reich, Robert B. 1991a. *The Work of Nations: Preparing Ourselves for 21st Century Capitalism.* New York: Alfred A. Knopf.

———. 1991b. "The Real Economy." *The Atlantic* (February):35–52."

Rosenfeld, Stuart, Philip Shapira, and J. Trent Williams. 1992. *Smart Firms in Small Towns.* Washington, D.C.: The Aspen Institute.

Ross, Doug, and Robert E. Friedman. 1990. "The Emerging Third Wave: New Economic Development Strategies for the '90s." *Entrepreneurial Economy Review* 9(1):3–10.

World Development Report. 1991. *The Challenge of Development.* Oxford, England: Oxford University Press.

SRI Reports

Center for Economic Competitiveness (CEC). 1984. *Choosing a Future: Steps to Revitalize the Mid-American Economy over the Next Decade.* Menlo Park, Calif.: SRI International.

———. 1985. *Success Factors in the Development of Silicon Valley.* Menlo Park, Calif.: SRI International.

———. 1988a. *From Bystander to Leader: Challenging Higher Education To Join in Building Baltimore's Economic Future.* Menlo Park, Calif.: SRI International.

———. 1988b. *Understanding Southern California's Economy: How Converging Forces Drive the Region's Dynamic Industrial Clusters.* Menlo Park, Calif.: SRI International.

———. 1989a. *Building Prosperity: A Five-Part Economic Strategy for Hong Kong's Future.* Menlo Park, Calif.: SRI International.

———. 1989b. *Cornerstone Florida: Foundations for Economic Leadership.* Menlo Park, Calif.: SRI International.

———. 1989c. *Enterprise Florida: Growing the Future.* Menlo Park, Calif.: SRI International.

———. 1990a. *Economic Success in the 1990s: A New Perspective and Analytical Approach.* Menlo Park, Calif.: SRI International.

———. 1990b. *Assessment of Alberta Technology Centres.* Menlo Park, Calif.: SRI International.

———. 1990c. *Crossroads: Designing Florida's Tax Structure.* Menlo Park, Calif.: SRI International.

———. 1991a. *The Changing Southern California Economy: Implications for Southern California Edison.* Menlo Park, Calif.: SRI International.

———. 1991b. *New Foundations for Arizona's Future: Defining Economic Development for the 1990s.* Menlo Park, Calif.: SRI International.

———. 1991c. *Achieving Leadership in Information-Intensive Industries: A Plan to Establish the Nebraska Applied Information Management Institute.* Menlo Park, Calif.: SRI International.

———. 1992a. *Understanding the Dynamics of Economic Regions.* Menlo Park, Calif.: SRI International.

———. 1992b. *New York State Centers for Advanced Technology Program: Evaluating Past Performance and Preparing for the Future.* Menlo Park, Calif.: SRI International.

———. 1992c. *Economic Leadership in Illinois: New Approaches for the 1990s.* Menlo Park, Calif.: SRI International.

———. 1992d. *Maribor Jutri: Creating a New Economy for the Region and Its Citizens.* Menlo Park, Calif.: SRI International.

———. 1992e. *Oregon Connects: A Telecommunications Vision and Plan for Oregon.* Menlo Park, Calif.: SRI International.

_____. 1992f. *Joint Venture: Silicon Valley—An Economy at Risk.* Menlo Park, Calif.: SRI International.

_____. 1992g. *Creating an Enterprise Network: Palm Beach County's Economic Strategy.* Menlo Park, Calif.: SRI International.

_____. 1992h. *Creating a 21st-Century Economy: Arizona Strategic Plan for Economic Development.* Menlo Park, Calif.: SRI International.

10 Building Industrial Competitiveness in Rural Areas

STUART A. ROSENFELD

Industrialization as an economic development strategy is not new to rural America. As early as 1914 the Smith-Lever Act, which authorized a national cooperative extension service for agriculture, also provided for assistance for industrial development to counties with low concentrations of farm employment. At the time the Smith-Lever Act was passed, concentrations of manufacturing plants in rural areas were rare exceptions. Most rural employment was on the farm or related to farm production. That has not been the case over the past half century, and manufacturing now employs many times more people than does agriculture, even in rural areas. Manufacturing plants and industrial parks can be found interspersed among farms and small towns in almost any region of the nation. The U.S. Department of Agriculture now lists 678 nonmetropolitan counties as "manufacturing-dependent" counties, in which more than 30 percent of the work force is employed in manufacturing. Off-the-farm manufacturing jobs also provide many farm family members with added income, making it possible for them to operate part-time farms that produce only marginal income from farming activities.

The road to industrial jobs—that is, recruitment of branch plants to rural areas—was paved with industrial revenue bonds and tax breaks nearly sixty years ago. It began in Mississippi with the state's Balance Agriculture with Industry legislation, passed in 1936. Ever since, rural areas have been handing out generous

Stuart A. Rosenfeld is President of Regional Technology Strategies, Inc., a nonprofit organization in Chapel Hill, North Carolina, dedicated to researching, designing, implementing, and assessing technology-based development strategies.

and ever-escalating amounts of subsidies, free training, and other inducements to lure branch plants. Rural areas aggressively—and successfully—recruited branch plants seeking to escape the higher costs and better-organized labor in the cities. The book *Industrial Invasion of Nonmetropolitan America* (Summers et al. 1976) documented examples of rural industrialization and its impacts, most of which were viewed by rural areas as beneficial. But today manufacturing employment is in decline in these same rural areas that once attracted branch plants. Even in much of the rural South, where the most vigorous recruitment took place (much of it in nondurable, agriculture-related manufacturing), employment has been declining. *After the Factories* (Rosenfeld et al. 1985) documented the decline, and *Shadows in the Sunbelt* (Autry 1985) coined the term *buffalo hunt* for branch plant recruitment. Sad to say, much of the loss of jobs has been caused *not* by innovation and rapid productivity growth producing much more with less labor input, as was the case in American agriculture, but by *lack* of innovation and competitiveness.

This paper focuses on the following arguments:

1. Our industrial policy has been misdirected by concentrating too much on branch plants and on making *locations* competitive, and by paying too little attention to small independent firms and to making *industries* more competitive.

2. The historical lessons and experiences of agriculture apply not only to industry; they represent promising elements of any comprehensive industrial policy.

3. New approaches and policies that enhance industrial competitiveness and improve the comparative advantage of rural and agricultural areas will, in the long run, have a greater impact on those areas.

The Situation Today

Most of the manufacturers that located in rural areas were labor-intensive branch plants attracted by low wages, an available labor force, and a strong work ethic of rural people. Competition primarily was among cities and states, not among regions or nations. In addition to the industrial jobs that resulted from recruitment, many children of farmers put the entrepreneurial and mechanical skills they acquired on the farm and in agricultural education to use by becoming artisans. With little fanfare and little government assistance, many started small manufacturing firms, which now supply larger corporations and specialty markets. About 90 percent of all manufacturers in the United States are small or medium-sized (fewer than 250 employees), independently owned manufacturing enterprises that produce parts and components for original equipment manufacturers and fill important niche markets. These companies are commonly called SMEs (small- and medium-sized enterprises). More than 350 thousand SMEs in the United States employ about eight million workers, which represents about two-fifths of the nation's manufacturing employment; these firms contribute about one-third of the value added in manufacturing. Across the nation, about one-fifth of all SMEs are located in nonmetropolitan counties, but that varies considerably by region. In the Deep South states of Alabama, Georgia, and Mississippi, for example, 51 percent of small- and medium-sized manufacturing plants are located in nonmetropolitan counties. In the nonmetro counties of those states they employ 41 percent, 38 percent, and 32 percent, respectively, of the nonagricultural work force. While some of these smaller plants are branches of large corporations, most are independently owned.

For both the giant corporation and the SME, the world is changing. Customer preferences and expectations, the nature of the competition, and the markets are not what they once were. The first two factors potentially favor smaller firms, while the changes in market loom as an obstacle to many small and rural firms.

First, customers—both consumers and next-stage producers—are becoming more discriminating, and manufacturers must be much more responsive to their demands for quality, design, reliability, and timeliness. As a result, American industry is moving away from mass production by giant corporations toward specialized production by smaller and more agile companies, and from vertical integration and heavy investment in plant and equipment toward contractual arrangements with SMEs for parts, components, or services.

But small firms operate according to principles different than those of mass production industries. They generally have many customers and shorter lot sizes, thus SMEs must be able to adapt more quickly to changes in customer demand and design. To operate efficiently, they seek economies of scope (the ability to produce short runs as efficiently as long runs), not economies of scale. Workers are expected to do a wide array of tasks and must be more flexible and adaptable. Unfortunately, neither managers nor operators have been prepared for this new style of manufacturing, and governments are not organized to encourage or support an innovative small-firm industrial economy. Both the public and private sectors are looking for new relationships and organizational structures to improve the competitiveness of their industries.

Second, competition for plants is becoming more intense than ever before, and firms are shifting from lower costs to product differentiation and quality for their competitive advantage. Firms that still seek lower costs can and do go to less developed regions, and the stakes (and costs) of "winning" are rising dramatically as states are forced to offer more and more incentives to compete with an increasing number of sites. Many of the other firms want close proximity to suppliers, skilled labor, and scientific expertise, and therefore they gravitate toward urban locations. Thus, many rural sites are losing their historic advantage of low cost. Even North Carolina, one of the most successful recruiters, has been hit hard by plant shutdowns. In February 1992, for example, a Procter Silex plant in Southern Pines, North Carolina, announced it was moving its production to Mexico, where labor costs are thirty-five dollars per week. At the same time, independent firms began to feel the squeeze of foreign competition. The United States in 1970 was home to 20 percent of the world's machine-tool industry, much of which was small, family owned, and rural, and which imported only 4 percent of its stock. Today the nation has only 6 percent of world production (ranking sixth among nations), and half of those firms in the United States are foreign-owned.

Third, a point now obvious, markets are more segmented and global, and firms that are not willing to look for market niches or to look abroad for opportunities are at a disadvantage. Small- and medium-sized manufacturers often lack the means to scan markets and the capacity to produce to foreign standards. Variations in consumer tastes are both increasing and changing more frequently. For example, a decade ago generic brands filled the shelves at supermarkets; today consumers can choose from among low-salt, low-fat, low-cholesterol, and low-calorie products for a given item. Fashion seasons in the apparel industry have gone from four to eight per year. Further, the steps a business must take to enter international markets and deal with different languages, customs, and regulations are complex and often confusing.

Despite the potential that SMEs hold for achieving flexibility and economies of scope to meet the new demands of changing markets, few have reached their potential. Small, and especially independently owned, manufacturers have been slow to adopt the new technologies and business practices that characterize high-performance firms. It is not just that they are not on the cutting edge; the majority do not yet use conventional computer-aided equipment that has been commercially available for decades: computer numerically controlled machines, robotics, and computer-aided design and engineering (Tables 10.1 and 10.2). Most do not use statistical process control or just-in-time inventory methods. Few are capable of meeting Europe's ISO 9000 standards.

The path to becoming a high-performance firm is often called *modernization*, a process of continually upgrading management practices and process technologies in order to give producers advantages in the marketplace over their competitors.

Table 10.1. Percentages of firms using specified technologies, various surveys

	Rural South (1989)	Rural VA[a] (1989)	WV[b] (1989)	WI[c] (1989)	Great Lakes[d] (1987)	U.S.[e] (1988)	Germany[f] (1987)	Japan[g] (1988)
N=	262	40	148	340	1388	9682	1069	n/a
CAD	36	20	27	33	48	39	31	—
CNC Machines	32	25	21	20	19	41[h]	40	49
Robots	5	3	2	6	7	13	11	26
Programmable Controllers	37	23	17	—	18	32	11	—
Automated Material Handling	18	20	4	11	7	2	11	14
Microcomputers	29	—	18	12	16	27	36	—
Automated Data Collection	16	—	5	—	—	—	30	—
Statistical Process Control	34	13	8	31	26	—	—	—
Automated Inspection	13	—	—	—	29	13	—	—
FMCs	12	8	2	2	11	4	1	—

[a] Respondents limited to wood products firms in western part of Virginia. Sinclair (1989).
[b] Respondents limited to durable goods manufacturers in West Virginia. Shapira and Geiger (1990).
[c] Unpublished survey data collected by Nelson (1989).
[d] Respondents limited to firms of more than 19 employees in Wisconsin, Minnesota, Michigan, Illinois, Ohio, and Indiana. Center for Social and Economic Issues (1987).
[e] U.S. Department of Commerce Bureau of the Census (1989).
[f] Schulz-Wild (1989).
[g] Shapira (1990b).
[h] The U.S. question asks about either CNC or noncomputer NC equipment.

Table 10.2. Rates of adoption of technologies by ownership status and size, rural
             manufacturers in South, 1989, percentages

	All Firms		Independent Only	
	Independent	Branch	≥ 100	≤ 99
CAD	25	52	21	41
CAE	17	39	14	36
CNC Machines	22	40	18	33
Robots	2	10	1	8
Automated Material Handling	11	28	4	36
Programmable Controllers	28	53	18	59
Shop Floor Microcomputers	19	44	16	49
Automated Data Collection	7	30	4	23
Automated Inspection	9	17	5	21
Statistical Process Control	22	53	13	49
Group Technology	6	18	2	15
Flexible Manufacturing Cells	5	24	3	21

SOURCE: Survey conducted by the Consortium for Manufacturing Competitiveness,
1989.

Modernization focuses on the ways that manufacturing firms process material,
organize people, use information, integrate systems, and accommodate innovation.

There are many explanations for the slow rate of modernization among rural
manufacturers (Shapira 1990a; Rosenfeld 1992a, 1992b). For example, SMEs are
unable to support specialists and staff to share administrative work load and free
up time for management to think about and act on strategic goals. The typical
owner or manager of an SME works in production as well as designing the products,
managing and administering the operation, and hiring personnel. He or she lacks
the time and/or expertise to read what the experts have to say, much less follow
their advice: monitor technological and market trends and developments, develop
strategic plans, carry out product or process development, and carefully analyze
investment opportunities.

Small-firm owners typically are fiercely independent. As modern-day versions of the Jeffersonian yeoman farmer, these owners are wary of universities that
are too "ivory tower," of government agencies that force them to comply with
regulations and fill out too many forms, and of banks that neither understand nor
are sympathetic to their needs. Many will not return industrial directory forms and

consequently are omitted from listings in state publications. Rarely are they members of chambers of commerce, local business groups, or trade associations, and they have little time for management seminars.

Rural SME owners also lack sufficient and timely access to capital. Thirty-seven percent of firms in the rural South cited lack of capital as a reason for rejecting investments in new technology. In a survey of firms in rural Virginia, more than 40 percent cited lack of capital as an obstacle; at a meeting of small and rural manufacturers in Oklahoma in the fall of 1991, participants cited financing as their most pressing problem. Too many bankers in rural 'areas are unfamiliar with the value of production technologies or technology-based accounting practices, and they are reluctant to consider strategic benefits. Capital gaps for modernizing SMEs are more likely to exist in working capital than in investment in plant or equipment, and the small firm with a number of small loans secured by its new assets has no funds for operating costs and receivables until the investments begin to pay off. Few local banks are willing to make those loans.

Information, even where available, is difficult to use unless someone is able to help access, translate, and evaluate it. Few small firms will avail themselves of information systems, no matter how good those systems are. Under these conditions, vendors who knock on doors are the most common source of information about new technologies. Lacking objective information about investment alternatives or knowledge of how to integrate a vendor's equipment into the firm's overall production system and its long-term strategy, the firm is likely to invest piecemeal rather than systematically toward an integrated system.

Labor markets are much more limited in rural areas. Educated workers and business are drawn to cities where, if internal opportunities for advancement are not available, there are other opportunities. Moreover, current patterns of working spouses now exacerbate the problems of rural plants in recruiting good staff. Even if an excellent opportunity is available and the recruit is willing, there may not be suitable or acceptable employment for a professional spouse. Thus, the rural manufacturer generally faces great difficulty in attracting professional or technical staff, unless the location is within reasonable commuting distance of large labor markets or the recruit chooses a rural location for personal reasons.

Rural, small, and independent manufacturers are not well served by training programs. They cannot generate large enough enrollments to justify public expenditures in tailored programs, and they do not invest in such training themselves because they underestimate its value to their productivity or they fear losing the trained worker to their competitors. Furthermore, rural SMEs do not provide high enough wages or good enough benefits to attract highly skilled workers or, if they do acquire or train skilled workers, to prevent high turnover.

Rural SMEs lack sufficient information about markets and market trends. Market information is available but often is too costly or too time-consuming for the small manufacturer to access. Most states try to provide technical and financial assistance, but they get few takers. As Nothdurft concluded after studying SMEs in Europe and the United States, "The primary barriers to exporting are internal to firms, not external to markets," and the firms have too little knowledge about export opportunities (Nothdurft and Friedman 1991).

Distances from technical resources such as research centers, and from large labor pools, financial institutions, and transportation hubs hamper modernization efforts. Trade shows and professional conferences—events that urban manufacturers take for granted—are rarely attended by isolated firms.[1] Just a few industrial extension services provide substantial rural outreach. Only about 10 percent of SMEs in the rural South surveyed replied that they received any help with technological decisions from either colleges, universities, or state agencies. Nearly two-thirds never received assistance from any public-sector institution or agency. In a 1992 survey of 300 machining and tooling companies, most of which are family-owned and rural, not one reported using information or assistance from any government agency or institution when purchasing automated equipment. Finally, the market system works to the disadvantage of the rural firm even when services are available. With fewer possibilities from which to choose for services that do exist, there is less competition to drive up quality and less chance that the service will fit a firm's special needs.

Despite these barriers to modernization associated with scale and distance, some rural SMEs have become world class and do compete with the best in the world. The challenge facing rural areas is how to move the average firm to the level of the best. What policies will best enable that to happen, and on what strengths and resources can rural and agricultural areas draw?

Learning from Agriculture

American agriculture was faced with many of these same problems a century ago, and the nation found a way to respond. It is a story that is often repeated but also often misunderstood. Cooperative extension, for example, is regarded by many as the nation's most effective government program; it is cited frequently as a model for a whole host of efforts to effectively reach large segments of the population. The success of cooperative extension, however, was not due only to its innovative design or scale. Much of its strength derived from the fact that it was only part—though an important part—of a complex social and economic web that linked farmers, businesses, and rural communities.

There is a movement under way to create a national technology extension program at the federal level based on cooperative extension, with some funds already authorized and additional legislation in process. A formal memo of understanding between the National Institute of Standards and Technology (NIST) and the U.S. Department of Agriculture paves the way for joint projects between cooperative extension and industrial extension, and a few states have agreed to host pilot projects. Cooperative extension is already an integral part of NIST's Manufacturing Technology Center in Kansas, and Kentucky will include cooperative extension in its plans to develop a technology extension program. These new joint efforts are based on the assumptions that cooperative extension has better access to SMEs in rural areas, that it knows how to stimulate demand for new technology, and that the skills of cooperative extension can be transferred from agriculture to manufacturing. There is more to extension service than meets the eye, however, and the hidden functions and conditions may be even more important than those that are most visible and discussed.

To better understand what it will take to modernize an entire sector, it is useful to review the history of cooperative extension and to identify both conditions that existed when it was developed and its original goals. Some appreciation of the scope of cooperative extension's activities and objectives in the early days might lead to more effective adaptations for American industry.

First, bear in mind that, although the goals of cooperative extension are almost always measured in terms of productivity growth, the primary mission was education. As one expert wrote, the county agent "is the interpreter of the agricultural college teachings and the experiment station discoveries to the farmer" (Herick 1918). But long before that, both the Grange and the Farmers' Alliance implored farmers to study and learn about new methods and to teach each other. They employed traveling lecturers to teach about crop rotation, careful seed selection, new machinery, and cooperative marketing (Ferguson 1942). The 1874 platform of the Grange included a plank stating that "the Grange is a school at which every farmer in the land can acquire information, establishing advantages relatively and placing himself in the current of human affairs." Farmers were encouraged to subscribe to technical journals and to debate economic issues and the pros and cons of new technologies. Each suballiance had its own lecturer and each county had its own county lecturer, and these lecturers often invited popular outside speakers for one- to four-day seminars that drew large audiences. A northern alliance advocated a "Chautauqua," with organized classes and supervised home study comparable to a national university.

The Farmers' Union announced that it was first of all an educational organization. The Union began its efforts with basic literacy, then extended them through economics and science. When Dr. Seaman Knapp began introducing scientific farming methods to Louisiana rice farmers and later organizing demonstrations of new crop rotation methods, it was seen as a natural extension of the educational process, a new experiential method of instruction (Herick 1918). The railroads, trying to improve their poor image among farmers that carried over from the days of Populism, carried institutes and agricultural shows to the most remote rural areas to spread the gospel of scientific farming. In 1915, according to U.S. Department of Agriculture records, nearly three million farmers attended demonstrations of new production methods and modern equipment. And the USDA experiment stations also used education to get their results into practice. In addition to millions of bulletins distributed directly to farmers, they conducted farmers' institutes to teach farmers scientific farming principles (True 1897).

The Grange and the Farmers' Alliance repeatedly petitioned schools to include principles of scientific farming and domestic science. Rural constituents opposed the industrial education movement that educated workers for mass production jobs because farm work was dramatically different. Farmers were entrepreneurs; not only did they have to know how to use new technology but they had to decide when and where to use it, which equipment or supplies to purchase, and how to finance them.

Second, learning—both from experts and from each other—was viewed as vital to innovation and long-term growth. Much learning took place as a collective or collaborative process. An important goal of the agricultural organizations and of cooperative extension later on was to organize farmers to become a self-sustaining, regionwide learning system. The president of the Farmers' Union wrote that each farmer assumes "an obligation to help his fellow members in every way possible without jeopardizing his own interest." The USDA farmers' institutes were organized so that farmers learned best methods directly from other farmers who were already using scientific principles.[2]

Seaman Knapp instructed county agents to work with groups of farmers and leaders, not individual farmers, in order to achieve the greatest impact. At about the same time, the state director of extension for New York urged his agents to organize farmers for the following reasons: "(a) It multiplies effort—especially self-help effort. (b) It establishes close contact with localities. (c) It makes leadership most effective. (d) It provides a clearinghouse" (McConnell 1953). Just as industrial extension engineers have discovered that they can reach only a very few manufacturers, the county agent system—even though much larger in scale and more dispersed—could maintain contact only with a small percentage of the farmers. The solution was organization, to reach farmers collectively instead of individually.

This was consistent with the emphasis among farmers and cooperative farm organizations. The numerous farm organizations established to educate farmers also encouraged the formation of economic cooperatives, both to strengthen famers' bargaining power with banks, railroads, and middlemen and to promote business efficiency (Saloutos and Hicks 1951). (Farmers also attempted to manufacture equipment in cooperatives, but with no lasting success.)

Third, the federal government did not create cooperative extension, but it did turn it into a national program. County agents worked in many counties long before the federal Smith-Lever Act of 1914. The federal government supported limited extension activities through its experiment stations and provided some funds to encourage diffusion, but it was a minor player. The first direct support for county agents came mainly from foundations and banks (McConnell 1953). Gifts came from the General Education Board, philanthropist Julius Rosenwald, and many businesses. In fact, the private sector at times did more than just encourage cooperatives and extension; banks and merchants sometimes threatened to withhold credit to farmers unwilling to partake of these opportunities (Hofstadter 1955). Thus, there is precedent for wide-ranging private-sector support for economic activities that further the nation's economic interest.

The methods used by cooperative extension, invoked repeatedly for an array of other outreach efforts, can be useful for other programs if adopted with a full understanding of what made them work. Although agriculture tends to cluster more by product than does manufacturing, and thus cooperative extension agents generally have a more homogenous client base, the underlying principles can be applied to many generic problems facing manufacturing. Further, a social infrastructure in which manufacturers are able to trust one another, exchange information, and share resources is a necessity.

Building Competitive Industries in Rural Areas

If we assume (1) that a vibrant and competitive high-value-added manufacturing sector is necessary to the long-term growth of regional economies, (2) that SMEs represent the base of the emerging industrial economy, and (3) that these SMEs will have to adopt better and more advanced production technologies and management techniques to secure their future, then what sorts of rural public policy will be most effective? I believe that rural regions will have to consider the following shifts in how they organize their programs and build their economies. They will have to shift the imbalance that exists in current policy:

- Balancing competitive sites with competitive industries
- Balancing investments in research centers with investments in demonstrations and outreach programs
- Using government less as a service delivery and more as a catalyst
- Balancing emphasis on specialized skills with breadth of knowledge and learning systems
- Balancing industrial diversification with industrial clustering
- Balancing function-based services with sector-based services
- Balancing individual effort with collective efforts

Balancing Competitive Sites with Competitive Industries

That competitive industries are at least as important as competitive sites is a fundamental principle of a growth strategy that is difficult to sell to economic development officials in rural areas. For too long, competitiveness has had a very different meaning: communities and states competing with each other for a fixed number of jobs. Economic development trade magazines such as *Site Selection* and *Plant Location*, along with performance measures such as the Grant Thornton Index, reinforce the traditional view of competitiveness. Nearly all economic development programs are based on improving a location. Industrial parks built on speculation, tax abatements, enterprise zones, airports, and extended sewer lines may help attract branch plants, but they do not meet the needs of the SME. Government officials gain more recognition for cutting the ribbon at a new plant than for promoting slow, but steady, job growth through incremental improvements in production methods.

Harvard economist Michael Porter (1990) makes the very persuasive argument that the only way a region can be truly competitive is to make sure its industries are competitive. This exchanges the conventional units of analysis of economic development policy, the individual firm and the site, for less conventional units of regional relationships and industry sectors. In this new vision, the three critical factors of location, location, and location must be modified to give equal weight to innovation, innovation, and innovation.

Balancing Investments in Research Centers with More Investments in Demonstration and Outreach Programs

Most strategies for technology transfer have been supply-driven, motivated by the assumption that research centers and laboratories have a wealth of good ideas that simply are not known to the typical manufacturers or, if they are known, are not appreciated or used to their potential. Consequently, government resources have gone into building and supporting centers and finding ways to transmit the knowledge developed more effectively. Technology transfer programs designed for laboratories, however, have not been very successful. For example, the Stephenson-Wydler Act, passed by Congress to encourage greater commercial application of the research in federal laboratories, has not resulted in a flood of innovations into commercial markets.

For rural businesses, there are two flaws in the emphasis on research centers. First, most rural SMEs have little contact with major research centers, which often are located in metropolitan centers or large research universities. Second, most rural SMEs are not at a stage where they can use the latest technological developments; they need to learn how to use technologies that are proven and available and to receive help in solving very specific production problems.

What is needed is demonstration and outreach, a means to reach the SME and help its management assess its strengths and weaknesses, identify its problems and long-term needs, observe newer and better methods, and develop long-term strategic plans. The sources of technical expertise must be trusted and accessible. The National Institute of Standards and Technology's program to establish manufacturing technology centers around the country has discovered that these centers cannot operate alone. The current views at NIST are that manufacturing technology outreach centers are necessary if the technology centers themselves are to have a regional impact. These outreach centers would be located at existing institutions such as community colleges, business associations, or local development offices.

Technology outreach programs and demonstration centers do exist in some places. Most operate out of land-grant universities and are modeled on cooperative extension, but they receive support that is equivalent to only a little over 0.5 percent of the revenues that cooperative extension receives from state and federal governments. The majority of the extension-type programs are centralized or, if decentralized, they operate out of small regional offices with one professional staff person (Chapman et al. 1990). Using a very loose definition of technology extension, a survey conducted by the National Governors' Association found only forty-two programs in twenty-eight states, and most state programs had fewer than ten staff members. The U.S. General Accounting Office (1991) found that just seven states operated programs providing direct help to clients with their problems.

Nowhere in the United States are extension services provided on a scale necessary to meet the challenge. In some places, technical colleges with advanced manufacturing centers and industrial training programs serve as extension and demonstration centers. A few colleges, such as Southern Arkansas University–Technical Branch and Somerset Community College in Kentucky, have combined the two by using mobile technology units to go to sites, much as the railroads moved agricultural demonstrations from town to town eighty years ago. But these, too, are constrained by funding mechanisms of college systems based on student enrollments, not services provided. Pending federal legislation, if passed and funded, would establish 150 teaching factories across the country that would give demonstrations, provide a shared facility for prototypes or developmental production, and train workers.

Many of our competitor nations have applied America's cooperative extension model to industry much more effectively than has the United States. Denmark, for instance, operates technology information centers in each county with three to six staff people, and the centers can call on the services of the Danish Technological Institute or the universities for technical assistance. The Steinbeis Foundation in Baden-Württemberg, one of Germany's most industrialized regions, operates more than one hundred far-flung technology transfer centers to work with SMEs (Rosenfeld 1990).

The Omnibus Trade and Competitiveness Act of 1988 charged NIST with helping states to develop technology extension programs, and it has awarded grants—all under $100 thousand—to assist with design and implementation (Shapira et al. 1992). But until the federal government makes a serious investment, states will continue to operate what are mostly marginal efforts and will be unable to reach most rural areas.

Using Government Less as a Service Delivery and More as a Catalyst

In the latest paradigm of government policy, which some call "third-wave economic development,"[3] the public sector relinquishes some of its direct services to the private sector. Government in this model is catalytic and, as Osborne and Gaebler (1992) suggest, concerns itself with "steering rather than rowing." Some states are redesigning and redefining their development agencies so that they are enablers and facilitators of innovation and learning, rather than problem solvers.

Governments as catalysts are not passive. They do not tell firms what they need, but neither should they wait for requests of help. They have to stimulate demand—with leadership, information, opportunities, and incentives. Minnesota Technology, Inc., operates through five rural outreach offices to help firms think strategically about their future. If SMEs need special assistance, Minnesota Technology will provide a list of sources and even subsidize some of the initial costs. But they are not experts in their own right to provide direct assistance. The organization also raises the level of understanding among members of the state legislature and the public about industrial policies, and it generates demand for the services that are needed.

Oregon's new twin industrial competitiveness programs, the Wood Products Competitiveness Corporation and the Key Industries Program, are examples of the changing role of government. The former was established by the government as an independent, nonprofit organization governed by SME owners who have responsibility for administering the state appropriations. Both programs are authorized to award challenge grants and service vouchers to firms based on their plans for becoming more competitive and for working collaboratively.

In Oklahoma, the Alliance for Manufacturing Excellence was established by the legislature in 1992 as a nonprofit, also governed by the private sector and managed by a staff selected by its board, to administer state funds appropriated to promote manufacturing modernization. The guiding principles of the legislation include using existing resources to deliver programs, promoting collaboration, expecting self-help and commitment from SMEs, and being customer-driven.

Typically, governments have responded to economic problems in rural areas with new programs. These examples all demonstrate that governments can operate effectively as enablers and catalysts, helping to frame questions and identify needs but not providing solutions. There is also a need for government to make sure that any direct services provided outside of government are available to rural SMEs. Services cannot be left to the market because the scale of demand would make the cost prohibitive in sparsely settled areas. Governments as catalysts, therefore, may have to pay special attention and devote additional resources to rural areas.

Balancing Emphasis on Specialized Skills with Breadth of Knowledge and Learning Systems

Perhaps the most important lesson industry has to learn from agriculture is how to educate the work force. Agricultural education has always had unique features unappreciated by its industrial counterparts. While industrial education adapted to mass production methods and emphasized narrow skills and work habits appropriate to a hierarchical and authoritarian management system, agriculture prepared youth to manage their own businesses; to make decisions about new technologies; to solve production and business problems; to understand the entire system, from seed to store; and generally to become community leaders (Rosenfeld 1984). Further, industrial education lacked the pedagogical focus on technological change and experimentation of vocational agriculture. Youth enrolled in vocational agriculture learned the value of innovation, experimentation, and cooperation and learned to make decisions. Youth enrolled in industrial programs learned to operate equipment and follow instructions.

Today industry is realizing that the skills and knowledge it needs in manufacturing are more similar to what agriculture has always taught, but it is faced with a system still deeply entrenched in a mass production mindset. This education system never served the nation's SMEs well, because their employees need much broader skills and knowledge and are much more likely eventually to open their own shops. But it was the giant mass production corporations that influenced curriculum development.

With the shift from mass production to specialized flexible production, much of the current educational reform effort is moving toward the agricultural model. Instead of the narrowly trained operator, high-performance businesses want something more akin to a Renaissance technician, who can take on a range of responsibilities and continually learn new skills. The basic skills of tomorrow's technician are "abstraction, system thinking, experimentation, and collaboration" (Reich 1992). One reason for the success of European SMEs is that technical training is based on the assumption that the student someday will become a manager or owner, and the training programs include leadership and management skills.

In addition to addressing the educational needs of individuals, firms can be considered learning systems. The rate at which SMEs in rural areas develop into high-performance firms depends largely on the rate at which they absorb and use new information. As one economist notes, "Because problems and solutions cannot be defined in advance, formal meetings and agendas won't reveal them. They emerge out of frequent and informal communications among team members. Mutual learning occurs within the team . . ." (ibid.). But will "the team" include production employees? The knowledge of firms is the collective knowledge of its employees and the degree to which that knowledge is freely exchanged, appreciated, and used. Without a firm organized as a learning system, employers will not have a chance to reap the benefits from employees' new skills.

Firms also learn from each other, a lesson that was learned early in the United States not only in agriculture but in the modernization of two mid-eighteenth-century American industries, muskets and paper. In Europe, SMEs frequently learn from each other, both intentionally, if the information is not proprietary, and informally in the normal course of the social interaction among workers and owners. In the United States, SMEs are learning again to trust and to learn from each other. In a survey administered to sixty-five SMEs in rural parts of Minnesota and Washington about reasons for considering collaboration with other SMEs, learning from one another was the reason cited most often.[4] The CEOs of thirty metalworking firms in the panhandle of Florida meet regularly to exchange information, and firms with special expertise train the workers of other firms. The concept of a region as a learning system may be one key to long-term competitiveness.

Balancing Industrial Diversification with Industrial Clusters

The conventional wisdom in rural development has been diversification. Small towns have been warned that reliance on a single sector is dangerous because the economy will rise and fall with the fortunes of that one sector. That advice, however, was based largely on a branch plant development strategy in which single employers dominated towns, which were then subject to the whims of management as well as the market fluctuations of the sector. Thus, even though the value of agglomeration economies is accepted by business and planning schools, the impact on industrial clusters in the Midwest during the last recent recession and the performance of New England and Silicon Valley in the current recession serve as warning signals.

At the same time, Western Europe and Japan not only have allowed clusters of like firms to grow but they have encouraged concentration. They believe that large concentrations of SMEs give a region a marketable name and reputation and that if the SMEs are flexible, they ought to be able to adapt to the markets and new competition. Large numbers of firms provide the external economies of scale for the region to develop specialized factors: services, skills, capital, and capital goods manufacturers. For example, as Porter (1990) points out, "Simply having a general work force that is high school or even college educated represents no competitive advantage in modern international competition. To support competitive advantage, a factor must be highly specialized to an industry's particular need. . . . These factors are more scarce, more difficult for foreign competitors to imitate— and they require sustained investment to create." It also provides the head-to-head competition to drive innovation. In Europe, well-known concentrations of firms around the towns of Sassoulo and Fiorano in Italy produce 30 percent of the world's ceramic tiles. When competition from developing nations cut into its market share, the region moved into higher-end tiles. In the rural region surrounding Castel

Goffredo, 150 miles north in Italy, 250 firms produce 40 percent of the women's hosiery sold in Europe.

As in Europe, such clusters do exist in some rural areas of the United States. The furniture manufacturers clustered around Tupelo, Mississippi, the hosiery firms around Catawba, North Carolina, the carpet manufacturers in and around Dalton, Georgia, and the wood products firms in the Olympic Peninsula of Washington are all examples of clusters in rural areas that could be further strengthened. Some states—namely, Arizona, Florida, and Illinois—are identifying industrial clusters on which to build their strategies for the twenty-first century.

Balancing Functional Services with Sector-Based Services

A lesson closely related to the advantages gained from industry concentration is that services are more efficiently delivered when organized by sector rather than by function. Currently an SME must go to one state agency for training, another for technical information, another for marketing, and another for finance or business advice. At present, few state agencies are storehouses of information for an industrial sector. In contrast, many European nations have established sector-based hubs. They help firms scan markets, learn about new technologies and quality standards, test products, train workers, and provide access to highly specialized services and capital. Europe, which coordinates services and pays more attention to interconnections between technology, design, marketing, and training, has set an example that is now having a positive effect on U.S. industry and public policy. A few states are moving toward sector-based approaches. Massachusetts' northern tier industrial policy selected three sectors: furniture, food processing, and metals. Oregon's new state program for the wood products industry represents a comprehensive sector-specific approach. Illinois is establishing sector "desks" for its key sectors, and new development plans in Arizona and Florida focus on services for specific industrial clusters.

Although a sector-based service for more than a small number of industries is beyond the resources of any state, it does open the door for regional collaboration. States could develop hubs for their key industries and rely on other states for their secondary industries, as four Appalachian states are about to do.

Balancing Individual Efforts with Collective Efforts

The most important change that SMEs in rural areas may have to make is the way they behave toward one another. Agriculture learned the value of collective action more than a century ago. Similarly, small manufacturers worked together, but as corporations grew larger the fears of charges of price fixing and manipulating the market loomed larger than the technological advantages of collaboration. The SME owners in the twentieth century—independent, rugged individualists—believe that capitalism and coorperation are inconsistent at best and illegal at worst.

Economist Lester Thurow (1992), however, notes that there are not one but two forms of capitalism: one that is based on individualistic values and features profit maximization, entrepreneurship, Nobel Prizes, and job mobility, and one that is based on communitarian values, featuring strategic planning, long-term investments in training, and firm loyalty. It is the latter, as practiced by Japan, Italy, Germany, and Scandinavia, that he predicts will be the more successful. The successful small-firm economies in these nations, many in small cities and rural areas, are strongly related to their willingness to work collectively. Firms band together to solve common problems, enter markets, acquire information, capital, technologies, or specialized services, or simply to learn from one another. The term commonly used to describe this form of collaboration is *flexible manufacturing network*, or just *network*.

Efforts to organize firms and develop linkages began in the mid-1980s. Accounts of the success of small-firm industrial clusters in northern Italy (Piore and Sabel 1984), bolstered by the efforts of consultant Richard Hatch to design programs modeled on the public and private services and interfirm relationships in northern Italy and on support from the German Marshall Fund for study tours of policymakers to Europe, played a major role in introducing the concept in the United States. Denmark's government program to encourage network formation and a scattered but growing number of small-scale collaborative activities here have strengthened the base of support in the United States. Increased visibility and growing credibility at a time when industrial policy is beginning to gain respectability, combined with the potential of funding from foundations and state and federal agencies, have attracted many more players into the game.

The fledgling networks that are emerging in the United States can be classified according to five generic forms: the trade association, the cooperative, the joint venture, the shared resource, and the grange. Most, however, are hybrids. The first category, modeled after trade associations, includes large numbers of firms in a common sector paying membership dues to obtain the benefits and power base of a larger organization. One reason this type of open-membership organization has become popular is that many large national trade associations have concentrated on lobbying and have failed to provide sufficient value and access to small and rural businesses. Another is that an association provides some potential income to support the on-going activities of a network broker.

The local or regional trade association model has the added benefit of providing a social environment in which firms can interact, learn from one another, and facilitate deal making among members that can lead to production networks. Two examples are the Metalworking Connection in Magnolia, Arkansas, and the Tri-State Manufacturers Association in Fergus Falls, Minnesota. More than fifty metalworking firms, brought together by the economic development directors of two local colleges, began with collective insurance and benefits packages to reduce costs but quickly moved into a shared apprenticeship training program, and joint marketing of capabilities and problem solving. Tri-State, supported by foundation grants and modest fees, represents more than one hundred firms in western Minnesota and eastern North and South Dakota. Firms meet monthly to learn about new technologies and techniques. Within the association, firms subcontract to each other.

The second form is modeled after the agricultural cooperative, an organization with limited membership that acts in the market as a single entity to give it greater leverage. Groups of firms may purchase parts or supplies together to get price breaks, create a common pool of funds with a bank for working capital, or contract with an exporting agent. Technology Coast Manufacturing and Engineering Network in Fort Walton, Florida, is thirty firms in two counties that purchase cooperatively. The North Carolina Sewn Products Network is contracting with marketing agents to sell their products overseas. MechTech is a cooperative youth apprenticeship training program in which youths receive basic education in classes together and then rotate among assignments with small manufacturers to gain broader on-the-job experience. Those who complete the program are employed by a single member firm. Despite these successes, industrial networks have little contact with more conventional rural cooperatives, and few have made any attempt to learn from their wealth of experience.

The third form, joint ventures among SMEs, is the model most likely to lead to innovation and is the most dynamic. Small numbers of firms that either manufacture complementary products or have expertise in specific phases of production of a single product join together to take advantage of a market opportunity for which each firm alone lacks the internal capacity or capability. This form of network is sometimes called a vertical network to distinguish it from the other forms of horizontal networks. Such networks may rely on brokers to bring firms together and generate ideas, but in the long run firms are able to identify areas for collaboration without further assistance. Several new and existing firms in an eleven-county region of southern Ohio, organized by the Appalachian Center for Economic Networks in Athens, are designing and building a new line of accessible kitchen units for disabled people. Individual secondary wood products firms in the Olympic Peninsula of Washington perform certain functions for the others that require special equipment or skills. For example, one SME does edge gluing; another, finger joining; and another, rough cutting.

In the fourth form, firms in a network share targeted resources that they could not afford individually. For instance, three wood products firms in southern Arkansas are sharing the expense of developing computer numerically controlled routers; a group of hosiery firms in North Carolina jointly contracted with a consultant to develop new computer monitoring equipment; and sawmill products firms in western Virginia are planning to share the costs of a new dry-kiln facility.

The last, and perhaps the most overlooked, type of network is based on the historical adult education efforts in agriculture. The Grange, the Farmers Alliances, and the farmers' institutes mentioned earlier brought isolated, independent, and suspicious farmers together to address common problems and begin cooperative ventures. Businesses, too, need an environment in which they can learn from each other, challenge each other to be more innovative, and address common problems. A group of firms in the Olympic Peninsula of Washington, for instance, meets regularly at member plants to talk about problems and pressing needs. The Technology Coast Manufacturing and Engineering Network in Fort Walton Beach, Florida, is another collective learning system. Members assemble regularly to exchange information and learn about new technologies and market opportunities. Despite the competitive nature of the firms, ultimately they face common external threats, and the need to be more creative and to innovate overrides the threat of disclosure of generic production problems.

Despite the explosion of interest in collaborative modernization strategies, it is still a new and difficult goal to attain, and the process for achieving it is still evolving. Cooperation requires a great deal of effort and trust, and there are many obstacles along the way. Most networks look for start-up support—or without it, early successes—to maintain interest. This pushes firms initially toward cost savings rather than strategic goals. Impediments to progress include difficulties with interpersonal relationships, paucity of resources, lack of trust among firms, fear of antitrust action, resistance from existing trade associations who view networks as competition and from departments of economic development that refuse to look beyond recruitment, lack of accurate measures of impact in terms of jobs and wealth, and the failure of some network brokers to follow through. Yet despite these obstacles, numerous successes clearly demonstrate the potential for an industrial policy that focuses on SMEs and strengthening interfirm linkages.

Implications for Rural and Agricultural Areas

In some respects, rural regions have unique strengths that could serve them well in helping SMEs overcome the barriers to modernization and strengthen their industrial bases. Traditional agricultural education is more appropriate for new and small businesses than are industrial courses, and the networks maintained by organizations such as the FFA Alumni Association can serve as models. Agriculture has a long history of learning and continual improvement from which industry can take lessons. And, in the nondurable goods–producing industries, the processing of farm products would be located near the sources of materials and expertise. What principles can be derived from agricultural and rural experience and history for a technology-driven manufacturing sector?

The first principle is that modernization is an educational process, not simply a technology transfer system. More important, it is an educational process that features the firm as learner. Too often adaptations of cooperative extension feature engineers and engineering students trying to convince managers to use the newest manufacturing or management concept instead of focusing on how to facilitate continual learning. The real strength of agricultural communities was in learning from each other. Cooperative extension was an important part of that system, not an outside influence.

The second principle is that in most places the solution is not to create more new programs. There is a plethora of programs available to businesses already, but most are not specifically geared to the needs of SMEs and are not used by them. A survey of SMEs in Kentucky, for example, found that only 2 percent had used any government service. What is needed is a way to coordinate, integrate, rationalize, and motivate the services and programs that already exist, and to make sure that they understand and serve SMEs. The state of Oklahoma has drafted a plan to do just that (Fig. 10.1).

The third principle is that any actions taken should be taken on a scale that can make a difference. Although there are many excellent new practices across the nation, none really has the scale to meet the needs of the manufacturing base it addresses. The best programs can reach only a small number of a state's manufacturers with anything more than access to information. Most states and localities continue to view modernization not as an economic program or a rural development program that leads to job creation, but as a technical program that may even result in fewer, not more, jobs. States have been unwilling to allocate to modernization even a small portion of what they offer branch plants as subsidies to locate, or what they include in advertising budgets to promote tourism. The federal government expresses interest in helping SMEs but has committed only a small fraction of the

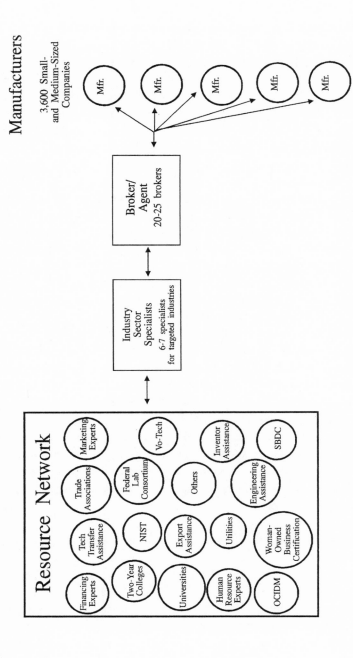

Figure 10.1. Planned organization of Oklahoma's technology extension system.

funds needed to deliver or even leverage services. Where it does invest, it expects programs to become self-sufficient too soon. As a result, states look at federal funding as short-term grants rather than as the foundation for new, on-going programs. Further, many programs are tied too closely to political sponsorship; if that sponsorship disappears as a result of the political process, programs die. The Michigan Modernization Service, often highlighted as the most promising program in the nation, was ended abruptly when a new governor was elected. To achieve scale, modernization must be debated and discussed as an economic development policy, not as a technology policy. And it must be given sufficient time to prove or disprove its worth.

The fourth principle is to involve the SMEs and trade associations early in the process. SMEs are not used to looking at the public sector as a helper, much less as a partner, and therefore they must be actively engaged in the process. It is absolutely essential to involve SMEs early and in all stages, in focus groups and as members of advisory boards, and to allow the customers to guide the process. In some places and for some industries, trade associations may be able to represent SMEs, although such representation is rare in rural areas. Most states that are now formulating modernization strategies are working closely with SMEs. Oregon's Wood Products Competitiveness Corporation, which has the responsibility for administering the state's $2.3-million modernization program enacted in 1991, is governed by seven SME owners. The Oklahoma Alliance for Manufacturing Competitiveness was designed with active participation of SMEs, and its board is predominantly manufacturers. Similarly, the Montana Competitiveness Council is dominated by SME owners.

A fifth principle is that success depends on high-level state and local support. It is important, for example, to know the state's political environment and to build constituencies among government, community organizations, trade associations, labor organizations, SMEs, and large producers. If state leadership is not present to build such constituencies, it must emerge from the process. No program succeeds without strong leadership.

The sixth principle is that in a demand-driven environment that depends heavily on private services, rural and poor areas will not be able to generate the scale of demand necessary to justify all the services they need. Governments have a continuing interest in ensuring that a reasonable level of access is available to all communities, either through partial subsidies or special services. Technology can compensate for some of the disadvantages of distance. Information, responses to inquiries, and education can be provided through telecommunications channels, but there will always be needs that require face-to-face contact.

The seventh principle is that associative behavior must be encouraged and supported by governments, not discouraged. This can be done by providing incentives in existing programs and challenge grants for new forms of networks, and by acting as brokers. Economies of scale, strength of numbers, and exchange of ideas provide a region with a synergy and scale that allow it to modernize more quickly and develop a collective reputation. Firms intuitively understand this and work together on an as-needed basis, but they also miss out on many other opportunities that are outside of their own experience or because they lack someone to act as a broker. But small businesses, which generally mistrust government agencies, must be convinced that government is involved for the long term. Programs that meet their accountability requirements must not end before they have achieved their desired ends.

These principles represent emerging third-wave development theories, in which the private sector delivers services and the market drives demand, but there is a clear role for the public sector as catalyst and broker, and it should be held accountable for its efforts. In the best and most promising practices, government agencies listen to their clients, are catalysts of change and innovation, are responsible for a support infrastructure, and work to change attitudes of SMEs toward each other and the public sector to enhance cooperation, learning, and partnerships; government agencies also ensure accessibility of services to firms in rural and agricultural communities. These principles constitute an ad hoc industrial policy toward which states are leading the federal government and for which bipartisan support is mounting. The best and most promising experiences of states, bolstered by the experiences of American agriculture, establish a frame of reference for formulating new and more effective rural and regional strategies to improve industrial competitiveness.

Cooperative extension and agricultural cooperatives both offer important lessons and experiences for industrial modernization. Both have considerable resources at their disposal, along with expertise in facilitating collaboration, learning, and innovation, and both have won the trust of rural communities. These attributes, if in part redirected to rural development based on industrial competitiveness, could fortify fledgling modernization programs. For instance, some extension agents could become brokers for existing industrial support services. Similarly, modernization resources could be brought to bear on more traditional, agriculture-related industries, giving rural communities opportunities to add value to their existing agricultural products.

Notes

1. Although many land-grant colleges are located in small towns, these are exceptional, not usual, circumstances.

2. There was considerable competition between the institute of farm organizations and the government. The latter drew smaller audiences and reached mostly the larger farmers.

3. See special issue of *The Entrepreneurial Economy Review* on third-wave strategies, volume 9, Autumn 1990, Corporation for Enterprise Development, Washington, D.C.

4. Survey carried out in 1991 by the author, under contract to the Northwest Policy Center.

References

Autry, George. 1985. *Shadows in the Sunbelt.* Chapel Hill, N.C, MDC, Inc.

Center for Social and Economic Issues. 1988. "Frostbelt Automation: The ITI Status Report on Great Lakes Manufacturing." The Industrial Technology Institute, Ann Arbor, Mich.

Chapman, Robert, Marianne Clarke, and Eric Dobson. 1990. *Technology-Based Economic Development: A Study of State and Federal Technical Extension Services.* NIST Special Publication 786. Washington, D.C.: Government Printing Office.

Ferguson, James S. 1942. "The Grange and Farmer Education in Mississippi." *The Journal of Southern History* 8:497–512.

Herick, W. O. 1918. "The Tutored Farmer." *The Scientific Monthly 7:158–65.*

Hofstadter, Richard. 1955. *The Age of Reform.* New York: Vintage Books.

McConnell, Grant. 1953. *The Decline of Agrarian Democracy.* New York: Atheneum Press.

Nelson, Orville. 1989. Unpublished survey data. Center for Vocational, Technical, and Adult Education, University of Wisconsin-Stout, Menomonie.

Nothdurft, William E., and Robert Friedman. 1991. "Lessons from the Export Masters: How Europe Helps Small Firms Become Exporters." Draft Report for the German Marshall Fund, Washington, D.C.

Osborne, David, and Ted Gaebler. 1992. *Reinventing Government.* Reading, Mass.: Addison-Wesley.

Piore, Michael, and Charles Sabel. 1984. *The Second Industrial Divide: Prospects for Prosperity.* New York: Basic Books.

Porter, Michael. 1990. *The Competitive Advantage of Nations.* New York: The Free Press.

Reich, Robert. 1992. *The Work of Nations.* New York: Random House/Vintage Books.

Rosenfeld, Stuart A. 1992a. *Competitive Manufacturing: New Strategies for Regional Development.* Piscataway, N.J.: CUPR Press.

_____. 1992b. *Smart Firms in Small Towns.* Washington, D.C.: The Aspen Institute.

_____. 1990. "Regional Development, European Style." *Issues in Science and Technology* 6:63–70.

_____. 1984. "Vocational Agriculture: A Model for Educational Reform." Commentary, *Education Week* 4:24.

Rosenfeld, Stuart, Edward Bergman, and Sarah Rubin. 1985. *After the Factories: Changing Employment Patterns in the Rural South.* Research Triangle Park, N.C.: Southern Growth Policies Board.

Saloutos, Theodore, and John D. Hicks. 1951. *Agricultural Discontent in the Middle West: 1900–1939.* Madison: University of Wisconsin Press.

Schulz-Wild, Ranier. 1989. "On the Threshold of Computer-Integrated Manufacturing." Draft paper. Institut fur Sozialwissenschaftlicht Forschung E.V. Munchen, Munich, Germany.

Shapira, Philip. 1990a. *Modernizing Manufacturing: New Policies to Build Industrial Extension Services.* Washington, D.C.: Economic Policy Institute.

_____. 1990b. "Japan's Kohsetsushi Program of Regional Public Examination and Technology Centers for Upgrading Small- and Mid-Size Manufacturing Firms." Research Paper 9019. Regional Research Institute, West Virginia University, Morgantown.

Shapira, Philip, and Melissa Geiger. 1990. "Modernization in the Mountains? The Diffusion of Industrial Technology in West Virginia." Research Paper 9007. Regional Research Institute, West Virginia University, Morgantown.

Shapira, Philip, J. David Roessner, and Richard Barke. 1992. *Federal-State Collaboration in Industrial Modernization.* Atlanta: Georgia Institute of Technology School of Public Policy.

Sinclair, Steven A. 1989. "Preliminary Needs Assessment Survey for the Wood Products Industry in Central Appalachia." Unpublished paper. Department of Wood Science and Forest Products, Virginia Polytechnic Institute and State University, Blacksburg.

Summers, Gene F., et al. 1976. *Industrial Invasion of Nonmetroprolitan America: A Quarter Century of Experience.* New York: Praeger Books.

Thurow, Lester. 1992. *Head to Head.* New York: William Morrow and Company.

True, A. C. 1897. "Popular Education for the Farmer in the United States." *Yearbook of the U.S. Department of Agriculture.* Washington, D.C.: Government Printing Office.

U.S. Department of Commerce, Bureau of the Census. 1989. "Current Industrial Reports: Manufacturing Technology 1988." Washington, D.C.: Government Printing Office.

U.S. General Accounting Office. 1991. *Technology Transfer: Federal Efforts to Enhance the Competitiveness of Small Manufacturers.* GAO/RCED-92-30. Washington, D.C.: Government Printing Office.

11 An Emerging Framework for Economic Development: An LDC Perspective

GORDON C. RAUSSER

Over the past decade or so, a number of prescriptions have been offered to less-developed countries for reforming their economic systems and achieving a sustainable growth path. The World Bank has advocated "getting the prices right" and "light" governmental intervention. Many bilateral donors from western democracies have offered the prescription of privatization as the answer to sustainable growth. In this paper, I argue that these and other similar prescriptions are incomplete and will not achieve sustainable growth paths unless the "governance structure" of these countries is realigned. In fact, the prescription offered here is that countries or various regions should be most concerned about setting their governance structure right, not about prices or privatization.

The opportunities for worldwide cooperation have never been greater. Trade liberalization, international competition, capital and labor mobility, and enhanced asset diversification all point to increases in the underlying trend of worldwide economic growth. Individual countries and regions that will continue to gain more than their fair share of this growth can be distinguished by (1) their encouragement and response to competitive forces; (2) their creation of institutions that support and regulate a thriving market economy; and (3) their introduction and maintenance of a constitutional order that is conducive to free inquiry, agreement on basic values, and processes for conflict resolution (or, equivalently, the estab-

Gordon C. Rausser is the Sproul Distinguished Professor at the University of California, Berkeley, and President of the Institute for Policy Reform, Washington, D.C.

lishment of a governance structure that can be characterized by accountability, openness and transparency, predictability, and the rule of law).

Research undertaken at the Institute for Policy Reform, Washington, D.C., has shown that major obstacles to economic growth emerge not in the design of particular policies or the reform of policies. Instead, the obstacles are inherent in the constitutional foundation and accompanying institutions that promote and protect economic and civil freedoms, as well as common property resources. At the core of any sustainable policy reform is the underlying constitutional framework or governance structure. Sound policies cannot be sustained unless the public sector places sufficient weight on the public interest. In turn, the public interest can be articulated only if societal, cultural, political, and economic forces do not violate basic freedoms—especially those associated with ease of entry to the economic system, the political system, and the ease with which the legal foundations of new institutions can be established.

Current Consensus

Throughout much of the world, the winds of change over the past five years have never been more dramatic. Democracy has won the political battle; markets have won the economic battle. Some serious scholars have even argued that the history of thought about first principles, including those governing political and economic organizations, has come to an end (Fukuyama 1989). For those who hold this view, Hegel was simply too early in forecasting the end of debate about first principles nearly two centuries ago. The entire Marxian experience from this perspective was nothing more than a 150-year detour. Hegel's view that the "end of history" coincided with the emergence of liberal democratic states following the French and American Revolutions would appear to have been corroborated.

Regardless of whether the history of ideology is over, a new consensus on economic, political, and civil freedoms has emerged. This consensus means more than simply adjusting public policies, achieving stability, and selling off a few government-owned enterprises in an attempt to set countries off on a path toward broad-based economic growth. Instead, it means creating a vision of an open economy underpinned by an open political system; identifying and removing the obstacles to economic participation, obstacles that place citizens in straitjackets; enhancing the availability and utility of information resources by shaping incentives, helping to establish the basic rules of social transactions; encouraging more efficient organization of economic activity, whether by market, hierarchy, or hybrid modes in ways that lead to fundamental restructuring of an economy; and fostering institutional frameworks that expand the role of human choice and promote entrepreneurial energies.

Major Lessons

This consensus emerges from the empirical evidence, not through the tunnel vision of theoretical constructs. In building on this experience, a number of economic "lessons" must be kept in mind. The lessons are drawn from countries that differ not only in the details of their economic policies, but also in their whole approach to growth and development. The first irrefutable lesson is that institutions matter. The historical evidence shows that, while many less-developed countries have stagnated, other developing countries have achieved spectacular economic growth. These striking differences in economic performance have not been due to the varying amounts of capital or other resources available to different countries. Normally it is not the countries who are given the most financial capital, or whose populations save the most, whose performance is best. Neither is it the countries with the most land and natural resources in relation to population. The same kinds of labor forces and culture exist in the parts of China, Germany, and Korea that have failed to grow as in the parts that have succeeded. The economically successful countries have, on the other hand, always had different institutions— different legal and organizational arrangements and economic policies—than those that have failed. Thus, the quality of a country's institutions principally determines its economic performance.

In the final analysis, development is a long-term process. One cannot get from "here" to "there" through quick fixes. Long-term investment is required. Such investment will not take place in a country where institutional risk is unacceptable!

The second principal lesson is also institutionally related. Specifically, bad governments have been a serious—if not the most serious—obstacle to economic development and broad-based growth. Third, all public sectors pursue a mix of predatory and productive activities, bad governments emphasizing the former and good governments finding a way of promoting the latter. Predatory, or redistributive, policies (PESTs) involve the transfer of wealth and income to special interests and are not explicitly concerned with efficiency. Productive policies (PERTs), or political-economic resource transactions, are intended to correct market failures or to provide public goods; these policies have neutral distributional effects, at least in design (Rausser 1982).

In terms of nuts and bolts, deSoto (1989) has shown that government regulations create serious roadblocks to economic participation. In many instances, cleverly disguised regulatory roadblocks provide significant deterrents to entry. To demonstrate this problem, de Soto tried to open a clothing business in Peru, legally and without paying bribes along the way. It took a lawyer and three other people a total of 300 days, or 1,200 man-days, to complete all the necessary forms and to obtain all the signatures that were needed to start the business. For comparison, de Soto performed the same task in Florida. Here it took only three hours to start a new business. Peru is not unique.

Given that governments are a major obstacle, reform and restructuring of their policies by definition also represents a major opportunity. A review of the history of major public policy reforms throughout the world (whether in countries developed or developing) shows that reform is motivated by one or more of the following events or forces: first, a major crisis (usually a precipitous deterioration in the economic environment), such as the 1986 oil crisis in Indonesia, the 1989 economic crisis in Argentina, or the 1986–1989 economic crisis in Poland, the (then) Soviet Union, and East Germany.

Second, a creative new design in the implementation of policy mixes and/or compensation schemes. A wonderful illustrative example here is South Korea's implementation of public policies in the late 1950s and 1960s. In essence, to implement reforms from this source, we need more Edisons who will invent the intellectual and political machinery that will allow policy reform to be profitably supplied. Reform may be accomplished by demonstrating the feasibility of alternative, more efficient programs of wealth transfer. To be sure, in some instances there may be no satisfactory means of satisfying all interest groups because the stock of ideas is inadequate.

Third, the emergence of new political factions or major institutional changes. A major means of generating sustained political reforms is through changes in the relative benefits and costs of organizing those interest groups that might be involved in the political process. In this respect, third parties (AID, World Bank, etc.) may motivate changes in the relative costs and benefits of interest group formation and articulation. Essentially, this third source alters the political power relationships by changing the effective interest group or political-economic landscape.

New Paradigms

Any new paradigm for sustainable policy reform must identify policies that are robust and important, not only economically but, in a fundamental sense, politically. An appropriate framework must address group processes and model collective decision making. The collective decision making always represents a multilateral bargaining problem among alternative interest groups. Institutions and constitutional rules set the governance structure, which determines how major issues are resolved. The governance structure specifies (1) the interests that should be represented in the bargaining process; (2) the breadth of issues over which these interests can negotiate; (3) what degree of consensus is sufficient to conclude negotiations; (4) who will represent the state or government; and (5) what will happen if the negotiations break down or, equivalently, what is the default option.

Throughout much of the world there is now a clear vision of where each country wants to arrive; unfortunately, there are few clues about the path that should be traveled to get there. The clues that do exist, and are undeniable, focus on the underlying constitution that establishes the guidelines and mechanisms for economic, political, and civil freedoms. In this setting we must be concerned with the enforceability of such freedoms and whether the legal and regulatory infrastructure that emerges from the underlying constitution provides an environment that is conducive to a vibrant market economy. In the selection of the constitutional framework (or, equivalently, of the guidelines and mechanisms for the "rules by which rules are made"), the political-economic landscape, the culture, the natural resource endowment, and the customs of the country in question must be formally recognized.

The interrelationships that must be considered in economic development, rural development, or the selection of industrial policies can be represented schematically (Fig. 11.1). In this representation, culture, custom, and natural resource endowments are treated as predetermined. The schematic representation addresses primarily group processes and attempts to model collective decision making. Four relevant spaces are

1. The result space, which characterizes the outcomes of the economic system and is referred to in Figure 11.1 as asset stocks and growth and distribution.
2. The governmental intervention or policy instrument space, which represents the design and implementation of public actions.
3. The constitutional space, which structures the collective choice or constitutional rules.
4. The institutional and organizational structures needed, along with the constitutional rules, to complete the formation of the governance structure.

This comprehensive framework for economic development allows us to focus on the explanation of governmental intervention, treating specifically the trade-off

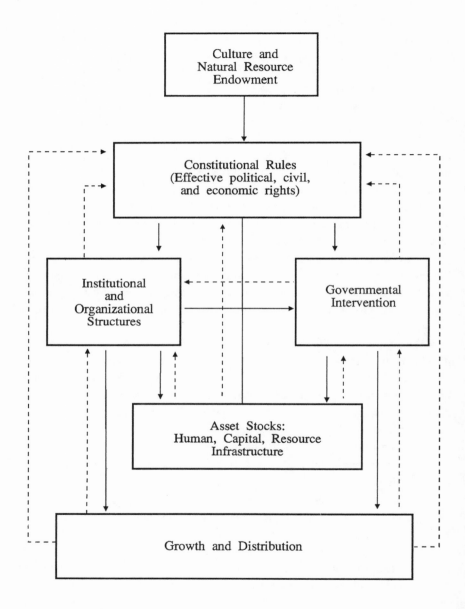

Figure 11.1. Causal linkages of governance structures and paradigms.

between public interests and special interests. The framework, perhaps more importantly, allows us to conduct prescriptive investigations of alternative constitutional or collective choice rules, institutional structures, and organizational designs. The latter prescriptions, in effect, set the governance structure.

The negotiators must select a vector of institutional variables. Each institutional vector is a complete description of the commercial and legal environment within which the private sector and individual enterprises will operate. Each vector must encode a vast array of information about items such as legal institutions (e.g., conflict-of-interest law, commercial code, bankruptcy law), the administration of justice, and so on. Commercial institutions such as capital markets and stock markets are examples of institutional or organizational structures, while investments in infrastructure industries such as telecommunications, data services, transportation, and education are productive governmental interventions. Government policies on such matters as antitrust regulations, foreign trade, and capital mobility also must be included in the governmental intervention component.

The elements of each box in Figure 11.1 are not determined passively. Consider, for example, the role of political-economic forces or interest groups seeking to exercise political power and influence for their own personal gain. Such interests are formed in the "result" boxes; they attempt to influence not only the setting of policy instruments but also institutional and organizational structures and, in many countries, the underlying constitutional rules.

In the constitutional box, the basic questions that this framework must be designed to answer are as follows:

1. Is the constitutional order of the country conducive to free inquiry and social experimentation, or is it fundamentally repressive?

2. Does the constitutional order provide ease of entry into the economic system and the political system, as well as ease in establishing the legal foundation of new institutions?

3. Does the constitutional order provide any self-correcting mechanisms for excessive predatory activities by government?

4. Does the constitutional order motivate an agreement on basic values and processes for conflict resolution—a sense of civil order that effectively reduces the cost or risk of innovation?

5. Does the constitutional order encourage and facilitate self-governance, as well as the facilitation of entrepreneurial and political leadership?

There are a host of basic political-economic questions that must be addressed. They include:

1. What are the constraints and obstacles to broad balanced economic growth that are the direct result of powerful interest groups?
2. Who wins and who loses from current policies?
3. What is the sustainability of the institutions and policies that support these constraints and obstacles?
4. What are the policy reforms that will promote economic efficiency and counter the constraints and obstacles that currently exist?
5. If the policy reforms are implemented, who wins and who loses, in the short run as well as in the long run?
6. Who are the influential socioeconomic and political interest groups that are likely to oppose the reforms? What mechanisms or approaches can be utilized to obtain political consensus for the implementation of the proposed reforms?
7. Does compensation make sense for those groups harmed by the adjustments that emerge after the policy reforms are implemented?
8. With the implementation of growth-promoting policy reforms, are there public goods that might be offered to improve social services (e.g., health, population, education, etc.) that would ease any pain of adjustment resulting from the policy reforms?
9. How can the interest of those groups who will benefit from reforms be appropriately articulated and channeled?
10. What institutional changes are required for the reform policies to be sustainable?
11. Do these institutional changes effectively alter the level and distribution of political power within the country?
12. How might the relative influence of those groups who benefit from economic policy reform be increased?
13. Do current institutions impede or promote innovations, the development of new products, new methods of production, and the emergence of pricing signals that properly reflect opportunities?
14. What institutional changes are required to promote economic and civil freedoms?
15. Are the current civil and economic freedoms sufficiently well developed to make participation in the political process effectively irrelevant?
16. If the country does not have the managerial or technical capacity to collect and analyze relevant information, determine the impact of policy alternatives, make wise choices and manage their implementation, what should be done to acquire this capacity?

17. Are there any compensation schemes and safety nets that can be designed to make institutional changes resistant to external shocks and to painful adjustment paths for specific groups?

Legal and Regulatory Infrastructure

At the core of the emerging framework for economic development are constitutional, institutional, and organizational reforms. To be sure, constitutional reform is a necessary, but insufficient, condition for protecting and enhancing political, civil, and economic rights. A judiciary must be designed that reinforces the constitution in a reliable, responsible manner, securing political, economic, and civil rights. Clearly legislation alone cannot create a favorable environment for enhancing resource allocations and entrepreneurial initiatives; there also must be mechanisms and designs for infusing confidence in the underlying constitution and the rules by which rules are made. Here the needed institutional and organizational structure pertains to the legal system. The three pillars of the legal system underlying every market economy form the core of any viable legal and regulatory infrastructure (LRI): security of private property, enforcement of contracts, and assignment of liability for wrongful damage. Each of these pillars is needed to achieve effective rights.

One of the striking features of many developing countries is that LRI mechanisms are designed to protect monopoly, inefficiency, and corruption. That is, they run in exactly the wrong direction. Mechanisms required to enhance credibility, confidence, and market efficiency are ineffective or absent. Citizens not sharing in the locus of political authority have little confidence that their property is secure; that their legitimate interests will be upheld if another party violates a contract; that they will be able to collect damages from another party responsible for a tort; that they will be subject to approximately similar treatment under various types of regulations; or that they will have similar access to concessions offered by the public sector to encourage economic activity.

Throughout much of the world, an inadequate LRI has proven to be a major barrier to broad-based economic growth. Such barriers are many and often are subtle in their design. A thriving market economy requires, *inter alia*, institutions or the rules themselves that secure individual rights. Enforcement, security, and protection of these rights via LRIs often distinguish one country's market economy and economic growth from that of another. Without the security of basic rights, compatible incentives will be impossible to achieve. Individuals thus can advance their interest only if they and the organizations they may create can secure rights that are undeniably enforceable. Any incentives to save and invest will not exist without private property rights.

Unfortunately, there is no private property without sufficiently strong government. Neither are there contracts, torts, or patents. But, just as governments through their underlying constitutions and implementable LRIs are essential for freedoms and liberties, so governments are also the greatest threat to these rights (Olson 1991). Throughout history it is governments that have expropriated property on a grand scale, systematically restructured advantageous trade among private citizens, and unilaterally changed the covenants of private contracts. Hence, to achieve sustained economic development, governments must be sufficiently powerful to implement LRIs but must also be limited and restrained by the judiciary so that individual rights are not abrogated. As James Madison noted in 1798, "The people, not the government, possess the absolute sovereignty."

Constitutional guarantees for property and contract—as well as basic political, civil, and economic freedoms—can be achieved by an effective judiciary. An effective judiciary is measured by the confidence it instills throughout the citizenry. Confidence is enhanced by creating a judiciary as a separate branch of government, assigning ultimate appeal for disputes over property and contract to the courts, reducing the self-interest of judges by assigning long tenure, making judicial decisions subject to the scrutiny of their peers and the press, and compensating judges well and placing them in positions of honor within their respective societies. Judges must be subject to stringent conflict-of-interest laws, screened for their integrity, and required to disclose their wealth and sources of income to the general public. Any legal reform that does not include these basic features is not likely to achieve sufficient credibility. A violation of any one or more of these features can be expected to lead to laws being ignored, masked, or simply suppressed. Without credibility, LRIs will fail to take on substance and improve the underlying conditions for sustainable and effective public policy implementation.

The most fundamental element of the LRI package is the system of property rights. The economics of property rights play a crucial role in the literature of institutional economics. In essence, a system of property rights is economically efficient if the rights are universal, exclusive, and transferable. As one country or region after another has learned, property that has no legal owner is likely to be abused. However, the experience of some countries has suggested strongly that property rights need to be qualified where, for example, concentration of land holdings passes certain limits. Empirical evidence in Japan, Korea, and Taiwan shows that state-imposed land redistribution, apart from its merits on grounds of equity, can lead to more efficient use of factor resources.

In contrast to the theoretical and empirical work that has emerged on property rights, the economics of contract law has received much less attention. Nevertheless, contract law plays a crucial role in promoting market economies by spelling out the terms of implicit contracts, establishing procedures for implementing the terms of both implicit and written contracts, settling disputes about implementation, determining remedies for breach of contract, and responding to contingencies that arise naturally from incomplete contracts. Effective contract law maximizes predictability and enhances credibility, reducing significantly ex post opportunism. As Leonid Hurwicz (1973) demonstrated some time ago, efficient exchange can be realized if one of the parties to the exchange behaves in a rule-bound way that is reliably free of opportunism. If the judiciary reliably enforces a purposive approach to contract law, opportunism will not be a serious concern, nor will strategic threats.

Another component of the LRI that has proven to be a significant barrier to broad-based economic growth is tort law. Tort law covers the space of individual relationships that is not admitted by contract law. It identifies wrongful damages caused by action or inaction and sets procedures for assessing their value. To the extent that tort law leads to predictable consequences, the basis is established for insurance contracts to spread risk efficiently. The first economic test for tort law is whether it ensures that parties whose interests are wrongfully harmed receive adequate, but not excessive, compensation. Second, the law should provide incentives for agents to undertake efficient precautions to avoid causing damages. These two tests cannot be met if basic economic and civil freedoms are not maintained; otherwise, the court can be bent easily in favor of powerful operators.

After the three cornerstones of the LRI come the remaining components of the institutional and organizational structure. For the private sector these components include a commercial code (company laws, bankruptcy, various business regulations), and, in the case of the public sector, conflict-of-interest laws, safety-net institutions, and (in some countries) significant civil service reforms. The need for a sound commercial code is self-explanatory, whereas the essential function of company law is to limit the liability of shareholders to their equity position. Bankruptcy laws are crucial in automatically triggering conditions under which a firm will be liquidated or will undergo a significant reorganization, and contract law provides incentives for owners and management to self-enforce efficiency.[1] Secured transactions are needed to facilitate the availability of credit and liquidity. Investments will not be financed in part by credit if lenders doubt their ability to secure available collateral if a borrower defaults.

As part of the LRI, regulations of the private sector cover the gamut: licensing and concessions, labor regulations, financial market regulations, environmental regulations, and antimonopoly or antitrust regulations. In structuring each of these regulations, the trade-off must be recognized explicitly between serving special powerful interests versus the public or collective interest (Rausser and Zusman 1992). In many instances, these regulations can also serve to establish safety-net institutions. In effect, if major transformations and new regulations harm some individuals, the issue of compensation naturally arises. If the costs experienced by disadvantaged individuals and interested observers are slight, compensation is unnecessary. However, if the costs are great and losses can be easily ascertained, then compensation may be warranted. From a political-economic perspective, compensation may be required to maintain political support and stability. Otherwise, the transition may well reach a point at which public dissatisfaction over unemployment and the cost of living forces expulsion of the current political leaders.

It must be recognized, too, that antimonopoly and competition regulations are critically related to official conflict-of-interest laws. As witnessed in country after country, the participation by public officials in business activities for their own account is a serious obstacle to the development of competitive markets. With such conflicts often come the establishment of monopoly rights in well-protected industries. The institutional structure must create and support the authority and means to ferret out such activities and to impose stiff penalties.

Along similar lines, civil service reform is another necessary component of the institutional and organizational structure. These reforms are needed to promote the transparency that in turn enhances the integrity, timeliness, and predictability of economic regulations. To be effective, the public sector must provide accurate and timely data on the performance and health of the economy. The accuracy and quality of the provisions of these public goods must be seriously investigated by external institutions such as the free press. Economic journalists should be rewarded for exposing corrupt and self-interested actions of governmental officials. The free press also should be actively engaged in assessing the investment in and production of useful statistical data on various sectors of the economy. Perhaps more importantly, the free press has a role to play in the maintenance of civil, political, and economic freedoms. As Thomas Jefferson observed in his 1801 inaugural address as president of the United States, "If there be any among us who wish to dissolve this union, or to change its republican form, let them stand undisturbed as monuments of the safety with which error of opinion may be tolerated and where reason is left free to combat it."

Governance Structures

In addressing governance structures, let me restrict the focus to a key strategy pursued by various developing countries in their attempts to jump-start their economies, to move from here to there, to make the transition to self-sustaining, broad-based economic growth. This strategy has been referred to as privatization. In fact, the war cry throughout much of Eastern Europe and the Newly Independent States (NIS) has been *privatize, privatize, and privatize*. Essentially this focus is misplaced. The focus should be on getting the governance structures right, not on prices or privatization.

What is the experience from other countries? It is, by and large, that growth has taken place primarily through the emergence of new activities, not through the adaptation of older ones. Countries seeking to implement major reforms have looked at the great success of the Thatcher privatizations—British Airways, British Steel, Housing Jaguar, even British Telecom and the water companies—and they have liked what they have seen. Nationalized British Airways and British Steel began the decade of the 1980s as about the worst performers, in terms of productivity and profits (i.e., losses), among the OECD countries. In the 1990s these privatized companies are among the best performing corporations in the West. Privatization clearly was thought to be the essential ingredient that worked such miracles. The main lesson, often neglected, is that under Thatcher the reform of the nationalized corporation was carried out while these companies were still in the public sector. The reductions in work force, the elimination of unprofitable plant and equipment, and the sharp increases in productivity, quality, and service all were achieved while the enterprises were owned by the state.

In essence, if we allow, and even encourage, free entry into the same activities of state-owned enterprises, the competitive standard for the latter is changed. In this case, there is no need for all privatization to happen tomorrow.

In another example, despite the Turkish government's stated and apparent determination to privatize, almost all state economic enterprises have continued to operate in the public sector and to produce at an estimated economic efficiency much lower than that of private firms. Economic growth of the late 1980s has originated largely from new economic activities that were started since incentives changed; the state-economic-enterprise *share* of output has declined. Even within the private sector, some small firms grew very large, while some large firms stagnated. While some producers continued to use the same combination of inputs as before, shifting output mix and lengthening production runs to the newly profitable export market, a much larger fraction of growth originated from new economic activities. It may be, therefore, that the biggest drawback many countries face is a misplaced fixation on old assets. Accordingly, it can be argued that, if the Turkish reforms in the 1980s had consisted solely in privatizing state economic enterprises, Turkey would have failed!

An important question is what the old assets are worth and whether they are worth enough to occupy as much time, attention, and scarce resources of politicians, finance ministries, and ministries of ownership as they have, in fact, been given. It is highly plausible that attention first should be placed on rapid adoption of a commercial code, establishment of assured legal procedures, and other arrangements to assure small businesses that they will indeed be rewarded if they succeed.

This leads immediately to the question of the timing of transition. Insofar as the creation of new earnings streams by people in different places or doing different things is the objective, it is important that those people be rewarded adequately for making changes. The focus on the generation of new earning streams places emphasis on new entrants and, thus, on effective joint design of competitive policy, trade policy, foreign investment policy, and privatization policy. It may well be impossible to achieve an effective privatization policy without an active competition policy, open trade regime, and a reasonably open foreign investment regime.

Governance Structures and the Political Economy

Governance structures are determined by political-economic forces and the influence exercised by various interest groups. To be concrete, let us focus again on Eastern Europe and the NIS. Given the pervasive bureaucratic structures that remain throughout that region, there is a natural propensity to overmanage all economic and social policies, especially the privatization process. The bureaucratic conditions throughout Eastern Europe and the NIS suggest that a major feature of the political-economic landscape will continue to involve bureaucratic interest groups of one type or another. The only effective means of overcoming the obstructionist behavior of bureaucratic interests is to move rapidly along the transition path. Only a successfully reformed economy will provide the incentives and conditions for breaking bureaucratic coalitions and reducing their effective power. Unless various interest groups secure a stake in the success of reform, the bureaucracy can be expected to position itself effectively to delay and obfuscate policy reforms. Overmanaging is a powerful, insidious way to defeat reform.

Throughout Eastern Europe and the NIS, centralized executive authority has been thoroughly discredited among the citizenry. As a result, the pendulum has swung toward greater decentralization and autonomy for provincial and local governments. This suggests that the bureaucratic propensity to overmanage economic and social activities during the transition must be avoided. Although a generic constitutional design must emerge from the center of the public sector's organization, the LRI and specific policies can be designed and implemented at the provincial or local governmental levels. If powerful self-interests cannot be opposed effectively at the centralized level, they may well be countered locally. In any case, the battle lines should be drawn wherever the political-economic landscape admits the possible implementation of significant reforms. If one provincial or local government is able, through implementation of an LRI and specific policies, to lead to a more sustainable path for economic growth than that experienced in some other province or locality, the demonstrated effects may create beneficial spillovers that will lead to enhanced LRIs and growth-promoting economic policies in other provinces.

Whereas traditional factions may have a stake in opposing change, viable alternative factions within the political system that might benefit from major reforms often fail to emerge. Peru's Hernando de Soto (1989) has detailed the enormous political and institutional hurdles that must be overcome by individuals and businesses when they are not a part of the dominant political-economic faction. His prescription is to mobilize alternative factions so they can represent their own interests. However, this may not be feasible without reforms to remove the barriers to such advocacy. Even in a democracy, alternative constituencies must be enlightened as to what various policy options would imply. They also must be given the means to voice their concerns and interests within the constitutional process. Finally, there must be checks and balances that limit the ability of any single faction to gain and retain unchallenged political and economic control.

Available evidence suggests that when domestic constituencies have emerged that favor and benefit from new policies, reforms have been sustained and credible. Occasionally, special inducements (e.g., export subsidies and export-processing zones) have succeeded in creating those new constituencies. Often the objective is not to achieve a trade-neutral regime but is instead to bias the system in favor of exports, at least temporarily, in what might rightfully be called redistributive governmental policymaking. This policy in isolation, however, generally has not been successful. It is crucial that comprehensive economic reforms be designed covering the mix of policies across all sectors as well as fiscal, monetary, and exchange-rate policies. When accompanied by appropriate exchange-rate and macroeconomic policies, special inducements can assist in sustaining export-oriented policies in the initial stages of structural reform. Successful practitioners of this tactic in the 1980s include the Dominican Republic and Costa Rica.

In the final analysis, the constitutional design and the institutional and organizational structure, as defined here, set the initial governance structure for the public sector. However, in any structure that is dictated by the underlying constitutional design and institutional and organizational framework, the public sector will be exposed to attempts by various interest groups to exert their influence. In this setting, because not all power resides with policymakers pursuing only the collective interest, some degree of organizational or bureaucratic failure will arise. Economic policies, then, can be viewed as the outcome of a political-economic process, conditional on the underlying constitutional design and institutional and organizational structure. This process is at work, regardless of how sound any particular policy proposals might be from a perspective purely of economic efficiency. And, while each governmental decision has impact on the evolutionary process, only if the underlying structure is well designed can we reasonably expect policies that serve the collective interest to dominate policies that serve the self-interests of powerful groups.

Note

1. One of the distinguishing features of developing countries is their unwillingness to close down inefficient firms. In many of these countries, bankruptcy laws are actively debated and passed, but implementation is grossly inadequate (Mitchell 1990). Many developing countries are unable to achieve a sustainable path of economic growth simply because the link between actions and consequences is broken by various governmental interventions. The risk of failure does not exist in many of these countries. As a result, irrational investments are undertaken (Woods 1989).

References

de Soto, Hernando. 1989. *The Other Path: The Invisible Revolution in the Third World.* New York: Harper and Row.

Fukuyama, Francis. 1989. "The End of History?" *The National Interest* 11:3–18.

Hurwicz, Leonid. 1973. "The Design of Mechanisms for Resource Allocation." *American Economic Review* 63:1–30.

Mitchell, J. 1990. "Managerial Discipline, Productivity, and Bankruptcy in Capitalist and Socialist Economies." *Comparative Economic Studies* 23:93–157.

Olson, Mancur. 1991. "The Hidden Path to a Successful Economy." In *The Emergence of Market Economies in Eastern Europe*, Christopher Clague and Gordon Rausser, eds.

Rausser, Gordon C. 1982. "Political Economic Markets: PESTs and PERTs in Food and Agriculture." *American Journal of Agricultural Economics* 64:821–33.

Rausser, Gordon C., and Pinhas Zusman. 1992. "Public Policy: Explanation and Constitutional Prescription." *American Journal of Agricultural Economics* 74:247–57.

Woods, A. 1989. *Development and the National Interest: U.S. Economic Assistance into the 21st Century.* Washington, D.C.: Report by the Administrator, U.S. Agency for International Development.

PART V Institutional Innovations

IF AGRICULTURE and agriculture-related industry are to prosper and grow, scientific researchers, managers of technology, and players within political, social, and economic institutions must accommodate each other in working toward a common goal of dynamic comparative advantage of the nation or region. This section contains three papers that describe new forms of public-private partnership that allow public resources to augment private capital while retaining the incentive structure provided by market discipline. University relationships with the private sector are highlighted in the papers by Dennis Olson and Don Hadwiger, and by David Gibson and Raymond Smilor. The paper by David Schroder discusses innovative methods for meeting the capital needs of rural business.

12 University Centers, Technology Transfer, and Agricultural Development

DENNIS G. OLSON
DON F. HADWIGER

In this paper, the development of university centers as a natural growth and maturation of agricultural research is discussed. The role of centers and, in particular, of utilization centers, is described. In illustration, the development and functions of the Utilization Center for Agricultural Products at Iowa State University are described in relation to technology and information development and transfer, as well as barriers to that process.

The success of American science, and of agricultural science in particular, is due in no small measure to the way it is organized. University research centers have become a prominent adaptation of that successful system. American scientists have captured more than half of the Nobel prizes that have been awarded since 1946 (*World Almanac* 1986), and U.S. agricultural science in particular has been a pathbreaker in world agricultural development. Studies of U.S. public agricultural research productivity show amazing rates of return on investment, usually in excess of 35 percent per year (Ruttan 1982).

We are challenged now to sustain this high productivity, and also to fill research gaps such as the large gap in applied and developmental research. A modern structure designed to meet these contemporary challenges is the university research center. University centers are elaborations of the traditional U.S. research structure, which is decentralized, competitive, and fragmented (Friedman and

Dennis G. Olson is Director of the Utilization Center for Agricultural Products, Iowa State University, and Professor of Animal Science. Don F. Hadwiger is Professor Emeritus of Political Science, ISU.

Friedman 1988). These centers follow the "associationalist" pattern of the agricultural experiment stations and federal agricultural research bureaus, which together were our country's first large science establishment. Those who first established agricultural research and extension institutions followed four major principles:

1. Dedication to a specific goal: increased efficiency and productivity in agriculture. It was assumed that farmers, by increasing their efficiency and productivity, would achieve other important goals such as higher income and relief from hard labor. Efficiency and productivity remained the goal of research even after it was learned that an efficient agriculture meant fewer farmers, and that greater productivity sometimes resulted in lower prices and incomes.

2. Identification of a target audience: the innovative producers. These would be the first users of new technology. They would also be its main beneficiaries because, by the time that new technology was widely disseminated, its savings would have been largely passed along to consumers. Innovative producers required continual technological change.

3. Building of a close relationship with that target audience. This was neccessary in order to share information, to improve decisions as to what research would be useful, to cooperate in implementing research findings, and not least of all, to develop political and financial support for public agricultural research.

4. Guarding of autonomy from electoral politics and macropolitical institutions. Research institutions insisted that research decisions were to be made by those associated with the agricultural industry, including rural legislators, agricultural agencies, and agricultural organizations (Hadwiger 1992). Intervention by presidents or political parties was unwelcome and was likely to be long resented.

Beyond the achievement of productivity and efficiency, however, there were unforeseen results. For example: upgraded consumer expectations, in response to the possibilities for higher quality and improved consistency of the finished product; improved environmental protection, as new technology reduces natural-resource inputs, permits flexibility in choosing safer technologies, and encourages a longer planning horizon for integrating emerging technologies; and added public programs to deal with increased productivity by stabilizing production, increasing exports, and opening secondary markets such as industrial uses.

These unforeseen results offer the possibility of political support from external groups intent on using the results to achieve their own group goals. External groups with potentially compatible goals include most environmental groups; groups seeking secondary uses for agricultural products, including industrial uses; groups seeking transfer of food in kind, both domestically and to developing countries; most groups seeking to achieve improved human health and nutrition; and rural development groups seeking alternative rural employment to compensate for the decline of labor in agriculture. Groups with incompatible goals might include some that wish to preserve a traditional social or economic structure in agriculture, some that champion animal rights, and those that oppose on general or theoretical grounds the introduction of new technology to agriculture.

The Role of University Centers

Experience suggests that public agricultural research has been most prolific within a structure that guards its autonomy from political regimes while maintaining a close relationship with a designated target audience, and which has increasingly close contacts with many of the groups that are unintended beneficiaries of new agricultural technology. It is within this modern structure of functional relationships that university research centers can play a major role. Complementing older research structures, university centers can form a partnership among producers and users of new agricultural technology to achieve a public goal. Capitalizing upon their developmental performance, they can mobilize the public and private resources they need for future operation.

One can describe a university research center in terms of its potential contributions, which include the following:

- Centers can focus upon particular developmental goals; for example, putting together the technologies that enable industrial uses of agricultural products.
- Centers can accelerate the process of creating new technology, by training future researchers, developing adequate research facilities, and providing a vision or plan for recognizing new research needs and opportunities.
- Centers can mobilize interdisciplinary research, which otherwise would be declining under pressures from academic disciplines.
- Centers can provide communication and information systems through which to coordinate efforts of university research, private research, producer and processing groups, and public agencies.
- Centers, in close cooperation with producers and processors, can develop, incorporate, and disseminate the new technology which they and other research groups have originated.

- Center research can help to mesh compatible goals of external groups, thus expanding the supportive coalition and warding off potential opposition.
- Centers can generate research funding from multiple sources, including private industries, trade associations, producer checkoff funds, state and federal research appropriations, and financial returns from patents.
- Centers, by virtue of their organization, can buttress the autonomy of the research establishment against occasional efforts to "centralize" research.

The Basis for Utilization Centers

To make the contributions described, it seems obvious that university centers need strong entrepreneurial leadership. They need the support of forward-looking constituencies, constituencies that exercise patience during the indefinite periods in which promising technologies are under development. On the one hand, group aspirations for industrial uses of agricultural products have often run ahead of the prospects as revealed in the laboratories, leading critics to charge that funding is being wasted, and tempting researchers to puff up their findings in order to blunt these criticisms. On the other hand, research centers can sometimes create opportunities where prospects once seemed poor, just as research on low-input agriculture has fashioned new farming system options and has borrowed technologies from fields such as biotechnology, monitoring from outer space, and computer science.

The frustrations, successes, and prospects for research centers are exemplified in the history of research on the utilization of agricultural products. Wartime scarcity has usually prompted interest in new uses and substitute products, leading to new industrial uses of some commodities and to new food packaging such as concentrated and dehydrated foods, which does not always prove to be immediately cost-efficient in a postwar environment.   Peacetime surpluses also have evoked enthusiasm for research on new product uses, sometimes accompanied by unrealistic expectations. In more deliberate fashion, public utilization research has been institutionalized over the years as a result of leadership initiatives within the U.S. Department of Agriculture, Congress, and the private sector. For example, regional utilization laboratories established within the Agricultural Research Service have provided remarkable benefits to the agricultural industry.

A recent initiative in the 1990 agricultural act (Public Law 101-624; the Food, Agriculture, Conservation, and Trade Act of 1990, Title XVI, Subtitle G) created a center for research and commercialization on nonfood, nonfeed, and nontraditional uses for agricultural products. This center will focus upon increasing sales and profits for agricultural commodities but will also consider other potential contributions such as rural economic development, conservation of depletable resources, and avoidance of environmental pollution. The center is directed in numerous ways to engender a partnership among manufacturers, financiers, universities, and private and government laboratories, all of whom are represented on the governing board. The board can make grants directly, and is also mandated to establish from two to six regional centers located at USDA laboratories or at universities, experiment stations, or state cooperative extension service facilities or in consortia. The structure and goals of these regional centers will be like those at the national level.

The State of Iowa in 1989 created a unit for technology transfer called the Wallace Technology Transfer Foundation. This foundation also invites—indeed requires—participation from the universities. The foundation will help Iowa businesses gain profits through adopting new technologies, and it will support the formation of new businesses which utilize technology resources such as those produced at university research centers within the state.

Iowa State University has adopted the research center concept. While there have been centers for specialized programs for decades at ISU, in the past decade a host of centers has been developed to bring multidisciplinary researchers together to address specific problems. While these centers are diverse in their mission and organization, they have commonality in engaging expertise from various disciplines, in having targeted objectives to achieve, in being evaluated by the return (in economic measures) on investment in their efforts, and in being closely linked with the private sector.

The rationale for centers at Iowa State arose when the political sector formed the precept that state universities could (and should) be a driving force for economic development and job creation. This precept emerged during the economic depression in Iowa of the early 1980s. The role of universities as an engine for economic development came from the assumption that basic science produced technologies that then laid dormant in university laboratories. This assumption was reinforced by myriad examples of technologies created in the United States but developed into commercial successes in other countries. Therefore, the drive developed to identify technologies lying idle in university labs that could be commercialized locally. An extension of that basic drive was for university researchers to develop technologies that could be commercial successes.

Iowa State University accepted the state's mandate to become involved in economic development and formed several research utilization centers that ultimately would lead to increased jobs. Through efforts at the state and federal levels, both numbers of centers and funding levels for centers increased dramatically. In addition to expanded programs, the centers provided the means to expand research capabilities by obtaining funds for capital construction. In so doing, Iowa State had the outstanding services of capable individuals, a strong political placement on key Congressional committees, and, the political "advantage" of being in a depressed agricultural economy; nonetheless, the commitment to technology development as a means toward a more diversified economy and more jobs was the primary factor in expanded center funding. Hence, the success of utilization centers is measured by the extent of job creation that occurs or the increase in the value of agricultural commodities by those external to the university. Internally, success is determined by grants received and external support for utilization centers.

Agriculture-Based Centers at ISU

With the success of several centers in obtaining funds from state, federal, commodity, and private sources, the centers developed quickly. Centers and related bodies were developed in almost every college. Some examples:

- Institute for Physical Research and Technology (IPRT)
- Biotechnology Council
- Center for Applied Technology Development (CATD)
- Center for Industrial Research and Service (CIRAS)
- Committee for Agricultural Development (CAD)
- Office of Intellectual Property and Technology Transfer (OIPTT)
- ISU Research Park–Iowa State Innovation System (ISIS)
- Leopold Center for Sustainable Agriculture
- Small Business Development Center (SBDC)
- Utilization Center for Agricultural Products (UCAP)
- Center for Agricultural and Rural Development (CARD)

While some of these centers have existed for many years, most have been developed within the past decade.

Within the agricultural arena, there are four basic multidisciplinary research thrusts. These are biotechnology, public policy and rural development, sustainable agriculture, and value-added utilization of agricultural commodities. The research thrusts are based within the College of Agriculture but extend to many programs in the university. Some of these programs have federal and private support, and all have some state funding. Of these significant research thrusts, the value-added utilization of agricultural products has the most direct impact on commercialization and creation of new jobs. Only in this agricultural center is the creation of jobs a criterion that is used to measure success.

Utilization Center for Agricultural Products

UCAP, as it is known, has four focused research programs. These are the Meat Export Research Center, the Center for Crops Utilization Research, the Food Safety Research Center, and the Linear Accelerator Facility. Each of the programs involves researchers from different departments and colleges that work together on targeted research projects.

Meat Export Research Center. Research at the Meat Export Research Center (MERC) has focused on developing products and processes that meet the specifications of different international markets. Considerable efforts have been made in assessing demand characteristics of international meat markets and in evaluating public policy alternatives related to international meat trade.

The Meat Lab Pilot Plant has about thirty thousand square feet, with full slaughter, cutting, and processing capabilities. This is one of the best-equipped public meat laboratories in the world. A series of short courses is held each year that brings about five hundred people from the meat industry (10 percent international) to the Meat Lab. Private companies use the facility (on average, once per week) to develop products; to test ingredients, casings, or equipment; and to educate their personnel or clients.

Through MERC, meat marketing manuals have been developed for Japan, South Korea, Taiwan, the former Soviet Union, Eastern Europe, Singapore, and Mexico. Conferences have been held in relation to some of these manuals.

The Meat Lab has been instrumental in developing the conditions and parameters for using blood plasma in various products. This has resulted in growth in market demand for plasma and in the rapid growth of the American Meat Protein Corporation, Ames, Iowa, which manufactures the plasma. Some of the processes used by Iowa Quality Meats, Des Moines, have been developed at the Meat Lab and have resulted in significant success in value-added, processed pork loins. There has been considerable effort to expand the export of high-quality chilled beef to Japan. These efforts extend from producers to transportation companies. Iowa holds a percentage of the expanded beef trade to Japan significantly higher than that of other states.

Center for Crops Utilization Research. The Center for Crops Utilization Research (CCUR) has brought new research capabilities and programs to Iowa State University in the past five years. New and remodeled facilities have been added at a cost of fifteen million dollars. Five pilot plants (35 thousand square feet) have been added: Wet Pilot Plant, Dry Pilot Plant, Industrial Products Pilot Plant, Hazardous Solvents Pilot Plant/Laboratory (one of only three in the United States designed to work safely with 120 gallons of flammable solvent), and Fermentation Pilot Plant/Laboratory. These pilot plants are designed to take products or processes from the laboratory and to scale them up to near-commercial use. A theater and classroom attached to the Industrial Products Pilot Plant will be used for workshops and other activities geared toward technology transfer. These facilities include chemistry labs dedicated for technology transfer activities. All of these facilities are available for use by commercial companies. Other CCUR facilities being constructed are state-of-the-art research laboratories.

Researchers work to develop products and processes applicable to the manufacturing and food industries, among them projects intended to replace petroleum-derived products and biotechnologies to enhance corn and soybean characteristics. Project areas include sequential extraction of corn for ethanol production; improving adhesive properties of soy protein; structure of starch granules that affect functional properties in food and industrial products; production and utilization of propionic and acetic acid from fermentation of corn-based substrates; technologies for degradable plastics from corn starch; thermally molded plastics from corn and soybeans; improved processing technologies for crambe; and screening corn germ plasm for unique starches.

CCUR has worked with several companies in various research projects. Nichii has invested in a soy foods plant in central Iowa and is using CCUR facilities for some of its research and development activities, in addition to funding research projects by ISU researchers. With new facilities, technology transfer activities will expand.

Food Safety Consortium. The ISU program in food safety has an emphasis on pork and is part of a consortium with the University of Arkansas (poultry emphasis) and Kansas State University (beef emphasis). Research is under way in the following areas: (1) evaluate potential health risks from infectious agents and toxins contaminated in the animal product food chain; (2) determine effective intervention points to prevent or control contamination; (3) develop rapid identification methods for contamination; and (4) develop techniques to control contaminants. Technology transfer activities are used to help the meat industry to improve the safety of its products.

Some of the projects being conducted at ISU: development of a rapid latex bead ogglutination test for presence of different pathogenic bacteria; study of survival of viruses in pork; identification of pathogenic bacteria on pork carcasses in three midwestern packing plants; measurement of consumer willingness to pay for safer pork products; development of modified-atmosphere packaging of fresh pork to control pathogenic bacteria; and analysis of survival of heat-stressed bacteria.

The Food Safety Consortium does not have dedicated facilities. Researchers are scattered in office laboratories around campus. Technologies to be transferred to industry relate to preventing contamination and developing methods of rapid detection of contaminants.

Linear Accelerator Facility. The Linear Accelator Facility (LAF) is a unique facility attached to the Meat Laboratory that gives the university the capability to irradiate food and nonfood materials. The facility opened in fall of 1992.

Irradiation has many potential applications in food, industrial, and medical products. Food is irradiated primarily to improve food safety (eliminating pathogenic bacteria), to extend shelf life (reducing spoilage bacteria or inhibiting sprouting), or to satisfy quarantine requirements (eliminating fruit fly larvae). There are many different industrial applications. Some examples are cross-linked polymers for heat-shrink films, rubber products, insulation on wires, and metal hardening. Medical applications are primarily for sterilization.

The facility can be used on a fee basis for research, demonstration, and short-term, short-run commercial production. This is one of only two linear accelerator facilities that is of commercial size yet is located at a public institution.

UCAP Functions

The primary goal of all UCAP centers is the creation of new jobs. Secondary objectives are value-added utilization of agricultural commodities and enhanced quality and safety of agricultural products. Technologies must be developed, transferred, and commercialized. The establishment of research centers has accelerated the development of potentially useful technologies. Centers have close industrial linkages that influence the direction of research efforts toward problems in the commercial sector. Hence, research efforts in centers are directed toward potentially patentable inventions.

An incentive for researchers to develop patents is the potential for later monetary rewards to the inventors. As technology develops and becomes more promising, competitive researchers enter into development, and the drive toward and necessity for patent applications accelerates to protect the invention. Hence, centers are attractive to innovative researchers who stand to benefit from their efforts. This is not unique to agriculture. In the mechanical, chemical, and electrical engineering fields, patents are sought more intensely. In agriculture, the development of technologies to utilize raw materials often involves innovations in process development. Unfortunately, process patents typically are not easily protested. Hence, inventors of process patents may not realize monetary rewards of any significant magnitude.

Another potential detractor from the goals and objectives of centers is the need for researchers to work towards tenure on university faculty, which occurs from four to six years after an initial appointment as assistant professor. Faculty researchers are expected to contribute to the advancement of their discipline. Technology development, because it emphasizes application of knowledge, may not be deemed academically important by peers making judgment on a tenure recommendation.

Barriers to Technology Transfer

The economic benefits of technology developed in centers are realized only when that technology is transferred to the commercial sector. Technology transfer is a most difficult task, and there is no one model that is successful for every technology.

Historically, technology transfer occurred passively. Technologies developed at universities may or may not have potential for commercial use. Commercial firms may have learned of potential technologies through scientific journals or scientific meetings, or through engaging university researchers as consultants. Those avenues of technology transfer are still active today. Technology developers in agriculture in the past generally have gained more by acting as consultants than by trying to patent technologies.

Patents for agricultural products or processes are difficult to obtain and enforce, in part because the basic science, which may be patentable, may have originated outside of agricultural disciplines. Agricultural research in land-grant universities historically has aimed to improve technology for commodity producers, at little or no cost to the producers. When technologies have been developed that could be transferred to the industrial agricultural sector, land-grant universities generally have not emphasized the need to patent those technologies and then license them and gain royalties on the license. Land-grant universities have widely ranging philosophies on the sharing of royalties among the inventors, research sponsors, and the university. Experience has shown that when a higher percentage of royalties is returned to the inventors, more patents are filed. The net royalty gain to the university may not be significantly changed, but the university gains because the researchers may obtain more grants, from which the university gains overhead.

Technology transfer can be easy and effective if a commercial firm is a partner in seeking the technology. Proposals for technology development are more easily funded from federal and state resources when a commercial firm participates in the technology development, because the technology to be transferred to the commercial sector is clearly identified. To transfer technology that was developed with no single commercial firm in mind is more difficult. However, technologies that have multiple users and multiple industry applications have much greater potential for monetary return to the inventors and the university.

There are a number of barriers that can develop to slow or inhibit technology transfer. Among them:

1. Failure to establish ownership and partnership in intellectual property. This includes patents, licenses, publications, and selection of the institutional researchers and industry partners or their competitors. Issues of discovery and development must be differentiated to encourage product and process development and commercialization. Compensation for individuals and companies for discovery, development, and capitalization risk must be balanced, fair, and predetermined.

2. Insufficient understanding of the technology and applications. Researchers (inventors) may overestimate the value of a technology due to a lack of understanding of the costs in utilizing the technology. Industry may underestimate the technology due to a lack of understanding of the technology's potential.

3. Characterization as a high-risk investment and/or a long-term return on investment. Industry tends to favor short-term returns on investment. Technologies that have uncertainty about the long-term returns on investment may be passed over by companies investing in the development of the new technologies.

4. Lack of pilot plants or field testing. Accurate production and economic assessment, along with a true estimate of expected results, are essential for industry to estimate and justify expansion, expenditure of funds, and time for return on investment.

5. Lack of a systems approach for assessing the technology. Technologies that solve a problem, improve a product, or decrease input costs may create new problems or costs upstream or downstream in the production and marketing system.

6. Inhibitory regulations. Technologies may create problems or conflicts with requirements related to labeling, environment, and subsidies of competitors.

To overcome these barriers, centers must build close relationships with industry. The industrial linkages must be multidisciplinary to include not only the industry technologists, but also contacts in marketing and finance. Such linkages are not easily formed, but input from these sources is essential to overcoming the barriers to technology transfer.

In summary, technology development and commercialization can become an integral extension of a university's research and outreach program. Imposing the center structure—with its multidisciplinary efforts, targeted objectives, and pilot plant capabilities—across academic departments facilitates both technology development and commercialization. Centers can generate support for funds from government, association, and private sources to benefit the university. The success of centers can be based on the return on investments and jobs, as opposed to alternative measures on academic programs. While centers can enhance and accelerate technology development and commercialization, the barriers that must be breached relate to intellectual property, academic/industry communication, returns on investment, pilot plant trials, and systems analysis. Universities, through centers, can effectively enhance technology development and commercialization if multidisciplinary industrial linkages can be created.

References

Friedman, R. S., and R. C. Friedman. 1988. "Science American Style: Three Cases in Academe." *Policy Studies Journal* 17(1): 43–62.

Hadwiger, D. F. 1992. "Technology in a Fragmented Politics: The Case of Agricultural Research." *Technology in Society* 14: 283–97.

Ruttan, V. W. 1982. *Agricultural Research Policy*. Minneapolis: University of Minnesota Press.

World Almanac 1987. 1986. New York: World Almanac.

13 Key Factors in Successful Technology Transfer: The Case of MCC

DAVID V. GIBSON
RAYMOND W. SMILOR

This paper presents behavioral and structural factors which are considered central to the fast and efficient transfer of technology across organizational boundaries. Discussion focuses on our study of the MCC (Microelectronics and Computer Technology Corporation) research and development consortium. R&D consortia represent a new organizational form that highlights and clarifies solutions to interorganizational technology transfer. We use interview, archival, and survey data collected on MCC to identify four variables—communication interactivity, physical and cultural distance, technological equivocality, and personal motivation—as being central to accelerating inter-organizational technology transfer.[1]

MCC—one of the nation's largest and most complex for-profit R&D consortia—began operation in Austin, Texas, in 1983. MCC was organized to pursue long-term (seven to ten years) precompetitive research aimed at significant advances in computer and semiconductor technologies. As of 1992, the consortium was funded by 22 shareholder companies, 59 associate members, and several government sponsors at about $45 million per year. The consortium was staffed by about 372 full-time employees, had spent about $450 million of its member company funds, had been awarded 56 patents, and had been issued more than 50 licenses for

David V. Gibson is Associate Director of the Center for Technology Venturing, Graduate School of Business, and Senior Research Fellow, IC² Institute, the University of Texas at Austin. Raymond W. Smilor is Vice-President, Center for Entrepreneurial Leadership, Ewing Marion Kauffman Foundation, Kansas City, Missouri.

its technologies. While this paper presents research findings on technology transfer at MCC, it does not evaluate the overall success or failure of the MCC's performance (for an in-depth description of MCC, see Gibson and Rogers 1993).

In addition to MCC, other prominent U.S. R&D consortia are the SRC (Semiconductor Research Corporation), Bellcore (Bell Communications Research, Inc.), the National Center for Manufacturing Sciences, the Software Engineering Institute, and SEMATECH (Semiconductor Manufacturing Technology). Well-known European consortia are ESPRIT (European Strategic Programme for Research in Information Technology) and RACE (Research and Development in Advanced Communications) in information technologies, JESSI (Joint European Submicron Silicon Initiative) in semiconductors, and BRITE (Basic Research for Industrial Technology) in advanced materials and manufacturing. These European and U.S. consortia were motivated by Japanese success with their VLSI (Very Large Scale Integration) Project in the 1970s and the threat of ICOT (Japan's Fifth-Generation Computer Project) which was formed in 1982. MCC motivated the passage of the National Cooperative Research Act (NCRA) that was signed into law by President Reagan in 1984. By 1992, over 275 R&D consortia had registered with the U.S. Department of Justice. About 40 percent of U.S.-based consortia are two-member organizations, while about 15 percent have 3 to 5 members, 20 percent have 6 to 10 members, and 25 percent have 11 or more members.[2] Worldwide R&D consortia represent a new organizational form that identifies traditional barriers and suggests innovative solutions to efficient and timely technology transfer within and between organizations (Peck 1986; Dimancescu and Botkin 1986; Evan and Olk 1990; Souder and Nassar 1990a, 1990b; Bopp 1988; Pinkston 1989; Smilor et al. 1990; Smilor and Gibson 1991; Gibson and Rogers 1993).

Traditionally there have been several key motivations for forming R&D consortia, such as (1) to allow member firms to leverage R&D investments, (2) to reduce the amount of duplicate research, (3) to promote long-term basic research, (4) to leverage costly and scarce intellectual resources and talent, (5) to better monitor the proliferation of new technologies and the research activities of competitors, (6) to reduce risk by allowing participants to diversify their portfolio of research projects, especially given increasingly short product development cycles, (7) to increase the ability of smaller companies to compete with giants like IBM, AT&T, and NEC, and (8) to enhance corporate image by emphasizing access to state-of-the-art technology (Murphy 1987; Fausfeld and Haklisch 1985; Gibson and Rogers 1988; Evan and Olk 1990; Gibson et al. 1988).

While getting technology transferred to member companies in an efficient and timely manner is a key managerial priority of most R&D consortia, it has also been one of the major challenges facing these new organizational forms (Hecker 1988; Kozmetsky 1988b, 1989; Noyce 1989; Inman 1987, 1988). Indeed, one of the main criticisms of R&D consortia is that in terms of return on investment, research results have been sparse given the amount of funds and research talent invested (Leiborvitz 1990).

Technology transfer is a complex, difficult process even when it occurs across different functions within a single product division of a single company (Zaltman et al. 1973; Kidder 1981; Smith and Alexander 1988). Moving innovative ideas from the research lab through production, marketing, and sales to the customer in a timely, profitable manner has proven to be a difficult challenge even for the best-managed U.S. firms (Peters and Waterman 1982; Leonard-Barton 1988; Leonard-Barton and Deschamps 1988). The challenges of technology transfer are magnified when crossing organizational boundaries, such as is the case in federal laboratories, research universities, and R&D consortia (Williams and Gibson 1990).

Consortia are commonly composed of personnel from different research and managerial (company culture) backgrounds. Consortia are supported by a range of member company investors with different technology and strategic priorities. These member company investors often have a long history of competition with one another. Consortia researchers and the member companies that fund these researchers are separated by a variety of professional, technological, strategic, distance, cultural, and competitive barriers. Such barriers also exist in technology transfer between federal labs and industry, universities and industry, and a firm's own research laboratories and the marketplace (Bopp 1988; Kenny 1988; Williams and Gibson 1990).

This paper describes technology transfer from the perspective of technology researchers and users in terms of three levels of involvement. Past attempts to model technology transfer are discussed and contrasted against a new approach to understanding and managing the transfer process. Based on our case study of MCC, four variables are presented as being central to technology transfer: communication interactivity, physical and cultural distance, technology equivocality, and personal motivation. Four hypotheses are presented for accelerating technology transfer across functional and organizational boundaries. Managerial implications are presented for the four variables that are depicted in a technology transfer grid. Finally, these barriers and facilitators to technology transfer are discussed in a case description of the transfer of an MCC-developed expert systems "shell" to funders of the research.

A Conceptual Framework

While there is a growing awareness that effective technology transfer is essential to the survival of U.S. business (Reich 1989), there is confusion over (1) what is actually meant by the words *technology transfer,* (2) the responsibilities of researchers and users regarding technology transfer, and (3) how to positively affect the technology transfer process (Williams and Gibson 1990). To begin to appreciate the challenges of technology transfer, one needs to get past the view that it is simply handing off a piece of hardware from Point A to Point B. In the present research, *technology* is defined to include knowledge or ideas as well as physical products (Weick 1990; Pinkston 1989). *Transfer* is the movement of technology via some type of channel: person to person, group to group, or organization to organization. Technology transfer is fundamentally the application of knowledge (Segman 1989).

Technology transfer can be ranked in terms of three levels of involvement (Fig. 13.1). Research is the most fundamental level. Here the transfer process can be largely passive through such means as research reports, journal articles, and computer tapes. A second, more involved level of technology transfer, known as acceptance, includes the responsibility for making certain that the technology is made available to a receptor(s) that can understand the technology and that has the potential for using it. The third and most involved level of technology transfer, application, includes the profitable use of the technology in the marketplace, as well as other applications such as intrafirm processes. Analysis of technology transfer must consider the rights and responsibilities of technology researchers and users given these three levels of involvement.

Three models of technology transfer have been most prevalent in the United States (Devine et al. 1987). The Appropriability Model (developed 1945–1950s) emphasizes the importance of quality research and competitive market pressures in achieving successful transfer. Such a model is consistent with a Level I research perspective. Deliberate technology transfer mechanisms are viewed as unnecessary. The challenge for the scientist is to do state-of-the-art research so that the user will "beat a path to the researcher's door." The argument is that good technologies sell themselves. Over the years, however, it has become increasingly apparent—whether we are talking about federal laboratories, research universities,

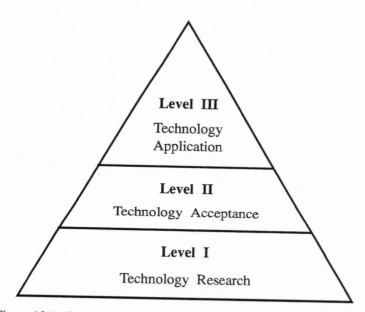

Figure 13.1. Technology transfer at three levels of involvement.

R&D consortia, or corporate laboratories—that good technologies usually do *not* sell themselves.

The Dissemination Model (developed in the 1960s and 1970s) emphasizes the diffusion of innovation (Rogers and Kincaid 1982). This model relates to a Level II acceptance perspective. The objective is to disseminate innovations to individual users. Once the linkages are established, the model says, the technology flows from the expert to the non-expert like water through a pipe. Yet in an age of complex technology it is becoming increasingly apparent that cooperation among many technology experts from a range of disciplines and functional responsibilities is required for successful technology transfer. One-way communication from an expert to a user does not characterize the process, if it ever did.

Most current literature on technology transfer describes what Devine et al. (1987) call a Knowledge Utilization Model, which emphasizes the importance of (1) interpersonal communication between technology researchers and users, and (2) organizational barriers and facilitators of technology transfer. While this model begins to appreciate the complexities of technology transfer from a Level III perspective, it suffers from an inherent linear bias (Dimancescu and Botkin 1986). The stated or implicit notion is that technology moves hand-to-hand, in one direction, to become a developed idea and eventually a product. This model tends to reduce a very complex process to chronologically ordered stages.

Each of these three technology transfer models has limitations in terms of applicability to technology transfer across organizational boundaries in contemporary high-tech industries. However, each also describes current beliefs and practices in R&D consortia, federal laboratories, research universities, and even corporate laboratories. For example, it is still commonly believed that the scientist's responsibility is to publish cutting-edge scholarly research and that once the appropriate linkages are established the technology will flow to the appropriate users in a timely fashion.

Level III technology transfer supports the view that many different sets of functions, activities, and networks must occur simultaneously to overcome obstacles and barriers to the transfer process (D. Rogers 1989; Kozmetsky 1988a, 1988b). The effective commercialization of new technology is considered less of a relay race, where players hand off a baton to the next player, than it is a contact sport like football, where the person carrying the ball (the technology champion) is met with active resistance (transfer barriers) while trying to score a touchdown (introduce the technology into the marketplace in a timely fashion) (Takeuchi and Nonaka 1986). Technology transfer is a contact sport.

Several important characteristics of interpersonal communication underpin Level III technology transfer (Gibson and Rogers 1993). First, successful technology transfer is a continuous, interactive process where individuals exchange ideas simultaneously and continuously. Feedback is so pervasive that the participants in the transfer process can be viewed as "transceivers," thereby blurring the distinction between the source and the destination of information. Feedback helps participants reach convergence about the important dimensions of the technology (Rogers and Kincaid 1982). The model is not unidirectional.

Also, often the technology to be transferred is not a fully formed idea. Researchers, developers, and users are likely to have different perceptions about the technology. As a result, technology transfer is often a chaotic, disorderly process involving groups and individuals who may hold different views about the value and potential use of the technology. Given such an orientation, technology transfer can be viewed as a particular case of the "garbage can model" of decision-making proposed by March and Olsen (1976). Transferred technology, then, is more the result of an unplanned mixture of participants, choice opportunities, problems, and solutions. Both problems looking for solutions (technology pull) and solutions looking for problems (technology push) are encountered.

Components of the MCC Study

In this case study, our objective is to understand the phenomenon of technology transfer in the context of an R&D consortium and its member companies (Weick 1984). To this end we employed a grounded theory approach (Glaser and Strauss 1967; Argyris 1972; Alderfer and Smith 1982; Pfeffer 1982; Martin and Turner 1986), and we collected multiple forms of data to uncover and explain technology transfer relationships across organizational boundaries.

For more than six years, archival documents, research publications, company statistics, and interview data have been collected on MCC.[3] The corporation is an extremely dynamic organization that has gone through three distinct eras: (1) its start-up phase, 1982–1986, when MCC was headed by Bobby Ray Inman (retired four-star admiral); (2) a stabilization and reassessment phase, 1987-1990, when MCC was headed by Grant Dove, a twenty-eight-year industry veteran of Texas Instruments; and (3) a reinvigoration phase, 1991 to the present, when the consortium aggressively explored new initiatives under the leadership of Dr. Craig Fields, former director of DARPA (Defense Advanced Projects Research Agency).

For this study we collected archival data, conducted interviews, and administered a survey to MCC researchers, managers, and company representatives. Interviews were conducted with MCC and member company personnel who were associated with MCC's research program areas.[4] Interviewees included MCC direct hires, shareholder representatives, and assignees. Direct hires are paid by MCC and come from industry, academics, and government. Shareholder representatives are paid by the member companies and are assigned to particular research programs at MCC for about two years. Assignees are shareholder company employees who become full-time researchers in residence at MCC. Direct hires made up about 70 percent of MCC personnel at the time of the present research. About 20 percent of MCC's researchers were shareholder representatives, and about 10 percent of MCC's personnel were assignees.

All interviews were open-ended requests that the interviewee give his or her opinions, observations, and experiences about technology transfer between the MCC and the shareholder companies. The objective was to obtain "deep and rich" data which would contribute to theory building (Weick 1984; Eisenhardt 1989; Muir 1991). We asked asked for and received available research reports, documents, and personnel files from the interviewees. Interviews were tape-recorded and transcribed for content analysis.

Based on interview and archival data, a survey instrument of Likert scale questions was constructed. The survey was pretested with personnel at MCC and with people knowledgeable about technology transfer and survey research. There were sixteen questions on the effectiveness of different methods of technology transfer, thirteen questions on factors facilitating technology transfer, nineteen questions on the importance of barriers to technology transfer, and thirteen questions on ways to improve technology transfer between the research consortium and the shareholder companies. The survey had a target population of 430 respondents, which included MCC scientists and managers, shareholder representatives and assignees that resided at MCC, and members of MCC's board of directors and research program advisory panels that were composed of shareholder personnel.

One hundred forty-seven respondents completed and returned the survey for a response rate of 34 percent. Seventy-one of the respondents were MCC direct hires, or full-time employees of the consortium. Seventy-six respondents were MCC shareholder representatives and assignees, and shareholder employees on MCC's board of directors and program advisory panels. The respondents were divided almost equally across research program areas.

Findings of the MCC Study

Effectiveness of Different Methods of Technology Transfer

The first column of Table 13.1 shows the mean scores of all respondents rating the effectiveness of various methods for technology transfer between the MCC and the shareholder companies (1 = very ineffective, 6 = very effective). The six methods considered most effective all concern MCC/shareholder interpersonal interaction: shareholder/MCC collaborative research projects, shareholder visits to MCC of more than two-week duration, shareholder site demonstrations, receptor organizations within shareholders, MCC/shareholder meetings, and shareholder representatives at the MCC.

The respondents rate the following methods least effective in transferring technology: proprietary technical reports, program technical advisory boards, nonproprietary technical reports, newsletters, the Technical Advisory Board, and refereed journal articles.[5]

MCC direct hires and shareholder employees share similar attitudes on the perceived effectiveness of most of the technology transfer methods. There is, however, a statistically significant difference of opinion on three of the methods:

Table 13.1. Effectiveness of methods for technology transfer

Survey Question	All Respondents[a] Mean	s.d.	Direct Hires[b] Mean	s.d.	Shareholder Employees[b] Mean	s.d.
Shareholder/MCC Collaborative Projects	5.4	0.9	5.4	0.7	5.4	0.7
Shareholder Visits to MCC of More Than 2-Week Duration	5.2	0.8	5.2	0.8	5.2	0.8
Shareholder Site Demonstrations	4.9	0.8	4.9	0.9	5.0	0.8
Receptor Organizations within Shareholders	4.9	1.2	4.9	1.4	5.0	1.1
MCC/Shareholder Meetings	4.6	1.2	4.7	1.2	4.5	1.2
Shareholder Representatives	4.6	1.2	4.4	1.3	4.7	1.1
Tutorials	4.3	1.1	4.5*	1.1	4.1*	1.0
Program Technical Panels	4.3	1.1	4.2	1.2	4.4	1.0
Technical Videotapes	4.3	1.1	4.4	1.1	4.2	1.0
Demonstrations at MCC	4.2	0.9	4.4*	0.9	4.0*	0.8
Proprietary Technical Reports	3.9	1.2	4.0	1.2	3.8	1.3
Program Technical Advisory Board (PTAB)	3.7	1.3	3.5	1.4	3.8	1.1
Nonproprietary Technical Reports	3.4	1.2	3.5	1.3	3.3	1.2
Newsletters	3.4	1.1	3.5	1.2	3.3	1.1
Technical Advisory Board (TAB)	3.1	1.5	3.2	1.6	3.0	1.3
Refereed Journal Articles	2.9	1.2	3.3**	1.4	2.6**	1.1

[a]N = 146–147.
[b]N = 52–75.
*p < .05, **p < .01, ***p < .001.

MCC direct hires consider tutorials ($p < .05$), demonstrations at MCC ($p < .05$), and refereed journal articles ($p < .01$) more effective means of technology transfer than do shareholder representatives/employees.

Importance of Factors Facilitating Technology Transfer

Table 13.2 shows the mean scores of all respondents ranking the importance of various factors in facilitating technology transfer (1 = very unimportant, 6 = very important). The five factors considered most important in technology transfer are highly interactive and personal in nature: person-to-person contacts, shareholder "pull" for the technology, a product champion at the shareholder company, cooperative activities between MCC personnel and shareholder companies, and knowing who to contact. Also, a sense of common purpose between MCC and the shareholders, shareholder representatives, concreteness of the technology, a service/customer-oriented attitude, MCC understanding of shareholder's business involvement, product champion at MCC, and MCC "push" for technology are important. Current incentives for technology transfer are considered most inadequate in facilitating technology transfer processes.

Generally, MCC direct hires and shareholder representatives and employees share similar opinions in ranking the factors facilitating technology transfer. There is a notable difference of opinion on two of the factors: (1) MCC direct hires consider knowing who to contact more important than do shareholder representatives/employees ($p < .001$), and (2) shareholder representatives and employees consider a service/customer-oriented attitude more important than do MCC direct hires ($p < .05$).

Importance of Barriers to Technology Transfer

Table 13.3 shows the mean scores of all respondents ranking the importance of barriers to technology transfer at MCC and at the shareholder companies (1 = very unimportant, 6 = very important). For every variable (except that of elitist attitude) the respondents indicate that the barrier is greater at the shareholder company than at MCC. The greatest barrier at the shareholder company is lack of a champion for the specific technology, followed by different research goals between the shareholder companies and MCC, and lack of support for technology transfer. Other barriers that are considered important at the shareholder company are technology transfer being seen as somebody else's job, the "not invented here" syndrome, no clear definition of technology transfer, not knowing who to contact,

Table 13.2. Importance of factors facilitating technology transfer

Survey Question	All Respondents[a]		Direct Hires[b]		Shareholder Employees[b]	
	Mean	s.d.	Mean	s.d.	Mean	s.d.
Person-to-Person Contacts	5.6	0.8	5.6	0.8	5.5	0.8
Shareholder "Pull" for the Technology	5.5	0.8	5.5	0.8	5.5	0.7
Product Champion at Shareholder Company	5.4	1.0	5.4	1.0	5.4	0.8
Cooperative Activities between MCC Personnel and Shareholder Companies	5.3	0.7	5.4	0.7	5.3	0.8
Knowing Who to Contact	5.2	0.9	5.5***	0.9	5.0***	0.9
A Sense of Common Purpose between MCC and the Shareholder	4.9	1.0	4.9	1.2	4.9	0.9
Shareholder Representatives	4.8	1.0	4.9	1.1	4.8	0.9
Concreteness of the Technology	4.7	1.2	4.6	1.3	4.7	1.1
MCC Understanding of Shareholder's Business Environment	4.6	1.4	4.6	1.3	4.7	1.3
A Service/Customer-Oriented Attitude	4.6	1.3	4.4*	1.4	4.8*	1.3
Product Champion at MCC	4.4	1.3	4.3	1.5	4.5	1.2
MCC "Push" for the Technology	4.3	1.1	4.4	1.4	4.2	1.3
Current Incentives for Technology Transfer	3.6	1.5	3.8	1.5	3.5	1.4

[a]N = 122–147.
[b]N = 63–76.
* $p < .05$, ** $p < .01$, *** $p < .001$.

Table 13.3. Importance of barriers to technology transfer

Survey Question	All Respondents[a]		Direct Hires[b]		Shareholder Employees[b]	
	Mean	s.d.	Mean	s.d.	Mean	s.d.
Lack of a Champion for the Specific Technology at MCC	3.9***	1.4	3.9	1.5	3.9	1.3
Lack of a Champion for the Specific Technology at the Shareholder Company	5.2***	1.0	5.2	0.9	5.1	1.1
Different Research Goals between the Shareholder Companies and MCC	4.9***	1.1	4.8	1.3	5.0	0.9
Lack of Support for Technology Transfer at MCC	3.9***	1.4	3.9	1.7	4.0	1.3
Lack of Support for Technology Transfer at the Shareholder Company	4.9	1.3	5.1	1.1	4.8	1.4
Technology Transfer Is Seen as Somebody Else's Job at MCC	4.2	1.4	4.1	1.5	4.3	1.3
Technology Transfer Is Seen as Somebody Else's Job at Shareholder Company	4.6	1.3	4.7	1.2	4.5	1.3
"Not Invented Here" Syndrome at MCC	3.8***	1.4	3.6	1.5	4.0	1.4
"Not Invented Here" Syndrome at Shareholder Company	4.6***	1.3	4.8*	1.4	4.4*	1.2
No Clear Definition of Technology Transfer at MCC	4.0	1.5	4.0	1.6	4.0	1.5
No Clear Definition of Technology Transfer at the Shareholder Company	4.5	1.3	4.8**	1.1	4.2**	1.5
Not Knowing Who to Contact at MCC	3.8***	1.4	3.9	1.5	3.7	1.3
Not Knowing Who to Contact at the Shareholder Company	4.5***	1.2	4.8*	1.2	4.3*	1.3
Technology Transfer Process Seen as Too Time-Consuming a Job at MCC	4.1	1.4	4.1	1.5	4.1	1.3
Technology Transfer Process Seen as Too Time-Consuming a Job at the Shareholder Company	4.2	1.4	4.4	1.2	4.1	1.3
Elitist Attitude at MCC	3.9	1.4	3.8	1.5	4.0	1.3
Elitist Attitude at the Shareholder Company	3.4	1.4	3.7	1.5	3.5	1.3
Secrecy at MCC	2.8	1.5	2.6	1.5	3.0	1.4
Secrecy at the Shareholder Company	3.3	1.5	3.5*	1.5	3.0*	1.5

[a]N = 142–146.
[b]N = 68–76.

* $p < .05$, ** $p < .01$, *** $p < .001$.

and technology transfer being seen as too time-consuming a job. The greatest barriers at MCC are technology transfer being seen as somebody else's job, the process being seen as too time-consuming, and lacking a clear definition of technology transfer.

Less important barriers at the shareholder companies are elitist attitude and secrecy. Less important barriers at MCC are lack of a champion for the specific technology, lack of support for technology transfer, an elitist attitude, the "not invented here" syndrome, and not knowing who to contact. Secrecy at MCC was considered a relatively unimportant barrier.

The widest difference in the ranking of a barrier at MCC as opposed to that at a shareholder company concerns the lack of a champion ($p < .001$), lack of support ($p < .001$), the "not invented here" syndrome ($p < .001$), and not knowing who to contact ($p < .001$).

MCC direct hires and shareholder representatives/employees share similar perceptions in ranking most of the barriers to technology transfer. However, MCC direct hires consider the following barriers more important than do shareholder representatives/employees: the "not invented here" syndrome at the shareholder company ($p < .05$), no clear definition of technology transfer at the shareholder company ($p < .01$), not knowing who to contact at the shareholder company ($p < .05$), and secrecy at the shareholder company ($p < .05$).

Ways to Improve Technology Transfer

Table 13.4 shows the mean scores of all respondents ranking ways to improve the technology transfer process (1 = strongly disagree, 6 = strongly agree). The respondents strongly agree that involving shareholder researchers more with MCC and increasing the awareness of the importance of technology transfer within shareholder companies would improve the process. Respondents also support greater shareholder communication with MCC, providing more incentives to shareholder and MCC personnel for transferring technology, increasing awareness of the importance of technology transfer within MCC, sharing success stories of technology transfer among program areas, and involving shareholder marketing and product planning personnel more with MCC.

MCC direct hires agree more strongly than do shareholder representatives and employees that the following would improve the technology transfer process: involving shareholder researchers more with MCC ($p < .05$), providing more incentives to shareholder personnel for transferring technology ($p < .001$), providing more incentives to MCC personnel for transferring technology ($p < .05$),

Table 13.4.   Ways to improve technology transfer

Survey Question	All Respondents[a] Mean	s.d.	Direct Hires[b] Mean	s.d.	Shareholder Employees[b] Mean	s.d.
Involve Shareholder Researchers More with MCC	5.1	1.0	5.3*	0.9	5.0*	1.1
Increase Awareness of Importance of Technology Transfer within Shareholder Companies	5.0	1.2	5.1	1.1	4.9	1.3
Have Shareholders Communicate to MCC More	4.7	1.2	4.9	1.0	4.5	1.3
Provide More Incentives to Shareholder Personnel for Transferring Technology	4.5	1.3	4.8***	1.1	4.1***	1.4
Provide More Incentives to MCC Personnel for Transferring Technology	4.5	1.3	4.3*	1.3	3.8*	1.4
Increased Awareness of Importance of MCC Technology Transfer within MCC	4.4	1.4	4.2	1.5	4.6	1.3
Share Success Stories of Technology Transfer among Program Areas	4.3	1.4	4.2	1.5	4.3	1.3
Involve Shareholder Marketing and Product Planning Personnel More with MCC	4.2	1.4	4.1	1.7	4.2	1.5
Set Up a Technology Transfer Office for Each Research Program	3.8	1.5	4.0	1.5	3.6	1.6
Establish a Technology Transfer Committee for Each MCC Office	3.4	1.6	3.7*	1.6	3.1*	1.6
Set Up a Technology Transfer Office at MCC	3.3	1.5	3.4	1.5	3.1	1.4
Establish a Research Program in Technology Transfer at MCC	2.4	1.5	2.7*	1.5	2.1*	1.4
Use Outside Consultants	2.3	1.3	2.3	1.3	2.4	1.4

[a]N = 142–146.
[b]N = 69–76.
* $p < .05$, ** $p < .01$, *** $p < .001$.

establishing a technology transfer committee for each MCC program ($p < .05$), and establishing a research program in technology transfer at MCC ($p < .05$).

Components Essential to Technology Transfer

Research on technology transfer has concentrated traditionally on effective linkage and information movement, usually to the exclusion of management theory (Levinson and Moran 1987). An exception is Creighton et al. (1985), who isolated nine elements that were stated or implied repeatedly in descriptions of technology transfer models. These elements were organization; project; documentation of information; distribution of information; linking; capacity to transport or receive and to act; credibility of parties or organizations in the transaction; willingness to transmit, receive or implement ideas; and reward.

Smilor et al. (1990) emphasize the importance of differences between consortia and their member companies in terms of academic and business values, networking and information sharing, long-term versus short-term perspectives, universal versus particular research objectives, and performance evaluation. Differences in these dimensions are seen to inhibit the flow of technology between organizations, even when communication linkages are established. Other variables such as risk, cost, and timing of the transfer process have been cited as being important to successful technology transfer (Inman 1987; Pinkston 1989).

In the present study, an analysis of the survey data, combined with the interview, archival, and observation data, led to four variables being identified as critical to the technology transfer process. They are communication interactivity, physical and cultural distance, technological equivocality, and personal motivation. In the following, each variable is discussed in terms of relevant literature primarily from the perspectives of organization and communication theory. Four hypotheses are developed and presented for future research consideration.

Communication Interactivity

Communication between MCC researchers and shareholder receptors can be ranked on a continuum from more passive to more interactive. Communication interactivity is closely related to information-carrying capacity, which refers to how well a medium is able to convey task-relevant information efficiently and accurately (Daft and Lengel 1984; Huber and Daft 1987). Media richness (Daft and Lengel 1986) also is a factor.

Passive links are media based and have the capacity to target many receptors. They are not constrained by geographic proximity and they can be asynchronous (not time dependent). The audience of possible receptors can be increased with minimal expense and commitment on the part of the message senders. Included in the passive category of communication linkages are research reports, journal articles, and computer disks and videotapes. Although such passive linkages can rapidly communicate the same message at the same time to a widely dispersed audience at a relatively low cost, the message sender often has no way of knowing who received the information and how the shareholder receptors receive and utilize the transferred technology. Prepackaged communication may go out, but little or no feedback returns. Such passive linkages are representative of Level I modes of technology transfer.

Interactive technology transfer links are defined as person-to-person, media-rich interactions. Such interactive modes of technology transfer relate to Level III (technology application) involvement between technology developers and users. Examples of interactive links range from cooperative research activities to on-site demonstrations. Interactive links encourage interpersonal communication in terms of fast, focused feedback; that is, researchers learn from the potential users and vice versa.

Hypothesis 1: *The more interactive the communication linkages between technology developers and users, the more likely there will be successful application of products and processes.*[6]

Physical and Cultural Distance

Distance involves both physical and cultural proximity (Rogers and Kincaid 1982; Hatch 1987). At MCC the wide-ranging geographical dispersion of shareholder operations exacerbates the problem of targeting an appropriate recipient for MCC-developed technologies (Smilor et al. 1990). However, as important as the variable of physical proximity is to technology transfer, spatial distance has not correlated with technology transfer success of MCC. That is, the shareholders located closest to the consortium have not been most successful at transferring MCC–produced technology. Cultural differences loom as the more important dimension (Albrecht and Ropp 1984; Pinkston 1989).

At the time of the present research, MCC shareholder companies were classified into four categories: mainframe computer manufacturers (e.g., Hewlett-Packard, NCR, Control Data, Digital, and Honeywell); semiconductor manufacturing companies (e.g., AMD, Motorola, and National Semiconductor); large aerospace manufacturers (e.g., Boeing, Rockwell, Martin-Marietta, Hughes, and Lockheed); and conglomerates that also have large computer, aerospace, or semiconductor operations (e.g., General Electric, Harris, Eastman Kodak, 3M, and

Westinghouse). Another member, Bellcore (Bell Communications Research, Inc.), was itself a research consortium that conducted research for the seven regional Bell operating companies. The shareholder companies differed in such fundamental characteristics as the industry or technology represented, the MCC research programs that they supported, the number and locations of divisions and their preferred markets, and the percentage of company funds going to company-based research versus MCC. Shareholder differences in organizational structure, resource allocation, operating structure, and technological and market orientations have a great deal to do with individual shareholder evaluations of the cost/benefit analysis of MCC membership (Murphy 1987; Gibson and Rogers 1993).

While the present research did not measure the differences in corporate culture between MCC and its shareholders, interview and survey data suggest that the differing shareholder technologies, structures, and processes are reflected in cultural differences. We further suggest that the diversity of corporate cultures among MCC shareholders poses significant managerial challenges to technology transfer from a Level III perspective. Being physically close may or may not increase cultural proximity. On the other hand, technology developers and users can be physically distant but culturally close, thereby facilitating technology transfer (Elmes and Wilemon 1988).

In short, cultural similarity/dissimilarity is an important predictor of whether boundary-spanning communication will be facilitated or discouraged. The more technology developers understand the values, attitudes, and ways of doing things in the user company, and vice versa, the greater the chance of successful technology transfer.

Hypothesis 2: *The greater the cultural proximity between technology developers and users, the more likely there will be successful application of products and processes.*

Technological Equivocality

Equivocality refers to the level of concreteness of the technology to be transferred (Weick 1990; Pinkston 1989; Avery 1989). According to MCC's chief scientist (Pinkston 1989, 145), it takes more learning and understanding to acquire technological know-how than it does to learn to use a tool. This difference results in qualitatively different problems in getting new technologies into use. The challenge is one of encapsulation: the more the user has to deal only with the externals (as in the case of a tool), the easier technology transfer will be. The less encapsulated the package, the more the user has to understand and master the details of what is going on within the technology, and the more difficult technology transfer becomes.

Highly equivocal technology is harder to understand, more difficult to demonstrate, and more ambiguous in its potential applications. While such ambiguity may facilitate different users perceiving the same technology as suitable for unique needs, such ambiguity does not facilitate technology transfer in terms of a Level III perspective; that is, in applying the technology efficiently and in a timely manner.

Hypothesis 3: *The less equivocal the technology, the more likely there will be successful application of products and processes.*

Personal Motivation

Motivation involves incentives for and the recognition of the importance of technology transfer activities. Personal motivation for actively participating in and supporting technology transfer processes, as a developer or a user, can range from positive to hostile. Both technology developers and users typically ask, what's in it for me? Successful technology transfer is most likely to occur in "win-win" situations. Personal motivation varies according to such things as the importance of the transfer activity to the individuals and whether the organization's culture rewards those who engage in technology transfer activities. In our research on MCC we found that the greater the variety of incentives, rewards, and recognitions for Level III transfer, the higher the motivation for those engaged in the process (Dornbusch and Scott 1975).

Hypothesis 4: *Successful application of products and processes is more likely to occur when research and user organizations support and reward those involved in the transfer process.*

The Technology Transfer Grid

A technology transfer grid can be constructed to depict various combinations of the communication, distance, technology, and motivation variables key to the technology transfer process (Fig. 13.2). In Cell II all elements are right for the successful application of the transferred technology. Given highly interactive communication processes, a variety of incentives and recognitions for technology transfer, cultural proximity among technology developers and users, and a clear understanding of the technology and its applications, successful technology transfer is most likely to occur.

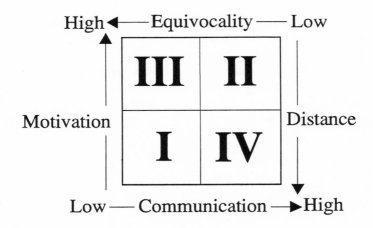

Figure 13.2. The technology transfer grid.

Successful technology transfer from a Level III perspective is *least* likely when there is low interactive communication, low personal motivation, high cultural distance, and high equivocality (Cell I). In this situation, technology transfer is not likely to occur because transmitters and receivers don't interact with one another, there are neither incentives nor recognition for those involved in the technology transfer process, there are wide cultural distances, and the technology is ambiguous and the applications uncertain. The technology may be developed, but it is neither accepted or commercialized.

In the two other cells of the technology transfer grid, there are combinations of two positive variables and two negative variables in relation to successful technology transfer and commercialization. Cell III describes the situation in which high motivation and low cultural distance combine with low communication and high equivocality. While there may be rewards for technology transfer as well as cultural closeness, communication processes tend to be passive and indirect. The technology is ambiguous and uncertain in its applications. In this situation, information may be passed from transmitters to receivers, but there is little or no feedback in dealing with highly equivocal technology.

Cell IV describes the situation in which high communication and low equivocality combine with low motivation and high cultural distance. While there may be interactive communication processes in conjunction with technology that has clear applications, personal rewards are minimal and cultural gaps are wide.

In this situation, people may interact and understand the technology, but the selling or marketing of ideas is blocked when unmotivated participants fail to reach across deep cultural barriers. Although demonstrations, on-site visits and person-to-person contacts may occcur, transfer is not likely because of attitudes such as the "not invented here" syndrome, a perception that transfer is somebody else's responsibility, and the feeling that technology transfer is a time-consuming and unrewarded task.

From Proteus to Design Advisor: Technology Transfer in Action

In mid-1987, MCC proudly and loudly announced that Proteus, a technology developed in the consortium's advanced computer architectures research program, was to be commercialized by NCR Corporation.[7] NCR, one of the founding members of MCC, was to use Proteus in a product called DesignAdvisor™.

Proteus was an expert system development environment, or software system "shell," that could be loaded with detailed knowledge about a specific problem area. NCR engineers used Proteus to develop an expert system for advising designers of integrated circuits. DesignAdvisor emulated expert knowledge in designing computer microcircuits. Installed on engineering workstations, the product reviewed proposed circuit designs and offered advice on how the design might be improved. DesignAdvisor was a significant product advancement given its ability to incorporate new facts and rules into its existing knowledge base and to revise its "expert thinking" based on new information.

Scientists, product development engineers, and managers had to work *very hard* as a team in order to effectively transfer the technology across organizational and functional boundaries. The process stretched from MCC's research laboratory in Austin, Texas, through an NCR product division in Fort Collins, Colorado, to NCR's customers. Important lessons are exemplified in the transfer of Proteus to NCR's product application in DesignAdvisor.

Birth of the Proteus Technology

Research leading to Proteus was begun at MCC in 1984 by three researchers in the Artificial Intelligence (AI) Laboratory of MCC's advanced computer architectures (ACA) research program. Charles Petrie was the project leader of ACA's expert systems group. David Russinoff was the principal designer and implementor of the Proteus system. Donald Steiner was a staff researcher. At the time, these three did not have a great deal of experience in developing AI software, but they believed that with their combined expertise and with the hardware and other resources available at MCC, they could design a more elegant, state-of-the-art expert system program than currently existed in the marketplace. Given their relative lack of AI experience, this assumption seemed presumptuous at the time.

MCC's shareholders funding the ACA research program indicated interest in the Proteus project. Funding was made available and Petrie, Russinoff, and Steiner were granted a one-year grace period before being expected to demonstrate results. Petrie, who had experience in managing advanced development projects in industrial settings, served as the interface between the shareholder company representatives and MCC researchers. Despite the agreed-upon grace period, within months the Proteus researchers felt caught between two seemingly opposing demands: to spend their time and resources (1) in conducting research on Proteus, or (2) in transferring research results to the shareholder companies.

As formalized in MCC's bylaws, it was the responsibility of the shareholders to build products that result from MCC research. However, the different shareholder companies funding the Proteus research had different uses and expectations for the same technology. Some shareholders were comfortable with the progress of Petrie and his team, but others pressured the MCC researchers to show the usefulness of their work.

Chuck Exley, chief executive officer of NCR Corporation, had helped to launch MCC in 1982. He was a strong supporter of the consortium. His company was a funding shareholder of three of MCC's research programs. One day in late 1984, he asked his vice-president for research, Tom Tang, what technology they were obtaining from the R&D consortium. By chance, MCC had recently mailed Tang (as well as several other individuals at NCR and other shareholder companies) an eight-minute videotape about the Proteus technology. Exley and Tang showed the videotape at the next staff meeting of NCR's senior executives. After viewing the video, Exley discussed the importance of MCC, then he looked at his senior managers and asked: "How are we going to turn this technology [Proteus] into a product?" With this high-level interest and support, it took just three months for NCR to develop a strategic plan for how the company could use the Proteus technology in a product application.

Ed Krall had worked for NCR for seven years as a senior consultant in corporate research and development. He joined MCC as NCR's liaison to the ACA research program in 1983. Based on his companywide knowledge of NCR's activities, Krall believed that an application of the Proteus technology could be made by NCR's Microelectronics Division at Fort Collins, Colorado. He knew the facility wanted to improve the productivity of their VLSI (very large scale integration) design process for semiconductor chips. Jack Mullins, NCR's liaison to MCC for computer-assisted design, helped Krall champion NCR's use of the Proteus technology.

NCR Makes a Commitment

In response to the recommendations of Krall and Mullins, Dan Ellsworth, manager of advanced development at NCR's Fort Collins Division, asked Robin Steele, a senior engineer, to investigate the Proteus technology. It was early 1985, and Steele had been employed at the Fort Collins facility for just eighteen months. Steele had a master's degree in electrical engineering; she was personable; and she was a world-class triathlete. As it turned out, her professional training, interpersonal skills, and athletic stamina all would be needed to extract the Proteus technology and turn it into a marketable product for NCR. The transfer of the Proteus technology to DesignAdvisor proved to be much more difficult than anyone could have imagined.

In April 1985, Steele presented to ACA's program managers her plan for using Proteus in a VLSI application. Petrie, Russinoff, and Steiner were enthusiastic about the potential application of their research. MCC's management supported Steele's plan. Steele returned to Fort Collins and sold the plan to her boss, Dan Ellsworth. Steele and Ellsworth then wrote a proposal about NCR's cooperative advanced development work with MCC. The plan had four main points: (1) NCR's need to learn more about AI, especially given the small size of the company's existing AI program; (2) the value of an NCR/MCC collaborative evaluation of representational approaches in computer software for semiconductor chip design; (3) the importance of technology transfer from MCC to NCR and the identification of this approach as a strategic experiment for NCR; and (4) the resulting contribution to NCR's prestige if the technology transfer from MCC proved successful.

MCC's Proteus software had been written in LISP programming language on a symbolics machine, neither of which were used by NCR in Fort Collins. Selling the idea of purchasing a LISP machine was a major barrier that Ellsworth had to overcome with his superiors. He argued that since NCR had already invested over two million dollars in MCC, the additional $120 thousand for a symbolics machine was justified. Tang agreed.

In July 1985, several NCR officials visited with Petrie, Russinoff, and Steiner at MCC. As a result of NCR's focused attention on the Proteus research, high-level MCC managers were becoming somewhat concerned about the issue of fairness to other shareholder funders of the AI research. There was also concern about protecting NCR's intellectual property. As a result, MCC managers established a visiting scientist position for Steele. This position was made available to all other shareholders who proposed similar joint research and technology transfer efforts. No other shareholders took advantage of the opportunity concerning the Proteus project.

MCC arranged for Steele to have an office and a workstation in its expert systems laboratory near the offices of Petrie, Russinoff, and Steiner. To prepare for her technology transfer role, Steele took several courses in expert systems and LISP. As Petrie commented, "Robin [Steele] was a highly-motivated young engineer who had a clear concept in her own mind of how Proteus could be incorporated into a specific NCR product that she was working on." Krall (NCR's liaison to MCC) observed, "She came down and interacted with MCC researchers. She grabbed hold of the technology and dragged it out."

Steele knew at the start of the transfer process that any deliverable product would have to be rewritten and ported to Apollo and Sun workstations, the main hardware used by NCR's customers at that time. So computer compatibility was a major problem to be overcome in the technology transfer process from MCC to NCR, as well as from NCR to its customers.

The Long Haul

Thus began a period when Steele spent one week in every six in Austin working with Petrie, Russinoff, and Steiner. The first day of each week was spent in downloading her computer tape, getting it running, and then giving demonstrations of NCR's applications of the Proteus technology to MCC's researchers. A second day was spent learning what had been happening with the Proteus research during the five weeks since her last visit. It took Steele a third day to incorporate these new developments into her software package. On the fourth day she conducted further demonstrations with MCC researchers based on the new ideas. On the last day of each week-long visit, Steele loaded code on a computer tape for her trip back to Fort Collins.

Once back in Colorado, Steele downloaded the revised version of Proteus and worked with Ballou and other NCR engineers to apply the Proteus technology to DesignAdvisor. Getting the MCC-developed technology to work satisfactorily at NCR was a difficult, time-consuming, interactive process. Proteus was not at industrial strength. As Ed Krall said, "By sheer dint of will, [Steele] got Proteus to work in a real product setting. It was very poor quality, a very bad interface. But it sort-of worked. More importantly, it convinced the [NCR] plant what was possible to do. Proteus continued to be developed and DesignAdvisor has evolved."

The trips between Fort Collins and Austin went on for twelve months. Steele liked Petrie and the MCC research team. She believed in the value of what she was doing. She appreciated the management support she was getting at NCR and from MCC. But it was long, hard, difficult work, and the tedium and the pressure got to Steele. During her visits to MCC she would often change into her running clothes and jog several miles on the track which wound through the cedar trees surrounding MCC's headquarters.

Initially, Petrie and his research team were leery of spending time with Steele. But gradually they learned to respect her considerable dedication to the Proteus transfer. They also came to realize that Steele made valuable contributions to their research by orienting them to the VLSI applications of the Proteus technology. As Ed Krall explained, "After visiting with the researchers in Austin [Steele would] take back a tape [to Fort Collins], spend some time getting it to work, do some data-analysis, deal with the problems . . . come back with the tape a month later and say, 'Hey guys, this didn't work . . . fix this, please.' And they [the MCC researchers] would learn from this feedback" (Krall, personal interview, July 1990). Thus MCC researchers got timely, useful feedback on the functions they were building into Proteus. They even began to look forward to Steele's visits to Austin.

In total, Steele and her collaborators worked on the commercial application of Proteus for over two years. The back-and-forth exchange demanded a deep, long-term commitment from both NCR and MCC personnel. But by mid-1987, Proteus had been successfully transferred to a market-strength product in Design-Advisor at NCR's Fort Collins facility.

Implications for Managers

Management can act to develop an infrastructure that is supportive of and conducive to Level III technology transfer. Their actions can increase communication interactivity and motivation, and can reduce cultural distance and technology equivocality. Recommendations for improving communication in interorganizational technology transfer are designed to increase the number and range of active mechanisms and to disseminate more broadly the passive communication. Technology development and user organizations are encouraged to

1.   Clearly identify and give authority to persons or groups to monitor, receive, and appropriately disseminate new technologies.

2. Emphasize the importance of technology transfer activities (such as in company publications) and increase awareness of successful cases of technology transfer.
3. Use visible and highly regarded technology champions during the transfer process.
4. Emphasize the use of highly interactive communication links.

While such recommendations seem reasonable, they are not all that easy to implement. For example, researchers and scientists are often motivated more by peer review and the need to publish their work in prestigious journals than by successful technology application. Technology user organizations may not want to assign their most capable and respected personnel to be "receivers" of technology. And although it takes the cooperation of many individuals representing a range of functions and hierarchical levels in *both* technology-producing and -receiving organizations, it usually only takes one well-placed "technology assassin" to frustrate successful application.

To decrease cultural distance between technology researchers and users, technology developing and receptor organizations are encouraged to

1. Expand the number and diversity of people interacting in the transfer process to increase mutual understanding of values, attitudes, and ways of doing things.
2. Involve product and marketing personnel in the transfer process.
3. Hold technology transfer seminars to bring together technology researchers and users.
4. Encourage and fund on-site visits to research and receptor organizations.
5. Conduct workshops to provide personnel with a better understanding of the culture and product strategy of technology transmitter and receptor organizations.

Once again, while these recommendations may seem obvious, they may be difficult to implement. For example "to increase mutual understanding of values, attitudes, and ways of doing things" across organizational and functional boundaries is a significant challenge for U.S. companies, which often reward individual or function-specific performance, not cooperative excellence.

To make technologies more understandable and less ambiguous across organizational boundaries, organizations are encouraged to

1. Clarify expectations for research activities and usability criteria, so that research and product development personnel have a better understanding of what each participant expects to get from involvement with the research and the transfer process.

2. Encourage collaborative projects in order to facilitate sharing of information and research results.
3. Require research programs to have technology transfer objectives.
4. Develop education and training programs on selling ideas early in the research process.
5. Encourage on-site demonstrations to make the technology more understandable to potential users.

Again, such actions may be easier said than implemented. MCC has worked for many years to encourage collaborative research projects, along with the sharing of research results both within the consortium and between MCC and its member companies.

Recommendations to heighten personal motivation focus on providing incentives, rewards, and recognition for those involved in transferring technology both in the technology developing and user organizations. Recognition may include monetary compensations such as bonuses and pay raises, special licensing or royalty arrangements, and honoraria for particularly noteworthy achievements in technology transfer. Recognition may also include featuring individuals and groups in newsletters, in the documentation of success stories, and in recorded accounts describing successful technology transfer activities. Situational incentives and rewards for those involved in technology transfer may include teaming opportunities with well-known and highly respected personnel, innovative collaborative projects that allow for interaction with a diversity of individuals and groups, training opportunities that expand an individual's knowledge and expertise, special allocation of funds for a pet project, and the allocation of time and resources to support on-site visits. The implementation of such actions may prove difficult. For example, while many companies may call for more efficient technology transfer, few may actually reward employees (in terms of meaningful peer recognition and monetary compensation) for crossing boundaries to enhance technology transfer processes.

Timely and efficient technology application, from the laboratory to successful product commercialization, is a key factor in determining successful interorganizational technology transfer. The organizational structure and technology transfer challenges of R&D consortia make these new organizational forms excellent "laboratories" for measuring barriers and evaluating solutions to interorganizational technology transfer. Management can accelerate the technology transfer process by developing an infrastructure that focuses on increasing interactive communication and personal motivation in the transfer process while decreasing cultural distance and technological equivocality. More research and experience will determine the validity and generalizability of these findings to other consortia, federal laboratories, and universities, as well as across a firm's functional areas from the research laboratory to the marketplace.

Notes

We appreciate the useful comments of the Technology Transfer Research Group at The University of Texas at Austin, and we thank Linda Teague of the IC^2 Institute for her valuable assistance in preparing this manuscript. Papers on this research project are published in the *Journal of Engineering and Technology Management*, "Key Variables in Technology Transfer: A Field Study Based on Empirical Analysis," 8 (1991), 287–312, and *IEEE Transactions on Engineering Management* (38), 1 February, 1991.

1. The authors thank the managers, scientists, and member company representatives of MCC (the Microelectronics and Computer Technology Corporation) for their cooperation in this research project. MCC provided the authors with unfettered access to obtain interview, survey, and archival data for our research on technology transfer at the R&D consortium.

2. The IC^2 Institute maintains a database on U.S. and international R&D consortia.

3. David V. Gibson and Everett M. Rogers (professor, Department of Communication, University of New Mexico) are co-authoring *U.S. Industrial Competitiveness on Trial: Texas High-Tech and the MCC*. This book will provide an in-depth description of the formation and operation of MCC.

4. These interviews included two researchers: one of the authors of the present paper and Christopher M. Avery (1989), who was collecting data for his dissertation, *Organizational Communication in Technology Transfer between an R&D Consortium and Its Shareholders: The Case of the MCC*.

5. Program Technical Advisory Boards and the Technical Advisory Board are made up of MCC shareholder representatives. They advise MCC research programs and MCC's board of directors concerning the operation of the consortia.

6. In the hypotheses presented in this paper, successful technology transfer refers to technology application, or Level III technology transfer.

7. This case analysis is based on published reports and archival documents as well as interviews and correspondence with Robin Steele (August 20, 1990) and Ed Krall (July 1990) both of NCR, and Charles Petrie (July 27, 1988) of MCC. The researchers also held a workshop at MCC that featured a discussion of the transfer of the Proteus technology to NCR. Please refer to *U.S. Industrial Competitiveness on Trial: Texas High-Tech and the MCC*, by D. Gibson and E. Rogers (1993), for a more complete analysis of this case and of barriers and facilitators of technology transfer at MCC.

References

Albrecht, T. L., and V. A. Ropp. 1984. "Communicating about Innovation in Networks of Three U.S. Organizations." *Journal of Communication* (Summer): 78–91.

Alderfer, C. P., and Smith, K. K. 1982. "Studying Intergroup Relations Embedded in Organizations." *Administrative Science Quarterly* 27:365.

Argyris, C. 1972. *The Applicability of Organizational Sociology.* London: Cambridge University Press.

Avery, C. 1989. "Organizational Communication in Technology Transfer between an R&D Consortium and Its Shareholders: The Case of the MCC." Doctoral dissertation. College of Communication, The University of Texas at Austin.

Bopp, G. R., ed. 1988. *Federal Lab Technology Transfer: Issues and Policies.* New York: Praeger.

Creighton, J. W., J. A. Jolly, and T. A. Buckles 1985. "The Manager's Role in Technology Transfer." *Journal of Technology* 10(1):67:65–81.

Daft, R. L., and R. H. Lengel. 1984. "Information Richness: A New Approach to Manager Information Processing and Organization Design." In B. Staw and L. Cummings, eds., *Research in Organizational Behavior,* vol. 5. Greenwich, Conn.: Jai Press.

_____. 1986. "Organizational Information Requirements, Media Richness, and Structural Design." *Management Science* 32(5):554–571.

Devine, M. D., T. E. James, Jr., and I. T. Adams. 1987. "Government-Supported Industry-Research Centers: Issues for Successful Technology Transfer." *Journal of Technology Transfer* 12(1): 27–38.

Dimancescu, D., and J. Botkin. 1986. *The New Alliance: America's R&D Consortia.* Cambridge, Mass.: Ballinger Publishing.

Dornbusch, S. M., and W. R. Scott. 1975. *Evaluation and the Exercise of Authority.* San Francisco: Jossey-Bass.

Eisenhardt, K. M. 1989. "Building Theory from the Case Study Research." *Academy of Management Review* 14:532–50.

Elmes, M., and D. Wilemon. 1988. "Organizational Culture and Project Leader Effectiveness." *Project Management Journal* 19(4):54–63.

Evan, W. M., and P. Olk. 1990. "R&D Consortia: A New Organizational Form." *Sloan Management Review* 31(3):37–46.

Fausfeld, H. I., and C. S. Haklish. 1985. "Cooperative R&D for Competitors." *Harvard Business Review* 63:60–76.

Gibson, D., and E. Rogers. 1988. "The MCC Comes to Texas." In F. Williams, ed., *Measuring the Information Society.* Newbury Park, Calif.: Sage Publishers.

_____. 1993. *U.S. Industrial Competitiveness on Trial: Texas High-Tech and the MCC.* Boston: Harvard Business School Press. *Forthcoming.*

Gibson, D., E. Rogers, and R. W. Smilor. 1988. "The Importance of Multiconstituency Communication to Research Consortia: The Case of the MCC." Symposium on Science Communication, the Annenberg School of Communication, University of Southern California, Los Angeles.

Glaser, B. G., and A. L. Strauss. 1967. *The Discovery of Grounded Theory.* New York: Aldine.

Hatch, M. 1987. "Physical Barriers, Task Characteristics, and Interactive Activity in Research and Development Firms." *Administrative Science Quarterly* 32:387–99.

Hecker, S. S. 1988. "Commercializing Technology at the Los Alamos National Laboratory." In G. R. Bopp, ed., *Federal Lab Technology Transfer: Issues and Policies.* New York: Praeger.

Huber, G. H., and R. L. Daft. 1987. "Information Environments." In F. Jablin, L. Putman, K. Roberts and L. Porter, eds. Newbury Park, Calif.: Sage Publishers.

Inman, B. R., 1987. "Commercializing Technology and U.S. Competitiveness." *High Technology Marketing Review* 1(2):83–98.

———. 1988. MCC interview with the founding president, CEO and chairman of the board. Austin, Texas.

Kenny, J. T. 1988. *Research Administration and Technology Transfer*. San Francisco: Jossey-Bass.

Kidder, T. 1981. *The Soul of a New Machine*. New York: Little, Brown and Co.

Kozmetsky, G. 1988a. *The Challenge of Technology Innovation in the Coming Economy*. Thirteenth Annual Symposium on Technology Transfer, Technology Transfer Society, Oregon.

———. 1988b. "Commercializing Technologies: The Next Steps." In G. R . Bopp, ed., *Federal Lab Technology Transfer: Issues and Policies*. New York: Praeger.

———. 1989. "Tomorrow's Transformational Managers." In K. D. Walters, ed., *Entrepreneurial Management: New Technology and New Market Development*. Cambridge, Mass.: Ballinger.

Leiborvitz, M. 1990. "U.S. Consortia: How Do They Measure Up?" *Electronic Business* (January 22):46–51.

Leonard-Barton, D., 1988. "Implementation as Mutual Adaptation of Technology and Organization." *Research Policy* 17:251–267.

Leonard-Barton, D., and I. Deschamps. 1988. "Managerial Influence in the Implementation of New Technology." *Management Science* 34(10):1252–65.

Levinson, N. S., and D. Moran. 1987. "R&D Management and Organizational Coupling." *IEEE Transactions on Engineering Management* 34(1):28–35.

March, J. G., and J. P. Olsen. 1976. *Ambiguity and Choice in Organizations*. Bergen, Norway: Universitetsforlaget.

Martin, P. Y., and B. A. Turner. 1986. "Grounded Theory and Organizational Research." *The Journal of Applied Science* 22:141–57.

Muir, N. K. 1991. "The Study of Technology Strategy, Technology Transfer, and Learning Processes in Shareholders of a Research and Development Corporation." Doctoral dissertation, The University of Texas at Arlington.

Murphy, W. J., III. 1987. "Cooperative Action to Achieve Competitive Strategic Objectives: A Study of the Microelectronics and Computer Technology Corporation." Dissertation. Harvard School of Business, Cambridge, Mass.

Noyce, W. M. 1989. Presentation to the Graduate School of Business by the founding and current president and CEO of SEMATECH. The University of Texas at Austin.

Peck, M. J. 1986. "Joint R&D: The Case of Microelectronics and Computer Technology Corporation." *Research Policy* 15:219–31.

Peters, T., and R. Waterman. 1982. *In Search of Excellence: Lessons from America's Best-Run Corporation*. New York: Harper and Row.

Pfeffer, J. 1982. *Organizations and Organization Theory*. Boston: Pitman.

Pinkston, J. T. 1989. "Technology Transfer: Issues for Consortia." In K. D. Walters, ed., *Entrepreneurial Management: New Technology and New Market Development*. Cambridge, Mass.: Ballinger.

Reich, R. B. 1989. "The Quiet Path to Technological Preeminence." *Scientific American* 261(4):41–7.

Rogers, D. 1989. "Entrepreneurial Approach to Accelerate Technology Commercialization." In K. D. Walters, ed., *Entrepreneurial Management: New Technology and New Market Development*. Cambridge, Mass.: Ballinger.

Rogers, E. M., and D. L. Kincaid. 1982. *Communication Networks: A New Paradigm for Research*. New York: The Free Press.

Segman, R. 1989. Roundtable on technology transfer and technology transfer research groups. The University of Texas at Austin.

Smilor, R. W., and D. Gibson. 1991. "Technology Transfer in Multi-Organizational Environments: The Case of R&D Consortia." *IEEE Transactions on Engineering Management* 38(1):3–13.

Smilor, R. W., D. Gibson, and C. Avery. 1990. "R&D Consortia and Technology Transfer: Initial Lessons from MCC." *The Journal of Technology Transfer* 14(2):11–22.

Smith, D. K., and R. C. Alexander. 1988. *Fumbling The Future: How Xerox Invented, Then Ignored, The First Personal Computer*. New York: William Morrow and Co.

Souder, W. E., and S. Nassar. 1990a. "Choosing an R&D Consortium." *Research-Technology Management* 33(2):35–41.

———. 1990b. "Managing R&D Consortia for Success." *Research-Technology Management* 33(5):44–50.

Takeuchi, H., and I. Nonaka. 1986. "The New Product Development Game." *Harvard Business Review* 64(1):137–46.

Weick, K. 1984. "Theoretical Assumptions and Research Methodology Selection." In F. W. McFarlan, ed., *The Information Systems Research Challenge*. Cambridge, Mass.: Harvard Business Review.

———. 1990. "Technology as Equivoque: Sense-Making in New Technologies." In P. S. Goodman and L. S. Sproull, eds., *Technology and Organizations*. San Francisco: Jossey-Bass.

Williams, F., and D. Gibson. 1990. *Technology Transfer: A Communications Perspective*. Newbury Park, Calif.: Sage Publishers.

Zaltman, G., R. Dundan, and J. Holbeck. 1973. *Innovation and Organizations*. New York: John Wiley and Sons.

14 Financing Industrial Development Initiatives

DAVID R. SCHRODER

The supply of capital can be successfully developed to support increased levels of start-up and expansion business activity in rural areas. However, if you intend to play, bring all of the pieces. The primary basis for this statement is my eight years of return-on-investment–oriented economic development experience with Kentucky Highlands Investment Corporation and, secondarily, eight years of focused venture capital fund experience with the Iowa Venture Capital Fund, L.P.

In general, private-sector financial institutions have not developed to provide much support for rural start-up businesses. Businesses are driven by the need to generate profits, positive cash flow, and growth under conditions that minimize the risk of failure. All other things being equal, businesses will cluster where it is easiest and most probable to be profitable. The elements that contribute to the ease of making money include high or growing levels of commerce; appropriate human and technical resources; resource, location, or cluster development advantage; and appropriate levels of support businesses. In many cases, rural areas offer few of these elements. Most business units are herd animals. They follow the group to locations that seem to offer these elements; without a bell cow, businesses in general will not head for rural locations.

Bell-cow support to increase the level of rural economic activity can come from the public sector, from the private sector, and from strong, disciplined local

---

David R. Schroder is a founding partner and current President of InvestAmerica Venture Group, Inc., a venture capital fund management company in Cedar Rapids, Iowa.

support. The best support comes from a coalition of all three of these elements. However, the most important of these elements is local initiative, an undying effort at the local level to muster resources over a long period of time to create a broadly based financial system.

Essential: A Broad-Based Financial System

The development of a successful broad-based financial system depends upon a number of elements working in concert. The first component of the system is a broad definition of capital. A broad definition should include the idea that capital can be defined both in terms of money and of in-kind human capital. Various types and sources of monetary and human capital should be provided to match the full range of balance sheet and operating statement financing needs of developing businesses.

The second component of a successful broad-based financial system is that of risk reduction through risk sharing. A "multiple deep pockets" approach should be followed so that many monetary and human capital sources are used to finance each investment. This approach will help to ensure that capital will be available for follow-on financings and that no single capital source will suffer a crippling loss from any single investment failure.

The third component of a successful broad-based financial system is the source and strength of the leadership supporting the system. To achieve success over a broad geography, the system should be supported at the highest levels of authority; that is, by state governors, town mayors, company presidents, university presidents.

The fourth element is that the individual components must work together and talk to each other in an interactive system. Additionally, support and rewards for the individual components should be based upon success. Various sources of monetary and human capital must be flexible, willing to take risks, and willing to support each other in order to help to build successful businesses.

Limited Financing Hurts Rural Networks

On the basis of actual fund-raising experience, I understand why a typical rural financial network may be inadequate to support increased levels of business development. A typical rural financial network is a collection of unassociated businesses that supply low levels of mortgage lending, typically little if any receivables and inventory financing, perhaps some form of narrowly conceived and remotely administered state-based financing, low levels of SBA financing programs, and no equity financing. Such a network supports the needs of existing basic businesses that depend on local markets, slow growth, and low levels of competition.

Some of the key ways in which financing in rural areas differs from financing in urban areas are the absolute lack of financial institutions, a different scale of financial operations, and a likely reduced level of financial risk-taking resulting from the lack of institutions and the difference in scale. Simply put, in urban areas there is a full range of financial doors upon which to knock. And there are many more doors! A large and fully developed system of financial institutions can sustain a certain level of losses attributable to the failure of high-risk business ventures. A rural financial system that is small and incomplete is less able to sustain the eventual losses resulting from high-risk lending and investing. Rural financial systems are probably more risk-averse than are urban systems.

Finance for Both People and Assets

A solution is to add more expansive and more innovative types of financing to the existing system in order to provide the full range of support required by rural business expansion. If the existing system is not getting the job done, more of the same will not resolve the problem.

Most businesses that already exist in rural areas depend upon local economies for their growth. The growth of most rural economies is relatively slow, so rural businesses grow slowly. These businesses have some stability, net worth, banking relationships, and mundane and understandable products and services. A rural business dependent upon a local economy has some disadvantages compared to a start-up business based upon new products or services being sold into larger markets. The slow-growth business won't create many new jobs with the expected high value added and profitability that is created by new products or technologies. These gains come with a cost. Compared to existing slow-growth businesses, start-up businesses require more financing, higher-risk financing, quicker financing, and many special support services.

Start-up and growth businesses require much different and more broadly based financial support than do slow-growth existing ventures. A major difference is that start-up and growth businesses require a financial system that will support people-based capital needs. Growth businesses require significant investments in research and development, product development, market research, business plan development, and technical support in the areas of accounting and financial forecasting and structuring.

A broad-based financial system should also provide low-risk debt financing solutions for appropriate asset-based cash needs. For instance, true asset-based financing should be available to supply cash needs based on receivables and inventory. Factoring should be available to support growth in receivables. Innovative inventory financing could be developed to include recourse for suppliers, thereby reducing lending risk. A "recourse" financing plan could be developed and enforced in which inventory financing would be provided to a new business if the key suppliers would agree to take back any unused inventory at full value. Thus, in the case of a business failure or upon the withdrawal of financing, the risk to the financing source would be minimized. Similarly, perhaps equipment financing could be developed with some recourse for manufacturers, also reducing lending risk.

For a rural financial system to be successful, it must make asset-based lending available on a broad scale. The reasons for this are compelling. First, cash needs for receivables, inventory, and equipment financing are generally the largest financing needs of many businesses. These financing needs also offer the most security to financing sources. Conversely, the largest amounts of available public and private funds are savings and short-term cash flows that can withstand only low-risk applications. The largest sources of low-risk funds should be matched with the largest uses of low-risk funds. While this is feasible and logical, lending sources frequently expect equity funds to be used to fund asset-based, growth-financing needs. This basic mismatch seems to be symptomatic of inadequate-growth business financial systems in rural areas.

The tendency toward overdependence upon and the overuse of equity is a mistake. The mistake is that equity funding sources are the small catalysts that must be used only to leverage larger amounts of secured debt financing. Asset-based funding sources must be convinced to take some of the risk. If a source of rural equity becomes tapped out, the catalyst that started the funding cycle will be extinguished and the new venture funding cycle will slow or stop.

Equity funds should be applied to high-risk needs and generally should not be used to fund asset-based needs. Asset-based borrowing presents a relatively low risk of total loss and should be matched with low-risk funds. Equity is usually available in small amounts and should be applied to smaller needs. Asset-based funding needs are relatively large and should be matched with large supplies of capital. This mismatch distorts the principle of risk sharing for a broadly based funding source. Equity funding should not be forced to bear a disproportionate share of the risk when many funding sources could legitimately bear a proportionate share of the risk.

Establish Systemwide Goals

A second element of the solution for a successful system is goals appropriate to the task. The goals must differ from the goals of the existing financial network. A first obvious goal of the system is to support increased levels of business growth and development profitably. A second goal is to craft elements of the system to work together in mutual support to achieve the business development goals. A third goal to spread risk over the entire range of the system to reduce individual risk and to increase the total amount of funding available in the system. Losses sustained in failures must be shared by many funding participants. If only one or just a few of the participants share all of the risk, then the risk-taking inherent in development, and thus the incidence of development, will be reduced. The system must have multiple deep pockets.

The ultimate question is, of course, can such a rural, broad-based, common-goaled system be successfully developed? The answer is yes. Some evidence to support this contention lies in the structure and performance of Kentucky Highlands Investment Corporation.

The Kentucky Highlands Investment Corporation

Kentucky Highlands Investment Corporation (KHIC) is a private development corporation that pioneered the development of a broad-based, primarily self-contained financial system to support both increased area business development and traditional financial returns. KHIC was established in 1968 and is headquartered in London, Kentucky. It provides traditional cash capital, people-oriented in-kind capital, and a full range of support to start-up or expanding businesses in eastern Kentucky.

KHIC started as a community development corporation. It was one of about thirty such organizations funded by the federal government's Office of Economic Development (OEDP). Initial funding was supplied by public sources. As KHIC developed, OEDP funding was replaced with various federal and private sources. Over time, KHIC has become able to support its operations with profits and investment gains.

Given funding constraints of the 1990s, funding for KHIC-type organizations is certainly feasible if supportive priorities are set by both public and private institutions. If we can support the Peace Corps and other major international initiatives, we can support a nationwide, locally based, rural economic development initiative with a public-private coalition.

To date, KHIC has invested $21 million in thirty-five business ventures, which have created twenty-three hundred jobs. KHIC has achieved notable successes. One of its first start-up ventures became the largest noncaptive tent manufacturer in the United States and is today a large air bag supplier to the automotive industry. Other start-up business successes include a kayak manufacturer, wood products companies, a successful injection molder recently sold for a substantial capital gain, and a sewing company that produced products ranging from unique stuffed toys to Laura Ashley blouses.

The Evolution of KHIC

An interesting aspect of KHIC's history is its evolution toward developing a broad-based system of financial support in order to increase rural business development. KHIC's initial development strategy was based primarily upon providing equity funding to support business development. Although KHIC eventually developed and now continues to expand and to refine a broad-based financial system, some of its early initiatives were less successful due to the lack of such a system. One of KHIC's early basic strategic beliefs was that the availability of venture capital would by itself create increased economic development. The difficulty was, of course, that venture capital alone could not provide enough financing if a full range of financing did not exist. Venture capital couldn't provide the human capital required, and by itself it couldn't attract an adequate quality and number of entrepreneurs.

A second early belief that proved inadequate was that KHIC should own and run businesses. KHIC did not have the human resources to both develop a broad-based financial system and build an industrial conglomerate. Even if it could have mustered the resources, a major KHIC goal—that of entrepreneurial support and development—would not be met by this approach. KHIC's current strategy evolved from the realization that a complete, broad-based financing system in support of entrepreneurial development was required to consistently and systematically achieve KHIC's development goals in eastern Kentucky. The KHIC financial system includes the following:

- Equity funding
- Factoring (the sale of accounts receivable)
- Secured lending
- Commercial real estate financing
- Business plan development
- Market research

- Financial analysis
- Accounting and legal support
- Relationship building with local, state, and federal funding sources
- Entrepreneurial search, assessment, and training

In retrospect, it is important to note that KHIC initially believed that merely supplying equity capital would support economic development. KHIC soon concluded that equity could not carry the entire burden of economic development, and it developed a more complete financial system. Many states and regions still misunderstand this reality and feel that the addition of equity capital is the major element required to support an increased rate of economic development.

The KHIC Financial System

Equity Funding through a Wholly Owned SBIC. Kentucky Highlands uses corporate capital and a small-business investment company (SBIC) to make minority and majority equity investments. Equity investing is used to support larger investments when institutional equity investing is appropriate and when a venture capital return on investment is possible.

A Factoring and Secured Lending Subsidiary. KHIC established a wholly owned subsidiary to provide factoring, the purchase of accounts receivable, and to make direct inventory and receivables loans to smaller businesses when equity financing was less appropriate and venture capital returns were not generally attainable. Factoring can be an excellent vehicle to provide high returns and good security to the lender and timely, growth-oriented financing for new and growing businesses. It is a financing vehicle that matches risk with security, reduces the need for equity, and shares lending risk. Every developmental financing system should include the availability of factoring.

KHIC's factoring company also can provide receivables and inventory financing to small businesses. This form of financing is not new, but its application to small businesses was innovative in that few area financial institutions provided receivables and inventory financing. KHIC thereby added in one more financing tool missing from the narrowly defined financial system available in rural eastern Kentucky.

To further support small-business financing, KHIC recently took additional innovative steps. KHIC has become an FmHA Intermediary Relender, is initiating an SBA Micro-Loan Demonstration Program, and has initiated an Aspiring Entrepreneur Program with local businesses.

Commercial Real Estate Financing. In a region of few available existing manufacturing buildings and even fewer available industrial sites, KHIC found that it was critical to participate in industrial site development and industrial building financing. To support this effort, KHIC founded a wholly owned real estate company that became the first certified industrial realtor in the region. Growth in business development depends upon this effort, which is just one more link in the establishment of a complete financial system.

In-Kind, People-Based Business Services Financing. New and expanding businesses require a set of business skills and services that may be lacking. These can include business plan development, market research, financial services, and financial modeling. The acquisition and support of these skills and services requires working capital financing. To supplement the lack of local working capital financing, KHIC in some cases will provide these services from experienced staff persons or through longer-term programs in technical assistance. While on the surface this may appear to be strictly technical assistance, this is actually a vehicle designed to provide working capital financing as one more link in the financial system.

Financial Relationship Building and Transferal to Developing Businesses. KHIC has been a prime mover in bringing outside federal, state, and private financing and support to the region and to the ventures that it supports. KHIC acts as a broker in this respect. These efforts have proven to be a key to achieving business development that includes support from multiple financial sources and the attendant risk sharing that is so important to the success of a financial network.

Entrepreneurial Search, Assessment, and Training. Investing in a person or a team that is able to build a profitable business is the focal point of a successful financial system. Searches for entrepreneurs and investment opportunities are not typically recognized as elements of a financial system. However, it is a cost of doing business that must be financed to support increased business development when development is lacking. Within KHIC's entire financial system, including formal business subsidiaries and financing programs and relationships, entrepreneurial and investment searches have been the cornerstone. A successful broad-based system must find a way to include and to finance searches that fit the goals of the financial system.

Building on KHIC in a Larger Geography

The KHIC financial model, or an appropriate equivalent, can be replicated on a statewide or regional basis. Although KHIC had the advantages of adequate financing, a private-sector philosophy, and a fairly self-contained identity, its elements and results can be developed successfully with a concerted public-private effort. A broad-based financial system to support rural economic development should include the following elements:

- Leadership that comes from the highest, most visible authority; from governors, from private company presidents, and from university presidents. Support should come from government, public institutions, and private companies.

- Public and private objectives that mesh. In general, the private sector must be rewarded with profits and the creation of economic wealth that can eventually be liquidated. In general, the public sector must be rewarded with attainment of sociopolitical economic development goals, which usually translate into job creation.

- Within a coalition, an understanding of how the public and private goals should be met, and who should control. The answer to this complex question was simplified in the KHIC case. Public goals were met if KHIC's capital was invested within a specified geography. The issues involving how to accomplish this goal were set by the participants, the KHIC board of directors, which was made up solely of representatives from the area served by KHIC. Thus the nature of the jobs to be created was up to the will of the people living in the area that was affected. How should the private-public decisions be made in other geographies? I suggest that the question is negotiable on a case-by-case basis, but that local people ought to be the key decision makers. Rural economic development will be successful only if it is managed and governed at local levels.

- A system that replicates the broad-based system that evolved at KHIC. The system must provide a full range of cash and noncash financing. The links that are missing in the region can be added. It is important that the system address both cash and noncash financing needs.

The Elements of a Complete Cash Financing System

Receivables and Inventory Financing. This is usually the largest financing need of growing businesses, but this need is seldom addressed in the design of developmental financial systems. Existing institutions or new solutions can be used to fill the need.

Factoring can provide the right kind of cash in the right amount at the right time. Factoring is secure and profitable for the lender. Ideas to help establish factoring could include (1) convincing local banking or financial institutions to establish factoring programs; (2) providing state funding to create a factoring operation (States now finance equity funds; why not fund a factoring operation?); and (3) providing state support to encourage an existing out-of-state or out-of-area factoring company to establish an office in-state, or in or near the targeted rural areas.

Receivables financing is the next link in the chain. Some means for increasing the availability of receivables financing could include (1) convincing existing commercial lenders to initiate receivables lending programs for developing rural businesses (Banks are set up to do receivables lending and they should be convinced to work with developing rural businesses); (2) state funding sources could provide a receivables lending safety net program by offering a partial guarantee on liquidated shortfalls; and (3) the lending community itself could develop a receivables lending program to fit the region.

As with receivables, inventory financing can be one of the greatest needs of an expanding business. Some rural financial institutions tend to underfund or not to fund this area at all. There is room for innovation within the area of inventory financing. For instance, lenders could negotiate a recourse program with key suppliers upon the return of inventory. This could enable lenders to loan 100 percent, or nearly 100 percent, of inventory value.

Lease Financing. For many businesses, equipment costs are large. Equipment lease financing may not be readily available for developing rural businesses. The potential solutions may be similar to those for increasing the availability of other types of asset-based financing. For example, we might convince existing lease financing companies to extend their services. State-based guarantee incentives could be used effectively. Another innovative tool could be the use of recourse by equipment suppliers to limit the down-side risk for lenders and guarantors. This would be a risk-spreading vehicle.

Equity Financing. I have deliberately placed equity financing as a link in the financial system toward the end of the discussion. While equity financing is important and is generally in short supply in rural areas, it seems often to be relied upon as the total answer to increasing rural business development. As experience has shown, equity capital is only one link in the chain of a complete financial system. A difficulty arises when the other participants in the financing system rely too heavily on equity to finance asset-based needs. Equity is in short supply and must be matched appropriately with riskier financing needs. In reality, if equity financing is available, but asset-based and other forms of financing are not available, equity will not carry the load and development will lag. Means for providing equity capital are many.

State and local governments have implemented numerous guarantees, direct funding, and incubator-oriented programs to fund product development and initial business development. In Iowa, the efforts of the Iowa Product Development Corporation, the Wallace Foundation, and the Center for Advanced Technology and Development are good examples. It is an easy task to research these efforts, to pick the best elements of their successes, and to design a program. Parenthetically, if the next link in the chain, growth-stage venture funding, is not available, early equity investment efforts may fail eventually.

Numerous states and some private sources have established state-oriented venture funds. Some of these have been successful. Examples of these efforts can be found, copied, and improved upon from states such as Iowa, Illinois, Indiana, Massachusetts, and Michigan.

Some state pension funds have invested in nationally oriented venture funds located outside of their states. The expectations of the pension funds have been that these out-of-state venture funds would search for and invest in companies in the pension fund's state. Apparently this strategy has not worked well in rural states. The problem is that venture funds are committed to only one goal, that of return on investment. They generally find it difficult to add economic development goals when the majority of their investors are not from the state making the investment and are interested only in their return on investment.

Elements of a Complete Noncash Financing System

Providing noncash or in-kind solutions to the operating needs of rural growth businesses is a legitimate element of a broad-based financial system. The advantages of noncash financing include providing for business cash needs not available from cash financing sources, spreading risk over a larger number of providers, reducing the amount of capital required from any one source, and adding needed links to form a broad-based system. Many innovative sources of noncash financing exist in the public and private sectors. These sources need to become integral elements of a broad financial system.

Accounting, Financial Management, Financial Modeling, and Auditing Assistance. Growth businesses usually are lacking in these areas. Hiring the expertise requires cash and creates a need for cash financing. Auditing and accounting firms can be convinced to provide reduced-rate, long-term accrued billings for rural growth ventures. This reduces some of the pressure on equity financing sources, decreases overall cash needs, shares risk, and matches the needs of the business with appropriate financing sources.

Legal Advice, Incorporation, and Patent Assistance. Corporate legal fees will grow if business development succeeds. Law firms should become a link in the financial chain. As with accounting firms, law firms can provide reduced-rate, long-term accrued billings to ease cash flow. The result is reduced risk for all of the players in the financial system and the addition of one more source of experience and assistance to ensure success.

R&D, Product Development, Market Research Assistance from Education Networks. Colleges and universities can play important roles by providing non-cash, in-kind financing in the form of research, product development, and technical information. These services should be provided at reduced rates and with accrued, long-term payment schedules in order to reduce the pressure on other financing sources.

Rental Space to Meet Building Needs. Incubator programs, if reasonably priced with accrual payment plans, are a widely used and successful link in the funding chain.

Entrepreneurs and Investment Opportunities. The search for entrepreneurs and investment opportunities is the element in the noncash financing chain most often taken for granted. Indeed, it is the beginning of the chain. Without an increase in the flow of investable deals, a financing system with increased capabilities will go unused. This link in a broad-based financial system obviously does not provide financing to individual businesses but must be financed itself. Ideally, support should come from public and private sources, but states may have to take the lead.

Long-Term Commitment. A final input. Successful rural business development requires a long-term commitment to achieve continuous, lasting success. The changes required to develop a broad-based financial system are substantial, and the process of business development requires time to produce a functioning system and significant results. The minimum commitment is probably five years. A more reasonable expectation is ten years.

Conclusions

My conclusions are simple and encouraging for rural economic development:

1. KHIC is a successful model. KHIC is no longer an experiment, but is instead a successful rural economic development corporation. KHIC is proof that it is possible to establish a rural development corporation that can support job creation and eventually become economically self sufficient.

2. A rural development organization must include a broad-based financial system. The organization must include a financial system that can supply a full range of monetary and in-kind, people-based types of capital.

3. KHIC can be replicated. Replication is only a matter of political will and fortitude.

4. Local control of a private-public coalition is a must. KHIC is successful for many reasons. In the end, local control and management of a broad set of public and private goals is the format that will bring success.

5. The long-term application of experienced management is important. Initial support must be committed for a minimum of five years, preferably ten. A core staff of people experienced in business development is essential.

VI Industrial Policy for Agriculture:
Policy Obsolescence and
Revisionist Approaches

THE TIME HAS COME for a reevaluation of the foundations of U.S. policy for agriculture and rural economies. In this final section, D. Gale Johnson examines how current policy, geared toward preservation, often works against the long-term interests of the industry and rural communities. In their conclusions, S. R. Johnson and S. A. Martin begin to structure a policy for agriculture and rural economies in the United States based on the framework provided by the economic and organizational theory of industrial policy. Elements of this revisionist policy will require new approaches by all agents in the policy process. The change in perspective will take time, but there is no doubt that it has begun.

15 U.S. Agricultural Programs as Industrial Policy

D. GALE JOHNSON

The opening paper by Sheila Martin and Stanley R. Johnson warns us that the term *industrial policy* does not describe a specifically defined set of objectives, nor the activities required to achieve those objectives. In other words, it is not something you can put your arms around and know what you have. They note three very different objectives or purposes of industrial policy, which I repeat:

- Preserving or restoring the existing structure for the industry and maintaining the existing political-economic equilibrium.
- Assisting the transition required by change or accommodating and increasing the efficiency of adaptation to change.
- Modernizing in anticipation of external changes—picking winners.

Clearly these three sets of purposes describe many of what are called industrial policies. But I believe that there is a fourth set of appropriate objectives for an industrial policy. This policy envisages (1) providing public goods; (2) supporting goods and services with significant externalities, such as primary education; (3) accepting a decentralized decision process for the provision of a major category of public goods, namely research and advanced education; and (4) creating institutional and legal conditions for the utilization of rural resources.

These four objectives constitute a description of what I believe was the rural industrial policy of the United States from the mid-nineteenth century until World

---

D. Gale Johnson is Eliakim Hastings Moore Distinguished Service Professor of Economics at the University of Chicago.

War I. These objectives are consistent with the decision process that created the land-grant universities (1862), the agricultural experiment stations (1887), the agricultural extension service (1914), and vocational agriculture (1917). The decisions that led to the land surveys and the setting aside of land every mile for a road, as well as the Highway Act of 1916, fit within the same mold, as did the gradual achievement of universal primary education paid for from public funds. There was also the requirement, at least in the Midwest, that every male adult had to contribute either labor or money to assist in the construction, improvement, or maintenance of roads. These measures constituted an industrial policy that was designed to complement the market—to carry out functions that the market, especially a competitive market, cannot carry out.

The emphasis upon the decentralized decision process for research and education merits special note. This approach, which has guided most publicly supported agricultural research, often has been criticized as resulting in duplication and lacking in direction. But as Evenson and Huffman have shown, it has given the nation an agricultural research system that is highly productive. It is a research system that has been able to respond to the particular needs of local areas. A unique aspect of the American agricultural research system is the large role played by the private sector. Would this have happened if the public system had been centrally directed? I don't know, but it is something to think about.

A clear lesson that we should learn from the Martin-Johnson paper is that to call something an industrial policy doesn't tell one very much. One must search for the objectives of that policy.

Agricultural Policy Has Focused on Losers

In spite of what one may gather from the rhetoric concerning industrial policy, the United States has a number of industrial policies affecting major sectors of the economy. One of those sectors is agriculture. If one were to characterize the objectives of some of the important industrial policies, one would have to say that the major objectives have been to preserve or restore existing structures or conditions. Our policies for textiles, automobiles, and agricultural commodities fit this category all too well. Except for the fond hope that time will cure everything, these industrial policies have not contributed transitional adjustment or increased efficiency, nor have they picked and supported winners.

U.S. agriculture has had some winners during the past half-century. These winners were nurtured by the efforts of the agricultural research enterprises and thus could be said to have resulted from the industrial policy described by the fourth set of objectives. These winners certainly include soybeans and broilers. Has the industrial policy for agriculture that includes the agricultural commodity programs, first promulgated by the Agricultural Adjustment Act of 1933, worked to support these winners by increasing their competitiveness? In the case of soybeans, the answer clearly has been in the negative.

To some considerable degree, our dominance of the world soybean market has been lost as a result of our industrial policies, specifically the feed grain and cotton programs. Because of the rules affecting set-asides and the incentives through the deficiency payments to devote the maximum permitted area to corn, the area devoted to soybeans was reduced during the 1980s. After increasing rapidly in the 1960s and 1970s, the soybean harvested area declined by ten million acres (15 percent) in the 1980s. Because U.S. production of soybeans has been reduced by the feed grain and cotton programs, the world market price has increased somewhat and competing producers in South America have expanded production and taken over an increasing share of the world export market for soybeans.

The feed grain and cotton programs have made participating in the acreage reduction program and idling land more profitable than expanding the area devoted to soybeans. The Export Enhancement Program also may have impinged upon the export market for soybeans. In a number of instances the EEP subsidy on wheat has lowered the import cost of wheat to that of feed grains, and it is possible that this has had a negative effect on soybeans. Have soybeans been hurt? Has anyone ever asked?

In the case of broilers, except for the support of the research community, policy has done nothing except to stand aside while a revolution has occurred in the production and distribution of poultry meat. This has occurred with a drastic shift in the location and concentration of poultry meat production. Should there have been an industrial policy for broilers? If you are a believer in industrial policy, should there not have been?

In our agricultural industrial policy we have put most of our considerable policy resources on losers, not winners. Most of the governmental expenditures on supporting agriculture, along with the added costs imposed upon consumers, have gone to support losers: dairy, wheat, corn, sugar, rice, and wool. Corn might not have been a loser had it not been "favored" by so much attention from the Congress and the Department of Agriculture.

Except for dairy our industrial policies for agriculture have not included livestock, unless you count bees as livestock. The exception here is the import controls on beef and veal. But for many years the efforts to increase the returns to grain production resulted in higher feed costs for livestock producers and thus reduced the competitiveness of our livestock products. This adverse effect was corrected when the use of deficiency payments became widespread, but the experience does indicate that often there are unintended consequences of an industrial policy when that policy seeks to maintain the existing structure of an industry and attempts to shield it from the winds of competition.

In our agricultural commodity programs we have continued to believe that we can have a significant influence on world market prices for grains and cotton by limiting the amount of land devoted to those crops. In other words, we are trying to act as though we are a monopolist. Like most monopolists, we are losing market share. In the late 1970s we produced about 21 percent of world grain; in the early 1990s we are producing about 17.5 percent. While our share of production in the part of the world where production and consumption is affected by world market prices is significantly greater than 20 percent, that share is sufficiently small that it is a very expensive arrogance on our part to assume that we can for very long have a major influence on the prices in world markets. Why do we continue to limit our production while farmers in the rest of the world are free to produce whatever amounts they wish? It is probably because given the commitments that have been made in legislation with respect to target prices, the budgetary cost is reduced by limiting acreage devoted to the price-supported crops. Consequently, the industrial policy that we have adopted results in our losing world market share. Is it, perhaps, time to reconsider the desirability of a policy that assures long-run erosion of our competitiveness in world markets for grain and cotton?

Rural Policy Lacks Coherence, Results

Can we say that the federal government has a rural policy? More to the point, can we say that the federal government has a coherent rural policy? The second of the questions can be answered unambiguously in the negative. We have been told that there are seventy-nine different rural programs, or perhaps one hundred or more.

Does anyone know what the effects of these programs have been? We didn't learn the answer to that question from the papers presented at this conference, and I fear that this question has not been answered anywhere. One of our papers did look at the factors associated with the distribution of funds or projects. But where the money went does not tell us what the consequences of spending the money were. A comment from the floor of the conference that those who supported the programs had no interest in finding out what the effects were is consistent with the lack of knowledge concerning the effectiveness of the programs.

Is it not likely that the most effective rural program the federal government has had in the past half century has been the interstate system? This system, combined with other improvements in highways plus rural electrification, may have done more for rural America than all the other programs, including the commodity programs with their huge annual budgetary outlays. The improvement in transportation and the availability of electricity has been a necessary condition for the expansion of manufacturing activities in rural areas. The increase in nonfarm job opportunities in rural areas has helped to maintain the rural population in the face of declining employment in agriculture.

I believe it can be said accurately that the numerous rural programs that we have seem to address symptoms rather than the underlying problems. The problems include the slow growth of productive earnings and job opportunities in rural areas and the relatively inadequate state of rural education. Our national rural policy has not emphasized the quality of primary and secondary education in rural areas. The quality of education is an important factor in attracting nonfarm enterprises to locate in or near rural areas. It is important because of its implications for the productivity of the rural labor force, but also because those who make location decisions are concerned about the quality of education available to the children of management who may relocate to rural areas. As we all know, there is great resistance to having the federal government play any significant role in primary and secondary education. As long as this position is maintained, it becomes the responsibility of state governments to assure adequate levels of educational performance in rural areas.

When there is a discussion of industrial policy, the pundits always refer to Japan. But if we want an example of an effective rural policy that is apparently cost-effective, we should look to Taiwan. Contrary to what one would assume from the pressure that the U.S. government has put on Taiwan in recent years to liberalize its agricultural trade, the average level of protection of Taiwan's agriculture is less than that of the United States. These are the findings obtained by the Economic Research Service of the U.S. Department of Agriculture. During the period 1984–1987 the difference between the returns to farmers and the world market price averaged 41 percent for the United States and 32 percent for Taiwan—Taiwan's agriculture was less protected than that of the United States. The protection of rice in the United States was more than double that in Taiwan: 114 percent versus 41 percent. In terms of land area, the average farm in the United States is somewhat more than one hundred times that of Taiwan, and the amount of labor per farm is about 50 percent more. Because of the high price of land in

Taiwan, the difference in the amount of capital required to establish a farm is quite small.

How has Taiwan established a relatively low-cost agriculture in spite of the limitations of its land area? Many factors have been involved: a successful land reform, a first-rate research and extension system, and a rural policy that emphasizes the relatively even development of the infrastructure in rural areas. This infrastructure involved the widespread availability of electricity and communications and the development of a road system that provided easy access to all rural areas. Nonagricultural enterprises are widely distributed throughout rural Taiwan. The majority of Taiwan's farms are part-time; only 10 percent of the farms are full-time. The average per capita real income of farm families compares favorably with that of nonfarm families, if one adjusts for differences in age and education. Taiwan also has made some mistakes. The sale and rental of land are impeded by a failure to change the land reform laws to reflect changed conditions. As a result, the sizes of farms have not been adjusted as they would have been in a market situation that permitted selling or renting as agreed upon by the parties involved.

We have heard references to the unsatisfactory state of rural life—relatively low incomes, loss of population, poor state of education. But what has not been noted is that after five decades of commodity policies that have become increasingly costly, farm consolidation has continued at a rapid pace. In 1990, 320 thousand farms (out of 2.1 million) accounted for 79 percent of farm sales; the 627 thousand largest farms accounted for 93 percent. For price-supported commodities, the largest 16 percent of the farms accounted for 71 percent of the sales. The farm population is now hardly more than 2 percent of the total, down from 10 percent in the late 1950s. I am not saying these outcomes were bad or that it would have been better if the farm population were larger now than it is. In fact, I sometimes think the best thing that can be said about our farm commodity programs is that they have not seriously inhibited the adjustment of farm families within the overall adjustment of labor to changing economic conditions.

But I doubt if anyone can argue that these were the outcomes that the programs were to achieve. Policymakers should learn much more about what the programs actually have achieved. For example, are the returns to farmers who obtain most of the benefits from the commodity program for their labor and management higher than they would have been in the absence of the programs? I think the evidence is almost certainly not. Anyone who understands farm families in terms of their management abilities has to know that they would not have accepted significantly lower returns for their labor and management than they could have obtained elsewhere. Net farm incomes have been increased by the programs, but the increased income has gone to increase the return to the farmland. Of course, if the commodity programs were halted suddenly, those now engaged in commercial farming would suffer losses in the value of their nonland assets and in the return to their labor and management. But no one I know of proposes an instantaneous phaseout of the programs.

Policymaking: Ripe for Scrutiny

In their paper, Martin and Johnson call our attention to the processes by which our rural (industrial) policies were formulated. They argue that if we are to understand our rural policies we must improve our understanding of how those policies are formulated and enacted. And they raise the provocative point that perhaps unless the present system of policymaking is changed, we cannot expect any significant improvement in the content of our rural policies. On this occasion, all one can do is to raise certain questions.

Why do the USDA and Congress, responding as they do to various interest groups, approve and maintain so many different rural programs? Why have not programs been consolidated over the years, even if multiple objectives remain? Why do we continue commodity programs that the Organization for Economic Cooperation and Development, of which we are a founding member, estimated cost U.S. taxpayers and consumers $36 billion in 1990? This was an average of $22 thousand per farm, but probably nearly $75 thousand for each of the largest thirty-two thousand farms. The average cost comes to more than one hundred dollars per acre of all cropland, or almost exactly equal to the cash rent paid for cropland in Iowa during recent years.

It is evident that over the past quarter century the formulation of agricultural policy has become more fragmented. Several factors have been at work. The general farm organizations have lost power and influence; commodity organizations have increased their influence. Discipline and control over the committees in Congress have been lost largely as a result of reforms enacted in the 1970s. There is some truth to the statement that the 1980, 1985, and 1990 farm bills were nothing more than a collection of discrete and uncoordinated pieces of commodity legislation. The fact that the executive branch and Congress have been controlled by different political parties has probably abetted this devolution of farm legislation into a collection of special commodity-interest legislation.

Stuart Rosenfeld raises the possibility of transferring the positive aspects of agricultural research, technology development, and extension to other rural productive activities. The rationale for our successful industrial policy for agriculture that was started in the mid-nineteenth century holds equally well for any competitive industry. In a competitive industry, the individual firms do not have and cannot have the resources to undertake research. In a competitive industry, research output is a public good; the research producer cannot capture the benefits of the research. It seems to me that a case could be made for research and extension activities in retailing, construction, and the service sectors generally, but especially for these activities in rural areas. I believe that Rosenfeld makes the case for a significant investment in research and extension related to the creation and maintenance of nonfarm jobs in rural areas. He does, I believe, even make the case for transferring resources from agricultural research and extension to the productive nonagricultural activities in rural areas. Overall, agriculture now has a minority role in rural life, yet it receives nearly all of the resources devoted to research and extension.

It is worth noting that some of the lessons that we might learn about industrial policy from the experiences of Europe and Japan cannot be applied so easily to the United States because of our antitrust laws. While there has been considerable relaxation of the application of those laws over the past decade, many forms of cooperation among large firms still are not possible or can be carried out only at considerable risk. Note that it was only fairly recently that restraints on cooperation in the development of catalytic converters were imposed upon General Motors, Chrysler, and Ford by a consent decree. With the increased role of international trade in our economy, one component of an industrial policy should be a systematic review of what now constitutes an appropriate antitrust policy.

Conclusions

It is evident from the papers presented at this conference that having an industrial policy is not a panacea for our ills. There are industrial policies and industrial policies; some contribute to adjustment and efficiency, while others attempt to protect what now exists and thus to protect inefficiency and high-cost production.

Japan generally is held up as having followed industrial policies that achieved great success in manufacturing. If we accept this, even recognizing some recent failures such as high-definition television and the fifth-generation computer, one might well ask why the service sector has remained so high-cost and inefficient. Employment in the services is now twice that of manufacturing and is still growing. Perhaps the maintenance of excessive employment in the service sector has been one of the safety valves that has permitted the remarkable progress in developing a highly competitive manufacturing sector.

Emphasis upon the apparent success of industrial policy in Japan should not dissuade us from looking at the policies of the other four East Asian economies that have performed so very well over the past four decades. These economies have not all followed the same policies, and there have been distinctly different involvements of the governments in the economies. On the one hand there are Hong Kong and Taiwan, where the governments have been relatively less involved in the micromanagement of the economies; on the other hand are Japan and Singapore, which have substantial governmental involvement through a variety of policies. Korea is an uncertain case that probably falls somewhere in-between these two groups.

There is much that we can learn from others, but in that effort we should look beyond the obvious. We must not permit ourselves to assume that a few slogans will suffice for policies and programs that contribute to our future growth and development.

16 Observations and Conclusions

S. R. JOHNSON
S. A. MARTIN

Industrial policy has been surprisingly productive as a framework for assessing the implications of agricultural and rural development policy in the United States. In addition to clarifying the rationales for many of the policy interventions based on traditional ideas of market failure, the chapters in this book point out the importance of U.S. institutions in raising standards of economic performance, and the unintended implications of the industrial policy of the past. In fact, as U.S. industrial policy for agriculture and the rural sector has unfolded, the role of institutions and external factors in agriculture and the rural sector has suggested fertile opportunities for research and for prescriptions for growth and development. Several authors reviewed the nature of the political-economic equilibrium governing industry policy. New institutions resulting from technology, from swings in population, and from constitutional change have affected this equilibrium as well as the differing circumstances for intervention designed to correct market failure.

Three themes for successful industrial policy in agriculture and the rural sector emerged from the symposium and the papers. The first is competitiveness. Competitiveness is increasingly important in economies governed by technologies and institutions that permit relatively free flows of resources to areas of highest productivity. If sectors or industries are to grow and develop in a more open

S. R. Johnson is Charles F. Curtiss Distinguished Professor of Agriculture, Iowa State University, and Director of the Center for Agricultural and Rural Development. S. A. Martin is Senior Economist at the Center for Economics Research, Research Triangle Institute.

317

economy, conditions that encourage efficient production must receive constant attention. Competitiveness extends not only to the production side of the economic equation, but also to consumption. The costs of obtaining particular bundles of consumption goods, including public and private services, are important to the location of industry. For example, a community's capacity to provide bundles of goods and services similar to those available in urban areas is a factor important to the growth and development of rural areas.

The second theme involves technology. Clearly, as Acker pointed out, agriculture in the United States has been highly influenced by technologies developed in both the public and private sectors. Institutions that govern the property rights to technologies are important in determining the relative roles of the two sectors in technological production and dissemination. Clear, too, is the unique historical role of the land-grant institutions in the United States as problem-focused engines for technology development and dissemination for agriculture. However, with technology, as with other ingredients for productivity on both consumption and production sides of the economic equation, institutional change and the openness of the economy have become increasingly important to strategies for growth of industries and sectors.

As Feller noted, technologies are more mobile, domestically and internationally, and the benefits of public investment in research are increasingly difficult to capture regionally. As a result, many land-grant universities have shifted their focus to applied research, specialized to the peculiar biological, geophysical, and institutional features of regions and industries. It is perhaps this aspect of technology and development, as much as other changes in the agricultural sector, that has resulted in the on-going reassessment of the research and dissemination missions of the land-grant institutions and an increasing number of private-public partnerships in science and technology.

The third theme is the idea of community. This theme emerged as a component important to the growth and development of agriculture and rural areas. It is clear from available county information that agriculture is not the primary source of economic activity in many of the rural areas of the United States. Thus, industrial policy for agriculture is a blunt and often inappropriate instrument for achieving growth and development of rural areas. Instead, more balanced development strategies that reflect alternative sources for community growth and change must be introduced. Also, communities must organize into cohesive economic areas that can provide public and private services efficiently. Despite an increasing mobility of resources and technology, communities remain the organizing vehicles for local areas, and they have important roles in fostering leadership, structuring social and economic activity, creating a local environment that is attractive for economic growth, and providing the continuity required for promoting efficient adaptation to economic change. Communities that are successful will likely adapt more rapidly and even have a capacity for reconstituting themselves in response to the political-economic equilibrium and the changes brought by their own actions and external factors.

Industrial Policy

Industrial policy can be advantageously viewed as addressing the issues of community, competitiveness, and technology. Industrial policy interventions can be considered in increasingly comprehensive contexts. The most narrow and traditional approach to industrial policy and assessment of the associated interventions is market failure. Industry policies can address, for example, monopoly, property rights for various technology development and dissemination, agglomeration, externalities of various types, and market segmentation or disfunction. There are clear circumstances under which government action to address market failure can be rationalized. Yet, while government intervention can be rationalized as an approach to market failure, there are concerns about the capacity of government to accumulate the appropriate information, to take the appropriate action, and to efficiently administer the associated interventions. These problems of administration or implementation argue for caution in substituting government for private activity, even in the presence of market failure.

The second approach to industrial policy has, as a focus, the political-economic equilibrium. Here, modern ideas of rent-seeking and productive, redistributive actions of the public sector are keys to understanding and evaluating industrial policy. Constitutions and institutions permit and define organized activity of interest groups and guide the political-economic equilibrium for sectors or industries. The industrial policy and the political-economic equilibrium adjust in response to external shocks. A productive area for inquiry is opened by recognizing the importance of the political-economic equilibrium as a target of government intervention, and as a force in shaping private and public actions in industries and sectors.

In addition to having significant predictive content, ideas of rent-seeking and political-economic equilibrium can be used to better understand the roles of agricultural and rural institutions and interest groups as influenced by technology, redistribution of population, changes in economic regulation, and linkages with other sectors or industries. For agriculture and rural communities, this framework is helpful in understanding the political dynamics that have resulted in current pressures to reduce subsidization and to achieve a fuller integration into world markets. At more local levels, the political-economic equilibrium supplies a framework for understanding the ways in which communities organize, provide public and private services, and show capacity for change and development.

The third and most general approach for industrial policy involves institutional or constitutional change. As Rausser argued, the technology, economic efficiency, and political-economic equilibrium are determined in a fundamental sense by the economic, political, and civil rights afforded by what may be broadly termed the constitutional setting. Constitutions affect the rights and roles of interest groups, and how these interest groups participate in the political-economic equilibrium. Current constitutional theory is not rich in indicating how to effectively change the institutional setting for rural communities, the agricultural industry, nations, or even relationships among nations. But, it is clear that the "rights structures" for individuals and organizations (institutions) have a clear role in the growth and development of sectors and industries. At this point, most of the empirical studies of institutions and constitutions use comparisons of the growth and development among nations. It is likely that research in this area will come to focus more on sectors and industries as the theory is developed.

Whatever the approach, industrial policies that have been applied to agriculture and the rural sector can be put rather easily into three categories: preservationist, modernization, and adaptive or facilitative. Preservationist policies are those that attempt to restore or maintain an industry or sector by countering more fundamental economic, political, and institutional forces. When these underlying forces have been persistent and real, the experience with preservationist policies has not been good. The costs of these policies progressively increase at the same time that the support for the policies in the political-economic equilibrium erodes. In many respects, the industrial policy for agriculture in the United States and other developed economies can be viewed as mainly preservationist in nature.

Modernization policies with the objective of "picking winners" also have a spotty record at best. As Ergas reported, close examination of experience in the European Community and Japan suggests that modernization policies have largely detracted from economic growth. The essential problem with modernization as an industrial policy is that it substitutes government for the private sector in economic decision making. The private sector has at comparatively low cost the information necessary for making efficient economic decisions. As the decision space for the private sector is transferred to the public sector, increasing costs of maintaining information and the bureaucracy for decision making tend to weigh on the policies' potential success. In general, caution is suggested by the experience with industrial policy aimed at modernization. Information costs, the need for flexibility, and the benefits of broad participation in markets strongly argue against substitution of government for private action in determining priorities for investment and economic initiative. Accordingly, the possibilities for economywide benefits from the modernizing type of industrial policy lie more with private-sector activity.

The final type of industrial policy seeks to adapt or facilitate private lead initiatives for growth and development. This is perhaps the most difficult category of industrial policy to define. But, in the case of agriculture, the adaptive or facilitative industrial policy would include increased incentives for investment in information, clear identification of property rights, and institutions supporting low-cost transfer of resources, contractual instruments for risk-sharing and risk-spreading, and public investments in research and dissemination. For rural areas as well as for agriculture, this facilitative or adaptive industrial policy would include the supply of infrastructure and services rationalized on the basis of market failure. It is this form of industrial policy that appears to have the most potential for supporting the growth and development of agriculture and the rural sector.

Thus, the nature of industrial policy can be characterized by a matrix of objectives and approaches, as shown in Figure 16.1. Consider the case of increasing returns to scale in agriculture. This economic phenomenon was the result largely of changes in the institutional and production technology for agriculture. Applying less labor and more capital to ever-increasing average farm sizes resulted in a shrinking farm employment force and a steady rise in the average farm size. A market failure approach to this situation would consider only the economic interactions between agents. A preservationist strategy in this case is to subsidize commodity prices in order to discourage farmers from leaving agriculture. This policy fights the technological trend head-on and is destined for failure, if the technology grows progressively more capital intensive. A modernization strategy would jump ahead of the current trend, trying to anticipate what factors will become most productive in the future, and move development resources before the market itself recognizes their potential. An adaptive policy would recognize the inevitable economic trend and work toward speeding the signals that prompt the flow of resources out of agriculture and into sectors in which they are more productive.

A political-economic equilibrium approach to this problem considers the social and political relationships that contribute to the formulation of policy. In response to increasing returns to scale, a political-economic equilibrium approach to a preservation objective would use the current institutional and constitutional arrangements to influence commodity and other policy through rent-seeking. A

APPROACHES

OBJECTIVES	Market Failure	Political Equilibrium	Constitutional Administrative
Preservationist	Increase commodity subsidies	Influence commodity policy through rent-seeking	Improve capacity for rent-seeking by changing property rights (i.e., through check-off program)
Modernization	Subsidize targeted research and development	Form new interest groups specializing in promoting research and development in agriculture	Change anti-trust laws to encourage formation of research and development consortia; change patent rights and trade laws
Adaptive or Facilitative	Provide placement assistance for displaced farmers	Organize displaced farmers and improve the efficiency of matching process	Relax jurisdiction definition to allow the formation of community coalitions, new forms of governance

Figure 16.1. Objectives and approaches for industrial policy.

modernization objective could be sought with the same approach, but the institutions, while theoretically empowered through the constitution, would have to be organized to effect a government-led change. An adaptation strategy would organize the process of matching displaced farmers (and supplying necessary training) with potential employers to improve the efficiency of the resource reallocation process.

The constitutional or administrative approach addresses changes in the institutional structure to promote growth and development objectives. For preservationist objectives, this approach might consider improving the capacity for commodity groups to perform rent-seeking by providing them added property rights through an additional funding mechanism (i.e., check-off program). The modernization objectives might be achieved in this context by revising antitrust laws to encourage the formation of R&D consortia, leading to new demand and increased uses of farm commodities. An adaptive objective might be achieved by breaking down organizational barriers and supplying infrastructure to allow communities to work together toward matching resources and applications in more productive areas led by private-sector activity.

The approaches, instruments, and targets of industrial policy can be interpreted as addressing market failure, political-economic equilibrium, or the institutional and constitutional setting. These policies in turn have the possible objectives of preservation, modernization, or adaptivity and facilitation. The history of U.S. agricultural policy suggests, as observed by Professor D. Gayle Johnson, that the primary emphasis has been preservation and that policy has been guided more by a political-economic equilibrium characterized by rent-seeking than by market failure or by the constitutional or institutional setting. But, this general orientation of the industrial policy for agriculture and the rural sectors is likely to change, largely due to the fact that the political-economic equilibrium is being eroded by redistributions of population, changes in technology, and increasingly open markets for capital, labor, and the outputs of agriculture.

Similar observations, perhaps not as strong, can be made for the rural sector. In some respects, the best evidence of this is an orientation for rural-sector policy that is preoccupied with agriculture, even though abundant evidence shows that agriculture, while important, is not the dominating industry in most rural communities. A better understanding of industrial policy and of the changes in factors impacting agriculture and the rural sector will likely result in a change in the orientation of associated government intervention. In this change is a real opportunity for research and public policy action that can reduce the present sense of

Competitiveness

The term *competitiveness* may be one of the most misused and poorly understood of those applied in connection with industrial policy for agriculture and the rural sector. Most analyses of competitiveness and industrial policy concentrate on productivity. In short, industries or areas that are more productive in resource use than others enjoy a competitive advantage. But in the context of rural communities and industrial policy, competitiveness must extend to the consumption side of the economic equation and to the cost of living. Clearly, high-wage employment, the target of many of the rural and agricultural development policies, is of more value in attracting the most talented people if the consumption bundle that the wages are used to purchase is relatively low in price; for example, if the costs of public and private services are low compared to similar costs in other areas. The consumption side of the economic equation is in fact a major linkage to the community as a factor in economic growth and development.

It is critical to the growth of the industry or economy that the "rewards" for services of mobile capital and skilled labor be relatively high. In the case of capital and labor used in the production of economic goods and services in a competitive environment, high productivity translates into high rates of return and wages, drawing additional capital and labor into the economic activity and resulting in growth of the industry or region. The one qualification in applying this simple logic to rural areas relates to the ownership and the flows of returns for labor and capital services. Normally in rural development analysis, the attention is primarily on labor services which, by virtue of their immobility compared to capital, tend to have owners located locally, resulting in the enrichment of the community.

The situation for returns to capital services is, however, different. Owners of capital or those receiving payment for capital services do not necessarily have to be located in a particular area, as Schroder indicated. In fact, issues of ownership of capital and the payment for these services as transfers between regions are an important and relatively unstudied aspect of local economic growth. For agriculture, questions of payments for capital services as affected by industry policy may be particularly important. The industry is highly capital intensive. A case in point is agricultural subsidies, which are to an arguable extent translated into increases in land value. If all of the benefits of agricultural subsidies are transformed into increased value of land (the payments for capital services) and if the owners are absent, the impact of the industrial policy may not be in the intended locality.

The cost of living is another aspect of rural development that has not been studied adequately. With increased communications and expectations for more uniform lifestyles, a major consideration for the development of rural communities is the cost of living. That is, what is the cost of a consumption bundle, taking into consideration the commitment of time and associated opportunity costs, as well as monetary outlay? Clearly, the relative prices of the bundles of services will be different between rural and urban areas, and there will be associated adjustments by those with similar preferences and incomes. Still, rural communities may need to provide a lifestyle, particularly for younger and more economically mobile people, similar to that available in urban areas, or something very different in terms of consumption opportunities. If this observation is correct, there are implications for the scale and diversity of the rural communities in relation to cost of living that merit additional attention as an integral part of rural development policy.

Most studies of consumption cost in rural areas have concentrated on public services. Clearly, if the full cost-of-living side of the economic equation is considered, efficiency in providing public services is an integral part of strategies to improve the competitiveness of rural communities. Organization of schools, health services, utilities, transportation, and other widely used services falls within this category. But, private services must also be considered. A substantial share of the income of rural consumers, in particular those who are younger and more mobile, is allocated to private goods and services. Between urban and rural areas what is the cost of a similar consumption bundle of private services? What are the unique consumption opportunities? Answering these questions may yield useful information on migration patterns within different age groups and may shed light on the attractiveness and competitiveness of rural communities.

Technology

Studies of returns on public and private investments in agricultural research and dissemination suggest a clear avenue for increasing growth in the agricultural industry and in rural communities. Even if the estimated rates of return, as reported for example by Huffman and Evenson, are halved, there is still strong justification for government participation in research and development. This argument follows from a market failure, the inability of private firms investing in research and development to capture the full benefits of their innovations. Exactly how the appropriation of benefits and areas of research investment are influenced by different institutions and laws on assignment of property rights remains an issue for added study, say Gibson and Smilor. For example, do patent laws that permit a fuller appropriation of benefits from research induce associated investment by the private sector, and somehow substitute for public investment in research? Clearly, there is some substitution. However, current instruments for appropriation of intellectual property rights are most influential for applied research, leaving the public sector largely responsible for funding basic research.

More analysis is required for understanding the benefits of research and development for rural communities. Treating the performance of agriculture and rural communities as one and the same is increasingly inappropriate. What is the level of public support for research on the development of regions or communities in comparison to support for research on industries? What are the rates of return to these investments, whether public or private? The focus of policies toward the rural sector in the United States is shifting from agriculture as an industry to rural areas and regions, and this shift will cause increasing debate.

Michael Crow has discussed the important changes in the system for public and private research and dissemination related to both agriculture and rural communities. How far will the new university and private-sector joint ventures go in changing the research and development enterprise? Will these joint ventures be confined primarily to industry, or is there an opportunity to forge added partnerships in relation to rural areas? Land-grant institutions in rural states are increasingly expected to serve as a source of economic development, say Olson and Hadwiger. Should associated initiatives by these institutions always be industry oriented, or is the appropriate area of research more oriented to the competitiveness of communities?

How much focused and in-depth research has been done on the growth and development of economies or local communities? Judging from the presentations and discussions at this symposium, Eisinger among them, efforts in rural development have received limited resources compared to agriculture. A conjecture is that in the future the focus of land-grant institutions will shift more to regional and geographical areas than to industry-based research and development as a stimulus for local economic growth. Clearly, research and development activity influences competitiveness and productivity, and for agriculture such activity has been a component of industrial policy, with a high payoff. Could the resources in the public sector which have been allocated traditionally to research and development for agriculture be at least partially turned to issues of growth and development of rural communities, with similar expectations for payoff? What would be the transferability of research results between rural communities or regions if such a change in the research and development portfolio of the land-grant institutions were to occur?

Community

Many of the specialized initiatives for stimulating growth and development of the rural sector are based on community, say Anderson et al. and Rosenfeld. Community can be variously defined. The relationships among individuals, organizations, and other economic agents that make up the community can be formalized in terms of governance or can remain informal as in the case of, for example, cultural or ethnic identity. Also, the aspirations of communities tend to be influenced by what is already present in terms of an economic base. From a political-economic equilibrium viewpoint, communities represent organizations in which there is a shared sense of participation and some implied shared ownership or property rights in commonly held beliefs and values. Changing the concept or understanding of community for purposes of an agricultural or rural development initiative is thus not an easy task. Because of the complexity of institutions and organizations, the local political-economic equilibrium is resistent to change. For example, there would likely be resistance to change that would alter the definition of the community and the implied rights structure even if the change were to be aimed at achieving improved economic performance.

Many times community initiatives designed to increase economic growth have concentrated more on social organization and the performance of the economic sectors than on enhancement of competitiveness as reflected in costs of living. Particularly in the case of cost of living, arguments can be made for reorganizing communities consistent with the achievement of attractive consumption bundles. These bundles can be defined in terms of comparative rural and urban sector costs of diversity and uniqueness of consumption alternatives in the rural sector. Perhaps studies of the competitiveness of the organization of communities can support the politically difficult arguments for restructuring communities to encourage economic development.

Rural communities in the United States developed and prospered based on the agriculture of the past century. Clearly, the agriculture that supported and was the source of the growth and development of these communities has radically changed. How can the communities adapt to perpetuate the features that are valued by the citizens and at the same time adjust to the fact that agriculture has changed, requiring less labor and using other services that can be supplied from a great distance? Communities can be viewed productively as enterprises. Then, the question is how do communities as economic and social enterprises organize themselves to have a diverse and resilient economic base, social institutions and services that are efficiently organized, and the sense of ownership and place that facilitate social interaction and contracting at relatively low transaction costs?

These are among the priority issues for community development, especially related to economic growth, that require answers as part of a general research and development effort aimed at improving the competitiveness and economic lot of rural areas as compared to urban areas.

Conclusions

Conclusions from the discussions during the conference and from the chapters in this volume can be grouped into three areas. The first is the dichotomy between industrial policy for agriculture and policy for rural development. It is obvious that agricultural policy in the United States is not rural development policy. Moreover, the evidence of the sustaining impacts of the industrial policy for agriculture clearly favors emphasis on research and development and infrastructure, not on subsidies. Subsidies fail because they are transfers with high leakage from rural areas and because they substitute government decision making for private decision making. This perception of the weakness of past industrial policy for agriculture is crystallizing at the same time that the political-economic equilibrium that produced agricultural policy in the United States is changing.

A future for U.S. agriculture that rests primarily on subsidies is, by most accounts, limited. Options that appear feasible involve reorienting the subsidies to areas of greater national and social payoff. An option for this reorientation is to directly address rural development and to allocate the resources now devoted to agricultural subsidies to broad rural development issues before they are lost or reduced by the diminished political capacities of agricultural and rural-sector interest groups.

The second conclusion concerns the objectives of industrial or regional development policy. Preservation and modernization, or "winner-picking," policies generally do not achieve their desired results in terms of growth and development, at least in the intermediate or longer run. This suggests a refocusing of the industrial policy for agriculture and rural areas to emphasize infrastructure, education and training, research and development, and other interventions to support productivity in the private sector. Also, industrial policy for agriculture and rural areas is likely to continue to embrace the environment and the natural resource base. This trend will offer opportunity for leveraging the political capacity of rural areas in influencing redistribution through federal and state government. Opportunities for the agricultural industry and for rural-sector development will likely be increasingly sought through policies that are facilitative or adaptive.

How can the government play a role in assisting agriculture and rural communities in adapting to economic reality and other realities? These interventions should not be confined to instances of market failure. The political-economic equilibrium and the social contract as related to the growth and development of rural communities and of the agricultural industry present opportunities for research and offer great potential for more effectively addressing the inequities that are emerging between rural and urban areas in the United States. This is a priority area for research that can lead to the kind of social change that will reverse the secular decline of rural areas.

The third conclusion involves competitiveness and the importance of a fuller understanding of its implications for the consumption and production sides of the economic equation. Productive inquiry and policy action must concentrate on costs of comparable consumption bundles and the uniqueness of consumption opportunities in rural areas as significant elements for competitiveness and the attration and generation of industry. In fact, equal attention to the consumption side of the economic equation effectively links issues of community, technology, and competitiveness. This focus can provide an organizing framework for more comprehensive prescriptions on rural development policy and the growth of industries that form the economic base of rural communities. But, broadening the scope of rural development to include cost-of-living requires an expanded characterization of economic systems. The computable general equilibrium model applied by Kilkenny and Schluter is promising in this respect. On the other hand, moving beyond traditional economies to rent-seeking and concepts of political-economic equilibrium for explaining the organization and functioning of communities, bureaucracies, and organizations holds promise for better design and implementation of policies to achieve rural growth and development.

In an even broader sense, there are significant gains to be made by better understanding the constitutions or the social contracts of communities as they relate to economic, political, and civil rights of individuals and, correspondingly, to local institutions. Institutions are both organizations and sets of rules by which collective and individual decisions are made. Solutions to persistent rural economic development problems and the problems facing agriculture's future in the United States and other developed countries, along with the husbandry of natural resources required for this industry, require broader policy frameworks. Also required is an expansion of the scope of research for support of rural and industrial development. Not only should political-economic equilibrium and community organization be more fully exploited for designing policies to stimulate growth, but this new research agenda should also include the basic rights conditioning the behaviors of the agents in industry and the agents and institutions in rural communities.

Conference Participants

Duane Acker
Assistant Secretary for Science and Education
USDA/217W Administration Building
14th and Independence Avenue, S.W.
Washington, D.C. 20250

Gary Anderson
Senior Economist, The Center
for Economic Competitiveness
SRI International
333 Ravenswood Avenue
Menlo Park, California 94025-3493

Varel Bailey
President
Bailey Farms, Inc.
Anita, Iowa 50020

Keith Barnes
President
AMPC, Inc.
ISU Research Park
2325 North Loop Drive
Ames, Iowa 50010-8612

Andrew Bernat
Agricultural Economist
USDA/Economic Research Service
1301 New York Avenue, N.W., #340
Washington, D.C. 20005-4788

Robert A. Burnett
    Retired Chair
    Meredith Corporation
    1716 Locust Street
    Des Moines, Iowa 50309

John Chrystal
    Executive Director
    World Agriculture Development Foundation
    601 Locust, Suite 1000
    Des Moines, Iowa   50309

W. D. Classen
    Retired Chair
    Rain & Hail Insurance Company
    4101 Greenview Drive
    Urbandale, Iowa 50322

H. D. Cleberg
    President and CEO
    Farmland Industries
    3315 N. Oak Trafficway
    Kansas City, Missouri 64116

Robert M. Colquhoun
    Vice-President
    ICI Seeds
    6945 Vista Drive
    West Des Moines, Iowa 50266

Michael M. Crow
    Vice-Provost for Research
    Columbia University
    402 Low Library
    New York, New York 10027

Steve Daugherty
General Manager, External Communications
Pioneer Hi-Bred International, Inc.
6800 Pioneer Parkway
P. O. Box 584
Johnston, Iowa 50131

Peter K. Eisinger
Director, La Follette Institute
of Public Affairs
Professor of Political Science and Public Policy
University of Wisconsin
1225 Observatory Drive
Madison, Wisconsin 53706

Henry Ergas
Conseiller pour la politique structurelle
Economic Affairs/OECD
2 Rue Andre Pascal
75775 Paris 16 France

Robert E. Evenson
Professor of Economics
Yale University
P. O. Box 1987, Yale Station
New Haven, Connecticut 06520

Irwin Feller
Director, Graduate School of Public Policy
and Administration
The Pennsylvania State University
N235 Burrowes Building
University Park, Pennsylvania 16802

Thomas Fretz
Associate Dean, College of Agriculture
Iowa State University
104 Curtiss Hall
Ames, Iowa 50011

Kenneth Frey
   C. F. Curtiss Distinguished Professor of Agriculture
   Iowa State University
   1401 Agronomy Hall
   Ames, Iowa 50011

Dick Gallagher
   Past Vice-President
   American Soybean Association
   2672 260th Street
   Washington, Iowa 52353

Eldean Gerloff
   Acting Director, Midwest Area
   U.S. Department of Agriculture
   Agricultural Research Service
   1815 N. University Street
   Peoria, Illinois 61604

David V. Gibson
   Associate Director, Center for Technology Venturing
   IC^2 Institute
   The University of Texas at Austin
   2815 San Gabriel
   Austin, Texas 78705

Don Gingerich
   Past President
   National Pork Producers Council
   P. O. Box 10383
   Des Moines, Iowa 50306

Leonard Goldman
   Director
   ISU Research Park
   2625 N. Loop Drive
   Ames, Iowa 50010

Donald Hadwiger
  Professor Emeritus of Political Science
  Iowa State University
  557 Ross Hall
  Ames, Iowa 50011

Kent Hall
  Director, Federal Relations
  Iowa State University
  222 Beardshear Hall
  Ames, Iowa 50011

Steve Halloran
  President and Director
  National Farmers Organization
  2505 Elwood Drive
  Ames, Iowa 50010-2000

Leroy Hanson
  President and COO
  Triple "F" Inc.
  10104 Douglas Avenue
  P. O. Box 3600
  Urbandale, Iowa 50322

Wallace E. Huffman
  Professor of Economics
  Iowa State University
  478C Heady Hall
  Ames, Iowa 50011-1070

Martin Jischke
  President
  Iowa State University
  117 Beardshear Hall
  Ames, Iowa 50011

Charles W. Johnson
  Deputy Assistant Administrator for Research
    and Development
  U.S. Agency for International Development, Room 4942
  Washington, D.C. 20523-0057

D. Gale Johnson
  E. K. Moore Distinguished Professor of Economics
  University of Chicago
  1126 E. 59th Street
  Chicago, Illinois 60637

Stanley R. Johnson
  Director, Center for Agricultural
    and Rural Development
  C. F. Curtiss Distinguished Professor of Agriculture
  Iowa State University
  578 Heady Hall
  Ames, Iowa 50011-1070

Marlyn Jorgensen
  Past President
  Iowa Soybean Association
  Rural Route 1
  Garrison, Iowa 52229

Maureen R. Kilkenny
  Associate Professor of Economics
  University of Colorado
  Boulder, Colorado 80309

Jack Kintzle
  Past President
  National Corn Growers Association
  5737 Highway 13
  Coggon, Iowa 52218

James Kirk
President
Omaha Farm Credit Services
206 S. Nineteenth Street
Omaha, Nebraska 68102

Herman Kilpper
Vice-President
World Agriculture Development Foundation
601 Locust Street, Suite 350
Des Moines, Iowa 50309

Dean R. Kleckner
President
American Farm Bureau Federation
225 Toughy Avenue
Park Ridge, Illinois 60068

Dan Kugler
Deputy Administrator
U.S. Department of Agriculture
Aerospace Center
14th and Independence Avenue, S.W.
Washington, D.C. 20250-2200

Ms. Myrt Levin
Executive Director
Iowa Business Council
100 E. Grand Avenue, Suite 160
Des Moines, Iowa 50309

Sheila A. Martin
Senior Economist
Center for Economics Research
Research Triangle Institute
P. O. Box 12194
Research Triangle Park, North Carolina 27709

Derryl McLaren
  State Senator
  Rural Route 1
  Farragut, Iowa 51639

Bob Mickle
  Consultant
  World Agriculture Development Foundation
  601 Locust Street, Suite 350
  Des Moines, Iowa 50309

William Northey
  President
  Iowa Corn Growers Association
  Rural Route
  Box 8201
  Spirit Lake, Iowa 51360

Dennis G. Olson
  Director, Utilization Center for Agricultural Products
  Iowa State University
  194A Meat Lab
  Ames, Iowa 50011

Dan Otto
  Associate Professor of Economics
  Iowa State University
  560B Heady Hall
  Ames, Iowa 50011-1070

Robert L. Peterson
  Chair and CEO
  IBP, Inc.
  Highway 35, Box 515
  Dakota City, Nebraska 68731

Bob Pim
State Director for Iowa
Farmers Home Administration
873 Federal Building
210 Walnut Street
Des Moines, Iowa 50309

Merlin Plagge
President
Iowa Farm Bureau Federation
5400 University Avenue
West Des Moines, Iowa 50265

Gordon C. Rausser
R. G. Sproul Distinguished Professor of Economics
University of California
207 Giannini Hall
Berkeley, California 94720

Michael V. Reagen
President and CEO
Greater Des Moines Chamber of Commerce
601 Locust Street, Suite 100
Des Moines, Iowa 50309

Joseph Roetheli
Acting Deputy Director
USDA/AARC Center
342 Aerospace Center
14th and Independence Avenue, S.W.
Washington, D.C. 20250-2200

Stuart A. Rosenfeld
President
Regional Technology Strategies, Inc.
218 Vance
Chapel Hill, North Carolina 27516

John Ruan
   Chair, World Agriculture Development Foundation
   Chair and CEO, Ruan Industries
   3200 Ruan Center
   666 Grand Avenue
   Des Moines, Iowa 50309

Gerald Schluter
   Head, National Aggregate Analysis Section
   USDA/Economic Research Service
   Room 912
   1301 New York Avenue, N.W.
   Washington, D.C. 20005

David Schroder
   President
   InvestAmerica Venture Group
   1001 Second Street, S.E., Suite 800
   Cedar Rapids, Iowa 52401

Kenneth R. Tefertiller
   Vice-President for Agriculture
   University of Florida
   1175 McCarty Hall
   Gainesville, Florida 32611

David G. Topel
   Dean, College of Agriculture
   Iowa State University
   122 Curtiss Hall
   Ames, Iowa 50011

Steven Zumbach
   Attorney
   Belin Harris Lamson McCormick
   2000 Financial Center
   Des Moines, Iowa 50309

Members of the Press

George Anthan
Des Moines Register
Washington, D.C., Bureau
1317 "F" Street, N.W.
Washington, D.C. 20004

Gene Johnston
Managing Editor
Successful Farming
1716 Locust Street
Des Moines, Iowa 50309-3023

Scott Kilman
Wall Street Journal
One South Wacker Street, 21st Floor
Chicago, Illinois 60606

Scott Pendleton
Christian Science Monitor
1503 Palma Plaza
Austin, Texas 78703

Lyle Schertz
Editor, *Choices*
12708 Oak Farms Road
Herndon, Virginia 22071

Jim Smiley
Omaha World Herald
World Herald Square
Omaha, Nebraska 68102

Conference Coordinators

Judith Gildner
  Manager, Information Services
  Center for Agricultural and Rural Development
  Iowa State University
  578 Heady Hall
  Ames, Iowa 50011-1070

Betty Hempe
  Staff Assistant
  Center for Agricultural and Rural Development
  Iowa State University
  578 Heady Hall
  Ames, Iowa 50011-1070